Published by Clachan Publishing

3 Drumavoley Park,
Ballycastle,
BT54 6PE,

County Antrim

© Seán O'Halloran and Mary Hudson
2016

Please acknowledge if using material from this publication.

ISBN: 978-1-909906-34-1
Email: sean.ohalloran@btinternet.com
mary.hudson1@btinternet.com

Front cover – Photo of Famine Memorial, Dublin

The Hallorans of Birstall & Aghamore:

A family history

Written and researched by Seán O'Halloran and Mary Hudson

This book is dedicated to the memory of five Halloran brothers who were born in Birstall, Yorkshire, England

James Halloran (1905-05) who died in infancy,

སོ་སོ་ལྦ་ལྦ་སོ་སོ་ལྦ་ལྦ་སོ་སོ་ལྦ་ལྦ

Thomas (Tom) Halloran (1908-74) who spent his adult life living in Birstall with William and Betty,

སོ་སོ་ལྦ་ལྦ་སོ་སོ་ལྦ་ལྦ་སོ་སོ་ལྦ་ལྦ

John Halloran (O'Halloran) (1911- 90), who married Eileen Sheehan and lived much of their lives in Kenya. He is the father of Maureen, Michael, Kevin, Eileen, Seán and Patricia,

སོ་སོ་ལྦ་ལྦ་སོ་སོ་ལྦ་ལྦ་སོ་སོ་ལྦ་ལྦ

William (Bill, Willy) Halloran (1913-72), who lived in Birstall and married Betty Walsh. He is the father of Mary and Bernard,

སོ་སོ་ལྦ་ལྦ་སོ་སོ་ལྦ་ལྦ་སོ་སོ་ལྦ་ལྦ

Bernard Halloran (1915-22) who died in childhood.

སོ་སོ་ལྦ་ལྦ་སོ་སོ་ལྦ་ལྦ་སོ་སོ་ལྦ་ལྦ

Contents

INTRODUCTION III

CHAPTER 1 1
ORIGINS 1
   The Irish ancestors of the Hallorans 1
   The Barony of Costello 7
   The parish of Aghamore 8
   The townland of Carrowbaun 9
   Education 18
   Viscount Dillon, Charles Strickland and Charlestown 23

CHAPTER 2 29
THE GREAT STARVATION 29
   The Hallorans in Carrowbaun in the autumn of 1845 29
   Potato blight 30
   The Poor Laws 34
   Black '47 40
   1848 – The third year 45

CHAPTER 3 57
THE HALLORANS WHO LEFT AGHAMORE 57
   Emigration or extinction - their journey from County Mayo 57
   Seasonal migration to Britain 61
   The navvies 64

CHAPTER 4 68
THE IRISH IN BATLEY 68
   Batley 68
   The 1841 English census - the Irish arrive in Batley 70

CHAPTER 5 74
THE IRISH ARRIVE IN BIRSTALL 74
   Birstall 76
   The first generation of Irish 77
   Thomas Halloran (1808/9-1887) and family in 1851 79
   Other Irish in Birstall 81
   Thomas Halloran (1808/9-1887) and family 1861 onwards 87
   Coach Lane, Brownhill – an Irish ghetto? 88
   Michael Halloran (1827-77), born in Oughamore (Aghamore) and family 90

CHAPTER 6 97
THE SECOND GENERATION - BIRSTALL 97
   Going down the mines 97
   Mining in South Yorkshire 97
   James Halloran (b. 1839) and Bridget Higgins 1842-1884/7 and family 106
   Halloran marriages and children of the second generation 108

Patrick and Bridget Halloran (b. 1837) and family *110*
Work, health and accidents *111*
The Morley pit mine disaster *112*
Women in the mills *113*

CHAPTER 7 114
THE THIRD GENERATION - BIRSTALL 114
The Catholic Church *117*
James Halloran (1862/3-1911) and Ellen Cuddy and family *119*

CHAPTER 8 125
THE FOURTH GENERATION – TOM, JOHN AND BILL 125
William, Lizzie and family life *126*
Religion and education *129*

CHAPTER 9 145
THE HALLORANS WHO REMAINED - CARROWBAUN 145
Introduction *145*
Hallorans in Aghamore parish in the 1901 Irish census *147*
Carrowbaun *149*
Michael Davitt and the Land League *153*

CHAPTER 10 165
THE HALLORANS OF RATH, CAHIR AND CORNAGEAGHTA 165
Post-famine Mayo *165*
Rath (Raith) *168*
Cahir (Caher) *174*
Cornageaghta or Mountain / Mountaincommon *183*
Appendices *188*
References *205*

Introduction

Acknowledgements

Mary Hudson started to work on this project when heavy snow kept her housebound during the winter early in the year 2010. Seán O'Halloran, at the time, was laid low with sciatica and a bad back. This coincidence of enforced idleness led to the collaborative working relationship that resulted to this history.

And what a fascinating, rewarding - even if obsessive - working relationship it has been. We started our research on the Internet, and were soon surprised at how useful a tool it is, particularly as we live in different areas. The Website *Ancestry.com* proved invaluable, allowing us access to the English census forms where we make our initial discoveries. Other websites that proved useful are cited in the text and acknowledged at the back of this book.

Many people have given us important information. We have to thank the parish priests at St Patrick's Birstall, St Paulinus, Dewsbury and St Austen's, Wakefield for helping us to search their parish records. We were helped with St Mary's records by Mr Finnegan, the Diocese archivist, as these records are held in Hinsley Hall in Leeds. Records of baptisms, marriages and deaths gave lots of information that was not available on the Internet.

We are indebted to Malcolm Clegg for the history of Birstall. Mary is especially delighted in his personal support and for his practical help in tracking down the answers to some of the mysteries revealed in the records.

Thanks go to those almost forgotten relatives who have been contacted and helped with stories, photos and information, notably: Margaret and Mike Cook from Morley; Patrick and Anne-Marie Halloran, of Leicester, and their families; Joan Tingle from Birstall; Joe Halloran and his sister Anne from Batley; Pat Halloran from Dewsbury and Paula Ashton, of Batley and Sligo great friend of the late Joan Halloran.

On the Irish side there are relatives we never knew of before we undertook this project. We were delighted to meet Martin Halloran and his sister Phil Reilly, from Aghamore, as a direct result of this study. Phil kindly gave us permission to make extensive quotations from her early experiences in *Retirement Reminiscences*, published in *Glór Achadh Mór* in 2002.

We are also indebted to Fr Pat Holleran who gave us some insights into the early connections between the Hallorans of Aghamore and those in Killasser.

We were very pleased to have met Joe Byrne, musician, local historian and much more, he was good enough to give us some of his time and insights into by-gone days in Aghamore. Ger Delaney of the South Mayo Family Research Centre shed light on the relationship between the Halloran men in Aghamore in the 1840s and 1860s.

We must also acknowledge the assiduous work of our proof-reader Malachy Scullion. However, it must be pointed out that the discovery of new material resulted in additions and changes to the text after he had done his valuable work. He cannot be held responsible for errors that appear.

Apart from the family photos, we have used a number of photos that were freely downloadable from the Internet. If we have inadvertently infringed anyone's copyright please let us know.

Mary has to thank Andrew for all his help rushing around Yorkshire and Mayo and other places, helping to note all the possibly relevant information, taking such an interest in the family origins, and making all those meals whilst she was glued to the computer, searching for the latest elusive records.

Seán wishes to thank all the members of his family and was very pleased that Helen, Ciaran, Mandy, Siobhan and Aibhne could accompany him on the first exploratory visit to Aghamore. They have all had to listen to his long accounts of our discoveries. Will they now read this book? Well, parts of it.

Preface

This is the story of a remarkable yet obscure family. Sean and Mary have doggedly unearthed much of our ancestry, beginning with those near starvation in 1840s Ireland. They have attempted to trace them through their hardships in industrial England, and the Land War in Ireland, finally leading on to the present educated generation, living comfortable lives in various parts of the world.

Thomas Halloran, born in 1808, and his wife Judy could have had no idea how their family would grow and prosper. Escaping the famine as illiterate peasants, arriving in England with a whole group of relations and friends, they recreated a mutually supporting community within the 'Heavy Woollen District' of Yorkshire. Here, they worked in appalling conditions as unskilled workers; almost inevitably the men were miners and the women 'rag pickers'. They lived in overcrowded slum housing, but always found room for relatives and friends escaping the terrible conditions in Ireland, and so recreated their Irish community in Birstall. These people had few skills, little money, and hardly any resources. What they had was a generosity of spirit and determination to work hard and to live life to the full.

This year has given us much excitement as historic records revealed the family links to Aghamore, in Mayo, where some Hallorans still live. It has also answered many questions such as why, in 1950s Birstall, Mary's dad's reply to queries about who local people were was, "Oh, it's your second cousin". As it happened, *everyone* was!

Records show a web of intermarriages between the same families in Birstall and Aghamore, so it is not surprising to see a clear similarity between Joe Halloran (Mary's brother Bernard's son) and John Halloran (Aghamore Martin's son), five generations apart. Facts have been unearthed which reveal terrible family tragedies: a mother dying at 33 leaving five young children; deaths due to smallpox, which killed small children who had just escaped the Great Famine. We have also seen how our forbears lived life to the full and supported each other in difficult times.

Memories have been jogged and stories remembered. We have been in touch with other relations, some of whom were also searching out our mutual ancestors. We witness the obvious skills and abilities of our untutored ancestors; skills that ensured the survival and achievements of later generations. This project has also given a different perspective on ourselves as a small part of the relentless roll-over of time; it has made us aware of the small part we actually have played in a great continuum; as our children and grandchildren take over from us.

Most of all, it has given great satisfaction to be able to reveal the achievements of the early family members, to keep their memories alive and to share with others our feelings of pride and gratitude. It is an opportunity to thank these groundbreakers who enabled our lives and our future generations to be so much easier!

Throughout, we have tried to cite the actual records and historical sources of all information given in the book. Where the source is family memory, we have indicated this. Where we have engaged in speculation, we have attempted to make this clear too. However, despite receiving so much help and information from others, we take responsibility for any errors.

Many names are spelt differently in different documents. Generally, we have used the spelling we found in the documents when we are referring specifically to them. Otherwise we have tried to use standard spelling

Introduction

The Gaelic Clann system

It is impossible to establish the distant origins of the particular Halloran family that is the subject of this book, i.e. our *Ó hAllmhuráin* ancestors. However, the family name itself derives from an ancient Gaelic *clann* and gives us a clue as to the family's ancient origins. Gaelic Ireland was organised around family clans that gave its members a sense of common identity and security. However, the clans eventually broke up into a number of distinct septs or groups.

The sept system was an integral part of Gaelic society and survived and was even propagated by the Norman invaders. These groups were headed by an original member of the *clann* and dominated a particular part of the countryside. It was common for septs from the same clan to be found in completely different parts of the country.

In *Crichaireacht cinedach nduchasa Muintiri Murchada*, a tract dating to the reign of its overlord, *Flaithbertaigh Ua Flaithbertaigh*, King of Connacht from 1092-1098 the lists of the main families and their estates within *Clann Fhergail* are found. The first listed was the family of *Ó hAllmhuráin*[1].

There are, however, two distinct septs of *Ó hAllmhuráin* - one in Galway and the other in Clare, where their present day descendants are still numerous. The county Galway sept, whose slogan was *Clan Fearghaile abu*, were chiefs of *Clann Fearghaile*, holding an extensive territory near Lough Corrib, comprising the baronies of Micelle and Galway, the parishes of Oranmore and Ballynacourty and Rahoon. They were the original proprietors of the lands on the western boundaries of Galway City and retained a leading position in *Iar Connacht* (Western Connaught) to the end of the 16th Century. They appear in the 'Composition Book of Connacht' in 1585. Remnants of this sept gradually spread northwards into Mayo, where our family ancestors are found.

The Clare sept were located in Ogonnelloe, on the southern shores of Lough Derg, and spread southwards into county Limerick.

After the arrival of the Normans many of the old Gaelic Chieftains lost their land, and the territory around Galway was taken over by the merchant families of the Kirwans, Martins, Blakes, Skerrets, Lynches, Frenches, Brownes and Darcys.

The great Cromwellian assault on Roman Catholicism and the Gaelic chieftains completed the process, and led to the impoverishment and fragmentation of the *Ó hAllmhuráin* clan. The Cromwellian settlement forced the great Irish chieftains to flee to France and Spain, while their lands were forfeited and given to Cromwell's supporters. Safe passage to the continent was given to ranking members of the Irish armies, and many of them subsequently fought for the Catholic cause in Europe. Many of the rest were slaughtered or sent as forced indentured labourers to slave in plantations in the West Indies, specifically Antigua and Montserrat. The sept system and the old Gaelic order, along with the ancient Gaelic names were destroyed and it became a disadvantage to have a Gaelic sounding name.

The presence of slaves and slave owners called Halloran in Antigua in the early part of the 19th Century gives evidence of this aspect of Irish history. Recorded there are Dick Halloran, born in 1793, a black male and 'owned' by John Gore; George Halloran, born in 1794, a black male and 'owned' by John Boyd; Tom Halloran, born in 1817, a black male and 'owned' by William Morris Trye Esquire; another Tom Halloran, born in 1804, a black male and 'owned' by H L Spencer Esquire; and Betsey Halloran, born in 1805, a black female and also 'owned' by H L Spencer Esquire. At about the same period, there was a widow Mary Halloran, who owned a number of slaves. This appears to indicate that some descendants of the original captives forced out by Cromwell managed to work through their indentured forced labour and gained freedom. Others, however, sank into slavery and intermarried with the African slaves who were imported later.

---

1 http://en.wikipedia.org/wiki/Clann_Fhergailf1f1

The Penal laws that were enforced by the British colonists were an attempt to completely subjugate the Gaelic way of life. They brought about a process of anglicisation that resulted in the destruction of the clan and sept systems. It was during this period that many Gaelic names changed to their Anglo equivalent or translation. The revival of Gaelic consciousness in the later eighteen hundreds then saw many Irish families reassume the Mac, Mc, Ó or other Irish form of their names, although this was reduced in a number of cases, depending on the sound of the name. Kelly is still much more prevalent than O'Kelly, Murphy more prevalent than O'Murphy, etc. It was John Halloran's (1911-1990) wife, Eileen neé Sheehan, who was largely responsible for persuading him to change his family's name back to O'Halloran in the 1960s.

The first *Ó hAllmhuráin* ancestors that we have located, however, were poverty-stricken peasants living in the parish of Aghamore in East Mayo in the 1830s. Previous generations had probably drifted north from areas around Lough Corrib in Galway to the remote regions of Mayo. Why this was happening is obvious from the table below, which lists a number of Hallorans evicted between the years 1827-1833, from County Clare.

Defendant (Surname)	Forename No. of defendants	Year	Nature of property	Total acres	Plaintiff(s)	Decreed or not (basis of suit)	Civil Parish/ Barony
Halloran	Michael/1	1830	house	not listed	George Perry	Decreed (overholding)	[none listed] Bunratty
Halloran	Michael/2	1832	land	not listed	John Healy	Not decreed (overholding)	[none listed] Bunratty
Halloran	Michael/3	1829	land	<one	Bindon Scott, Esq.	Not decreed (overholding)	Clouney Bunratty
Halloran	Michael/4	1830	land	not listed	Bindon Scott, Esq.	Not decreed (overholding)	Clouney Bunratty
Halloran	Michael/1	1833	land	not listed	John Clanchy	Not decreed (overholding)	Doura Bunratty
Halloran	Michael/1	1829	land	not listed	John O'Brien	Not decreed (overholding)	Kilfidane Clonderalaw
Halloran	Michael/2	1828	land	not listed	John Lucas	Not decreed (overholding)	Kilmaley Islands
Halloran	Michael/1	1829	land	>15	Peter Connellan	Decreed (overholding)	Kilmaley Islands
Halloran	Florence/2	1833	land	not listed	Stafford O'Brien, Esq.	Not decreed (overholding)	Kiltananlea Tulla
Halloran	Michael/1	1829	land	>15	George Perry	Decreed (overholding)	Tulla

Evictions as Court Proceedings, between the years 1827-1833, for County Clare, derived from the Enhanced British Parliamentary Papers on Ireland, 1801-1922[1].

Those who moved out of Galway drifted north. Our ancestors seem to have settled near or around the townland of Carrowbaun, an area of forests and boglands, forming a typical tight-knit *family-based* community, where land, i.e. a few acres, was parcelled out according to need. The people worked together to cut down the forests and drain the boglands to cultivate the potatoes on which they depended. There is a suggestion that some Hallorans moved on – probably forced by poverty, evictions and the pressure of over-population – to the more northern parish of Killasser.

Seasonally, a band of them probably travelled together to mainland Britain where they worked in bringing in the harvest to earn the cash to pay their rent. The young men would travel over longer periods to work as navvies on the canals and railways. Sometimes they chose not to come back; others had little choice.

---

1 http://www.clarelibrary.ie/eolas/coclare/genealogy/don_tran/court_rpts/ejectments1827_1833_surnames.htm

Introduction

There was little land to work at home. Many young women, if they were not too peasant-like, probably went to work with well-to-do families as domestic servants.

No remnants of *clann* pride remain among these unfortunates. Their loyalty was to their nearest neighbours in the townland of Carrowbaun, where they lived in a cluster of hovels called a *clachan* or *stráid* and struggled together to grow potatoes, keep a pig and perhaps a pony or donkey and pay the landlord his rent for bog lands for which they vied with each other. However, even that precarious existence was about to be threatened by catastrophic events, which overwhelmed not only their lives but altered the history of Ireland and changed the demographics of the English-speaking world.

This is primarily a story of how the horrors of the famine in County Mayo broke up this peasant Ó hAllmhuráin family, and how events shaped the lives of its subsequent members. It was a story that was repeating itself remorselessly all over Ireland and nowhere with such ruthlessness as in the western counties. The families from the townland of Carrowbaun had experienced hunger before the Great Famine or *an Gorta Mór*. Hunger and the pressure of population had forced them to this region, from whence they were again forced to move on in even larger numbers. The Great Famine meant that not just the men and boys, but now entire families had to move, and for most, permanently.

Two massive social upheavals of famine and industrialisation shaped the fortunes of this and countless Irish families in the mid nineteenth century. Entire townland communities were broken up as hunger and want forced many to flee to the newly industrialised regions in the United States and Britain.

Chapters 1 and 2 deal with the Halloran families before and during the famine. Chapters 9 and 10 deal with those who remained in Ireland, particularly with James and those who came after him. The remaining chapters (chapters 3-8) deal with Thomas and Michael, their families and neighbours who fled the famine to make a new life for themselves and their descendants in Yorkshire, England.

CHAPTER 1

Origins

The Irish ancestors of the Hallorans

Although we know little about the details of the people who came before us, it is impossible not to be intrigued by the humanity of ancestors long dead. This book is an attempt to make something of their lives accessible to their descendants and the descendants of countless others who lived like them; to shed some light on men and women who could not write for themselves and whose voices and lives have vanished in the obscurity and anonymity of illiteracy, drudgery and poverty.

We know the turning point in the story of the Hallorans in Mayo was somewhere between 1847 and 1851. We know it was around that time that at least two brothers - Thomas, with a large family, and his younger brother Michael Halloran (*Tomás agus Mícheál Ó hAllmhuráin*), left their home townland to seek new lives in England where they show up in the English census 1851 with a large group of family and neighbours from home. We also know that other Hallorans, specifically one called James, remained at home in Carrowbaun, a townland in Aghamore parish, County Mayo, possibly to look after parents or other elderly members of the family; staying on in the hope of surviving on the family small holding.

We also know that Thomas and Michael's father was called Michael. We know this from his son Michael's marriage certificate (see chapter 2). This marriage took place in the Roman Catholic chapel in Dewsbury, Yorkshire, to Honoria Stinshin [Stenson] on 13th November 1851. The celebrant was Fr Patrick O'Leary. This couple is discussed in more detail in chapter 5.

These were poor people. Neither the groom nor bride could write. The name Stenson was written as it was pronounced *Stinchen*, and is still pronounced in Aghamore parish, Co. Mayo, where it is still found. Interestingly, the father-in-laws, Michael Halloran and John Stinchen, were described as labourers, perhaps indicating they were still both alive. There is no evidence in the 1851 English census of either of them, nor indeed any men of the Irish community of their age. Presumably they were still in Co. Mayo, as labourers or landless cotters. This class of people were virtually driven to extinction by the Great Famine.

This man, Michael, Thomas' father, we have established, is the great, great, great grandfather of Mary and Seán, the writers of this family history. He was probably in his seventies at the time of this marriage, having been born around the 1780s - 230 years ago.

The Gallen and Costello Baronies showing Killkelly and Mannin in 1790

The English census

In looking for the ancestors of the Hallorans of Birstall, we turned first to the English census returns for Birstall and Gomersal in the West Riding of Yorkshire, as we knew generations of the family had lived and worked there since emigrating from County Mayo. The earliest reference was in the 1851 census, where we found a Thomas Halloran (b. 1808) and his wife Judy (b. 1809) and family living in 101 Low Lane, Birstall. Living with Thomas was his younger brother, Michael (b. 1827), aged 23. Living next door to them was Patrick Frain who was married to Catherine Halloran (b. 1821). She was identified as a

Chapter 1 – ORIGINS

Halloran through local parish records. Further examination of the census records allowed us to trace a direct line of descent from Thomas Halloran (1809-1887), to James Halloran (1837–1919) – both probably born in Aghamore, Co Mayo - to William Halloran (1877–1929), who was born in Birstall and was the father of the five brothers to whose memories this book is dedicated - James, Thomas (Tom), John, William (Bill, Willie) and Bernard. Only three of these brothers reached adulthood: Tom, the eldest, John and Bill. John and Bill married and are the fathers of Seán O'Halloran and Mary Hudson (neé Halloran) respectively, the authors of this book. Tom did not marry and lived with his youngest brother, Bill and his wife Betty in 11 King's Drive, Birstall.

The marriage certificate of Michael Halloran (b. 1827) and Honora Stinchen (Stenson) (b. 1832)

James died as a baby and Bernard as a small boy. The three surviving brother knew Bernard and spoke of him to us, their children. None of us, however, knew of the short life of James before we undertook this research, and wonder if his existence was known of by his surviving brothers. It is discoveries like this that have made the writing of this book so rewarding.

Apart from Thomas, we also know from the 1871 English Census that a Michael Halloran (b. 1827) was living with his family in 31 Church Street, Gomersal, Birstall. He was 44 (b. 1827) and described as the head of the family and a labourer. Subsequently, we found the same Michael and young family in the 1861 census under the surname 'Allen'. We know this because of the sequence of children's names. Luckily for us, and most unusually for a census entry at the time, specific details of his place of birth were recorded. The usual census entry for the Irish in Birstall was 'Co. Mayo' or simply 'Ireland'. In his case the entry was 'Ireland, Oughamore (Aghamore), Co Mayo'. His wife, Hannah, was recorded as born in Clamfullough (possibly Cloonfallagh), regions a few miles apart in east Mayo. Why these extra details were added is hard to tell. It is nice to believe that Michael and Hannah displayed such a sense of pride in their origins and emphasised it so forcefully that the recorder felt compelled to note them. What we do know from this is that in all likelihood Thomas, as Michael's brother, was probably also born, or at least lived in Aghamore, giving us a direct link to their origins in Ireland.

Origins in Aghamore

The first evidence of Hallorans in Aghamore appears in the Tithe Applotment book for around 1832. There we were informed that a Thomas Halloran and Co. paid tithes for the area of 'Caltragh', an area very close to Carrowbaun[1]. This is discussed in detail in chapter 9. Suffice to say here that the Thomas

---

1 Information from records in the South Mayo Family Research Centre, supplied by Ger Delaney

who went to Birstall (b. 1808) would have been about 24 at the time and it is possible the record refers to him.

Less specific information was found in Máire McDonnell-Garvey's book, *The Ancient Territory of Slaibh Lugha: Mid-Connacht*, (1995). There we find details of the Dillon Estate concerning leaseholders in the area in 1801 and 1803.

> 30a BALLYNACLOGH (pt. called Carrowbaun) [Ballynacloy, Carrowbaun, p. Aghamore] 1801: John Taffe and Garret Dillon & Co.
>
> 30b (pt. called Carrowbeg) [?Carnbeg, .p. Aghamore] 1801: George Stenson & Co.
>
> 30c (pt. called Carrowscully) Carrowscoltia, .p. Aghamore] 1803: John Burke

This tells us that John Taffe and Garret Dillon leased the land in Carrowbaun directly from the Dillon estate. George Stenson and John Burke leased land in the neighbouring townlands of Aghamore and Carrowscoltia. Another source is Bald's *Map of the Maritime County of Mayo*[1], made by William Bald between the years 1809-1816 but printed in 1830. The relevant part of it is reproduced here, with the modern townland names superimposed.

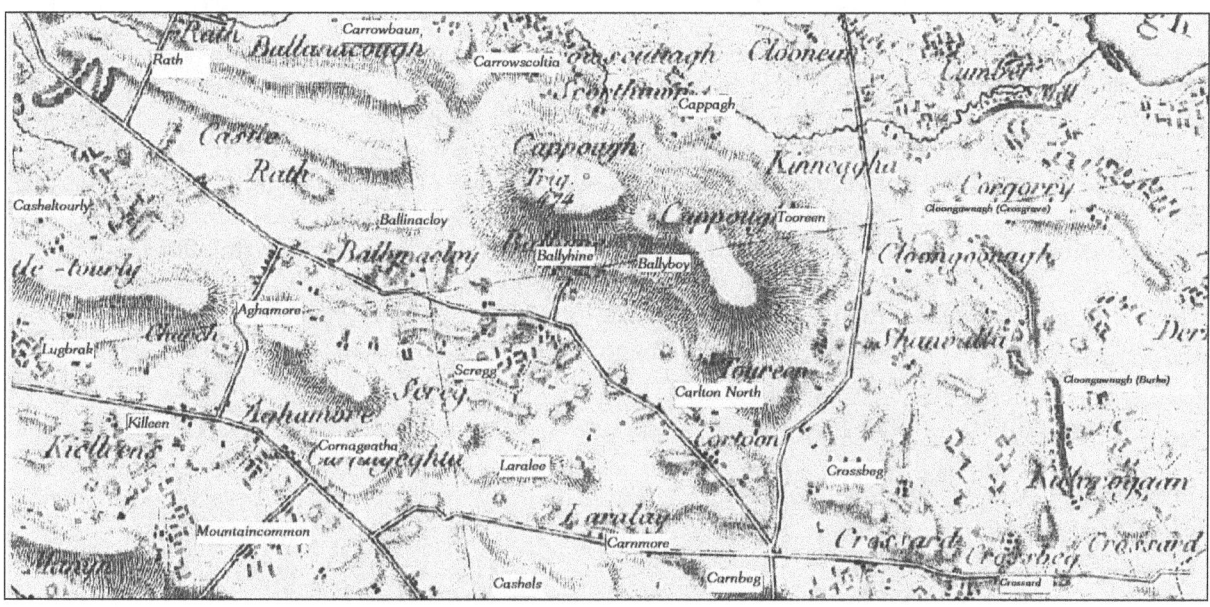

Bald's Map of the Maritime County of Mayo

This map clearly shows that there was only a scattering of dwellings between the more populated areas of Rath and Carrowscoltia, and there is no evidence of roadways in the Ballanaclough /Carrowbaun area. This, however, does not mean the area was not populated. Landless labourers and their families usually lived in temporary cabins known as *scalpeens* or *scalps*, which were often just holes cut in the bog, roofed with sticks and clumps of turf. This, coupled to the fact that only one Halloran family is found in Griffith's Valuation 50 years later, lends support to the idea that family moved to the area at or around the beginning of the 1800s. The earliest fact we can be sure of is that Michael Halloran, Thomas' younger brother, was born in Aghamore in 1827.

The area was not hospitable. In *Notes on the Parish of Aghamore* by John P. Jordan [2] we learn that in 1587, Sir Robert Bingham and the Commission appointed by Queen Elizabeth I for the Composition of Connaught, could not access the area, which he referred to as the Barony of Bellahawnesse in the County of Mayo, commonly called MacCostello. He reported that accessing the area was too difficult because of, 'great bogs, woods, moors and mountains, and other evil ways'. The people there were described as, 'very

---

1 Mayo County Library: http://www.mayolibrary.ie/en/LocalStudies/MapBrowser/OrdnanceSurveyMaps/

2 Notes on the Parish of Aghamore by John P. Jordan - http://www.aghamoreireland.com/history/overview.htm

Chapter 1 – ORIGINS

uncivil and barbarous, and the country there a very receptacle of Scots and a harbour of other louse and evil people'.

Sir Theobald Dillon, the landlord at the time, requested that despite their not being able to view the barony, the Commission would be content if he and his tenants would make yearly compensation to her majesty [Queen Elizabeth I], 'both for the better reducing of the people there to servility, and that they might yield obedience and know their duty unto her Highness'.

Whether the people were reduced to servility is arguable. However, they were certainly reduced to poverty through paying rent for land that had not been economically viable until they had worked it. The names of many townlands suggest the area had been heavily wooded, especially with oak trees. The oak gave its name to the many *doires* in the area: Derryclaha, Derryea, Derrykinlough, and Derrybrack, to mention a few. The trees had to be cut down and the stumps burnt or dug out. There was also bog land that required drains to be dug, the rushes and boulders removed. Then the land had to be worked, often using potato crops to break up the ground to make it fit for agriculture, at which point the rents were raised as more people flowed in. This influx allowed the rents to be raised again, and those who could not pay were evicted and new tenants brought in. Frequently, land that had taken massive amounts of manpower to prepare was turned over to grazing, leaving the families who had worked the farm, landless and destitute.

However, as we have seen, around 1801, the names Taffe, Dillon, and Burke are associated with fairly substantial landholders in the area, and their interests may have been largely speculative, as, unlike the Stensons who also leased land in the Dillon estate, their names do not appear in the parish in subsequent generations. It appears they leased out their holdings to larger groups, perhaps of families and the land would have been further sublet and subdivided among individual members. When these individuals had children to leave land to, it would have been subdivided yet again. Thus the rent flowed upward from those who had the smallest plots, through the hands of small farmers and then through the hands of larger farmers into the hands of an agent who would pass on a predetermined sum to the landlord. Rent was often a combination of money, crops and labour. At the bottom of the pile, and renting enough land to grow potatoes for the family was the farm labourer or cottier, who were also required to give of their labour.

These struggling people, working what had traditionally been sub-marginal land, were a new population. The displaced of Ireland were finding their way to remote regions and living on potatoes using a method of cultivation called lazy-beds. This involved turning over sods of peat and planting the seed potato while applying a fertiliser, often seaweed (desalinated) in coastal areas, to improve the ground. This was a very efficient way of breaking open new land to cultivation. It involved a huge amount of manpower, proving an ingenious way of absorbing the growing population. However, it created a dangerous dependency on a mono-cultural form of subsistence farming that ultimately proved to be catastrophic.

A typical 'scalpeen'

Within the social and economic structures of the day, small tenant farmers and cottiers had little access to other forms of food and were often without the means to grow cash crops. All such cultivation was done for the landlord as rent in kind. They also had to pay rent in cash, earned through seasonal work in England or with money sent by relatives in England, usually navvies or house servants. Quite simply, the land rented could not produce sufficient to feed the family who worked it and leave enough to pay for its rental. The peasants who created the wealth were constantly on the verge of poverty and hunger. Meanwhile, the landlords of Ireland, who were enriched by this process, became a major political force in Westminster - seat of the most powerful government in the world – and some of the richest people in the British Empire, rivalling the aristocratic families of Europe and the Indian Maharajas.

This situation appears to be unparalleled in subsistence farming elsewhere in Europe at the time and led a commentator in the *Illustrated London News*[1] to remark, 'the Irish cotter is as much a serf as the Russian peasant; with the difference he is worse fed'. It also meant there was no surplus cash for investment or improvement, particularly in view of the uncertainty of tenure and the refusal of Irish landlords to maintain dwellings and outhouses, responsibilities undertaken by landlords in England.

However, there may have been advantages in coming to an area that was so underdeveloped. According to Cousens (1961), famine depopulation was lowest in the eastern periphery of Mayo, because of the large amount of wasteland that could be reclaimed and converted into smallholdings by families that would otherwise have starved or emigrated. It may have been the existence of this wasteland that drew the Hallorans to the area in the first place and allowed those who remained to survive and acquire new land.

The present day generation of Hallorans in Aghamore

Having thus found evidence that there were Hallorans living in Aghamore in the 1830s, we were delighted to find much more interesting evidence. When we went to visit the area just after Easter in 2010, we discovered, to our delight and surprise, that Hallorans were still working the fields of Carrowbaun, nearly two centuries later. It was on that occasion that we met Martin Halloran, now a resident of Swinford, and his sister Phil Riley. They took us to Carrowbaun, where Martin still has grazing cattle. Both had been brought up there and they talked of other Halloran families in the area, in Raith, Cahir and Mountain.

They told us all these families were connected in the distant past, but the families had now died out locally. It is also believed that, in the very remote past, the Killasser forebears of Rev Fr Pat Holleran, parish priest in Rockfield, Coolaney originated from Aghamore. Killasser is north of Swinford and some 15 miles from Carrowbaun. Fr Pat Holleran told us his first parish was in Aghamore and, at that time, he and some of his family met an old bachelor on the Cahir crossroads. He was a Halloran and they all remarked how he was the splitting image of their own uncle in Killasser.

In Killasser, the Griffith Valuation records one Thomas Halloran in the townland of Magheraboy, another Thomas in Doonmaynor, a Michael Halloran in Cartronmacmanus and a Martin Halloran in Cartron. The areas into which they and the rest of the displaced of Ireland were being forced before the famine had developed very little social infrastructure. Schools and medical support, inadequate even in the rest of Catholic Ireland, were very rudimentary where they existed at all, especially outside of the towns.

This meeting with Martin and Phil was a real bonus as it was way beyond our expectations. Though Martin and Phil would be distantly related to us, we share a common heritage and were standing on the land that Thomas and James, our great, great grandfather had worked on and tragically seen fail during the Great Famine. It was also the land that James, Martin and Phil's great grandfather, continued to work, and was passed down to the present generation. Both men, James and Thomas, had probably worked this land, had known great hardship and survived to rear families - one in Carrowbaun and one in Birstall. We who were standing there owed our existence to their survival.

---

1 ILN - March 1847 - quoted in Donnelly 1996

Chapter 1 – ORIGINS

Aghamore, County Outline of relationship between Hallorans of Aghamore and Birstall

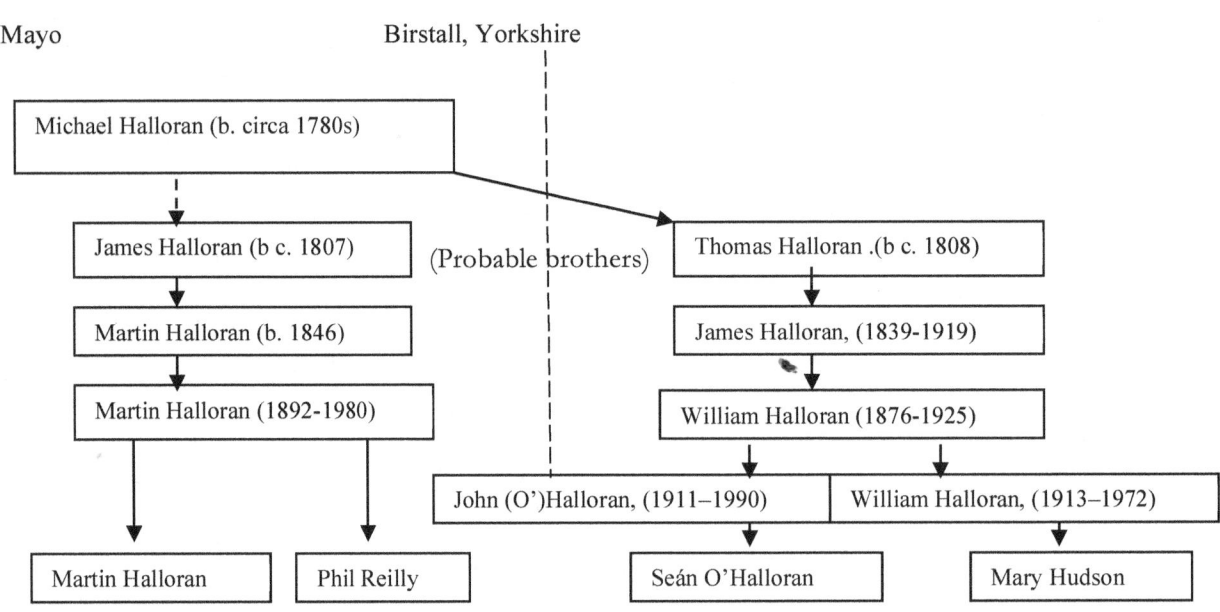

Mary Hudson (neé Halloran), Joseph & John Halloran, Phil Reilly (nee Halloran) Sean O'Halloran, Martin Halloran in Carrowbaun

In chapters 9 and 10, we will examine the family that Thomas and Michael left behind in Carrowbaun. At this point it is worth finding out a bit about the parish and townland where they grew up and the Great Famine that forced them to flee.

THE HALLORANS OF BIRSTALL AND AGHAMORE

The Barony of Costello

To understand the geopolitical context in which the Hallorans lived, it is important to realise that the administrative divisions in Ireland are unlike those of Britain. The counties themselves make up the four provinces of Ireland: Leinster, Munster, Connaught and Ulster. Mayo, of course, is in Connaught. These provinces are made up of counties that are divided into baronies, these in turn being divided into parishes that are themselves divided into townlands.

County	Electoral district	Barony	Civil parish	Townland
Maigh Eo	*Achadh Mór*	*Coistealaigh*	*Achadh Mór*	*Ceathnú Bán*
Mayo	Aghamore	Costello	Aghamore	Carrowbaun

Looking over the landscape of East Mayo at the beginning of the nineteenth century one would see a very different sight from today. People lived on the land in a very different way and the mark they left on it was different too. The main difference would be the number of people.

We can draw on contemporary sources that describe life in Mayo at the time in some detail in order to get a clearer picture of the type of life Thomas and James Halloran and their families and neighbours lived. One is the *Statistical Survey of County Mayo*, conducted by Dr McParlan on behalf of the Royal Dublin Society, who travelled throughout Mayo and analysed each barony. McParlan remarks:

> *The population of Costello in 1831 was 44,985. Houses numbered 8.655. Families employed chiefly in agriculture. 7,543; in manufactures and trade, 1,039; in other employment, 326. Males at and above five years could read and write numbered 1,313; who could read but not write 184, who could neither read nor write 17,334.*
>
> *On present day calculations, Connaught in 1841 contained 1.418,859 people, a large proportion of whom had become entirely dependent on the potato for their existence.*

We do not know if he was aware how prescient these words were, however, he continues with this description of the Barony of Costello.

> *The soil and surface of the whole barony, with a few exceptions, is either bog, reclaimed moor or mountain. These exceptions are Edmondstown, the seat of Mr. Costello; about the town of Balladerrin; at Lung and Cloonmore, where some good grounds are to be seen. Between Ballyhaunis and Donmacreeny there are some green grounds; and in that line towards Becon and Clare, there is a green aspect; but the soil is very light, of a moory quality, and seems to have been reclaimed. ...*
>
> **[Of navigations and navigable rivers:]** *...The river of Lung, which runs into Lough Gara, is navigable for eight or ten miles, from above the bridge of Crenan, for boats of ten ton, except in a few spots, not amounting in all to a mile. ... Lough Gara, near Boyle, touches on the borders of Roscommon, Sligo and Mayo; it is in some places five miles across; 'its banks are for the most part excellent for tillage and fattening; those banks are likewise in the neighbourhood of coal and iron ore, consequently opening this navigation might eventually prove an extreme public utility.*
>
> **[Of fisheries:]** *... Probably all the lakes and rivers of the county abound with all sorts of fresh-water fish, and many of them are the depots for all the salmon to deposit their spawn in. Cloonlomley river, in the barony of Costello, is the chief nursery for the Ballina fishery, and is now in the care of bargees, Those bargers, or persons appointed to watch the rivers where the salmon come up to spawn, are extremely troublesome, in entering the houses of peaceable inhabitants at late hours, abusing and beating them when not in bribe. This I write by desire of a gentleman of Carra, who is ready to prove it. ...Fresh-water fish of every kind, and the best qualities, abound in all the lakes and rivers of this county.*
>
> **Of manufactures – whether increasing:]** *The flax and yarn are here in very brisk plight; large quantities of both are sold raw and in linens.*
>
> *At Ballina, Costello, and different parts of the county, is abundance of fuel and water, and consequently every aptness of situation for bleach-greens, many of which are still necessary in this county, so extensive and considerable is grown the linen business.*[1]

---

1 The flax industry soon fell into sharp decline, unable to cope with competition from the newly industrialised linen production in Ulster.

Chapter 1 – ORIGINS

The villagers here, who are in partnership, divide themselves according to their numbers, into four or eight parties; each party keeps a horse, the joint property of the whole, which horses do in common the work of the village.

The parish of Aghamore

Lewis Topographical Dictionary of Ireland 1837 describes *Aghamore*[1] as follows:

AGHAVOWER, or AGHAMORE, a parish, in the barony of COSTELLO, county of MAYO, and province of CONNAUGHT, 4 1/2 miles (N.) from Ballyhaunis, on the road from that place to Swinford; containing 7062 inhabitants. St. Patrick is said to have erected a monastery here, for his disciple St. Loarn. The surface of the parish is varied with several small lakes; the lands are chiefly under tillage; there is a considerable quantity of bog, also a quarry of black marble. The gentlemen's seats are Cooge, the residence of James Dillon, Esq.; Annach, of Thomas Tyrrell, Esq.; and Oahil, of James McDonnell, Esq. Fairs are held at Ballinacostello on June 3rd, Aug. 8th, Oct. 19th, and Dec. 18th.

The parish is in the diocese of Tuam, and is a rectory and vicarage, forming part of the union of Kiltullagh: the tithes amount to £158. 4. 10. The ancient church is in ruins, but the cemetery is still used. In the R. C. divisions it is part of the district of Knock; the chapel is an old thatched building.
There are seven pay schools, in which are about 550 children. At Cloonfallagh there is a mineral spring.

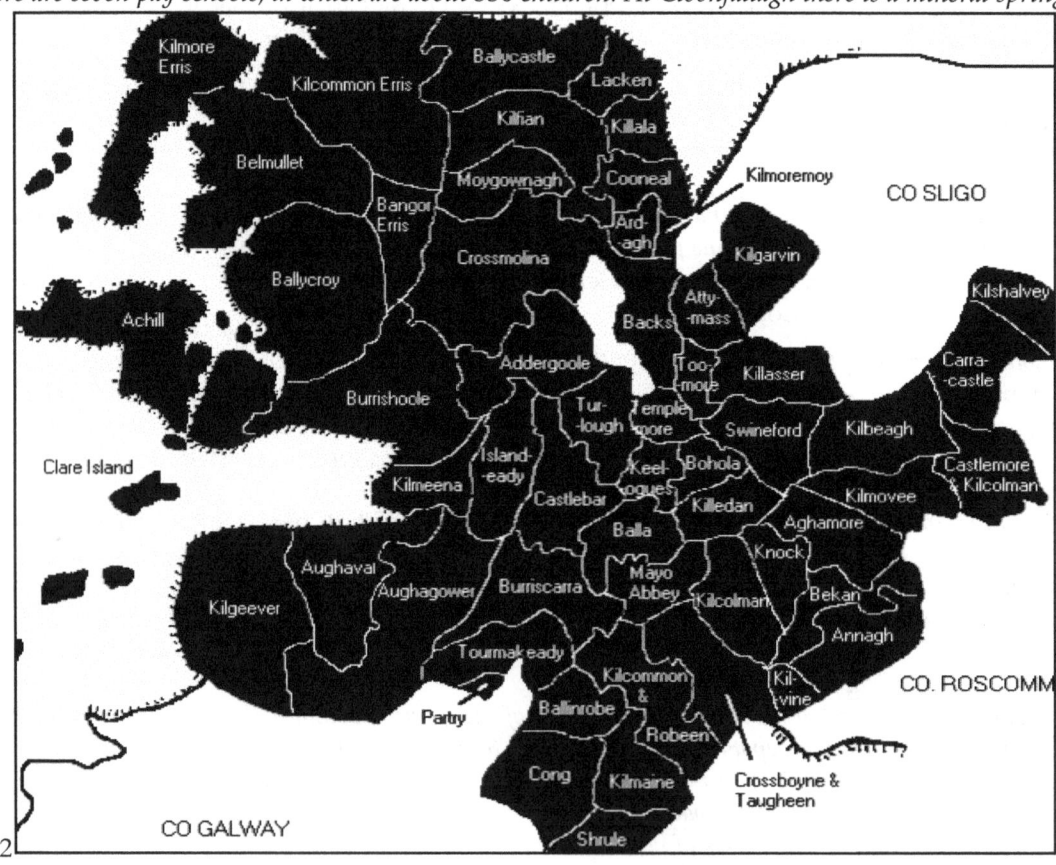

The Roman Catholic Parishes of County Mayo

Jill Dale (2010) in *Country Mayo beginnings*[3] describes Aghamore civil parish - part of Aghamore Roman Catholic Parish - at the time of Griffith's Valuation in 1856, when it contained 74 townlands. Most of the

---

1 A possible source of confusion is that Aghamore is the name of the parish that also contains a townland called Aghamore. This is adjacent to Carrowbaun, but we have no record of Hallorans in the townland of Aghamore. In Irish, Aghamore means 'the great field'.

---

3 http://www.rootsweb.ancestry.com/~irlmayo2/aghamore_cp_characteristics.html

townlands, like Carrowbaun, were quite small, though some, like Caher, Mountaincommon and Falleighter - to mention only townlands relevant to this story - were quite large.

The population was scattered throughout the countryside in *clachans*. These are clusters of dwellings, largely associated with particular families and associates. Unlike in England, the rural population was not concentrated in villages, where one found townhouses, shops, a church, post office, mills and other buildings associated with rural life. Rural life in the west of Ireland was sustained by subsistence living. For the ordinary people, there was little commerce or paid employment. Money was used primarily for the rent.

Joe Byrne, local historian and musician, tells us the more usual term for *clachan* in Mayo is *stráid*, or street, because of the road that connected the houses. In Carrowbaun, this road was called the *Bridle Road*, as it was down it the agent, the one man with a horse with a bridle, rode to collect the rent.

At that time, the only Roman Catholic Chapel was in the townland of Killeen and there were graveyards in the townlands of Aghamore, Carrownedan, Cloongawnagh (Cosgrave) and Boleyboy.

Four fairs were held in the townland of Ballinacostello in the late 18th century. (Gillespie; Crawford, 1987, p. 84). When the *Statistical Survey of County Mayo* was conducted in 1802, Ballinacostello didn't have a market for grain or cattle, but fairs were listed as taking place on June 3, August 9, October 9 and December 16. (McParlan, 1802; 2007, p. 47-51).

When the Griffith's Valuation was conducted in Aghamore civil parish, it listed in various townlands a 'Fair Green' and a 'Customs of Fairs', as well as a corn mill, kilns and a forge. Ballinacostello was the hub of commercial activity for the parish. The townland of Aghamore was the location of the Courthouse, and the townland of Tober had a pound for stray livestock. Other townlands had corn mills, forges and kilns. Herds' houses were present in many townlands indicating a fair amount of pasture for grazing. (Griffith, 1847-1864; 2003, Aghamore). It also indicated that cereal crops were grown, probably for the landlord.

Multiple lakes were scattered throughout Aghamore civil parish in greater profusion than at present, as many have been drained. Samuel Lewis, in his 'A Topographical Dictionary of Ireland', describes 'a considerable quantity of bog' in this civil parish. (Lewis, 1837; 1984, p. 18).

The townland of Carrowbaun

We focus on this townland, as it is where we find James Halloran in 1856. Townlands are believed to have originated as farms held in common by a number of families. They were thus very important social units, identifying a family group with a particular piece of land, an emotional association that was much more powerful in the eyes of the cottiers and those with smallholdings than the relationship between the landlord and the land.

Griffith's Evaluation of Ireland – a primary evaluation (1847 – 1864)

Griffith's was the first full-scale valuation of property in Ireland compiled in order to facilitate the collection of taxes, especially to levy the county cess[1] charges and Grand Jury Rates. It is the most comprehensive survey of Irish households available for the middle of the nineteenth century and is a principal tool of genealogists and local historians. It became very controversial as the values it put on properties became a great source of contention between the tenants and the landlords, as the latter frequently charged rents much higher than the evaluation determined by the Griffith Valuation.

The valuation was overseen by Richard Griffith and published between 1847 and 1864, a critical period in our investigations, as it spanned the period between the Great Famine and the first mention of Hallorans in the English censuses. Its survival is a small compensation for the loss of the nineteenth century Irish census records that were destroyed in the Irish Civil War in 1922, when the Public Records Office was burned down and one thousand years of Irish state and religious archives were lost.

---

[1] The cess is something equivalent to local taxes, used for the upkeep of roads etc.

Chapter 1 – ORIGINS

It is in *Griffith's Evaluation of Ireland – a primary evaluation (1847 – 1864)* that we find James Halloran, the only Halloran in Aghamore who rented enough land to register in this survey, though there may well have been others who were small cottiers or landless labourers.

Bridget Kelly and James Halloran

When we look at the map that accompanies the written entries in Griffith's Valuation, we clearly see Bridget Kelly's holdings marked 1, 2, 3 and 4 - plot numbers used to identify each occupier's parcel of land on the Ordinance Survey Maps. Bridget Kelly rented a house, 5 acres of arable land and 30 of pasture from Viscount Dillon. She had sub-let two of these plots, 3 and 4, to James Halloran, with who she is bracketed. James is marked as holding a house, a cottage and an office. His house rent of £10 indicates he and his family are living in a more substantial dwelling than Bridget. The cottage, perhaps occupied by a son or landless labourer, may well be such a temporary structure that it does not get recorded. There are houses marked on plots 1 and 2. She probably lived in one of these.

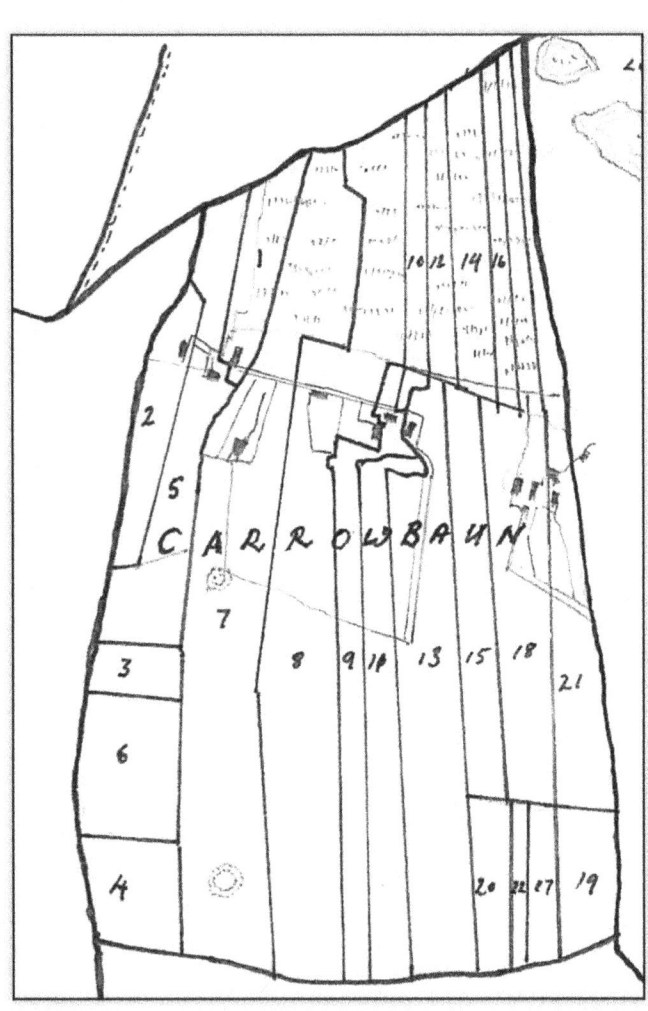

We know James was a sub-tenant because Bridget Kelly's plot is marked with a lower case *a*, an indication that she is the principal tenant and a small farmer. The letter *b* indicates a worker on the farm, suggesting that James' home is on Bridget's farm where he is both a sub-tenant and labourer. It appears another individual has a home or garden within Bridget's farm and is listed as *c*. This may be James' son or close relative. It was common in County Mayo for small farmers to hold their land in what is termed a 'rundale,' (discussed below) where land is sub-divided and each partner was given a portion of land based on the rent paid. Theirs is the only example in the townland of three levels of tenancy. There are two examples of subletting. One involved Timothy Glarey, though the name of the subtenant is not given, possibly because it was a son. The other is where James Cox is a subtenant of Thomas Prendergast.

Map of Carrowbaun based on Griffith's Valuation

Land was measured in acres, roods and perches (the column a, r, p). The total annual rateable valuation was £4.10s and £5.00s, equalling £9.10s between the two of them. Her land's rateable value was £1.10. No rateable value was given for her property. James property was valued as £ 2.15 and his land at 5 shillings.

So it appears James rented land, a house, an 'office', and a cottage from Bridget Kelly and that Viscount Dillon was the landlord. The land consisted of 5 acres of arable land, 3 of bog, and 7 of pasture. The total rateable value was £4.10 shillings. The term 'office' refers to some sort of outbuilding such as a factory, mill, turf shed, or a farmer's outbuilding like a cowshed, stable or even a privy.

The total amount of arable land was 20 acres. There were 30 acres of pasture and 8 of bog land. The question then arises of how well this could support Bridget Kelly as well as James and his family. The Devon Commission received evidence that 10½ acres was needed to support a family of five. Presumably this refers to arable land. By this standard, Thomas appears relatively better off than some, depending on

THE HALLORANS OF BIRSTALL AND AGHAMORE

the size of his family. However, it must be remembered that this is a snapshot of a famine-depleted townland; the potato crop first failed in 1845 and repeatedly for a number of years thereafter. Prior to the famine the townland was more heavily populated by a number of young families, possibly including that of Thomas Halloran, and his brother Michael, who fled the Great Famine, and settled in Birstall, Yorkshire.

No. and Letters of Reference to Map.	Names.		Description of Tenement.	Area.			Rateable Annual Valuation.		Total Annual Valuation of Rateable Property.
	Townlands and Occupiers.	Immediate Lessors.					Land.	Buildings.	
	CARROWBAUN. (Ord. S. 82.)			A.	R.	P.	£ s. d.	£ s. d.	£ s. d.
1				5	0	30	1 10 0		
2 1 a	Bridget Kelly,	Viscount Dillon,	Land and house,	5	3	7	2 15 0	0 5 0	4 10 0
3 – b	James Halloran,	Same,	Land, house, & office,	3	1	10	1 10 0	0 10 0	
4 – c		Same,	One cottage,	7	2	0	2 15 0	0 5 0	5 0 0
5 a	Michael Stenson,	Same,	Land, house, and office,	12	0	15	5 0 0	0 10 0	
6	Michael Stenson,	Same,	Land,	8	1	25	3 15 0	—	9 5 0
7 a	James Tigue,	Same,	Land, house, and offices,	41	1	33	17 10 0	0 10 0	18 0 0
8 a	Timothy Glavey,	Same,	Land and house,	31	1	0	12 10 0	0 10 0	13 5 0
– b			One cottage,	—			—	0 5 0	
9 a	Patrick Fahy,	Same,	Land, house, and office,	10	1	37	5 0 0	0 10 0	6 0 0
10	Patrick Fahy,	Same,	Land,	3	3	20	0 10 0	—	
11 a	Owen Keane,	Same,	Land, house, and office,	11	2	15	5 0 0	0 10 0	5 0 0
12	Owen Keane,	Same,	Land,	4	0	10	0 10 0	—	
13 a	Thomas Regan,	Same,	Land, house, and office,	20	2	30	9 10 0	0 10 0	10 10 0
14	Thomas Regan,	Same,	Land,	7	1	26	0 10 0	—	
15 a	Owen Linskey,	Same,	Land, house, and office,	7	3	20	3 10 0	0 10 0	
16	Owen Linskey,	Same,	Land,	3	2	25	0 5 0	—	5 10 0
17	Owen Linskey,	Same	Land,	4	0	20	1 5 0	—	
18 a	Owen Stenson,	Same,	Land, house, and office,	20	3	9	8 10 0	0 10 0	
19	Owen Stenson,	Same,	Land,	5	0	0	1 10 0	—	10 0 0
20	Owen Stenson,	Same,	Land,	3	3	5	1 10 0	—	
21				9	1	30	3 0 0		
21 a	Thomas Prendergast,	Same,	Land, house, & office,					0 5 0	2 8 0
– b	James Cox,	Same,	Land, house, & office,					0 5 0	2 8 0
22				3	1	20	1 6 0		
			Total,	231	0	27	87 1 0	5 15 0	92 16 0

Griffith's Evaluation of Ireland – a primary evaluation (1847 – 1864) – Carrowbaun townland Sheet no. 82, Map Ref 1,2,3,4.

Nonetheless, the map does not seem to account for the 30 acres of pasture, which was probably located on a nearby hillside or bog land. This is typical of an aspect of the rundale system known as *booleying*. This involved the movement of livestock, usually cattle, to mountain summer pastures. This system relieved pressure on the growing crops and provided fresh pasture for livestock, particularly where farms were small.

We also know the valuation in this part of count Mayo took place in the first half of 1856. As the valuation proceeded, smaller properties were excluded from its investigation. Properties of less than £3 annual value were only included up to 1831. Those with an annual value of £5 were excluded from 1836 onwards, that is before the valuation took place in Aghamore. This means that a great number of small subsistence holdings did not appear in the records, nor did the smaller holding of landless labourers, cottiers, who lived in very primitive *scalpeens*, often just a lean-to propped against a wall.

Clachan and Rundale

A typical feature of the townland was the rundale, or open field system centred on family based clachans. According to Freeman (1957), land around these was leased to one or two tenants who then divided it up amongst 20-30 others so that the land was held in joint tenancy, being distributed amongst the tenants based on the amount of rent contributed. An 'infield area' that was composed of land to grow crops and an 'out field' area further out that was used for grazing usually radiated out from the homes, (Jordan, 1994, p. 56). Originally, as the name 'open field' suggests, there were no dividing walls or fences and animals were tethered, to keep them in the right spot, though they often broke free and ate the neighbours crops or vegetables, resulting in frequent disputes. The different pieces of land were shuffled periodically to promote a fair distribution of poor, middling and quality land. Rundale land division was in its most extreme form in Co Mayo and Co. Donegal.

The rundale system, ultimately, could not survive the demands of a growing population. Over the generations it resulted in multiple sub-divisions of farms. In *Facts of Gweedore*, Hill (1887) claims that a man might have his holdings in as many as thirty or forty patches of different quality, good, bad or indifferent. He states:

> *the farms were also frequently, at the death of the parents, reduced to atoms at once; being divided amongst all the children, in such cases when the farm was small, it left to all a mere 'skibberlin' (a shred of a coat) and by this simple process, the next generation were beggars.*

Hugh Dorian, a schoolteacher, wrote a 'true historic narrative' of the transformation of his home community in the nineteenth century in 1889. It has been edited and published under the title *The Outer Edge of Ulster*. He describes how, as money was not in use, land was divided and handed down each generation to the children in a family.

> *The old man, the father was the owner – the tenant. The receipt, if such could be produced, was in his name, the son or the daughter at marriage got the land, as best as pleased him, and were sub-tenants and were accountable for a proportional share of the rent. Next, the grandson got a share and was likewise accountable for his addition to the general purse when the time arrived [to pay rent] … Anyone having land could divide it and following up this old system, field after field, piece after piece was divided and subdivided, until at last one man might have fifty or more pieces in a townland, either by bequest or by purchase. … Those plots of land varied in size and of every shape possible, and to point out or define the property large stones or other marks were set up here and there to mark the boundary. This was the Rundale System.*

More expensive items, like horses and carts, and even donkeys, were held in common and shared out in the *meithal* system. Though these systems of collective and shared ownership are now idealised and romanticised and represented as belonging to an era of communal simplicity, the pressure of a growing population and the encroachment of outsiders resulted in conflicts and even pitched battles. It was a system born out of necessity. People needed each other to do some of the most basic things, like getting products to markets. This sense of mutual dependence fostered strong bonds between people; bonds that served them well when times got hard. And times did get hard. It is difficult to imagine how people with virtually nothing survived the famine and fled to new counties creating new Irish communities in places like Birstall, if it had not been for the ingrained habits of mutual support and dependency that marked their lives in Ireland.

The landlord class, however, believed that this system encouraged dependency and discouraged individual initiatives and improvement and many of them made attempts to 'square the land' through consolidating the holdings. This is visible in the map of Carrowbaun above. The fact that the land in Carrowbaun was divided into long strips and that tenants leased two strips each, suggests that the landlord, or at least his agent, Charles Strickland, had begun an assault on the rundale system, had begun to 'square the land', in the belief that self-reliance and initiative would be encouraged by the development of individual farms. Certainly, the process of subdivision was not as bad as described in Gweedore. This was probably not the case in pre-famine times. However, the massive depopulation resulting from the famine reduced or completely removed the need to subdivide land after the 1850s, as much more land was available.

Coulter (1862), who is not uncritical of the excesses of the landlord class, but does not see it an inherently flawed, tells us of the Dillon estate more than a decade after the famine.

> *The rundale system existed here, as on other properties in Mayo, and led to that minute subdivision of holdings which has been found to be productive of so many mischievous effects. The striping of the lands was commenced systematically in 1840, and has been carried out over at least two-thirds of the estate; and wherever the old system still remains, it is owing to the existence of old leases. The people are fully alive to the benefit of having their lands properly divided, and in some instances they have voluntarily surrendered their leases for the purpose of having this effected. In the laying out of the new farms on the various townlands at the fall of the old joint tenancy leases, great pains were taken by Mr Strickland [Dillon's agent, discussed at greater length later] that perfect justice should be done to all parties. The proportionate rights of every tenant were strictly observed, and care was taken that each should have in one division a fair proportion of the good and inferior qualities of land, with bog attached, for fuel and future reclamation. It was so arranged that each holding should, if possible, abut on the public road; but where this could not be done, accommodation roads were made at the landlord's expense, to be subsequently maintained by the tenants.*

Neighbours

The Halloran's neighbours in Birstall were the very same neighbours they had in the townlands of Aghamore, as we will see in chapter 5. The table above is a list of those townland neighbours and the rateable value of their land and buildings.

21-22	Prendergast, Thomas	£2.08		11-12	Keane, Owen	£8.00
22	Cox, James	£2.8		5-6	Stenson Michael	£9.50
1-4	Kelly, Bridget	£4.10		13-14	Regan Thomas	£10.00
1-4	Halloran, James	£5.00		18-19	Stenson Owen	£10.00
15-16	Linskey, Owen	£5.10		8	Galvey, Timothy	£13.05
9-10	Fahy, Patrick	£6.00		7-8	Tigue James	£18.00

Residents of Carrowbaun townland

Also in the townland we note a Michael Stenson, in possession of plots 5 and 6, totalling 20 acres, and an Owen Stenson, in possession of plots 18, 19 and 20, totalling over 28 acres; quite substantial holdings for the time. These two men may have been relatives of Judy (neé Stenson), Thomas Halloran's wife. Thomas and Judy, as well as a number of other members of the Stenson family had, as we know from the 1851 English census, fled the famine and were, by the time of the Griffith Valuation, living in Birstall.

We already know that John Taffe and Garret Dillon leased the land in Carrowbaun directly from the Dillon estate in the early 1800s. At the same time, George Stenson and John Burke also leased land in the neighbouring townlands of Aghamore and Carrowscoltia at that time. Phil Reilly tells of how her father, Martin Halloran (1892-1980), talked of seven Stenson brothers from Co. Leitrim coming into Aghamore and settling in the area between Falleighter, Carrowbaun and Cappagh. It appears these families settled and spread into the neighbouring townlands. There remained a strong association between the Stenson and the Halloran families for generations after the famine in both Birstall and Carrowbaun.

We also see two clusters of nucleated dwelling, *clachans*, or *stráids* typical of a County Mayo townland. Probably the impermanent nature of the dwellings meant the settlement pattern changed comparatively often (Freeman. 1957). What, however, is remarkable is that when we compare it to maps on Google Earth, the modern layout of the main fields reflects that of the 1850s. A similar map of Carrowbaun found in chapter 9 gives more detail and some of the names of the Halloran fields as given to us by Phil and Martin Halloran.

Conacre and labourers

After the famine, James, it would appear, was on the fringes of the cottier class, a labourer, like Thomas and Michael's father, Michael, but in possession of two small plots held by Bridget Kelly; subdivisions of the rundale system. It was members of this cottier class who were to be virtually wiped out during the famine, and we can only wonder how it was he and his family survived.

McParlan reports that before the Great Famine:

> the general price of labour all through the country… is eight pence per day without food, six pence per day and dinner; the cottiers have about six pence per day short and long, but have good bargains of house, land, and turbary. Occasional workers, such as shearers and mowers get from ten pence to twelve pence with food.

Landless labourers would often rent land using the conacre system. This is a system of letting a portion of a farm to a landless labourer to grow potatoes, who would, as well as paying the rent, be obliged to work on the landlord's land. Frequently such labourers would move to England or Scotland at harvest times to raise the money for this rent.

It is possible that Thomas Prendergast and James Cox, neighbours of James in Carrowbaun, who both had smallholdings in Carrowbaun, were in such a position. In view of the small size of James Halloran's holding and the fact that he was member of a larger family before the famine, might suggest that he and or at least some of his brothers rented land using the conacre system before they emigrated.

Chapter 1 – ORIGINS

Another useful contemporary source is Fr. Durkan's *Deposition to the Devon Commission*. The commission took evidence all over Ireland and examined 1100 witnesses. Its brief was 'to inquire into the law and practice with regard to the occupation of land in Ireland'. In 1844, Fr. Durcan, PP and Mr. Ormsby from Kiltimagh gave evidence to the Royal Commission in Swinford. Fr Durcan reports:

> *The con-acre system prevails here. Manured land for potatoes costs between £6 - £8, but if the land is very good it can be as high as £10.*
>
> *Mr. Ormsby has some of his land set to labourers at the same rent as any other tenant, and they are obliged to work when called upon at any period of the year at 6d a day, without diet ... and if they refuse when called on at the most pressing time for his own business, he is fined 1s and his crop is distrained to make him pay. So far as their houses are very much neglected, and they do not exert themselves so much as those who have separate holdings in improving them. One idle person may prevent other persons exerting themselves where they otherwise would. They cannot make fences or anything of that sort.*
>
> *Rent is fixed, in general, by proposal. The highest offer is accepted; when a lease terminates the landlord gives preference to the occupier, but expects him to give the highest offer.*
>
> *For average land rent varies from 25s to 35s, and in some cases as high as £2. Rent is due in May and November. The May rent is demanded in October, and the November rent in March or April.*

Fr. Durcan noted that rents are:

> *usually 40%, 50% or 60% above poor law valuation[1], and in some cases 100%. If tenants default rent is recovered by distraint[11].*

However, the clachan and rundale system was more than a system of farming; it was the expression of the culture and values of the people of rural Ireland. Hely Dutton (1824) concluded they led to:

> *Such strong attachments, generally strengthened by intermarriage, that though they may have had some bickering with each other they will, right or wrong, keep their companions.[2]*

And keep their companions they did, even in the face of famine. As we will see in detail, the close-knit dependency that characterised *stráid* life was extended and transferred to the back streets of Birstall where the immigrant Irish community supported each other and supplied a network to those at home. This was happening throughout Ireland, especially in Connaught, the result was that the system was magnified in a huge network of mutual support that crossed lands and seas and ensured the continued existence of families and neighbours driven from their townlands by hunger and disease.

Interior of a peasant's cottage.
Pictorial Times - 1846

As Whelan reports[3,] the *clachan* settlement and the rundale farming system was part of a face-to-face world where communication skills were valued and a rich oral culture was encouraged. The non-material arts like singing, story telling and dancing emerged as prize art forms. *Clachan* and rundale were cohesively inter-woven into communal, customary and contextual modes

---

1 Derived from Griffith's Primary Valuation

2 Hely Dutton (1824), A statistical and agricultural survey of the county of Galway, http://books.google.co.uk/books?

3 Pre- and post famine landscape change The Great Irish Famine

of organisation. Though these were being challenged by political economists and improving (or exploiting) landlords, and though they were severely disrupted by the famine, the values of clachan and rundale system prevailed, at least for a few generations. Though transformed, these self-same values emerged in small towns like Birstall, where a sense of mutual dependency and family alliances created a cohesive network of family alliances that allowed young families and people whose families had been decimated, an extensive system of family connections that provided shelter, sustenance, companionship and shared experience. It was these things perhaps beyond all other that allowed the Irish to emerge anew in scattered diasporas around the world, and is ultimately responsible for their survival and the existence of such families as the Hallorans of Birstall.

Relative to the congestion and size of farms, Carrowbaun was not the most impoverished township in Mayo, but again it must be remembered that the picture captured by Griffiths Valuation is of a famine-stripped land. Presumably, James' land in the post-famine era was larger than that held by the family, or families, in pre-famine times. This suggests that the Halloran holding in pre-famine days was very small, perhaps just a couple of acres and perhaps these were held according to the con-acre system. Some of the family may have been landless labourers. However, the family we know was quite large, and there were probably other members we know nothing of. This suggests subsistence would have been difficult.

Dwellings

In these prevailing conditions, there was generally neither the cash nor the incentive for the cottiers[1] and those with smallholdings to improve their land or dwellings. Regarding the buildings and dwelling houses we can note that the 1841 Census divided the 'houses' of the country into four classes: the fourth grade consisted of mud cabins with only one room; the third grade consisted of mud cottages with two to four rooms or windows; the second grade consisted of houses with 2 to 4 rooms and windows; and the first grade consisted of houses of even greater dimensions.

In County Mayo nine out of ten dwellings were in the third and fourth grades and half were in the lowest grade (Freeman, 1957). The information from Griffith's Valuation suggests that James Halloran's status was such that he would probably have been in a low grade.

There are numerous contemporary reports of the pitiful state of the Irish peasantry, who endured possibly the worse living conditions in Europe. Gustave de Beaumont in *Ireland: Social, Political and Religious Parts 1839* describes the lowest and probably the most common form of cabin in the west of Ireland; the sort that landless agricultural labourers like the Hallorans may have lived in before the Great Famine.

> *Image four walls of dry mud, which the rain as if falls restores to its original physical condition, having for its roof little straws and sods. For its chimney, a hole cut in the roof. ... the door through which alone the smoke finds an issue.*
> *One single apartment contains a mother, a father and some children and sometimes a grandfather or grandmother. There is no furniture in the wretched hovel. A single bed of straw serves the entire family. In the midst all lives a dirty pig, the only thriving inhabitant of the place, for he lives in filth.*

Slightly up the social system were the small farmers. This is how McParlan described farmhouses:

> *Habitations in general, though bad, not the worst in the country. Fuel, plenty of turf; food, potatoes, oaten bread, milk, flummery, cabbage mixed with salt and butter, thin gruel. The cost (and this computation too may stand for the county) of six in a family will come to about twenty seven pounds, calculating on the average price all, that the potatoes, meal, milk, and butter they consume, at two cows to a family, if sold would bring. But although the articles, if sold, might bring prices to make up that sum, a more reasonable calculation might be from fifteen to twenty pounds.*

Of Gallen, a Barony just North West of Costello, he remarks of small farmers:

> *The houses are made of dry walls, and dashed inside with lime and mortar; they have generally a chimney and two partitions, with a little suite of cowhouse, barn and stable, besides a little recess called a hag, which is made into the side wall opposite the family fire, for one bed; this is divided from the fire and the body of the house by straw mats, which hang parallel with the wall from the roof, by way of curtain.*

---

1 A smallholding under cottier tenure (the holding of not more than half an acre at a rent of not more than five pounds a year).

Chapter 1 – ORIGINS

Regarding their general condition Fr Durcan reports:

> *The people eat potatoes. Some have milk. Many people have no bedsteads. If the land is good a family can live off three acres: if not they need at least ten acres.*

Generally, dwellings were built on the side of a hill above the fields. The health and security of any chickens, ducks, geese, and pigs they owned were virtually a matter of life and death. Hence, they were kept within or next to the house; the manure they produced carefully collected and placed just outside the front door where an eye could be kept on it, as it was vital for the success of the next crop.

Most landlords felt no responsibility to make improvements. Fr Durcan continues:

> *Ireland is different from England. The houses are invariably repaired by the tenant ... at his own expense, never by the landlord; and by an express clause in every determinable lease, the tenant is bound to keep his house in repair, and all the improvements of the farm.*
>
> *Some habitations are very poor, made of turf sods, badly roofed and thatched, and full of smoke and dirt, as they have neither chimneys nor offices, except a very few; but since the commencement of separate tenures, the cabins begin to improve, and a separate cowhouse and barn are not infrequently seen. The main fuel used is turf. Food consists of potatoes, oaten bread, milk, and flummery (boiled oatmeal).*

As leases were generally quite short there was little incentive to make substantial improvements to land or dwellings. However, there is evidence that on the Dillon estates that as the century progressed, tenant farmers, at least, had somewhat better living conditions and more incentive to improve their holdings. Coulter (1862) reports of the Dillon estates:

> *The building of a better class of houses has been encouraged by giving the tenants timber, and, in some instances, slates, together with a money allowance according to the style of cottage that has been erected. Limestone abounds everywhere throughout this district, and there are numerous little lime kilns scattered over the estate, in which the people make their own lime. Lord Dillon allows his tenants for making their new mearing fences – an act of liberality which is not very common on large estates in Connaught. The tenants have a strong encouragement to improve, in the custom, which may be considered to be permanently established on this estate, of making the lettings for twenty-one years. Although the farmer is nominally a tenant from year to year, he knows that he will be allowed to remain undisturbed for twenty-one years at his original rent, and that, no matter how much more valuable he may have rendered his holding, the rent will not be increased until the expiration of that time. In consequence of this encouragement, a great deal of bog has been reclaimed, and every year more of it is being brought into cultivation*

McParlan adds:

> *Clothing very good; the men wear friezes, and some a finer cloth, thickset breeches, and red coating and pressed cloth waistcoats; the women too are neatly dressed, many of them in cottons and red cloaks. It should be added that apart from employment provided on the land there was virtually no other work available outside the little supplied by linen manufacture.*

Farms

McParlan describes farms and farming in Costello as follows:

> *There is in this barony some little degree of improvement in its mode of tillage. But still the implements of husbandry, and execution of work, are both of a very inferior kind; in the mountainy parts being too soft for horses, and also in many other parts, which are too rocky, the spade is used; the plough in the open parts of the country, which are not very many. This very bad description however does not apply to Mr. Costello, and a few other gentlemen, residents of this barony,*
>
> *The only extent of agriculture is now in potatoes and oats. Formerly this was a great barley country, but the prohibition against malting, which prevented the gentlemen from taking from their tenants barley in payment of the rent, has completely stopped the culture of that article, and materially hurted the tillage of this barony; as, before that act, the tillage was double as much as now. Edmondstown alone is, perhaps, the only place where wheat is grown,*

The plough referred to is the Irish wooden plough, which left half the vegetative surface, unturned. The pins of the harrow were made from wood.

> *The chief extent is in oats and potatoes. In some parts they grow flax and barley; wheat is only grown by a few gentlemen, for their own use. Great quantities of oats and potatoes are sent to Castlebar market, which, together with some flaxen yarn, are the principal means of providing for the rent.*

THE HALLORANS OF BIRSTALL AND AGHAMORE

In pre-famine Mayo most of the holders worked only with a spade, so it was impossible to cultivate more than a limited area in potatoes, oats and other crops. As the potato could be grown in a wide variety of places, including steep hillsides and around rocky outcrops, there developed in Ireland an extraordinary variety of spades for different types of ground.

A long-beamed, heavy wooden plough from Co. Kilkenny, drawn by Donal Mac Polin after the illustration from W. Tighe, 1802.

Causes of Poverty

The ordinary people of Mayo, of nearly all of Connaught in fact, were accustomed to hunger and the fear of famine, as the accompanying newspaper report of 1831 – twelve years before the Great Famine demonstrates.

MEAL DESTINED FOR KILTAMAGH LEADS TO RIOTS [1]

A quantity of Indian meal procured by Mr. James Jourdan at Westport for the poor of the parish of Killedan led to a riot and three deaths.

Mr. Jordan states that he asked for military protection before leaving Westport, as on previous occasions country people had carried away foodstuffs. He was given an escort of twelve soldiers and one policeman. About one and a quarter miles outside Westport, on the Castlebar road, 'he met an immense crowd of people who said he should give up the meal.' Mr. Jourdan told the crowd 'the people it was intended for were in a state of actual starvation, that they (the crowd) were near the stores in Westport, and could get meal for themselves much more readily than the poor people up the country; the crowd became clamorous and said if he gave them part of it, they would take the lives of the soldiers and began to carry off the bags'. At this point Mr. Jourdan rode back to Westport for additional military support. When he returned he was accompanied by an official, Mr. Clendining, as well as the soldiers. They found that a great quantity of the meal had been carried off. From the great numbers of people about the crafts, and their threats and apparent determination, Mr. Jourdan 'thought they would have all been murdered', and that they would not have escaped had he not gone back for more assistance. The soldiers took several people prisoners, especially those who had been most violent and who had some of the meal in their possession. 'Mr. Clendining ordered them to take the few bags that were on some of the carts, and added them to others, so as to make up the full loads. The police and soldiers then went on towards Castlebar with the meal.

The Riot Worsens:

The crowd reassembled further up the road. Mr. Bourke and the officers in charge tried to persuade the crowd to let them pass, 'But the stones came thicker than ever, so a volley was fired over their heads,' somebody cried that the soldiers only had powder. The crowd continued to throw stones. The officer's horse began to plunge from the barrage. The crowd closed in, and the soldiers fired. Three people were dead or dying - a man and two women.

Ballina Impartial, 2nd July, 1831

Fr Durcan summarises the causes of poverty as follows:

> *The poverty and miserable conditions of the people appear to me to have two causes. First, the exorbitantly high rents and the other burdens on lands. Second, the want of employment, or a remunerative price for labour ... The county cess (tax), which is collected twice a year, presses with particular severity in summer; so much so that people are often obliged .... to sell the potatoes they require for their own use, and in consequence to purchase meal at a usurious rate of interest, so high as 50%. The second cause of distress is the want of employment and low rate of wages. The highest rate is 6d per day, without diet; and even at that low rate constant employment cannot be procured.*

---

[1] Kiltimagh: Our Life and Times, Eds. Peter Sobolewski & Betty Solan, Kiltimagh Historic Society

Chapter 1 – ORIGINS

What is required is remunerative employment, and the question is how it may be given. The simplest and best mode of doing so appears to me to be to give the holders of small farms security of tenure. I am convinced, that if the people has sufficient tenure, and if on the termination of their tenure they were entitled to compensation for all the valuable improvements they would have made, labour would be enhanced, the waste lands would be brought into cultivation, the necessity of going to seek wages in England would be removed, and the general condition of the people, both physical and moral, would be improved beyond calculation.

Fr Durcan comments:

A large proportion of the labouring class go to England. If they go for the hay harvest, and remain there the whole season, in a good year they might bring £4 -£5 home; a person going for the harvest alone, from £2-£3. It is the dire necessity that compels them to go. If they got even moderate remuneration for their labour at home they would prefer it.

In bringing his testimony to a close Fr. Durcan recommended the following:

Useful public works, such as canals, railroads and inland navigation.
The introduction of manufactories, which would employ the surplus population.
Bring rents to their proper level. Check the undue competition for land.

Education

The evidence from the 1851 census returns in England suggests that Thomas and Michael were both illiterate and were unable to spell their own names in English. Their family name only appeared in a standard anglicised form 'Halloran' a decade later, by which time their children had had some schooling. The parish priests of Aghamore used this spelling and slight variations of it in the parish records from the 1860s. The first generation of Irish in Birstall probably spoke very little English and the generation after them in Aghamore were described as illiterate in both English and Irish - even in 1901.

McParlan comments regarding education in Costello in 1801:

Petty schools, kept and paid for by the poor, are the only source of education here, except Mr. Costello's school, supported by him for the poor of his estate in this barony.

It is unlikely that any of the Halloran children attended these.

Attending School

Figures published in 'The Report of the Commissioners of Public Instruction' 1836:

532 are attending school in Kiltimagh parish, 349 boys and 183 girls. Four of the schools are hedge schools, which means school is conducted in the open air. One is an all girls school, that of Jane Robinson. The girls pay her 1/- to 2/- (5p to 10p) per quarter, which gives her an annual income of about £ 10 to £12. The teachers in the other hedge schools are John Philben, John Sheeron and Patrick Flagherty. All these schools teach English reading and writing, arithmetic and catechism. Although none of them are under the national board, nevertheless Irish is not taught.

However, according to Griffith's Valuation, there was a schoolhouse in the townland of Rath that adjoined Carrowbaun. 'A Topographical Dictionary of Ireland' describes Aghamore as having seven pay schools. (Lewis, 1837, 1984, p. 18). Perhaps Thomas' parents were not in a position to send their children to school.

To get a flavour of what the schools were like we can turn to an account given by Charles McGlinchey (2007) about his father's experience in Inichowen.

In my father's time and before it there was always some kind of a school kept going in Meentiagh Glen. It would be held in a barn or some 'cró' of a house with stones round the wall for seats. The last of the old teachers was a man by the name of Graham. He was a well educated man and a poet but he was greatly given to the drink. I don't know where Graham went to; or what happened to him. He was a good teacher and turned out better scholars than what's going now.

Everybody attending Graham's school spoke Irish and knew nothing else. But he taught English and figuring. When they were learning the English letters they picked from the names of things that had the same shape as the letters: - A – the couple of a house, B – spectacles, C – the shape of the moon …

It was all slates they used till they got on a distance and then they wrote with quill pens. The teacher would have a bunch of feathers and trimmed them himself, as they were needed. They made some sort of ink, as far as I remember hearing, from the seeds of the elder tree. ... A neighbour of ours at the same school learned to measure land well. That was Mickey the Man. He could measure a field that was a round circle. Very few could do that.

Marriages

Among the poor there was every reason to marry early and have many children. Archbishop Oliver Kelly reported to the parliamentary commission that produced the Second Report on the State of Ireland (1825):

I did frequently observe that in those prosperous districts the marriages were not so frequent as I found them in more impoverished districts ... I have perfectly on my recollection that the circumstances [in the prosperous districts] struck me at the time, and I did enquire among the people how it happened; and the reply I received was that they had no idea of entering into the matrimonial state until they could acquire a competency for their own support, and the support of their family. In other parts of the country, where I observed very considerable poverty, I found a greater indifference about their future comforts than among persons in a more prosperous situation in life.

A Catholic curate giving evidence to the Poor Inquiry (Ireland), (1836), reported that the poor were:

Induced to marry by the feeling that their condition cannot be made much worse, or, rather, they know they can lose nothing, and they promise themselves some pleasure in the society of a wife

Donald Jordan (2000) comments that in impoverished counties like Mayo, where land was easily subdivided and where the practice of the impartible inheritance of land had not yet found acceptance, there were few constraints on early marriages. Couple would have little difficulty in obtaining a potato patch. It can be added that early marriage allowed the orderly transfer of land from one generation to the next.

Beer and spirits

McParlan comments regarding Costello:

The clearness of provisions for the last three years, the suppression, or rather the suspension of the distilleries, and the act against malting, have completely over-ruled the use of both beer and spirits throughout this country in consequence of the dearness of price, to which those causes have raised them. In the barony of Tyrawley, and the interior of the county, the vigilance of the revenue- officers has kept down private distilleries, but in the remote and mountainous parts they went on in the worst of times, and are now working in full plight in the baronies of Clanmorris, Costello, and in many other places; so much so, that now once more, as they have plenty to eat, they are resolved to have plenty to drink.

Young children working at an illicit still

There is a deal of beer brewed in Castlebar; a great deal has been brewed in different parts, for instance, in the barony of Costello, until the act had been made against malting, which in a great measure prevented the growth of barley, the use of that innocent and nourishing beverage beer, and checked in some degree the career of agriculture

Chapter 1 – ORIGINS

Development of National Schools

As the restrictions against Catholics were gradually removed, it became possible to set up schools run by Catholic clergy. However, many in the Catholic Church opposed these, as, though they allowed Catholic clergy to run schools for the first time, they focused on the teaching of English and things British, and did not permit the teaching of Irish. They were therefore perceived to be a powerful tool in the anglicisation of the Irish, and a weapon used to undermine the Irish identity.

Application for Boys' School [1]

Nat. Arch ED 1/61 No. 12

8 April 1839

Rev. B. Durcan has made an application to have a boys' school for Keltimaugh. In the application he states that the Girls' School is being built at present.

He mentions that there are two pay schools (hedge schools) in the Parish. The cost of the school is £77 6s. 8d., furniture £9 7s. 6d., and the school will cater for 120-150 boys.

Application for Girls' School

The Telegraph or Connaught Ranger 1838 [2]

An application has been made to the Chief Secretary, Dublin Castle for aid towards building a national school for girls in this parish.

To date £15 has been collected locally towards the school and a grant of £59 is being sought. In the statement for aid the following information:

'Nowhere could a school be more wanted. The village of Keltimaugh containing a population of about 600 persons. The Parish contains a population of 5743 persons who are all, it may be said, deprived of the benefits of education. The hedge schools already existing scarcely deserve the name of schools. The district is so poor that it is utterly impossible to procure any subscriptions from the people. The Landlords possessing property in the Parish, the major part of whom are absentees, have been applied to for assistance, but with little success. All that could be obtained from them in subscriptions towards this school is included in the £15 already received'. The site for the school has been obtained from John Mooney. Mooney's land has a lease of three lives from Mr. Browne of Brownestown.

The building, which will cost £74.0s.4 $\frac{1}{2}$d., will cater for 120 girls. The dimensions are 30' long, 24' wide and 10' high.

At present there are three schools for boys and none for girls in Keltimaugh village. These schools are 'depending solely for support on the very precarious payment of the parents of the children, who are in general poor, under the patronage of the Catholic clergy'.

Signed: Thomas Vizzard, Anthony Vizzard (Protestants), Bernard Durcan

The Roman Catholic Church – the Penal Laws

Over the years, starting in 1695, a series of laws, collectively referred to as the Penal Laws, had been enacted to eliminate Catholicism in Ireland and Britain. Catholicism was seen as a source of disloyalty and a threat to the established Protestant order in Britain. Ireland, which remained a predominantly Roman Catholic country after the Reformation, was naturally most affected by these laws, which resulted in a near total divide between the mass of the Roman Catholic population and the ruling Protestant elite. Catholics were forbidden an education, or to keep arms, or even own a horse of greater value than five pounds. To these laws were later added restrictions on Catholics entering the professions, holding public office, engaging in trade or commerce and leasing or buying land. In 1710, to prove their loyalty to the Williamite cause, all Catholic priests were required to take an oath of loyalty to King William. Unsurprisingly, very few did this, thus all priest were liable to arrest and deportation and there were prohibitions on Catholic services.

---

1 The following extracts appear in Kiltimagh: Our Life and Times, Eds. Peter Sobolewski & Betty Solan, Kiltimagh Historic Society

2 Lord Frederick Cavendish founded the *Connaught Telegraph*, or *Mayo Telegraph* as it was originally named, on March 17th, 1828, and used it as an organ to help fight the battles of the lower classes.

The remoteness of the region allowed some of the major landlords in the area, like the Dillons and Costellos, to remain Catholics, so the full brunt of these laws was not always applied. Also, there were very few Protestants in rural Mayo to fully enforce these laws. Yet, the Catholic population was seriously disadvantaged and excluded from avenues to power and commerce, the vast majority of whom remained true to their Roman Catholicism, practicing their faith in secret.

Mass in the Penal Days at St. Mullins, Co. Carlow

Joe Byrne gives an interesting account of aspects of parish life in Aghamore in *Páirc an Teampaill: The Ancient Cemetery of Achadh Mór* in *Glór Achadh Mór* (2002). In Aghamore, there was no permanent Catholic Church in the 18th Century and Fr Kneafsey, Parish Priest, said Mass in the open air in *Páirc an Teampaill* and at a Mass Rock and in souterrains in Falleighter, a townland neighbouring Carrowbaun. The parish priest who followed him between 1774 and 1893, Fr Richard Kirwin, had neither church nor house and was arrested and condemned to death for his priestly activities in 1891. However, a member of the local gentry, and a fine dualist, challenged the judge to a duel over the matter. The judge, unable to face a more accomplished dualist, released the priest[1]. Fr Kirwin may well have baptised Michael Halloran, the father of Thomas and Michael, sons who fled to Birstall during the famine. It is quite likely James and Thomas Halloran were baptised by Fr Henry Burke around 1807/8, and Michael by Fr O'Grady in or around 1827.

The account gives extracts from a short memoir by one of Fr. Pat O'Grady's mass servers, Daniel Campbell of *Sean Mhachaire*, who was born in 1818. No doubt he was well known to members of the local Halloran families. He tells us about Sunday Mass -

Many of them had to travel three or four miles to hear mass of a Sunday. A Farmer that was well-to-do would ride, and his wife and daughter would sit behind him on a pillion. Mind you, those were the respectable part of the congregation. Others would walk with their shoes under their arms until they reached the little village of Knock. Some of them coming from the northern part of the parish would wash their feet at Tobberfoorly and put on their shoes and stockings there, just by the parish pond. Others would go to a friend's house and put them on - I mean the women, and some grown up boys also and women too went barefoot altogether to hear mass on Sunday.
There was only one mass at Knock each Sunday in my time and that was at 12 o'clock. Sometimes one priest had to serve both parishes, Knock and Achadh Mór, the churches nearly four miles apart. Then the clergyman officiated and said early mass at Knock about 9 o'clock, Achadh Mór at 12. The next Sunday, Knock 12 and Achadh Mór 9. There was no evening service, but the religious portion of the congregation performed the Stations of the Cross, said the Rosary and taught the catechism.
The two parishes Knock and Achadh Mór are about seven miles long from north to south, and about four miles wide from east to west, and at the time I was there they contained about 2000 families. And until Fr. Pat O'Grady became a middle-aged man he had but one curate or coadjutor to attend at least 10,000 persons large and small. Some of them of course were not very troublesome to him, but between baptisms, marriages, deaths and confessions, the two priests had enough to do.
How the priests managed the confessional

---

1 Notes on the Parish of Aghamore by John P. Jordan - http://www.aghamoreireland.com/history/overview.htm

Chapter 1 – ORIGINS

They were divided into districts or stations of three or four little villages, about 20 or 30 families as it might be, some more and some less. The priest visited each district and gave a whole day at that station to hear confession and give Holy Communion to the people. The priest announced from the Altar on the Sunday where he was to call next and the person's house he was to call to also, so that they might prepare on the day mentioned to attend to their religious duties, and likewise the party to whose house the priest came, might have time to prepare for the priest's breakfast and dinner, and if they liked to invite their friends also to a cup of tea or a glass of whiskey...

It took nine or ten weeks to hear the Christmas confessions and about the same time to hear the Easter confessions, for I remember the Easter Indulgence used to end on 29 June, St. Peter and St. Paul's Day.

The PP's salary as I said before was 2/2d (2 shillings and 2 pence) per year with a collection on Easter Sunday and Christmas Day, and Masses, marriages and baptisms which amounted to a good sum for the 12 months. The curate's salary was £30 per annum with a collection at one of the churches on Easter and Christmas Day. Then he went from house to house to collect oats for his horse, which amounted to a good sum...

For it was a general rule especially by the respectable class to do so. And the priests always expected to be provided with a good breakfast and dinner and they were not teetotallers either. For if there was no whiskey to make punch, there would be no merriment, for Fr. Pat always liked his glass of punch in a moderate way.

Daniel Campbell also explains the delicate matter of priests' salaries.

Now for the PP's salary and how he received it, he always carried his book with him which contained the names of each householder and after Mass he called the name of each householder and each man came forward that was present, and paid his 1/1d [1 shilling and 1 pence] which cleared himself and his family for half a year. If they did not answer, the priest put an X down opposite the name, which showed he was absent and did not attend to his duties. And also he could see at a glance how many times he absented himself, and how much money he owed the priest. 2/2d [2 shillings and 2 pence] per year. And he always reckoned up the absentees and how much money they owed him, and always gave the absentees a good scolding for not complying with their religious obligations and also for not paying the priest's salary.

He goes on to describe a demonstration that was" got up in Aghamore" against church fees.

I remember some parties striking against the priest's salary and wanted to reduce his 2d. per year and give him but 2/- instead of 2/2d. I do not know who began it, but I know that it was got up at Achadh Mór and a procession was formed and it was getting larger as they marched from house to house and extorted a promise from the owner of the house to pay no more than 2/- per year, but did not interfere with the collection at the church on Easter or Christmas Day. They were not satisfied with the promise above mentioned, for each house had to send one with the procession until they went to a certain number of houses. I forget how many.

But I, though a boy, which I am sorry to say, had to go for fear's sake, for my father would not go on any account on such an errand. And for fear of doing us an injury, I was advised to go instead of my father. It had the desired effect and instead of the half-yearly 1/1 d it was 1/- for the whole family ... There was no collection on the Sunday. The church was free except on Christmas Day and Easter Sunday, an on those days there was a collection at the eastern door.

Old Church in Aghamore

Campbell also has stories of how the priests dealt severely and publicly with sexual immorality, and with "fairy women" or *fios* women, whom it was believed practised elements of witchcraft. There are also details of an attempt at proselytisation or conversion to Protestantism within the joint parishes of Aghamore and Knock.

Viscount Dillon, Charles Strickland and Charlestown

The landlord of Carrowbaun at the time was Charles Henry Dillon, 14th Viscount Dillon, born in Dublin in 1810 and died in 1865. He was a descendant of Charles II.

A fuller account of their history is given in chapter 10. Suffice to say here they were an Irish-Norman landlord family from the 13th century and had supported the Catholic King James II of England. They fled to France after the defeat of the Catholic cause by William of Orange. There they formed the Jacobite Irish Brigade in the French Army, which was supported by the exiled Irish Army.

Despite their associations with France, the family regained royal favour, one of them serving as Lord Lieutenant of County Roscommon. The main part of their estate was in county Mayo, in the parishes of Aghamore, Annagh, Bekan, Castlemore, Knock, Kilbeagh, Kilcolman and Kilmovee in the barony of Costello. Carolan's air *Lady Dillon* was composed by the harper on a visit to his patron Viscount Dillon in the Dillon house of Loughglynn.

There are different reports about which Dillons converted to Anglicanism and when. The twelfth Viscount is said to have conformed to Anglicanism in 1767, however, Cathal Henry (2009) reports that at least one later holder of the title was Roman Catholic and attended Mass at a chapel in Loughlynn[1]. Two detectives, Henry reports, were sent to find out if this were true. All the neighbours would tell them was that they could hear his footsteps coming into the chapel, but they never saw him at Mass; the reason being that a screen separated Lord Dillon from the people.

The Dillons became less involved with Ireland in the mid eighteenth century, when the Eleventh Viscount married an English heiress. Charles Henry Dillon, 14th Viscount Dillon, moved the family out of Ireland completely. Thereafter, the Dillons become absentee landlord for much of the nineteenth century.

Loughglynn

They left the running of their estates to the English Roman Catholic Strickland family. In 1818 Jarrard Edward Strickland was bought to Ireland as agent to the estates in Mayo and Roscommon. Charles Strickland became agent after his father's death. As such, he was the agent who was responsible for the tenants of Carrowbaun townland. It is clear that, unlike many agents of the time, he saw his duties went beyond the collection of rent.

The fullest, if not least partial, account that we have found of the condition of the tenant farmers of Aghamore can be found in Henry Coulter's (1862) *The west of Ireland: its existing condition, and prospects* to which we have already referred. He has an extensive description of the work of Charles Strickland. In tone, the study is generally supportive of the landlord system, but Coulter is prepared to be critical of the abuses and cruelty of individual landlords. His comments may be read in this light.

> I believe there are few men having the management of property in Connaught more generally esteemed and popular than this gentleman. Mr. Strickland succeeded his father in the management of this large estate. It was under his charge when the famine of 1846-47 swept over the land; and the manner in which it passed

---

1 http://towns.mayo-ireland.ie/WebX?50@33.fzYibyQd5s3.0@.ee88298

Chapter 1 – ORIGINS

through that terrible ordeal speaks volumes for the care, solicitude, and ability that were displayed in the preservation of the people. In the year 1841 the population on Lord Dillon's estate numbered nearly 33,000 persons; and in 1851 it showed a decrease of only six or seven hundred, whilst, within the same time, neighbouring estates were almost depopulated.

An active man with an interest in the wellbeing of the tenantry, Charles Strickland succeeded in getting a site for a school from Viscount Dillon at *Cnocán na mBráthhair*, Friars Hill, near Castlemore. This became the School of the Sisters of Charity and opened on 1877. This, it appears, as not a one-off occurrence. Coulter (1862) states:

Lord Dillon has interested himself much in the education of the people, and has built seven new schools on his estate, besides repairing several old ones previously in existence, and enclosing the grounds. The master of the school near Lough Glyn demesne gives practical instruction to the boys in agriculture, and a piece of land is attached to the schoolhouse for that purpose. The pupils carry out in their little gardens at home the instructions they have received, and there is an annual exhibition of their produce, for the best specimens of which prizes in money and agricultural implements are awarded.

Strickland was also a town planner and was responsible for establishing Charlestown. The manner in which he did this is highly indicative of the man. The tenants of Lord Dillon were Mayo men and were therefore disadvantaged by the rules of the existing market in Bellaghy in County Sligo. They had to carry their sacks of potatoes and grain to the town and then wait till all the Sligo men, tenants of Lord Sligo, had had their produce weighed before they could go to market. Complaints were made by the tenants to the agent, who put their case to Lord Sligo who did nothing to rectify the matter. After receiving an insult, Strickland is reported as saying, 'I will wipe out Bellaghy' and determined to set up a rival market town. Lord Charles Dillon gave him permission in 1845 to establish a town on the Mayo side of the Sligo boarder (Henry 2009).

He initiated the town's development by offering several acres of land rent-free forever to the first person to complete a house. Naturally this brought in settlers from the neighbouring towns and the winning house was later the Imperial Hotel, which still stands in the Town Square. It was further directed by Strickland that all new buildings should stand two stories high and be of a uniform design and that public houses should have private and public entries. The roads were wide and provided access to both the front and rear of each premise, converging in a spacious square in the centre of town. By 1856 the town had the appearance of a small modern town with close to 60 houses. In the same year, with encouragement and some financial support from Charles Strickland, the foundation stone was laid for a Catholic Church[1].

Church Street, Charlestown

The Knox Estate attempted unsuccessfully to sue the Dillon Estate for the ruination of the market in Bellaghy. The case was held at the local Petty sessions and the Dillon Estate won.

The town, originally named Newtown Dillon, was renamed Charlestown in Strickland's honour. This is an unusual tribute to a landlord's agent and an indication that he, unlike most of his contemporaries, showed a keen interest in the tenants' welfare. He also received warm tributes from Marie McDonald-Garvey in her book *Mid-Connacht* for the great work he did as Chairman of the Gallen and Costello Relief

---

1 http://www.irelandgenweb.com/~irlmay/townlands/Charlestown.htm

Committee for the relief of the poor during the Great Famine. This is evidenced by a resolution of the Gallen and Costello Relief Committee, made on the 13th October 1846, proposed by Edward P, McDonnell and seconded by Rev. Mr Coghlan PP.

> *That this being our last meeting, before we separate we deem it due to Charles Strickland Esq., agent to Lord Viscount Dillon, to hear our unqualified testimony, not alone to his indefatigable zeal and his valuable assistance in carrying into effect the objects of this committee, but for his very great and laudable exertions in being the means of procuring a large quantity of the provision for the poor in this, the barony of Costello, and thereby enabling many poor and destitute families to prolong for a short time a wretched and miserable existence*[1].

Charlestown was only a village at the time of the Great Famine; however, it is believed the tenants on Lord Dillon's estate were fortunate because Strickland personally laboured to get food to those in need and worked with the local Relief Committees, as is discussed in greater detail in the next chapter.

In 1860 Viscount Dillon and his agent Charles Strickland were also involved in the construction of the Cathedral of Ballaghaderreen, where large windows commemorate Charles Dillon, 14th Viscount Dillon, in the Baptistery, and Charles Strickland in a chapel on the south side of the sanctuary. The window was erected by the Bishop of Achonry and others to 'commemorate their respect and esteem for Charles Strickland and his wife Maria of Loughglynn and their zealous assistance in the erection of the Cathedral Church' in 1860. Though a famine commemoration of a landlord's kindness may appear a grovelling piece of sycophancy - the exploitive landlord system was deeply implicated in the deaths and departures of countless impoverished Irish men and women - it is gratifying that some individuals had sufficient humanity to use their wealth and power to reduce the suffering and deaths of some of the victims of the system which had enriched them. It might also be borne in mind that Strickland was well connected within the Catholic Church; two of his brothers were Jesuit priests. His generous support of it may well account for some of the esteem with which he was held.

What may be of significance is that the first wave of Irish immigrants into Batley came from the Charlestown area in the early 1830s. As is discussed in chapter 3, Batley is a town near Dewsbury that was experiencing a boom in woollen production and is two miles from Birstall, the town the Hallorans arrived at twenty years later. What is interesting is that Charles Strickland's brother, Thomas, operated a flax mill at Castlemore. This mill had been strengthened by an influx of about 2000 refugees from sectarian trouble in Ulster. Most of these refugees were weavers[2]. The Irish who moved to Batley were also weavers, recruited to break a strike at a local woollen mill. They had the same landlord and agent as those who, nearly two decades later, fled to Birstall from the famine. As we shall see in the chapter on the Irish in Batley, they appear to have arrived there as the result of a coordinated movement of people, perhaps arranged through contacts between mill owners. It is worth researching this area further.

The Stricklands remained agents for Dillon after this period. In 1876 Viscount Dillon owned 83,749 acres in county Mayo, 5435 in county Roscommon and 136 in county Westmeath. When the estate was sold in 1899, the 93,321 acres were sold for £29,000. In chapter 9 we will see how later agents of the Dillons reduced the tenants to abject poverty in the later part of the nineteenth century.

Landlords, middlemen and absentees

By 1856, the time of Griffith's Valuation, James was a sub-tenant of Bridget Kelly, and none of the rest of the family appeared on Griffith's Valuation, we can presume they did not hold as much as three acres of land. They appear to have been at the bottom end of a system that had the great British and Anglo-Norman landlords at the top.

The landlord's role, ostensibly, was to provide markets and roads to access them. Charles Strickland appears to have been diligent in this, establishing a market in Charlestown. However, landlords charged levies on market sales and the roads, where tolls had to be paid, were often not much more than cattle 3drives and could hardly take a laden cart.

---

1 Swords, Liam, 1999, In their own words: the Famine in North Connacht, 1845-1849, Dublin:Columba

2 Marie McDonnell Garvey Lecture (2007), The Towey Clan, http://www.toweyclan.com/MarieGarvey Lecture.pdf

Landlords were also responsible for providing security and law and order. Thus, many acted as Justices of the Peace, and they ensured militia were stationed in most towns. However, in reality, their most important function was to protect property and quell political unrest, often aimed at the landlords themselves. The better roads were usually designed to facilitate the rapid deployment of troops to quell unrest.

Another important function of the landlords was to alleviate distress. During the famine many worked as Guardians of workhouses and on relief committees. However, few of these landed families lived in the area, preferring to lease their lands to lesser landlords or put their estates into the hands of agents.

It appears the tenants in Carrowbaun were not typical. Though no doubt ground down by poverty and hardship and living in constant fear of hunger, they appear to have been better off than most of the peasantry in terms of their landlord and agent. The following description, taken from Hall and Hall (1841) is of the more prevalent system. Even where the landlord was not an absentee aristocrat and where the agent or 'middleman' was a local, terrible hardship was inflicted on the tenants.

A middleman was usually, in his origin, 'one of the people', who, having made money, took a farm or an estate, rented a hundred, or, as was often the case, a thousand acres. The landlord-in-chief, generally an absentee, looked to him alone for the payment of his half-yearly rent, and knew nothing whatever of the condition of the cottiers who dwelt upon his estate; if we add that he cared nothing as well as knew nothing, we shall not be far from the truth; for, while pursuing a course of pleasure in the metropolis, in Dublin sometimes but more frequently in London, he was far away from the sight of their sufferings.

The peasantry, badly housed, badly clothed, badly fed, were in no way necessary either to his luxuries or his necessities; the middleman was always a punctual paymaster, and he was the only person upon his estate with whom the landlord was brought into contact or called upon to correspond. This middleman had to transmit to his employer perhaps three or four thousand pounds, often more, every year. And how was he to procure it? First, his system was to parcel out the estate into small bits, seldom more than two or three acres to each but generally averaging an acre. These 'bits' were invariably let annually, and never on lease; the occupier, therefore, had no temptation to cultivate the land. His slip of ground seldom bore any other produce than potatoes; these were designated solely for the consumption of his own household and the support of a pig, which, if it lived and no unusual misfortune attended the family, was to pay the rent. Of course, the land was let at the highest possible rate, and to the highest or most thoughtless bidder; the middleman had to pay the landlord, and to grow rich himself; as the tenant was invariably in arrears, he was at all times in the power of the middleman; and the putting on a new coat, the addition of a trifling article of furniture, or the appearance of anything like comfort in or around his dwelling was a sure and certain notice that the bailiff would be 'down upon him' ere the sun had set.

The general want of employment, and the consequent anxiety of obtaining for their families the means of even temporary subsistence, produced such an eagerness on the part of the peasantry to get possession of land, as to induce them to engage for the payment of a rent, which the crops, even under the most favourable circumstances, must have failed to yield. This circumstance was too frequently taken advantage of; and the ultimate ruin of the miscalculating tenant was the invariable result.

The landlords' connection with the local population was, in most cases, minimal, if it existed at all. The infamous charge of 'absentee landlords' was justly made against a class of people, many of whom had no interest in their lands, except for the rent it would yield. Unlike many of their counterparts in England, there was little concern for agrarian 'improvement'. This indifference combined with contempt for the indigenous Irish race meant that the appalling living conditions experienced by Irish cottiers and those with smallholdings, though unacceptable in England, were widespread in Ireland.

Politics

It is hard to know if members of the cottier class and those with smallholdings like the Hallorans took any interest in politics. However, these improvements in education and medical facilities, slight as they were, indicated a growing sense of the possibility of civic improvement.

Among the peasantry, there would undoubtedly have been a sense of the loss of liberty and a yearning for a vanished past when they were not ruled by strangers, but by their own Gaelic chiefs, who spoke their language and were familiar with their ways. No doubt they looked back in pride to the romantic past when *Grana Uaile*, a historical figure from the 16th century also known as 'The Sea Queen of Connaught' and 'The Pirate Queen' ruled the seas and was courted by Queen Elizabeth of England. In folklore she represented a time when Connaught was independent and proud to be Gaelic and free from foreign oppression and landlords. There would have been an instinctive feeling of excitement at the prospect of their foreign rulers and landlords been overthrown. In the cabins there would have been tales of the more recent 'Races of Castlebar', when British troops were forced to flee Castlebar in 1798 when the French army forced General Lake to retreat and the French general Humbert proclaimed the Provisional Republic of Connaught. This was part of the general uprising of 1789, which ultimately was a failure. Such defeats of the British military and the discomfort of the landlords would have been met with great glee by the oppressed people of Mayo.

The 'King of the Beggars' however, was Daniel O'Connell whose belligerent and devastating attacks on the system which saw the suppression of the Catholic majority at the hands of - and to the profits of - a small Protestant elite electrified the cottiers and small landholders of rural Ireland, who flocked to his huge outdoor meetings and dipped into their meagre resources to support his campaigns for Catholic emancipation and later, repeal of the Union with Britain.

There was also agrarian unrest mainly related to the Ribbon men. This was a millennium secret society formed to prevent landlords from changing or evicting their tenants and opposed the payment of tithes to the Church of Ireland. They sent threatening messages, signed menacingly under such names as 'Captain Moonlight', and 'Rory of the hills'. Many of its members looked forward to the destruction of Protestantism in Ireland, which they saw as the source of most of their grievances. However, its sectarian orientation was not so marked in Mayo, there being very few Protestants in the area. Nonetheless, such was their power that a number of magistrates were under suspicion of paying off the Ribbon men in order to secure the safety of their own families.

Secret societies would hold mass meetings where whole villages would take secret oaths, often under pressure. They sent menacing messages and made threatening midnight visits. They were particularly hostile to 'land grabbers', bailiffs, those who collected the tithes for the Church of Ireland and those who sold goods at market at high prices. They often beat their victims, stole their firearms and damaged their property. This could involve houghing, which is cutting the tendons of the cattle of those who offended them and destroying the grain collected as tithes.

A night visit from 'Rory of the Hills'

Jarrard Edward Strickland, Charles Strickland's father, came to Mayo in 1818 to replace Mathew Wyatt as Lord Dillon's agent. As a magistrate he became disillusioned in his powers to persuade his tenants from associating with the Ribbon men. He and Charles Costello urged the government to strengthen the military barrack in Ballaghaderreen. However, the activities of the Ribbon men tended to decrease only in times of famine, as in 1821, when the potato crop failed, as it did quite regularly.

Repeal

The big issue of the day was the question of the Repeal of the Act of Union, whereby Ireland would have an independent legislature in Dublin. This particularly excited the slowly growing number of the Irish Catholic middle-classes. Its great advocate was Daniel O'Connell, who had previously championed the cause of Catholic emancipation, giving a small number of well-off Catholics the vote. However, he was one of the few great champions of Ireland who could speak directly to the oppressed peasantry, and his successes generated great hope and affection among the small landholders and cottiers as well as those who were gaining a new-found prosperity. The excitement generated by his visit to Mayo in 1845 is captured in the accompanying news reports.

Chapter 1 – ORIGINS

Though issues like Repeal of the Union and votes for a few well off Catholics may not have been of great relevance to farm labourers and cottiers, he brought about the prospect of hope.

Repeal Meeting At Castlebar - Daniel O'Connell in Mayo[1] *Connaught Telegraph, , 9th October 1845*

On Sunday last, at an early hour, the town of Castlebar began to assume a business-like appearance. Thousands flocking in from all directions as early as eight o'clock, ... Joy, hilarity, and enthusiasm pervaded every bosom, and all anxiously looking forward to the hour when the Trades were to move forward, to conduct the Great Liberator into town from French-hill, a spot remarkable in the annals of Mayo, from the fact of some Frenchmen having been buried there in the year 1798, who fell in a skirmish with the English army, while flying from Castlebar, at that memorable epoch. Thither, a distance of over two miles, the Trades marched at half-past ten o'clock to meet Him they so dearly loved. They left town without music or cheering - in fact a beholder, unacquainted with the cause of their movement, might look on it as a funeral cortege, so silently did they move along - and this was owing to the circumstance of the military being then engaged at divine worship in the Church, by which they had to pass. Not so, however, on entering Spencer Street. The bands struck up a merry tune, while the air was rent with shouts and long-continued cheering, which was renewed every other minute, as the immense multitude moved along for the place of rendezvous - the road, as they proceeded, becoming more and more thronged by the country people who were collecting from different directions, to greet the uncrowned Monarch who rules supreme in the hearts of our countrymen. Word of the day was, 'Repeal'. ...

Underneath the banners before mentioned, floating on the breeze: the hill, and the numerous eminences around, covered by a living mass of human beings. And here we must remark, that never did our hearts throb with more lively emotions than at that hour, when beholding the bone and sinew of Mayo, congregated together, with but one object in view- the freedom of their country from the galling bondage in which it has been held by an adverse nation, who would deny them that liberty so dear to Irishmen, and for which their fathers bled and died. That liberty which cost England so much gold in the purchase of, together with the conferring of titles upon those individuals who basely sold their country's rights.

The Great Liberator, 'the uncrowned monarch' was in town. He had secured Catholic Emancipation. Could he secure the repeal of the Act on Union and Irish self-government?

Repeal Candidate Wins Mayo Election

Mr. Joseph Myles MacDonnell has been elected to represent Mayo by a majority of sixty (477 to 417). Repeal has thus been triumphant after as hard a battle as was ever fought in Ireland... While we rejoice at the victory, we must condemn the conduct pursued on both sides. The freedom of election was disregarded; the freeholders were taken hold of, as the property of one party or the other, they were mere instruments, abject slaves, coerced to vote without having a will of their own. On the one side certain landlords, with their agents, Bailiffs, and Drivers, threatened utter destruction to their dependent serfs if they voted for a repealer; and when they murmured against such unconstitutional interference, they were taken prisoners and conveyed under a strong Military escort to the hustings to record their votes. Many escaped, determined not to be dragooned, retiring to the islands and to the mountains, abandoning their families and their homes to avoid being captured. Those who were brought forward to poll were intimidated; and yet we have heard those persons advocate the Freedom of Election. On the other side several of the Roman Catholic priesthood were arrayed, denouncing those who would vote against Repeal..., instilling into the minds of the voters that a repeal of the Legislative Union was necessary for the safety of the country, and to ensure prosperity and happiness to the people - that it was, in fact, a mortal sin to vote against Repeal. This declaration was confirmed by Mr. Robert Dillon Browne, who in the presence and hearing of Doctor MacHale, said, 'Those who voted for the anti-repeal candidate, and against his own conscientious feelings would, if he died the moment after voting, be hurled into perdition'.

However, the question of repeal was quickly abandoned by the even more urgent problem of simple survival. In the autumn of 1845 there was a major failure of the potato crop throughout Ireland. The situation was particularly bad in County Mayo. The potato crop failed repeatedly over the following years resulting in the Great Irish famine.

---

1 The following two extracts appear in Kiltimagh: Our Life and Times, Eds. Peter Sobolewski & Betty Solan, Kiltimagh Historic Society

CHAPTER 2

The great starvation

The Great Famine resulted in the wholesale depletion of the Irish countryside, and drove many members of the Halloran family from Ireland. Hundreds of thousands of men and women died of hunger, further hundreds of thousands died of famine-related diseases, and the number of people who fled the country was greater than the number who died from both. It was the last great famine in Europe; it took place in an agricultural country blessed with fertile soil and a mild climate. Furthermore, the country was administered by one of the most resourceful governments in the world and its infrastructure was more highly developed than those regions that have suffered great famine in more recent times, yet the Great Famine's duration was much greater. Throughout the populated regions there was a network of passable roads. There was a courthouse in nearly every rural town. Government officials were capable of mapping every field and coastal inlet and there was a yeomanry and militia that could be dispatched within hours to virtually any place where trouble or disorder brewed.

Furthermore, much of the land was owned by some of the wealthiest and most powerful people in the world. Hundreds of thousands of the people who were dying were tenants of men who were cabinet ministers in the government of a country that was well on the way to having one of the most far-flung and tightly administered empires ever seen. The question therefore arises as to how such a famine could take place and why it lasted so long? The fact that it did, however, resulted in the death, not only of countless Irish people, but also innumerable communities all over Ireland. But in an extraordinary struggle of survival, it also resulted in the painful birth of new communities of Irish men and women all over the English-speaking world, including an impoverished community of the displaced Irish in Birstall.

This chapter looks at some of these issues, while most of the subsequent chapters explore the lives of these same families involved in one of the most remarkable migratory achievements in world history. These people are of course the members of the Halloran family and those of their relatives and neighbours who fled the Great Famine to settle, live and work in Birstall in the west Riding of Yorkshire.

George Bernard Shaw created the following heated exchange in the play *Man and Superman*:

> Malone: *He will get over it all right enough. Men thrive better on disappointments in love than on disappointments in money. I daresay you think that sordid; but I know what I'm talking about. My father died of starvation in Ireland in the black 47, maybe you've heard of it.*
> Violet: *The Famine?*
> Malone: *[with smouldering passion] No, the starvation. When a country is full of food, and exporting it, there can be no famine. My father was starved dead; and I was starved out to America in my mother's arms. English rule drove me and mine out of Ireland.*

This smouldering anger against English rule was a major legacy of the famine. The term *famine* seems to suggest an impersonal, providential disaster. He, like many Irish, rejected this version of events. His preferred term *starvation* suggests not a providential event, but a man-made one. These two conflicting interpretations have haunted much of Irish history and politics. The purpose of this account is not to fix responsibility, but rather to explore the experience of one family and their descendants who survived it and celebrate their capacity for endurance and their resourcefulness in survival.

The Hallorans in Carrowbaun in the autumn of 1845

There were many mouths to feed in Carrowbaun. Apart from the Hallorans, of whom there were possibly three families in the district, there were families of Stensons, Kellys, Fahys, Keenes, Ragans, Linskeys, Prendergasts and Coxes. All these names appeared in Aghamore records and most of them were found in Birstall, Yorkshire after the Great Famine.

James Halloran (1807-1882), the eldest of the Halloran males we know of, had a family. From information supplied by Ger Delaney of the South Mayo Family Research Centre, we know he had sons called Thomas, Patrick and Martin. We know that Bridget, reported as aged 55, was the name of Martin's sister in the 1901 census, and was therefore James' daughter. There is another younger Patrick Halloran who is obviously from another Halloran family we know very little about. We later find him married in Rath. The following appear in marriage records in the Aghamore Parish records after 1865 and are discussed in chapters 9 and 10.

- Thomas Halloran (b. abt. 1839, aged about 6 at the outbreak of the famine.)
- Pat Halloran (b. abt. 1843, aged about 2),
- Martin Halloran (b. abt. 1846 - the beginning of the Great Famine)
- Another Patrick Halloran (b. late 1840s)
- Mary Halloran (b. ? but who married in 1868)
- Bridget Halloran (b. abt. 1842, aged about 3) recorded as Martin's sister in the 1901 Irish census.

There were almost certainly other children, probably some who did not survive to adulthood, others who never married and others who left the parish young. Many of the young women were pregnant during the early stages of the famine, but they successfully raised some of these children to adulthood.

We know about Thomas and Judy (neé Stenson) Halloran's children from the English censuses and baptism records. At the outbreak of the Great Famine there was James aged about 7, Patrick about 5, Michael about 3, Thomas about 2 and Mary, born just before the Great Famine in 1844. Bridget is cited in the 1851 English census as five, thus born in the first year of the Great Famine, though she was probably older. Catherine is recorded as three, and born in Ireland, a child of the famine. There is evidence from other records that the census recorder underestimated their ages. Having been hungry for much of their childhood they would have been undernourished and appeared less developed physically than more healthy children. Other children were born after the Great Famine in England and are discussed in Chapter 5. Catherine is the only child born during the famine who survived, though Judy gave birth to a living child every two years before that. Whether she was too weak to conceive or had lost other babies, or indeed this was because Thomas was working in England, desperate to earn enough money to bring his family out of Ireland, we will probably never know.

We can be certain that of a number of other Hallorans joined Thomas and Michael in Birstall. Whether they travelled as a large group or in smaller groups in the late 1840s and early 1850s is a matter of speculation. In the Birstall district there are marriage records of a Catherine Halloran, two Patrick Hallorans and an Ann Halloran. Furthermore, Hallorans named William, Joseph, Bridget and Mary are recorded as godparents in St Paulinus parish records, Dewsbury from 1851 to 1854. What little we know of these will be discussed in chapter 5.

Of course there is also the likelihood that Halloran womenfolk had married, and there were other cousins in Carrowbaun itself or in neighbouring townlands. We know nothing about the older people, but no doubt there were a good number of them who needed extra support in times of hunger.

Potato blight

In 1845, threats to the potato crop were not new. Partial failures of the potato crop had been experienced in 1817, 1822, 1831 (the year of the riots reported in the previous chapter), 1839 and 1841, causing widespread distress and hunger. There can be little doubt that as autumn progressed, James, Thomas and Michael, indeed all the members of this family, would have awoken every morning and surveyed their potato crop in trepidation.

However, there was a quiet optimism that any failure would be localised. As late as 16th September, the *Mayo Constitution* reported 'in regard to potatoes, we fear the disease so much spoken of prevails to a considerable extent, although much more limited than in England'.

It was probably in late September sometime that the Hallorans awoke to find parts of their field had turned black, and the dark decay was spreading rapidly from one neighbour's field to another. In shock and panic they would have scrambled to their neighbours' rough cabins, some clustered near them, others clustered a few fields away. All would probably have rushed to unearth the potatoes from under the plants that still looked good, only to find many of the tubers had already turned black and putrid. As they were unearthed a malodorous stench pervaded the land.

The initial false sense of securely came about because the crop was in a much worst condition than appeared on the surface. Once the harvesting began, a pattern emerged. The *Mayo Constitution* reported:

> *In some cases, although the potato stem appeared luxuriant, upon digging it became apparent that the root was rotten, and potatoes which had appeared so sound upon digging had, when stored, decomposed into a putrid, black mass*

In many cases, the full extent of the damage was not apparent right up to the day the potatoes were stacked. It blighted the green stalks of the potato. That year, 1845, about a third of the national potato crop was destroyed.

In many cases, as reported by Charles Strickland, Viscount Dillon's agent in Carrowbaun, the full extent of the damage was not apparent even when the potatoes had been stacked or placed in their pits.

All sorts of advice and suggestions were circulated, but they were based on the assumption that the blight had something to do with damp and humidity as suggested below in *The Connaught Ranger*.

A description of the disease[1] *Bristol Mercury - 28th October 1845*

I find, in almost every instance, that the epidermis of the stalk below the surface of the ground is more or less in a state of decay, often disintegrated and completely rotten; leaves and branches accord with the state of that part of the stalk below the ground. The tuber, beneath the outer skin, is first spotted brown (like a bruised apple); these spots extend and penetrate towards the centre, quite changing the nature of the potato. Those near the surface are most injured.

Advise concerning the potato crop *The Telegraph or Connaught Ranger*

The dreadful disease that has attacked your potatoes is one, the effects of which you can only stop by strict attention to the advice of those interested in your welfare. Many plans have been proposed, and after examining them all, we recommend the following as the best. All competent persons are of the opinion that the first things to bear in mind are the following directions: 1. Dig your potatoes in dry weather, if you can, and if you cannot, get them dry somehow as fast as you can. 2. Keep them dry and cool. 3. Keep the bad potatoes separate from the good. 4. Do not pit your potatoes as you have been accustomed to do in former years. 5. Recollect that if they get damp nothing can make them keep; and do not consider them dry unless the mould which sticks to them is like dust. 6. Do not take them into your houses unless you want them for immediate use.

Digging and Drying

As you dig the potatoes leave them in the sun all day. If possible throw them on to straw, turning them over two-three times. At night gather them together and cover with straw to keep frost off. Next day remove the straw and spread the potatoes in the sun. Do this for three days, weather permitting. If the weather is unfavourable use a day loft, if you have one.

However, none of the touted remedies proved effective. The agent responsible was later diagnosed as a killer fungus *Phytophthora infestans*. It simply drifted across the land with the breeze.

As the inhabitants of Carrowbaun realised the enormity of what had happened, fear must have gnawed in the pit of their stomachs. Without the potato there was nothing to eat. Perhaps they had a few cows, necessary for milk and buttermilk; in all likelihood they had a pig. But these were not for eating. The pig, if it lived, was to pay the rent and that was due in October. Furthermore, how could it be fed without potatoes? Eyes would have been cast over the children and pregnant mothers to watch out for the early signs of malnutrition. They were already hungry, having survived on meal during the summer months as the potato crop from the previous year only kept until April or May. Meal had to be paid for with hard-

---

1 Extracts from *Kiltimagh: Our Life and Times*, Eds. Peter Sobolewski & Betty Solan, Kiltimagh Historic Society

Chapter 2 – THE GREAT STARVATION

earned cash and it was often sold at exploitative prices by the despised meal, or 'gombeen men'. They were desperately hoping to be self-sufficient again.

Hopes of an early reprieve were dashed and immediate thoughts would have been on what else they and their children could eat. Cash not put aside for rent would have already gone on meal over the late summer. Some man may have just returned from harvest work in England. Would they be able to persuade the agent to lower the rents or allow delayed payment without having their pigs, donkeys and cows seized? The spinning and weaving of linen, once a source of additional income, was no more, as the linen industry had been ruined by cheaper mechanised means of production in Ulster. There was no prospect of any other employment. Perhaps some of them could gather and weave rushes, but they could not all turn to that to make enough money to buy food. If there were a few grazing cows, butter could be sold, but whatever milk they had was now even more precious.

The People - The Famine[1] *19 November 1845, The Telegraph or Connaught Ranger*

People of Mayo - impoverished and persecuted tenantry of Mayo - we have been endeavouring, for weeks past, to open the eyes of unrelenting landlords and hard-hearted agents, to the approaching prospect of starvation and famine that awaits you, but we regret to state, our appeal has been unheeded by them. ... Despairing of obtaining any alleviation of your unforeseen misfortunes from the landlords, we now turn our eyes upon the Government, and what, are they going to do for the poor of Ireland? ....

The immediate advisers of our Gracious Sovereign, Sir R. Peel in particular, as we learn from the English and Irish Journals, have in contemplation the giving of employment to our idle population, in Draining the Waste Lands of Ireland and in other useful works. May the rumour prove correct!

Happy will be the reflection, that even by getting employment our people will, in some measure, be rescued from the jaws of famine ... We do not, however, place implicit reliance in those rumours. There have been several Cabinet Councils held of late, but the results of their deliberations have been carefully kept enveloped in mystery. Rumours will have it that a serious division among the Ministry exists - that the Premier is for opening the ports, but that a majority of his colleagues are opposed to the scheme. Another on this is that Sir Robert Peel finding himself stranded on the ports propriety of question, is about laying before Parliament the granting of Three Million of Money for constructing useful public works in this country. This, we conceive, would be a most practical measure of relief, if immediately adopted and one which, in our opinion, would have the most happy effects. Without work the labourer will have no means to get food ...

If the poor be not employed what will become of them? ... How will they support their poor famishing and persecuted families, with the driver of the landlord impounding the cow or the ass for the present rectangle? We are not the advocates of outrage or plunder - but who could blame the miserable wretch who has not the wherewith to check the hunger of himself or his children; if by force, or by stealth, he had recourse to his rich landlord's well stocked pentold, or bursting granary, for the means of subsistence? ...

To the Government we would also say - do justice to the Irish – it's far more humane, honourable and just to prevent crime than to abet it. Better give the poor the means of earning an honest livelihood than be paying enormous sums to defray Commission expenses to try the shoals of hunger-made-thieves with which our prisons must be crammed. Better employ the people than be paying Doctors, ..., to check the spread of fever ...

The starving peasant applies to the landlord or his agent for relief, he is told with derision, to eat grass! Merciful God! do we live in a Christian country? ...

The alarm had already caused increases in grain prices. Famine prices were spreading over the land, the consequences of which were as deadly as the Great Famine itself. The *Mayo Constitution* reported that new oats cost 7s 8d in both Swinford and Foxford, but to buy food at that price involved a walk to those far off towns only to be at the mercy of the gombeen men there. Prices in the more conveniently located Kiltimagh and Killkelly were much higher still. The Quakers (the Society of Friends) reported that 'very often the poor people have, after earning their wretched pittance ..., to walk ten, twenty, even thirty miles to the nearest store to get a stone of meal, or to buy it off the small hucksters at an advance of as much as

---

1 Extracts from Kiltimagh: Our Life and Times, Eds. Peter Sobolewski & Betty Solan, Kiltimagh Historic Society.

thirty per cent market price'.[1] The families in Carrowbaun could buy from travelling sales men at even higher prices on credit - but at enormous rates. Hugh Dorian (2001) likens these men to the landlords.

The meal monger gives freely to one whom he expects to have some means of paying at the right time, taking good care to stipulate what price he must get at or about November. … It was no way disputed that fourteen shillings worth of meal at or after May became twenty shillings owing at November.

Appeals were made to the landlords to give relief on rents, and, judging from the above article *The People - The Famine* in the *Telegraph* or *Connaught Ranger* of the 19 November 1845 - the month the rents were due – these had largely fallen on deaf ears.

The potato: its strength

How was it that the loss of one single crop in an agriculturally rich and diverse country could have such devastating results? In the seventeenth century, Ireland was a country of tillage and pasture. Even the first Roman observers of Ireland reported that it was a country of cattle. The flat lowlands were ideal for the plough and pasture. This had been the traditional way of life for centuries. The remoter mountainous regions were regions of slopes, rocks and bog and were largely deserted as incapable of sustaining a human population (Whelan 1995). This all changed with the widespread cultivation of the potato. This crop, initially a fancy crop imported from South America for the gentry, had spread throughout Ireland and had become the staple food of the peasantry. The reason was simple enough, it could grow in places other food could not and it was easy to cultivate and needed no processing. However, unlike cereal crops, it did not store well over long periods.

The potato contains most of the necessary vitamins including thiamine, niacin, vitamin B6, and iron. The vitamin A it lacked was obtained through milk and buttermilk from the family cow. Whereas an acre of wheat or oats could feed a family of 2 or 3 for about 10 months, an acre of potatoes could feed a family of 5 adequately for 1 year.

Soon mountainous slopes were patterned with lazy-beds for the cultivation of the lumber potato – a high bulk variety that could tolerate poor soils and required little manure (Whelan 1995). Landlords were happy with this as it resulted in an increase in tenants and new income from formerly worthless land. As the population grew throughout the seventeenth century, the slopes and fringe bog lands of the West of Ireland became peopled with subsistence farmers who generally grew their potatoes in small plots for their own consumption and who kept a pig which they sold to pay their rent. A family may have had a cow grazing in common pasture and perhaps a few sheep. Many also went to England and Scotland to work on the harvest in order to earn cash.

Potatoes were grown in 'lazy beds'. This method involves placing the seed potatoes in rows on top of the existing sod or turf with the eyes facing upwards. Fertiliser, often seaweed, was added. The surrounding turf is then turned over them, forming rows of ridges and shallow furrows. These ridges can by increased in height by adding more turf from the shallow areas as the tubers develop, allowing additional tubers to grow. No soil preparation or ploughing is required. The ease with which this was done is the origin of the term *lazy beds* and this became a term of scorn, denigrating the Irish character. However, it was a very efficient system of cultivation and was an ideal way of breaking up previously uncultivated ground. So deeply has this means of cultivation become embedded in the Irish folk memory that memories of the Great Famine are stirred by a glance up the side of any mountain or over high bog lands where ancient outlines of lazy beds can still be seen.

This is how Hall and Hall described the situation in *Ireland, its scenery and character* (1841)

It is universally admitted that a finer or hardier race of peasantry cannot be found in the world; and although it is considered that their strength fails them at a comparatively early age, it is impossible to deny the nutritive qualities of a food upon which so many millions have thriven and increased. But there can be as little doubt that the ease with which the means of existence are procured has been the cause of evil. A very limited portion of land, a few days of labour, and a small amount of manure, will create a stock upon which a

---

1 Distress in Ireland: Extracts from correspondence published by the Central Relief Committee of the Society of Friends, II, P- 35-36,1847.)

family may exist for twelve month; too generally, indeed, the periods between exhausting the old stock and digging the new are seasons of great want, if not of absolute famine; but if the season is propitious, the peasant digs day after day the produce of his plot of ground, and before the winter sets in, places the residue in a pit to which he has access when his wants demand a supply. Nearly every soil will produce potatoes; they may be seen growing almost from a barren rock, on the side of a mountain, and in the bog, where the foot would sink many inches in the soil. Every cottage has its garden – its acre or half acre of land, attached; and as the culture requires but a very small portion of the peasant's time and still less of his attention, his labour is to be disposed of, or his time may be squandered in idleness. He can live, at all events – if his crop does not fail; and he can pay his rent, if his pig, fed like himself out of his garden, does not die.

We describe the lower classes of the Irish as existing, almost universally, on the potato; we have known many families who very rarely tasted flesh or fish, and whose only luxury was 'a grain of salt' with their daily meals; we do not speak of families in poverty, but of those who laboured hard and continually – the produce of whose labour barely sufficed to preserve them from utter want. Generally, however, they contrived to have a salt herring with their dinners; this was placed in a bowl or dish, water was poured upon it, and the potato, dipped into it, obtained a relish.

The potato: its weaknesses

Charles Edward Trevelyan[1], Assistant Secretary to the Treasury at the time, wrote of the risks inherent in the potato economy in *The Irish Crisis* (1848).

[T]hose who are habitually and entirely fed on potatoes live upon the extreme verge of human subsistence, and when they are deprived of their accustomed food, there is nothing cheaper to which they can resort. They have already reached the lowest point in the descending scale, and there is nothing beyond but starvation or beggary. Several circumstances aggravate the hazard of this position. The produce of the potato is more precarious than that of wheat or any other grain. Besides many other proofs of the uncertainty of this crop, there is no instance on record of any such failure of the crops of corn, ... showing that this root can no longer be depended upon as a staple article of human food.

The potato cannot be stored so that the scarcity of one year may be alleviated by bringing forward the reserves of former years, as is always done in corn-feeding countries. Every year is thus left to provide subsistence for itself. When the crop is luxuriant, the surplus must be given to the pigs; and when it is deficient, famine and disease necessarily prevail. Lastly, the bulk of potatoes is such, that they can with difficulty be conveyed from place to place to supply local deficiencies, and it has often happened that severe scarcity has prevailed in districts within fifty miles of which potatoes were to be had in abundance. ... The potato does not, in fact, last even a single year. The old crop becomes unfit for use in July, and the new crop, as raised by the inferior husbandry of the poor, does not come into consumption until September; hence, July and August are called the 'meal months', from the necessity the people are under, of living upon meal at that period. This is always a season of great distress and trial for the poorer peasants; and in the districts in which the potato system has been carried to the greatest extent, as, for instance, in the barony of Erris in the county of Mayo, there has been an annual dearth in the summer months for many years past.

Though potatoes may be nutritious, especially when eaten with their skin, to be the sole means of sustaining life, they had to be eaten in vast quantities. The Sixth Annual report of Poor Law Commissioners for England and Wales tells us that in the Ennistymon Poor Law Union[2] (establishments setup for the destitute) men and women had 5 lbs potatoes and 1 pint of milk for breakfast, the same for dinner (lunch) and supper, though supper was not always taken. Much the same figures obtain for other unions - that is between 10 and 15 lbs of potatoes per person per day.

The Poor Laws

The loss of the potato crop resulted in widespread destitution. Previous to the Great Famine, care for the destitute was organised around workhouses. This system was clearly inadequate to deal with the massive increase in poverty brought about by the failure of the potato crop in 1845. In the early stages of the famine, when Peel was Prime Minister, up to half the cost of relief work was met by the government, but

---

1 This is the same Trevelyan referred to in the famous ballad 'The Fields of Athenry' sung at Irish rugby matches and so many Irish sporting and social occasions.

2 Quoted in Kissane, Noel, 1995, The Irish Famine: a documentary history, The National Library of Ireland

the amount of money available was small - just over £10,000, mainly to be used on the construction or improvement of piers and harbours. There were also schemes to drain the bog lands, but they were few in number. In December 1845, the *'Mayo Constitution'* reported that 'Mr. Brett, the surveyor for Mayo, has been employed for making the necessary enquiry for this purpose. He recommends the deepening of the beds of several rivers, and the removal of obstructions by which many thousands acres of land will be relieved from the floods which render it almost useless.' Mr Brett went on to recommend that the Moy and some of its tributaries be deepened. As the situation worsened appeals were made for more help. It is unlikely that this sort of relief work would have assisted those in Carrowbaun as it was limited to those who lived in coastal regions.

In order to free up more food for Ireland, Peel's government had attempted to repeal the Corn Laws. The Corn Laws however had been introduced to protect British agriculture by placing a tax on imported corn. The fear was that cheap imported corn, particularly from the United States, would force down prices and thus reduce profits. The British landowners, the most powerful lobby in the land, resisted this in the House of Commons, as they perceived it as an attack on their interests. Thus without the support of his own party but with the support of the Whigs and the Radicals the Corn Laws were repealed after several month's debate. However, in June 1846, Peel was defeated on another bill, and resigned.

Under Russell's government, the 1838 'Act for the more efficient relief of the destitute poor in Ireland' was passed by the British Parliament. It created 130 Poor Law Districts administered by a locally elected Board of Guardians and financed by a levied rate on valued property. Five Unions were set up in Mayo, one of which was the Swinford Union which was created in 1840. It was here that the Poor House was built. Swinford Union consisted of an area of 330,000 acres with a population of 73,529. The Union's Board of Guardians, seven of whom were resident justices of the peace, consisted of twenty-eight members whose first duty was to levy a rate for the Union. Each area was represented, with Aghamore having two members.

Political economy and poverty

In order to understand the rationale behind the British government's policies, it is necessary to look at some of the prevailing beliefs. Attitudes to assisting the impoverished in the mid-nineteenth century were dominated by two beliefs prevalent among the political classes. The first was an absolute belief in *laissez faire* and the other was the concept of 'the deserving poor'.

Laissez-faire is characterised by the belief that supply and demand are a self-correcting mechanisms that ensure the proper running of the economy. Governments should therefore avoid interfering in the economy. Charles Wood, Chancellors of the Exchequer outlined his belief in the role of government, 'all we can seemingly aim at is to see that the people in every part of Ireland may have the opportunity to purchase food at current prices, if they have the means to do so'. It was this sort of belief that led Lord Russell, in the face of massive food shortages in Ireland, to declare, 'the government will not import food from other countries, we think it far better to leave the supply for the people to ordinary trade'[1].

However, such doctrinaire policies were not so ardently imposed when they conflicted with the interests of the landed classes, who, as we have seen, strenuously resisted the repeal of the tax on imported corn.

Moreover, in much of rural western Ireland the people lived at a subsistence level. There was only a very limited market economy. It was obvious that the required mechanism of trade simply did not exist, as money transactions were few. In January 1848, Lord George Bentinck declared in the House of Commons, 'in times like the present, when a calamity like the potato famine, unexampled in the history of the world, has suddenly fallen on Ireland, when there are no merchants or retailers in the whole of the west, when a country of which the population have been accustomed to live on potatoes of their own growth, produced within a few yards of their own doors is suddenly deprived of this, the only food of the people, it is not reasonable to suppose that suddenly merchants and retailers will spring up to supply the ordinary demands of the people[2]'.

---

1 The Radharc Documentary

2 The Radharc Documentary

Also, many – including the rural peasantry – saw the Great Famine as providential; an act of God with a social meaning. This 'providential' interpretation of the Great Famine was emphasised by many of the ruling class to support a policy of minimum intervention. If the potato blight was seen as the will of God, a visitation on an indolent, lawless people who stubbornly clung to superstitious beliefs, perhaps it were better that it should take its course. On the 1st February 1847 Charles Trevelyan in an attempt to console a disturbed Relief officer asserted, 'we must do all we can and leave the rest to God. I hope the Catholic priests are making this clear. It is hard upon the poor people that they should be deprived of knowing that they are suffering from an affliction of God's providence'.

This laissez faire approach was also supported by a sense of rectitude. Poverty was seen as often a moral defect, caused by laziness and fecklessness resulting in an overdependence on charity in the recipient. As far as those in London were concerned, this applied especially to the Irish who were considered to specialise in these traits. The virtue of charity was set against the greater virtues of hard work, thrift and self-reliance. Such prevailing attitudes in the governing classes helped inform the policies of Lord John Russell and his Liberal colleagues. This strict Protestant ethic was reinforced by a general view of the racial and moral inferiority of Irish papists.

Added to this was the view that there could be no improvement in Irish agriculture while farms were so small. Greater persuasion was given to these arguments by the fact that it was in the landlords' economic interest that the impoverished rural population of Ireland was removed. Even before the Great Famine many landlords were attempting to clear their land of surplus tenants and break up the rundale system of land allocation. Charles Wood, Chancellors of the Exchequer, told one landlord, 'I am not at all appalled by your tenantry going; that seems to be a necessary part of process. We must not complain of what we really want to obtain[1]'.

British public opinion

Within the traditions of Irish Nationalist politics as reflected in the Bernard Shaw's play quoted at the start of the chapter, and particularly in the views of men like John Mitchel, the Great Famine was seen as the result of a deliberate plan to transform Ireland and the Irish through ridding the countryside of its cottiers and small holders. In an age that accepted that some were born into slavery, there was an acceptance the Irish cottiers were born to endure poverty and hardship and their 'removal' was a necessary evil to bring about agricultural improvement.

There were some who found parallels between them and the African slave, the most degraded peoples in the European world: An Anglican bishop and philosopher, George Berkeley, reported that the 'Negros' of his plantation had a saying – 'if negro was not negro then Irishman would be negro'[2]. Charles Kingsley, an author and clergyman of Sligo while on a tour of the West of Ireland in 1860 was 'haunted by the human chimpanzees' he saw in the West of Ireland 'to see white chimpanzees is dreadful. If they were black one would not feel it so much, but their skins, except where tanned by exposure, are as white as ours.'[3]

As is often the case where racial characteristics are used to justify slavery and near slavery, the notion that the enslaved peoples were somehow less than human was common. The Irish peasant was describes in Punch in 1862 as '[A] creature manifestly between the gorilla and the negro'.

As with African slavery, people in Britain were not ignorant of the plight of the Irish agrarian workers. The radical MP, John Arthur Roebuck claimed Irish landlords were 'very much like slaveholders, with white slaves … and had been made so very much by British legislation[4]'. As Charles Orser (2000) points

---

1 The Radharc Documentary

2 George Berkeley, A Word to the Wise: Or, an Exhortation to the Roman Catholic Clergy of Ireland, in A.C. Fraser (ed.) The Works of George Berkeley, D.D. (Oxford, 1871) p. 439, quoted in An Archaeology of the Great Famine. Charles E. Orser Jr. (2000).

3 Quoted in Luke gibbons, Race Against Time: Racial discourse in Irish history, in Oxford Literary Revues, xiii (1991) p. 96 – quoted in Orser 2000.

4 Hansard's Parliamentary debates, 3rd series (1847), col. 1030 quoted in Morash and Hayes 1996.

out, outsiders who went among the African slaves and the cottiers of Ireland described their living conditions in startlingly similar terms.

Such parallels were made sufficiently often for Fredrick Douglass, the great African-American orator, to reject them. He repeatedly asserted the Irish cottier, though impoverished and disenfranchised, was not a slave in that he or she was not owned by the landlord[1]. Certainly, it is true that Thomas and Michael and their kin were free to leave, and were probably even encouraged to do so by their landlord. However, in so far as Black American slaves were economic assets, their lives and health were valued. This was not the case with the Irish cottiers, whose departure or death was beneficial to the landed classes. By evicting them from their cabins, in most cases, they were in effect condemned to death.

Much of the devastation of the Great Famine was attributed to the Irish landed classes and many felt the responsibility for dealing with the problem lay with them. The feeling in Britain that the Irish landlord class were feckless wastrels led to reluctance among the political classes to interfere in the great tragedy that was unfolding in Ireland. Thus, the cry was 'Irish Property must pay for Irish Poverty'.

'A creature manifestly between the gorilla and the negro' – the Irish, as represented in Punch

The tales of ejectments, clearings and all the long list of legal but heartless practices that reach England from the other side of the channel have hardened Englishmen against those who have for centuries held the fate of Ireland in its hands. The plain fact is here before us, too dreadfully evident to be overlooked: with the possession of property of the island an absolute monopoly of political power, patronage and place ... the dominant class in Ireland have reduced both England and Ireland to this.[2]

The basic problem as perceived in England was that many of the Irish landlords were severely indebted, and were too ready to seek help from the British government. Middle class English anger and resentment against the Irish landed classes grew to a fever pitch. It was generally believed that famine and evictions in Ireland were cynical evasions of responsibility by the Irish landlords, who were content to dump the poor of Ireland on the shore of England, Scotland and Wales to be supported by the English Poor Law and be a burden on the British tax payer (Donnelly, 1996).The *London Illustrated News* declared, '[T]hey are ready alike to hold out their hands for loans and grants.'[3] Were English workers, the *Times* asked, 'to sink into a nation of overworked, underpaid drudges, slaves, helots, mere mechanical operative animals, for the sole purpose of maintaining the landlords of Ireland in disgraceful luxury?'[4]

The Times fuelled the controversy by exclaiming, 'no argument that pen ever writ of heart ever indicted [about maintaining the Irish poor at home in Ireland] can match with the spectacle of England positively invaded, overrun, devoured, infected, poisoned and desolated by Irish pauperism'[5].

---

1 Blassingame, J.W. (ed.), 1979, The Frederick Douglass Papers, Series One: Speeches, Debates and Interviews, Vol. 1, 1841-46, New Haven – quoted in Orser 2000.

2 Times, 24 March, 1847 – quoted in Donnelly 1996.

3 ILN., 6 February, 1847– quoted in Donnelly 1996.

4 Times, 10 March, 1847 - quoted in Donnelly 1996.

5 Times, 24 March, 1847 – quoted in Donnelly 1996.

Chapter 2 – THE GREAT STARVATION

There were other concerns about the effect of the Great Famine on the mainland. Lord George Bentinck asked, 'we know that there are between three hundred thousand and four hundred thousand quarters of corn in stock on hand in the different ports of London, of Liverpool and Glasgow. I want to know then what was to have prevented ministers from sending any part or all of this food in to the west of Ireland to feed the starving there[1]'. In the face of this type of demand for greater government intervention, Charles Trevelyan replied, 'it is useless to transfer famine from one country to another. If food were bought for Ireland in the present scarcity, prices must be sent up and the English and Scots working classes would pay more'.

Relief works

However, to many politicians, administrators and observers, the most urgent need was to set up relief works whereby the hungry men could be set to work and thus earn money to feed their families. The new relief works proposed under Russell's Liberal government was organised by Trevelyan and outlined in the Poor Employment Act of 1846. Much of the work involved making and repairing roads. However, the guiding principal remained that each Irish county had to pay for the total cost of relief. Government loans could be applied for but they had to be repaid in full and with interest. The government was determined that the burden of maintaining the Irish poor should be borne by Ireland alone and would not be shared by the British taxpayer. The main point of the Russell Government's Labour Rate Act of August 1846 was to move the cost of public works onto the Irish Rates. However, £50,000 was set aside for the poorest districts. This led to a letter to Lord Russell from Archbishop McHale of Tuam in which he complained; '£50,000 to save a starving people. £20 million was spent to emancipate the Negroes of the West Indies'[2]

The Irish landed gentry, as the main ratepayers, had to pay for famine relief in full and make repayment to central government. As the drafting and operation of the Poor Laws illustrated not only was there great resistance in England to paying for the negligence of the Irish landlords but many of the law makers saw the Poor Laws as a necessary means of preventing the destitute of Ireland going to England.

Furthermore, a number of administrative problems delayed the relief works. On the 28th August 1846, Charles Strickland wrote to T. N. Redington, requesting 600 parchment tickets for the labourers to be employed on the public works in the barony of Costello 'Words cannot describe the distress of the poor who are waiting with the utmost anxiety to get work on these lines. The lists are prepared but there are no tickets to be had in Swinford.[3]'

---

1 The Radharc Documentary

2 The Radharc Documentary

3 Swords, Liam, 1999, In their own words: the Famine in North Connacht, 1845-1849, Dublin:Columba

> **Road Works to Go Ahead**[4]   *Nat. Archive RLF Comm. If 2: 228-6184 (1846)*
>
> 23 July, 1846
>
> The Relief Commission has forwarded the resolution 'that the Government be urgently called upon to order the construction of the line of road from Kiltymaugh to Ballyhaunis as the most urgent want exists, and there is no work in Mayo more required and that if not commenced many hundreds of deserving poor will be left without the means of purchasing the common necessities of life.'
>
> *The Board of Works replied that the works referred to have been approved and recommended.*

Thus sometime in late 1846, as a result of these schemes, the men folk from the parish of Aghamore probably went to work on roads or drainage projects. We know that at a meeting of the Gallen & Costello Relief Committee on Tuesday 14 July the following resolution was passed, 'that the Board of Works be requested again to approve the new road from Kiltimagh between the mill at Cloonfallagh and the main road at Cahir, as the inhabitants are in the greatest state of want.' It is not unlikely that the Hallorans and their relatives worked on this project. The men would have been paid according to performance but wages were set low so no one would choose to work on a government scheme if they could find other employment.

In so far as they were strong and healthy, the money earned might at least allow the purchase of food. But such an arrangement was likely to penalise those weakened by hunger and disease. Very soon the women and children of Carrowbaun were probably also at work on such programmes as they were also admitted, swelling the numbers employed in relief work to 441,000 by December 1846. In the tradition of the *clachan* system, child minding would likely be pooled and shared out by the older women to maximise the number who could go out to work. Children who could would go to work with their mother, perhaps those as young as five or six. Children of this age were working in mines and factories at the time. Obviously there was no question of schooling, as there was little enough of that for such children even before the potato blight. In March the number on relief works peaked at 714,000, a total of wage-earners, which must have supported close to three million.

However, the sheer numbers facing destitution and starvation were too great to be met by relief work. On Wednesday 7th October 1846, a memorial of the Costello Relief Committee to the Lord Lieutenant, signed by A. Holmes JP, J. Seymour JP, Vicar of Castlemore, Denis Tighe PP, Ballaghaderreen, Charles Strickland, JP, chairman, Thomas Philips JP, Cloonmore House, John Coghlan PP, Kilmovee 6- William McHugh PP stated:

> *Words cannot describe the famishing state of the people ... The works selected for immediate employment are quite inadequate to meet the immediate distress. Employment of 1,000 men in a barony with a population of 50,000 is a mere nothing ... The peace of the country is endangered. The patience of the people is now exhausted as they see no prospects of the works commencing. God only knows where it will end if the seriously threatened outbreak should once commence. (quoted in Swords, 1999)*

Though there is evidence of genuine humanitarian concern, many of these committees were equally concerned about law and order and keeping the cost to the rates down. There was also much public anger because projects, which involved public money, were often abused. In many cases relatively independent farmers with connections were taken in preference to the genuinely needy who had no such influential friends. A consequence of this was that many smaller farmers neglected their land and their planting, which, in a time of food scarcity, was obviously short-sighted leading to further shortages by the end of 1846.

A cynical Hugh Dorian (2002) writing in 1896 of his recollections of the Great Famine makes the following wry comments, probably reflecting the views of many of the ordinary people of Ireland.

> *Government engineers were sent out at a good salary to mark out the new lines of roads, through rocks and bogs and every other impediment. The greatest engineering and ingenuity used in laying out these were to find out the most difficult routes, impossible to make and impossible to tread. Then pay-clerks, check-clerks,*

> *overseers and gangs-men or gaffers were appointed according as they had real or supposed knowledge, or better still through intercession [connections]; and at long last, the hungry and the naked, in the cold depth of winter, were set to work; and a selection of those was made - those who were known to be in extreme necessity - and their daily wages fixed at not even that valuable coin – one shilling – oh no! but exactly nine pennies per day.*

It is questionable whether these relief works kept many destitute people alive. By early 1847 chaos prevailed. People began to ask if these projects were worth the enormous cost and would it not be more effective to simply subsidize food. Officially recipients were paid 10d a day but, as Dorian claims, often received less. Even this did not keep up with raising prices and people were still starving.

Hugh Dorian continues his account:

> *Here is where the government advisers dealt out the successful blow – and it would appear premeditated – the great blow for slowly taking away human life, getting rid of the population and nothing else, by forcing the hungry and the half-clad men to stand out in the cold and in the sleet and rain from morn till night for the paltry reward of nine pennies per day. Had the poor pitiful creatures got this allowance, small as it was, at their homes it would have been relief, it would be charity, it would convey the impression that their benefactors meant to save life, but in the way thus given, on compulsory conditions, it meant next to slow murder.*

Thus it was that many began to believe that there was an official but unspoken plan to depopulate the rural regions of Ireland. This reflected remarks made John Mitchel, an Irish nationalist activist, solicitor and political journalist, that 'the Almighty, indeed, sent the potato blight, but the English created the Famine'. Subsequently, many, especially the Irish in America, levelled charges of genocide against the British Government of the time.

Younger men and women had for many years been leaving the poorer rural area to work as navvies, domestic servants or as factory hands in England. At this stage this stream became a flood. Dorian writing of a similar situation in Donegal wrote:

> *The women and children were within doors; the able bodied male portion of the families were out in every known direction looking and applying for employment or for relief. A father or son who managed to make his way to Scotland thought himself lucky though absent – out of sight of his dear ones – so long as he could send home as soon as it was earned a few shillings to save his wife, his mother, his brother or perhaps his own little ones from starving, and how readily they would submit to the loss of his presence so long as the expected relief arrived.*

It is likely men from Carrowbaun, some of them Hallorans, their relatives or in-laws, had gone to work in England possibly as navvies on the railways, just as their forefathers had previously worked on the canals and as agricultural labourers over the summer months. Month by month, as famine tightened its grip; a conviction probably grew among them that to save their families they must make use of what they knew of England to get their families out of Ireland. In all likelihood the money for the eventual journey to England came from these men. In the meantime the more fortunate probably survived on this money, which was doled out within the family in the same manner as land was distributed in the rundale system, which is based on family connections, family responsibility and need.

Some of the able-bodied remained at home to work their plot in an attempt to ensure a new potato crop was planted in the spring. There would have been little or no seed potato to do this, but it was the practice in times when potatoes were in short supply to extract the eyes of the potato attached to small potato chunks. These were kept dry, allowing the cut potato to harden for planting. In this way the rest of the potato could be eaten.

Black '47

In Aghamore, our forebears eked out a living through 1846, desperately waiting for next crop of potatoes and the arrival of money from those working in England. However, when the crop came it was healthy in most places but small. In the spring of that year, the lack of seed potatoes from the previous year and the necessity of working on relief programmes during planting time meant that only small acreage had been sown. However, the new potato crop was again blighted in much of East Mayo. What healthy potatoes there were, were eaten too early, reducing the size of an already diminished crop, little of which could be stored for future use. The eventual yield was not much more than a quarter of pre-Famine levels and the Famine tightened its grip on the land.

Charles Strickland describes the following report of the situation in and around Aghamore.

Friday 23 January 1847. Charles Strickland to J. P Kennedy, Dublin Castle
Up to so late a time as the end of December, the loss of the potato crop, tho' severe in some places, did not much alarm me. Much use was made of the diseased potatoes in feeding cattle and pigs and in many cases for human food by cutting off the affected parts...Within the last fortnight and even the last few days the potatoes in pits are nearly all diseased or quite rotten ...When sowing time comes it may be difficult to find a sufficient quantity of sound seed for the next year's crop. .During the last fortnight we have had very unusually fine weather and warmer than any weather since the crop was dug and the disease seems to be much increased by it. (Quoted in Swords, 1999)

On 4th August 1846 the *Mayo Constitution* reported on the crop on which the people hoped to survive during the following year:

The Potato Disease [1]

We have been much alarmed during the past week at the fearful accounts of the potato crop. Within the last week large quantities of the tubers have become blackened, and the potatoes when dug are quite infected. The crops which a few days since were apparently safe, have, on investigation, been found diseased. We heard several of the guardians at the last poor law meeting state that the stench arising from the potato fields during the night was insufferable.

The Mayo Constitution, 4 August 1846

The disease presents the same appearance as that of the last year, except that decomposition is taking place much more rapidly, so much so that we fear a great part of the crop is already lost. Several farmers in the neighbourhood of this town sent early potatoes to the market, which when sold appeared sound, but on being boiled were unfit for food. The oat and wheat crops look very healthy, and promise an abundant return.

The realisation that the potato crop had failed badly for the second year running must have filled all with fear as people started to lose hope. Hugh Dorian gives this account:

In a very short time there was nothing but stillness, a mournful silence, in the villages; in the cottages, grim poverty and emaciated faces, showing all the signs of hardships. The tinkers disappeared – fled to the cities; the musicians of all and every description disappeared, and these classes of visitor have never since returned. Many of the residents also made their escape at once, finding employment or early graves elsewhere. But in general the people were drifting from bad to worse, no one having sufficient food for the family for the year within himself; ... they had to fall back upon anything they had for sale - a cow, a heifer or a few sheep - and take it to market being bound to sell at whatever price offered, and with this they would buy Indian meal, brought home in lieu of the pet animal which had to be parted with, but the love of offspring was dearer to the parent, and before seeing his children hungry he would sacrifice anything however valuable. ... A mournful silence, no more friendly meetings at the neighbours' houses in the afternoons, no gatherings on the hillsides on Sundays, no song, no merry laugh of the maiden, not only were the human beings silent and lonely, but brute creation also: not even the bark of a dog nor the crowing of a cock was to be heard - and why? These animals had nearly all disappeared.

The year 1847 saw the famine at it most widespread and a sharp increase in the number of people who actually died. This is how John Mitchel (1876) described a cluster of farmhouses he saw from a coach in the West of Ireland. It could have been a description of the dwellings in much of Aghamore.

Around those farm-houses which were still inhabited were to be seen hardly any stacks of grain; it was all gone; the poor-rate collector, the rent agent, the county-cess collector, had carried it off: and sometimes, I could see, in front of the cottages, little children leaning against a fence when the sun shone out, – for they

---

1 Extracts from Kiltimagh: Our Life and Times, Eds. Peter Sobolewski & Betty Solan, Kiltimagh Historic Society

> *could not stand, – their limbs fleshless, their bodies half-naked, their faces bloated yet wrinkled, and of a pale, greenish hue, – children who would never, it was too plain, grow up to be men and women. I saw Trevelyan's claw in the vitals of those children: his red tape would draw them to death: in his Government laboratory he had prepared for them the typhus poison*[1]. *(p. 147)*

It is hard to imagine the particulars of lives so different from, even if so closely connected to, our own, however Hugh Dorian (2001) who lived through and experience the Great Famine captures the haunting details of family life.

> *Many affectionate parents reduced themselves to mere skeletons from the too oft repeated act of withholding from themselves the necessaries they were so much in need of and giving them to their silent helpless children, thereby feeling great comfort in the act but unawares that feebleness would steal upon them. So overcome would they be from a weakness caused by want of food that apparently strong able-bodied men, on managing to get into a neighbour's house without any business whatever but to while away the time and be relieved, to be out of sight of the distress if only for a few minutes, would sit on a seat and soon fall asleep from exhaustion, and on attempting to get home again would have to lay hands on a wall or a fence to keep from staggering ...*
>
> *In persons reduced to this extremity, this weakness in the frame, the cheek bones became thin and high, the cheeks blue, the bones sharp, and the eyes sunk, arising from the deprivation of nourishment at the same time the legs and the feet swell and get red, and the skin cracks.*

There was also, as time went on, the sense that the famine was spreading and effecting people who had initially felt immune from its devastating power. Those with a middling size farm sold a pig and few cattle to get through the first years though food prices were high. But after a year of two these reserves were gone and the middling-sized farmer who had not emigrated early found himself and his family reduced to the level of those landless labourers and cotters who still survived.

Many were inclined to blame the worsening situation of the failed policy of relief works that had directed many cotters and small farmers away from food production. There was also anger that the government was failing to provide adequate seed for future crops.

The following is a letter of 4 March 1847 to the Editor of the *Mayo Telegraph*.

> *There is a disinclination to cultivate the soil in this truly afflicted parish, not arising from a conspiracy (for this notion is as absurd as it is ridiculous); but the reason is obvious. The great majority of the people have no seed, nor means for procuring it; and even if they had, they are well aware that when the crops would become fit for use they should pay 2s 6d. per day to what are called keepers or bailiffs, who would take good care of them. Under these circumstances, the people don't know what to do. To remain in the country they are afraid; - to emigrate they are discouraged. And how are they to blame, when the only encouragement held out to them is the grasping avidity with which the November rent is secured'? ... But, in justice, I must acknowledge there are some landlords whose sympathy for the starving poor cannot be exceeded. I have the honour to remain,*
> *Your obedient servant,*
> *'A Kiltimagh Man'*

---

[1] Mitchel, John, The Last Conquest of Ireland (Perhaps) http://www.libraryireland.com/Last-Conquest-Ireland/Contents.php

THE HALLORANS OF BIRSTALL AND AGHAMORE

Distress in Mayo [1]   *The Mayo Telegraph, 27 October. 1847*

From every quarter of the county the cry of distress is now daily on the increase. Turn to what direction you will gaunt figures or moving skeletons meet the eye. ... The late measures of the government relief for Ireland are now, alas, producing their natural results. We long since foresaw what would follow from converting the people into organised lazy pauper gangs, grubbing on the broken roads of this country. We foresaw, and declared our conviction that more ruin would be entailed on Ireland by these works than can be remedied for years to come. The labour of two millions of men for that time, directed by a government staff of twelve thousand officials, has not been productive of a stone of potatoes or a bag of corn or wheat additional for the sustenance of the people. The roads yield neither potatoes nor com, and will never yield either ...An ignorant and inert government, by turning the natural visitation of the elements into a scourge has forced the country through a succession of projects and trials that have emaciated and entirely destroyed it. ...

Last year the people trusted that the measures proposed by government would be of a beneficial nature to them. Fatal confidence. By the direction of government seed oats in Mayo was converted into meal, upon the understanding that at spring time seed would be supplied to the people.

This was not done, and now the poor of Mayo are destitute and dying from want. Nothing can equal the distress of the people in the rural districts.

The Poor Laws and soup kitchens

The fact of mass starvation was obvious by the spring of 1847 as was the failure of the relief works to address the situation. The cost of these schemes and the fact that they were diverting labour away from food production finally resulted in a radical change of policy and the government invested responsibility for relief to the Poor Law unions and the workhouses. The 1847 Poor Law Amendment Act was a further embodiment of the principle 'Irish Property must pay for Irish Poverty'. Irish landlords were seen as responsible over centuries of indifference creating the conditions that led to the Great Famine and must be made to pay for its consequences. Irish landlords dreaded the prospect of outdoor relief, aware that it would spiral beyond the limits imposed on relief delivered in workhouses. In line with the notions of 'political economy' prevalent at the time and citing arguments of the political economist, Nassau Senior, relief was still to be dependent on the workhouse test of destitution. There was a phasing out the relief schemes and a system of free food distribution, primarily involving soup kitchens, was created. The Soup Kitchen Act was introduced in January 1847 and soup kitchens were established in each of the electoral divisions. Later that year there were 1,250 soup kitchens in operation and by June this had increased to 1,850. However, the phasing out of relief works brought with it its own terrible consequences for some, and in some cases, had to be delayed.

THE PUBLIC WORKS [2]   *5 May, 1847*

On Saturday last, pursuant to the order of the Government, all the works in this county were stopped, and the poor wretches who toiled on them sent to die, for want of food. The appearance of this town in the afternoon of that day was truly awful from the number of poor creatures who flocked in quest of payment, many of whom were disappointed in their expectations. On Monday they again came in to the amount of some thousands. No act of violence or disorder of any kind was attempted by them, which, possibly may be attributed to the report that many of them would be re-employed on the works on this day.

The ending of relief works would have meant a drastic change for the Hallorans. By July the daily trudge to the relief works had been replaced by the daily trudge to soup kitchens. That year over 3 million people were collecting daily rations of cooked food.

---

1 Extracts from Kiltimagh: Our Life and Times, Eds. Peter Sobolewski & Betty Solan, Kiltimagh Historic Society

2 Extracts from Kiltimagh: Our Life and Times, Eds. Peter Sobolewski & Betty Solan, Kiltimagh Historic Society

Chapter 2 – THE GREAT STARVATION

Relief through soup kitchens had been well established previously, but had been run mainly by charities and religious bodies. A year after the first potato failure, the Irish Quakers became involved in relief efforts in an organised and extremely practical way. Now the method was made government policy. When the government decided to use soup kitchens as the main form of relief in the spring of 1847, the Quakers provided the boilers to make the soup[1]. Local relief committees were reconstituted to administer the scheme and the kitchens were supported by subscriptions that were matched with government grants. To get the process up and going, the government provided loans that were to be repaid from the rates.

Quaker soup kitchens

Charles Strickland was quick to avail of the Quakers' offer for the barony of Costello and on Monday 1st February he wrote to the Society of Friends.

> *I should like to put up two or three soup shops as soon as possible. We have practically ascertained the quantities of several articles to make a really good and nourishing soup and have got in a store of articles ready to carry us for a little time in anticipation of your kind and generous assistance.*
> *Draft note: 'Grant 1 ton of rice for immediate distribution. C. Strickland proposes to have boilers ferried by canal to Longford, 1 of 130 gallons, 1 of 100 gallons and 1 of 70 gallons*[2].

He received this reply on Monday 22 February from William Todhunter of the Society of Friends:

> *The ton of rice was forwarded to thee on the 6th inst. by canal boat to Longford. The boiler we had not yet been able to set off.*

From March to June the numbers employed on the relief works were gradually reduced and the workers paid off. By August, up to three million people were receiving soup daily. Even though the people regarded queuing with containers to be degrading, they swallowed their pride in order to fill their empty stomachs. The scheme made a very significant contribution to relief and saved the lives of many thousands, including members of the Halloran family. It may have allowed them to spend more time on reclamation of bog land within and around their townland. It is known that during the famine period, huge areas of bog land in East Mayo were drained and made ready for potato cultivation and pasture.

Despite the fact that theses kitchens saved the lives of so many, they have been stigmatised in the Irish folk consciousness with the label of 'souperism'. The charitable work of the Quakers was undoubtedly sincere and unconditional. However, a number of evangelical missionary groups made relief conditional on conversion to the Protestant faith. Among the most controversial proselytisers were Rev. Edward Nangle who established a missionary colony on Achill Island, Co. Mayo in 1831, and Rev. Alexander Dallas who established schools in Connemara during the Great Famine. They attracted some hundreds of converts, but their strident propaganda caused great resentment among the Catholic clergy. 'Souperism' remained an abiding source of indignation in popular folklore. It was considered the ultimate act of exploitation of the hunger and desperation. Instinctively, it appears, the ordinary people of Ireland felt that if an answer was to be found to their problems it was in solidarity; a principle put into practice in the following years by the Land League and the boycott.

By mid 1847, however, it appeared that the prospects of the future looked brighter.

---

1 UCD MultiTextProject in Irish History, http://multitext.ucc.ie/d/Private_Responses_to_the_Famine. Emancipation, Famine & Religion: Ireland under the Union, 1815–1870,

2 Swords, Liam, 1999, In their own words: the Famine in North Connacht, 1845-1849, Dublin:Columba

> **THE HARVEST - POTATOES**[1] *16 June 1847*
>
> Readers of *The Telegraph*, we are aware of the universal anxiety now felt throughout the kingdom about the growing crops. We have, therefore, gleaned from the public Journals the latest, and we are happy to add, the most satisfactory information on this most important subject.
>
> Before we direct the reader to the perusal of those accounts we would here state that at no former period within our recollection, did the crops in Mayo exhibit a more promising appearance than do the present. Potatoes, large tracts of which have been planted through the country, are, as yet, most promising, exhibiting no appearance of the fatal disease of the last two seasons. We confess we had our misgivings as to the quantity of land laid under cultivation in Mayo: and we are rejoiced to find, from personal observation, and by accounts from our country correspondents that our despondency on this head is now turned into joy. Green crops also are very promising, as is also the appearance of the fruit crops. In short, as far as we have gone in the season, every seed in the earth (if we except parsnip and carrots, which have in many instances failed) promises an abundant yield.

But within four months hope turned to despairing disbelief as it became apparent that the potato crop had failed for the third successive year.

Gregory clause

Integral to the new Poor Laws was the 'quarter-acre clause' - the infamous Gregory clause in the Poor Law Extension Act 1847, called after the man who proposed it, Sir William Gregory MP of Coole Park, Co. Galway. He was later the husband of Isabella Augusta, Lady Gregory the Irish dramatist and folklorist who co-founded the Irish Literary Theatre and the Abbey Theatre with William Butler Yeats. This clause excluded from relief anyone who had more than a quarter acre of land. Another clause, the £4 clause, made the landlord responsible for the all landholding tax on any holding valued at under £4. This latter clause covered most landholdings in Connaught. These two clauses effectively defined smallholders as parasites. They accelerated the process of 'clearance' (as it was called) as the starving had to abandon their holdings and go to the workhouse if they wanted a chance to survive. Many smallholders who needed relief were forced to give up their holdings in exchange for food and a place in the workhouse. So though the potato crop was better in 1847, the number of landless poor was greater and such an improvement did not bring them any benefit. For many, this clause clearly demonstrated the hidden agenda behind the policies purportedly aimed at bringing relief to Ireland, and that agenda involved clearing the land of cottiers and small land holders, that is people just like the Hallorans, even if, in many cases, it meant sending them to certain death.

1848 – The third year

The destruction of the potato crop in the autumn of 1847 meant that hunger and disease grew more widespread, as the resources even of those with larger farms were eaten up.

Fever and disease

Disease had become rampant from the winter of 1846 onwards and ultimately proved a bigger killer than hunger, which itself of course, impairs the body's immune system and makes it more prone to illness. Famine disrupts a community's habitual sanitary practices and routines, resulting in neglect of personal hygiene and a general deterioration in standards of sanitation. Furthermore, there was considerable dislocation as people were forced to move from place to place and to gather together in soup kitchens, on relief works and in workhouses, further spreading disease. Potentially fatal diseases were soon endemic in the famished population, including typhus and relapsing fever (famine fever) - which are transmitted by human body lice harbouring in filthy clothing and bacillary dysentery ('the bloody flux') - which is spread by flies, fingers or infected food, though the causes of these diseases was unknown at the time. Relapsing fever was characterised by recurring bouts of fever, aches, vomiting and bleeding. Also prevalent were tuberculosis, rheumatic fever, bronchitis, influenza, pneumonia, diarrhoea and measles (Geary, 2000).

---

1 Extracts from Kiltimagh: Our Life and Times, Eds. Peter Sobolewski & Betty Solan, Kiltimagh Historic Society

Chapter 2 – THE GREAT STARVATION

The Board of Health in Dublin was flooded with appeals for help of every kind but the superintendence of the sick poor was left to the Poor Law guardians, who were not experienced in such administration and often proved to be influenced by local interests. The government's persistent refusal to sanction emergency funding meant that the pandemic was free to flourish. The fever hospitals were underfunded and there was talk of peculation and jobbing (Geary, 2000). The Poor Law Dispensary in Kiltimagh had £152-8-0 expended on it and it administered to 2,463 patients (Sobolewski & Solan).

The epidemics peaked in most areas around the summer of 1847; however, Asiatic cholera appeared in the 1848-9, adding to the general pandemic. The sheer scale of number of deaths meant the disposal of infected bodies created additional hazards. The following account is given in the main collection of Irish Folklore Commission (1935-1971) and refers to the workhouse in Castlerea, Co. Roscommon

> *When a person was near death, he or she was removed from other parts of the workhouse to a large room at the gable end of the workhouse (the gable nearest the town of Castlerea). This room was called 'the black room', and the gable, 'the black gable', for in this room the sick person was allowed to die; sometimes there were up to seven persons in this room. From the window in this room there were a few boards slanting down to the earth, and beneath was a huge grave or pit. When a death occurred, the corpse was allowed to slide down the boards into the pit beneath, and lime was put over the corpse, along the boards and over the gable. This caused the wall to get black and gave the name 'the black gable'.*
> *(Johnny Callaghan; Main Collection Folklore Commission (1935-1971), Ms 1069, p. 255)*

In many areas there was neither dispensary nor resident apothecary. The under-manned dispensaries were partially dependent on local subscriptions and thus tended to be in the towns and more prosperous areas, not the poorer rural areas where they were most needed. These were the areas where there were no resident landlords and few medical practitioners. This is evident from a letter sent By James Jordan to the Lord Lieutenant on behalf of the Kiltimagh Local Relief Committee at the outbreak of the famine.

> *To his Excellency Lord Viscount Besborough Lord Lieutenant and General Governor of Ireland.*
> *We the undersigned members of the Keltimagh local Committee, respectfully beg leave to call your Excellency's attention to the following facts, and consequent distress of this Parish (Killedan) Co. Mayo.*
> *We may almost state that there are no resident landlords nor any relief whatever from them.*
> *That there are one or two instances of death caused by starvation and that unless immediate relief be given many will meet with premature graves.*
> *That there are many instances of families living during the last ten days on Turnips and Cabbage and that fever and other diseases are rife in the Parish; to all these facts we invite investigation.*
> *R. C. C. Chairman. James Jordan* [1]

The resident landlords must have resented the fact that so many of their class were absent. They were responsible for paying the Poor Law rates, yet many were not around, probably leaving this responsibility to their agents. The greater the destitution, the greater was the demand on the Poor Law rates. Smaller landholders could not afford to pay them, and increasingly demands were made on for more help from central government in the form of the Lord Lieutenant and on charitable institutions, like the Quakers.

Below are extract from another letter written in a similar vein by the same James Jordan, in his capacity this time as Guardian of the Electoral Division of Killedan in the Swinford Union to Joseph Todhunter of the Society of Friends advising him of the calamitous conditions prevalent in Kiltimagh.

> *27 April 1848*
> *Sir,*
> *… This locality is different. Situated from many other parts of Ireland, the peasantry generally hold from one to 5 acres, and many of them of course think the same as losing their lives to lose their little spot of land, they are the only class that are now suffering as the destitute persons holding no land are relieved by the existing poor law. I would also beg to remark that the landed proprietors here are all absentees. There is not a single small employer in this parish out of a population of 6,500 save a few by Sir Compten Domville*[2], *who in justice to him must be acknowledged as a good landlord. He is an honourable exception.*

---

1 (National. Archives, Distress Papers 5292 in Kiltimagh: Our Life and Times, Eds. Peter Sobolewski & Betty Solan, Kiltimagh Historic Society)

2 Sir Compton Domville is discussed in chapter 10

Several hundreds of these poor creatures would be glad to work for him morning till night for their support without a farthing wages. Fever and other diseases are making destructive ravages and t'is no strange thing to see a person dead more than a week without a coffin and many are buried actually without coffins...
James Jordan
Bushfield
(Nat. Arch. RLFC 2-5067)

During 1846 and 1847 people had lived in hope that next year's crop would be healthy, only to be bitterly disappointed. It appeared that the potato crop in the autumn of 1847 was good and largely free of infection auguring well for 1848.

POTATO PLANTING[1]

Telegraph or Connaught Ranger, March 1848

We have received accounts from all parts of the county, that the plantation of potatoes is carried on very extensively; and such is the anxiety evinced by the peasantry, who yet hold a plot of ground, that they have their land prepared, altho 'without seed, entertaining a hope that they will receive a supply from some benevolent quarter. We trust their fond hopes will not be disappointed. We find meetings have been held, assembled on the requisition of that benevolent and truly Christian clergyman, the Very Rev. James MacHale, Roman Catholic Rector of Castlebar, to adopt measures to obtain from the General Central Relief Committee a Loan with which to purchase seed for the very poorest and most destitute of the peasantry of the parishes of Castlebar, Ballyhean, and Breafy. We trust, with sincerity, their application will be crowned with success. A general plantation of potatoes should be encouraged by every benevolent person, which will, if it pleases Providence, prevent a recurrence of a famine which has depopulated the land and reduced our country to a charnel house. May God prosper the efforts of Mr. MacHale and his associated, and reward them for their praiseworthy exertions on behalf of the poor.

However, other factors were also at work. The potato of itself had never been sufficient to sustain life, usually only available for nine or ten months of the year. Crofters and small holders had depended on meal purchased with cash as well as milk to augment their diet. However, anything which could be sold off had been. Much of the population had depended on their pigs but these were fed on potatoes and had in many cases been sold off or had died. Much the same applied to the family cow which supplied the all important milk that complemented their monotonous diet. Laying chickens also would have vanished from the most of the households. Even a good crop would not provide enough potatoes or the cash to purchase food. Also there was the rent to pay and worse still, the soup kitchens and much outdoor relief was stopped as the harvest was considered good enough and the bad times over.

The workhouse

The workhouses created under the 1838 Act were designed to cater for a relatively small population of paupers, and had nowhere near enough capacity to deal with the massive numbers affected by the Great Famine. *The Times* of London reported, 'The workhouses are full and only hold 100,000, while 4 million are Starving'. There was considerable overcrowding, conditions were unsanitary, and disease was rampant. The situation was aggravated by a serious fever epidemic early in 1847. The government was determined to keep the numbers on outdoor relief to a minimum, as otherwise the costs would be more than the rates could support, unions would become bankrupt, and the government would again be forced to finance special relief measures.

---

1 Extracts from Kiltimagh: Our Life and Times, Eds. Peter Sobolewski & Betty Solan, Kiltimagh Historic Society

Chapter 2 – THE GREAT STARVATION

> **Famine in Mayo – The Poor Laws** [1] *Telegraph or Connaught Ranger, 13 December, 1848*
>
> Day after day, and night after night, the cries of the famishing, and the low moans of the dying, are heard in our streets, and in the public high ways! Yet the relief the law allows such is heartlessly denied them, owing to the stringent rules of the Poor Law Commissioners. For instance a poor man with a large and starving family will not get a pound of food so long as he presents the appearance of bodily vigour. Why is this so? Why are God's creatures thus hurried to their graves by process of law? … Why are those having the semblance of 'able- bodied' men, denied poor law relief? The answer is 'they are able to work' and, we reply - They are Willing to Work! Pray, Gentlemen! - you who administer the poor laws in Mayo - Where are they to get the Work? They are ready, even in the last stage of emaciation from starvation, to LABOUR! and notwithstanding all this you, -you who know those things as well as we can tell them to you - deny them a portion of that bread the law allows to the famishing children of men!

A report of a meeting of the Board of Guardians of the Swinford Union indicates there were 284 applicants for admission of whom 157 were admitted. The following resolution was approved, 'that as this Workhouse is now almost full we request our Chairman, G.W. Jackson, will represent to his Excellency the Lord Lieutenant, and the Poor Low Commissioners, the utter impossibility of our carrying on the relief of the destitute through the poor law owing to the unlooked for and unprecedented calamity in which we are plunged unless a loan is made to meet the intense urgency of the present moment, to be re-paid by the rate at a future period'[2]. It is interesting to note, the name Charles Strickland, Esq., Viscount Dillon's agent, was among the members of the Board of Guardians.

The main ratepayers were of course the landlords. They had a vested interest in keeping the cost of relief to a minimum; in some cases, boards dominated by landlords restricted admission to the workhouse and did not actively pursue defaulting ratepayers. An extreme example was the board of the Castlebar union in Co. Mayo, which was alleged to be both incompetent and corrupt. It was eventually dissolved, and replaced by paid officials known as vice-guardians.

As relief works and workhouse admissions multiplied, the burden on the ratepayers grew. 'So oppressive is the poor rate', Rev John Garrett reported to the Quakers, 'that a host of the better sort of farmers are daily emigrating to America.' Others complained that it was reducing even the better off farmers to the condition of paupers and forcing them to sell of the very means by which they could avoid destitution. A virtual war broke out between the ratepayers and the collectors. The collector in Loughglynn (the seat of the Dillon estate and the residence of Charles Strickland) and Frenchpark had to be escorted with a force of cavalry and infantry, amounting to 360 men as well as 100 policemen (Swords, 1999).

There was also particular concern about who should qualify for outdoor relief and about the exclusion the able-bodied. Many of the workhouse Boards devised a mechanism known as 'the workhouse test', whereby applicants for outdoor relief had to prove that they were destitute by becoming resident in the workhouse. The Gregory clause forced those holding even a small parcel of land to give it up in order to qualify for relief. This meant few could leave the workhouse because they had no home to return to. Once they had resided for a period, thereby showing that they were genuine paupers, they were usually turned out and put on outdoor relief, thus providing space for a new batch to undergo the test. When workhouses closed for lack of money the inmates were sent out with no prospects before them but death.

---

1 Extracts from Kiltimagh: Our Life and Times, Eds. Peter Sobolewski & Betty Solan, Kiltimagh Historic Society

2 Extracts from Kiltimagh: Our Life and Times, Eds. Peter Sobolewski & Betty Solan, Kiltimagh Historic Society

It appears that a number of auxiliary workhouses were set up outside Swinford, including one in Aghamore. The return of Destitute persons receiving outdoor relief in this Union shows that 218 Aghamore people, at a cost of £7 12s 0¾ are recipients of this help. The full statement, as published in *The Telegraph or Connaught Ranger*, appears above.

There is every reason to believe that people connected with the Hallorans, and possibly members of their family, saw the inside of this auxiliary workhouse. The custom-built workhouses were bad enough. It can only be imagined what the auxiliary ones were like. With terrible shortages at home, it was the old, the sick and the infirm who were most likely to end up in the workhouse. There were also the evicted - those who had had the roof torn from their dwellings because they had got behind on the rent.

SWINFORD UNION[20]

RETURN OF THE STATE OF THE WORKHOUSE AND

AUXILIARY HOUSES, 2nd DEC. 1848.

No. In the Workhouse, &c., Sat., 25th. Nov., 1848.- 2327
Admitted during the week 147
Total 2474
Discharged during the week,..................................471
Died 2
....473
Remaining at end of week,................................2000

State of the Sick.
In Fever Hospital, 87;   In Infirmary, 82.
Total under Medical treatment 139
General average cost of a pauper for the week, ...1s. 2¼.
Return of Destitute Persons relieved out of the Workhouse, under the 1st. section of the act, and the cost of Relief afforded in each Electoral Division and Union at Large, for the week ended Saturday, Nov. 25, 1848.
Board Room, Swinford, 2nd Dec., 1848   RICHARD KYLE, Clerk of the Union.

	Persons	Cost of Relief.				Persons	Cost of Relief.		
Swinford	207	£8	5s	8d	Knock	52	£1	13s	7d
Killasser	248	£7	16s	2½d	Aughamore	218	£7	12s	0¾d
Toomore	232	£7	4s	0½d	Kilmovee	280	£8	4s	2¾d
Meelick	239	£7	16s	2½d	Kilbeagh	185	£5	1s	0d¾
Bohola	225	£6	13s	8d	Achonry	225	£7	11s	3d
Killeaden	259	£6	13s	9d	Kilmactigue	284	£9	10s	0d

The Committee men

There were many problems about the way relief was distributed. Committees of clergy and other gentlemen supervised and controlled the allocation of most of the resources that were purported to bring relief to the poor and hungry. These included the allocation of places for the destitute in the workhouses, employment on relief works and the allocation of coupons for Indian meal or soup. Many of these committees made up their own rules that reflected the spirit of the Poor Laws and the 'quarter-acre clause'. Just as debarment of the able-bodied from relief led to the able-bodied growing hungry and weak; and just as the debarment of those with a quarter of acre of land drove many to abandon what little land they had, so some committees made laws debarring people with 'four-footed animals', excluding cats or dogs, from relief. The result of course was that in desperation for a little food for their families many had to give up their pony, donkey, cow or pig, driving more and more of the better off farmers to the same level of dependency and poverty as the destitute (Dorian, 2001).

There is no reason to think that the committees set up in the parishes around Swinford were any better or worse that those elsewhere. That there was abuse is certain. Dorian talks of the 'committee men'.

Chapter 2 – THE GREAT STARVATION

> *The 'committee men' were from all denominations. ... [they] were entrusted with small sums of money and at their discretion divided it among those supposed to be most in need, and if they had not the necessary goods to give in lieu themselves, they were watchful to find a friend who had and put the money his way...*
>
> *Those who had the distribution employed favourites to build fences, make drains and improvements, beautifying the approaches to their dwelling. ... This was the way in which a great deal of the relief fund being entrusted to those worldly-minded men was converted and smuggled into other uses. Yet such men were looked upon as good men for they gave employment – for their own benefit and with the charitable money bestowed by others.*

All relief schemes, however, were unfortunately ended in September; the rationale was that as the potato crop was relatively unaffected by blight in 1847 and that the crisis was over.

Evictions

If some were prepared to see the Great Famine as an act of providence the same could not be said of the evictions that accompanied it and became a feature of life for many in the West of Ireland for the next two generations. There is no doubt the land was massively overcrowded and could not sustain the population that struggled to survive on it. Apart from the sheer size of the population, other factors accounted for this. The unequal legal and social structures related to land tenure acted as a disincentive to any improvements in either the underdeveloped agricultural methods or the living conditions of the tenants. Nonetheless, the use of the law to eject the famished and impoverished from the land provoked a sense of outrage in an age and among classes of people not usually sympathetic to the poor. It soured relations between the indigenous Irish and the British ascendancy classes and government for decades to come. This report is by James Hack Tuke, in *A visit to Connaught,* Society of Friends, Dublin, 1847.

> *The extreme western portion of Erris is a narrow promontory called the 'Inner Mullet'. Upon this wretched promontory, a proprietor named Walsh, residing in another part of the country, has an estate from which he was desirous of ejecting a number of tenants by the usual summary process of unroofing and eviction. As no less than 140 families were to be turned out and cast forth to beg or perish, for the poorhouse was fifty miles distant and could not have contained them, it was natural to expect some resistance from persons with such prospects.*
>
> *Fifty soldiers, therefore, headed by the commanding officer of the district, are added to the force. It is thought the 'kindest' way to prevent bloodshed, by showing a superior power. Arrived at the scene of action, the troops are stationed in reserve behind a hill, and the landlord and sheriff, protected by forty policemen, proceeded to announce their errand. The tenants are commanded to quit – they are told that their landlord forgives all arrears, on condition of their quietly giving up possession of their hovels and holdings, and leaving their crops should they have any. ... The policemen are commanded to do their duty. Reluctantly indeed they proceed, armed with bayonet and muskets, to throw out the miserable furniture: dirty time-worn stools and bed-frame, if any, ragged cover-lid [coverlet], iron pot; all must be cast out, and the very roof of the hovel itself thrown down. But, the tenants make some show of resistance – for these hovels have been built by themselves or their forefathers who have resided in them for generations past – seem inclined to dispute with the bayonets of the police, for they know truly that, when their hovels are demolished, the nearest ditch must be their dwelling, and that thus exposed death could not fail to be the lot of some of their wives and little ones. But the signal is given to the soldiers, and, overawed by the unexpected sight, the tenants are compelled to submit, and in despair and dismay to see the ruthless work proceed.*
>
> *Six or seven hundred persons were here evicted; young and old, mother and babe were alike cast forth, without shelter and without the means of subsistence! A favoured few were allowed to remain, on condition that in six months they would voluntarily depart. 'A fountain of ink (as one of them has said) would not write half our misfortunes'.*
>
> *At a dinner party that evening, the landlord, as I was told by one of the party, boasted that this was the first time he had seen the estate or visited the tenants. Truly, their first impression of landlordism was not likely to be a very favourable one!*

An examination of what happened to Lord Lucan's tenants in Treenaglaragh in the neighbouring parish of Killedan illustrates how devastating eviction from one's smallholding was. The following is a letter dated the June 22, 1848 from Fr Daniel Mullarky, P.P. of Killedan to the Editor to the *Freeman's Journal,* the oldest nationalist newspaper in Ireland.

> *As you have been at all times the warm and unflinching advocate of the poor man, and the implacable foe of the oppressor. I strongly anticipate you will give insertion to the following startling facts. On the 14th*

instant the sheriff with a strong force of police, arrived in the townland of Treenaglaragh, parish of Killedan, evicting the poor inhabitants. This townland is now made the theatre of many a melancholy and heart rendering scene. The whole townland, may I say, presents the appearance of a battlefield the day after the fight - nothing to be seen but the shattered ruins of what were so lately abodes of men. No less than thirty-three families, numbering in all one hundred and forty-five human beings, have been thrown on the world. It would be impossible for me, sir, to give you a full and fair description of the wretched and deplorable condition of these unfortunate creatures, stretched along ditches and hedges - many of them children and decrepit old parents - falling victims to cold, hunger, and destitution.

The land in question, about 332 acres, was held in common (rundale), and, according to Fr. Durcan, the object of the ejectment was to consolidate this land into individual farms. Their rent was £3 an acre.

"I will not breed paupers to pay priests"

The following is a newspaper report of the incident:

Lucan evicts 145 Kiltimagh people[1]   *June 1848*

The Earl of Lucan, Lord Lieutenant of Co. Mayo and holder of 60,570 acres in this county, valued by Sir Richard Griffith at £12,940, is undertaking a most vicious and heartless clearing of his pauperised tenants. He has already evicted 33 families in Treenagleragh, consisting of 145 persons. Meanwhile his tenants in Cartoon, Gorrymore, Lisnamanigh and Pulrenaghaunmore, wait in fear and trepidation as they ponder their fate. ...

The Earl, who has done little to 'develop Castlebar, the villages on his estate or the agriculture of the country,' has said he 'would not breed paupers to pay priests.'

This was not an isolated event. The number of families evicted in Co. Mayo over three years is as follows:

Year	families evicted	families reinstated	families in total	persons
1846	263	39	224	969
1847	528	79	449	1944
1848	630	95	535	2317
1849	1,115	420	695	3010

There was a very steep rise in the number of convictions, especially in 'Black 47' in which twice the number were evicted that in the previous year. The estimated total number of persons evicted is based on the figure of 4.33 members per family, a figure derived from the average family size of families evicted from Treenagleragh. We can estimate that 8330 individuals were evicted over these four years. It is reasonable to assume that more than half of these were children.

It should also be added that those who were evicted and subsequently reinstated suffered terribly as the eviction process was accompanied by the destruction of the home, especially the roof, and it probably took some time to be reinstated, during which the families had to live under hedges and rebuild their homes.

In the popular Irish imagination, landlords like Lord Lucan have left an indelible mark as typifying the landlord classes, and not without a considerable degree of justification. However, even John Mitchel, famous for his remark, 'the Almighty, indeed, sent the potato blight, but the English created the Famine', had the following to say in *The last conquest of Ireland (perhaps)*, (1861):

Irish landlords, sir, are not all monsters of cruelty. Thousands of them, indeed, kept far away from the scene, collected their rents through agents and bailiffs, and spent them in England or in Paris. But the resident landlords and their families did, in many cases, devote themselves to the task of keeping their poor people alive remitted their rents, or half their rents; and ladies kept their servants busy and their kitchens smoking with continual preparation of food for the poor. Local committees soon purchased all the corn in the

---

[1] Extracts from Kiltimagh: Our Life and Times, Eds. Peter Sobolewski & Betty Solan, Kiltimagh Historic Society

government depots (at market price, however), and distributed it gratuitously. Clergymen, both Protestant and Catholic, I am glad to testify, generally did their duty; except those absentee clergymen, bishops and wealthy rectors who usually reside in England, their services being not needed in the places from whence they draw their wealth. But many a poor rector and his curate shared their crust with their suffering neighbours; and priests, after going round all day administering Extreme Unction to whole villages at once, all dying of mere starvation, often themselves went supperless to bed. (p. 30-33)

Crime and the Great Famine

Despite the horrendous conditions in which ordinary people lived; despite the obvious and enormous disparity between the rich and the poor and despite the often heartless and frequently illegal treatment of tenants, there was little agrarian unrest in the area. Many commented on the profound resignation of the most desperate, who showed a pious fatalism in the face of the calamity, reacting with quiescence to what they viewed was the 'wrath of God' for the 'sins of the people'.

However, many of the better educated were not so quiescent. The Young Irelanders staged an abortive uprising of their own in 1848. They were a group of young idealistic men who had broken away from Daniel O'Connell's Repeal Association with the intention of pursuing a more radical agenda. It was a year that saw rebellions in Paris, Berlin, Vienna, Rome, Prague, and Budapest. However, the planning of the uprising in Ireland was rushed as the government was about to suspend *Habeus Corpus*. The uprising failed to gain popular support, fizzling out after a stand-off at Widow McCormack's House in Ballingarry, Tipperary. Two protesters were shot and several of the rebel leaders convicted of sedition. Their death sentences were commuted and they were transported to Australia. John Mitchel escaped and emigrated to the United States in the early 1850s, where he served on the Confederacy side in the American Civil War.

Whether anyone in Carrowbaun even knew of this uprising is doubtful. Life had become totally disrupted for the rural poor, who were weakened by hunger, alarmed by the spread of disease and spent their entire waking hours conniving how they and their families were to survive.

Ribbon men activities also appear also to have become a victim of the Great Famine, as the newspaper report below suggests.

Mr. Justice Jackson - Crime in Mayo

The Connaught Ranger 23rd. March 1848

In the Crown Court on Saturday, Mr. Justice Jackson, while telling the Jury to acquit a prisoner charged with administering an illegal oath, said - 'Gentlemen, it is to me a source of much satisfaction to state that your county is free from outrages of the nature charged against the prisoner. I have it from the Grand Jury; I have had it from the gentlemen of the several petty juries, that your county is free from Ribbonism and Molly Maguireism, notwithstanding the awful state of destitution under which the poor are suffering.

It is gratifying, gentlemen; it is highly honourable and I feel much satisfaction in stating so to you.' Edward P. MacDonnell, Esq., Cahir House, and others of the Jury, remarked to his Lordship that many of the cases which came before him were got up for the purpose of getting prosecutions money from the county.

The learned, humane and excellent Judge nodded, and the issue paper having been handed down, he ordered the man to be discharged.

However, courts throughout the country were still convicting people for theft, which was usually motivated by the simple urgency of survival. The modern folksong, *The Fields of Athenry*, is sung at many Irish sporting occasions and is one of Ireland's most popular songs; testament to how the victims of the Great Famine, their hunger, the injustices done to them, still resonates with the heart of the Irish people.

Fields of Athenry *By Pete St John, 1979, published 1985*

1. By a lonely prison wall
I heard a young girl calling
Michael they are taking you away
For you stole Trevelyan's corn
So the young might see the morn.
Now a prison ship lies waiting in the bay.

Chorus
Low lie the Fields of Athenry
Where once we watched the small free birds fly.
Our love was on the wing
We had dreams and songs to sing
It's so lonely 'round the Fields of Athenry.

2. By a lonely prison wall
I heard a young man calling
Nothing matters Mary when you're free
Against the Famine and the Crown
I rebelled they ran me down
Now you must raise our child with dignity.
Chorus

3. By a lonely harbour wall
She watched the last star falling
As that prison ship sailed out against the sky.
Sure she'll wait and hope and pray
For her love in Botany Bay
It's so lonely 'round the Fields of Athenry.

Were the Hallorans and their neighbours evicted?

This question cannot be answered at present. It depends very much who their landlord was. The assumption has been made in this study that Thomas Halloran's family were from Carrowbaun. This is based on the fact that James Halloran was living in Carrowbaun in 1856. However, he may have relocated there after the Great Famine, as it resulted in a great deal of disruption. If the family were in Carrowbaun during the Great Famine, they would have been tenants on the Dillon estate, where Charles Strickland was the agent. His reputation is such that it is unlikely any of his tenants were evicted. He specifically denies having ever evicted a tenant in the following letter of Thursday 12th July 1849 to Bewley and Pim, of the Quakers[1].

> *The persons now in the greatest distress are the poor but small landholders who have suffered sorely in sowing a crop and have in very many instances left themselves completely destitute and are now more dead than alive... Relief should be given in food only, from 1 to 2 stones of meal weekly to families who are not receiving poor law relief and who have their lands cropped ... The poor landholders with a good crop sown is by far the most deserving object of relief and at present far the most distressed class ... I have already given out 6 tons of meal as a mere temporary relief in one district ... I have not thrown a house or turned out a tenant from Lord Dillon's estate in all these distressed years. A few have given up their land but are left in their houses.*

This last line is perplexing. Does it mean they had to forfeit their land, as they could not pay their rent? Was their land then leased to other tenants who could pay? To be left in their homes without land is to be left without any means of survival. They may have survived on relief for much of the famine but could not survive once the relief ended.

However, Charles Strickland was not free of the accusation of evicting tenants, as the following account shows.

> *Monday 1 March 1847. James Conlon, potter and tile maker, Crennane, to the Lord Lieutenant*
> *I took a holding of ground from Charles Strickland, made a boundary fence and drained it and possessed it for two and a half years and paid two years' rent ... .14 September 1846, Mr Strickland sent the bailiff who seized the effects, served notice for me to quit on 1 May 1847 and stripped my workshop of shelves and racks and left me unable to earn 6d. a day at my trade .. I went to Mr Strickland and asked him to put my son on the public works and myself as steward but he refused in order that I and my family might starve and perish. My son has read arithmetic, algebra, Euclid and mensuration (sic). (Swords 1999)*

Disregarding the extraordinary curriculum followed by his son, there is no reason to dispute this claim.

---

1 Swords, Liam, 1999, In their own words: the Famine in North Connacht, 1845-1849, Dublin:Columba

Chapter 2 – THE GREAT STARVATION

The prospects of evicted families were very poor. Eviction itself was a result of destitution. The only options for those so dispossessed were the workhouse or the open road in a famished land. In order to emigrate, a family needed some resources. Probably, most tenants avoided eviction by funding their emigration on money saved for their rent, perhaps supplemented by money sent by relatives working in England, and setting off on the long walk to Dublin docks. This may well have been the Halloran's situation. However, some travelled to England with absolutely nothing. We know that Michael Davitt's family managed to make their way to Lancashire having left the workhouse where they arrived after being evicted for non-payment of rent. Their story is discussed in chapter 9.

The story was probably different in each townland, depending to the severity of the landlord or his agent. According to Griffith's Valuation of the Aghamore civil parish a variety of different landlords were represented in Aghamore, many of whom were absentees, including Francis R. O' Grady, Mary Jane Olmsby-Gore, Annsley Knox and Sir Compton Domville Bart, among others. The landlords of Rath, Caher and Cornageaghta, townlands where Hallorans lived after the Great Famine, are discussed in chapter 10.

It is possible that a number of the inhabitants of Aghamore received some form of financial inducement to vacate the land, leaving perhaps the eldest sons to work on consolidated farms. Some landlords and their agents allowed a remission of rents during the famine years; this may have eased the financial burden somewhat.

When the families from Aghamore arrived in Birstall there is no evidence that they were joining an existing Irish community, like the one in Batley, though some individual members of the family may have already being working in the area. This supports the view, held by Bill Halloran and other members of later generations, that some of the Halloran men had worked as navvies on the Manchester/Leeds railway. As we shall see in chapter 5, after this was completed in the early 1840s, there were other railway projects in the Birstall area. The 1851 and other early censuses indicate that most of the men were labourers. Working on the railways would have been much better paid work than the relief works in Co. Mayo and would have allowed the accumulation of enough savings to bring some of the families out.

The fact that something drastic happened in Carrowbaun in the 1840s is clear from the decline in the number of households and population, as indicated in the various censuses from that date onwards. From 1841 to 1851 the population dropped by 12. This seems remarkable in view of the fact that we know Thomas emigrated with his family of 10 (though some of his children were born after 1841), including his brother Michael, and that he was surrounded in Birstall by many of his relatives and neighbours. It may be that his was the only family to leave Carrowbaun, and that most of his neighbours in Birstall were from surrounding townlands where conditions were much harsher. Furthermore, there is no certain evidence that Thomas and his family were actually from Carrowbaun. This is supposition, based on James' presence there in 1856.

Year	1841	1851	1861	1871	1881	1891	1900	1911
Population	107	95	100	89	99	94	86	82
Houses	17	15	14	14	14	13	14	13

Population and households in Carrowbaun

The population of Aghamore civil parish, like that of many other civil parishes in County Mayo, declined during the famine years and beyond. However, the population in Carrowbaun by 1851 had experienced an 11.2% drop in 10 years. The total population in the parish, however, was 7,675 in 1841, but dropped to 6,097, a 21.6% decline - significantly less than in Carrowbaun.

There is evidence that tenants on the Dillon estates did not experience the full hardship inflicted on tenants by many of the landlords who felt it their duty to maintain the rights of property and continued to demand market and even rack rents. Coulter (1880), in discussing the Dillon estates, informs us:

> *During the famine years considerable abatements were given to the tenants generally, and an allowance besides of half a year's rent. Provisions were also provided and sold at a cheap rate, so as to bring food within the reach of all, even the poorest amongst them.*

We do not know on what he based these comments, and it must be said his views on the landlord system were generally uncritical, except in cases where landlords actually broke the law. However, the decline throughout the parish did not stop after the Great Famine. By 1911 the population was down to 5,699; though not as significant a drop as in many other civil parishes in County Mayo, this was a huge proportion all the same (O'Hara, 1982, p. 7). Nowhere else in Europe experienced a similar decline.

The poorest parts of Ireland had the highest population. Generally in Co Mayo, 73% of the farms were less than 5 acres and a square mile of land supported 400 souls, or over seventy families. Coulter (1880) feels that Charles Strickland's approach to the problem of over-population and small farms was 'politic and wise'. He says:

> *The course pursued by Mr. Strickland, in nursing the tenantry during that period, was not only benevolent, but politic and wise. A great portion of Lord Dillon's property is such that it can only be cultivated profitably by a small class of tenants, and cannot be converted into those large grazing farms which are so much the rage at present, so that, if the people had been allowed to starve or emigrate, the lands might have been waste for years. Mr. Strickland, therefore, acted most prudently in preserving the tenantry; and though a vast number of the holdings are too small, he has never attempted to correct this evil and consolidate farms at the expense of any tenant who has a bona fide claim on the estate.*

The potato crop failed badly for successive years until 1851. It has been estimated by modern historian R.J. Foster (1988) that 'at least 775,000 died, mostly through disease, including cholera in the latter stages of the holocaust'. He further notes that 'a recent sophisticated computation estimates excess deaths from 1846 to 1851 as between 1,000,000 and 1,500,000...; after a careful critique of this, other statisticians arrive at a figure of 1,000,000'. It is further estimated ... in excess of one million Irish emigrated, while millions emigrated over following decades. Among those who emigrated were our own forebears, Thomas Halloran and family. They at least had survived and subsequently appeared in Birstall, Yorkshire. With them were relatives and neighbour: perhaps a sister Ann and another brother Patrick. We also know James Halloran, possibly Thomas' brother, also survived the Great Famine in Carrowbaun and his offspring continued to farm there and in the neighbouring townlands of Rath, Cahir and Mountain.

> **'Tá sinn ocrach'** [we are hungry].
>
> *Report by William Bennett on conditions in Belmullet, Co. Mayo, 16th of third-month, 1847, (Transactions... of the Society of Friends, 1852, p. 162-4.)*
>
> We now proceeded to visit the district beyond the town, within the Mullet. The cabins cluster the roadsides, and are scattered over the face of the bog, in the usual Irish manner where the country is thickly inhabited. Several were pointed out as 'freeholders'; that is, such as had come wandering over the land, and squatted down on any unoccupied spot, owing no fealty and paying no rent.
>
> We spent the whole morning in visiting these hovels indiscriminately, ... avoiding only such as were known to be badly infected with fever, which was sometimes sufficiently perceptible from without by the almost intolerable stench...
>
> The scenes of human misery and degradation we witnessed still haunt my imagination with the vividness and power of some horrid and tyrannous delusion rather than the features of a sober reality. We entered a cabin. Stretched in one dark corner, scarcely visible from the smoke and rags that covered them, were three children huddled together, lying there because they were too weak to rise, pale and ghastly; their little limbs, on removing a portion of the filthy covering, perfectly emaciated, eyes sunk, voice gone, and evidently in the last stage of actual starvation. Crouched over the turf embers was another form, wild and all but naked, scarcely human in appearance. It stirred not, nor noticed us. On some straw, saddened upon the ground, moaning piteously, was a shrivelled old woman, imploring us to give her something, baring her limbs partly, to show how the skin hung loose from the bones, as soon as she attracted our attention.
>
> Above her, on something like a ledge, was a young woman, with sunken cheeks, a mother, I have no doubt, who scarcely raised her eyes in answer to our enquiries, but pressed her hand upon her forehead, with a look of unutterable anguish and despair. Many cases were widows whose husbands had recently been taken off by the fever, and thus their only pittance, obtained from the public works, was entirely cut off. In many, the husbands or sons were prostrate under that horrid disease, the results of long-continued famine and low living, in which first the limbs, and then the body, swell most frightfully and finally burst ...
>
> Perhaps the poor children presented the most piteous and heart-rending spectacle. Many were too weak to stand, their little limbs attenuated, except where the frightful swellings had taken the place of previous emaciation. Every infantile expression had entirely departed; and, in some, reason and intelligence had evidently flown. Many were remnants of families, crowded together in one cabin, orphaned little relatives, taken in by the equally destitute, and even strangers; for these poor people are kind to one another to the end. In one cabin was a sister, just dying, lying by the side of her little brother, just dead. I have worse than this to relate, but it is useless to multiply details, and they are in fact unfit. They did but rarely complain. When we enquired what was the matter, the answer was alike in all: 'tá sinn ocrach', [we are hungry].

CHAPTER 3

The Hallorans who left Aghamore

Emigration or extinction - their journey from County Mayo

While the Great Famine was raging in Ireland, thousands, like the Hallorans and their neighbours, were fleeing the country. As the townlands fell silent, small country towns throughout the north of England were being transformed by unparalleled developments in railway building, coal and iron mining and the mass production of cotton and woollen goods. The two brothers who left Aghamore were of very different ages. The older, Thomas (1808) was about forty. He was already married to Judy Stenson and they had a young family of six. This young couple started the family line in Birstall and are the great grandparents of the five brothers to whom this book is dedicated: James (1905-05), Thomas (Tom) (1908-74), John (1911-1990) and William (Bill/Willy) (1913-72), Bernard (1915-22) Halloran of Birstall, Yorkshire.

The younger brother, Michael (b. 1827), was about twenty years Thomas's junior. Together, and no doubt with a large party of relatives and neighbours, they were forced to leave Mayo and take up a new life in England, where they struggled to make a living in the coalmines and woollen mills of Yorkshire. No doubt, they had considered going to the United States. Perhaps some members of these families had already left for the more accessible, perhaps interim, option of England. Many from the area had been to England before and had worked on the harvest, or perhaps on the railways. These experiences may have affected their decision. Perhaps some knew friends and relatives who were already there - a small ray of hope.

The Great Famine had threatened the very existence of countless families. In impoverished homes or in make-shift huts, groups met everywhere to discuss how to save their families and feed their hungry children; who should risk their lives and flee; and who would risk their lives by staying. There may well have been elderly parents and relatives to thinks about. We don't know who among the Hallorans were involved in this discussion. We don't know if it was held in response to a particular event - perhaps an eviction or death, or if it was in response to a general sense that hunger might well destroy them all. It seems most likely that it was a decision made in conjunction with relatives and neighbours, perhaps members of the Stenson family. Judy was a Stenson, and they were an extensive family with relatively large holdings. The discussion would have involved the Kelly, Frain or Brenan families. The Higginses, Kellys and Doughertys might well have also been involved.

Neither do we know why it was that James (and others) should stay nor why Thomas and Michael (and others) decided to leave, but is was often the case that the eldest brother would stay to look after elderly parents and work the land, which supports the idea that James, Thomas and Michael were brothers. However we do know that at least these three men survived, two to appear in Birstall, Yorkshire in 1851, where there are records of marriages involving an Anne Halloran, and shortly after a Patrick Halloran in 1853 and 1853 respectively. Other Hallorans who appeared as godparents on baptismal certificates in England between 1851 and 1854 include William, Joseph, Bridget and Mary. We cannot be certain of the relationship between these nine Hallorans who appeared in Birstall, but it is likely that James, who lived in Carrowbaun in the 1850s, was Thomas and Michael's brother, though we know there were at least two families of Hallorans in Aghamore before the famine.

It is possible that their departure was sudden, and not much discussed with outsiders. It may have taken place in early May, just before the rent was due and all the families had managed to put aside some money which they were not prepared to pay to the landlord. It was not uncommon for families to take flight at this time, using their rent money to pay for their passages instead.

Chapter 3 – THE HALLORANS WHO LEFT AGHAMORE

Whatever the case, it would be marked by some sort of farewell get-together. Charles McGlinshey (1986) of Inishowen, Donegal, describes what he had heard from his father about the family preparations for the departing emigrants.

> *Everyone took a supply of oaten bread with them. The whole townland would be baking and hardening bread for whoever was going away. They were baking for a fortnight beforehand. The bread would be hardened three or four times until you could walk on it. All the bread was packed into a small barrel that the coopers made for the purpose.*

If the Halloran preparations were similar, the oats must have been hard to come by in the middle of a famine, but provisions were necessary and had to be obtained in some form, though the cost to those who remained must have been great. They may have set off, as did the family of Michael Davitt of the Land League (see chapter 9), with nothing. His family had been evicted and did not have the wherewithal to pay the rent.

The Aghamore families' departure would have been seen essentially as exile. Though departures to England were less final than exile to America, leave-taking parties were similar throughout Ireland, and were viewed as wakes. Such occasions during the famine would not have involved the drinking and eating of less desperate times, but the families mentioned above would have gathered on the eve of departure, probably in the parents' homes, with what food and drink they could get to mark a special occasion. In less stricken times, relatives and neighbours would have been invited and there would be singing, smoking, storytelling and dancing, as well as lots of advice and expressions of sorrow. Evicted families would not have enjoyed this luxury, as it was often dangerous for neighbours to shelter an evicted family. It was, in all likelihood, a time of gaiety and grief, particularly the latter as whole families and young children were leaving. Early next morning, most of the townland would accompany the departing group to the edge of the village to make their final farewells.

We don't know how large the group was that left. There was almost certainly an element of 'chain migration', where those who had already gone suggested who should follow them, re-forging family and community bonds in England (Swift, 2002). What we do know is that by 1851 some members of virtually all the families from the townland and district appeared in a single community in Birstall, suggesting they travelled in either a large number of small groups or a smaller number of larger groups, the size and frequency of such departures determined by the amount of money that could be set aside or sent by those already in England.

To emigrate at all, particularly if the destination was America, implied some access to resources. Tickets had to be paid for with cash and some provisions - clothing, perhaps a cart and pony and some small quantity of food - had to be secured. Most financed this desperate venture with funds sent from relatives working in England, probably as navies. This may have been combined with unpaid rent money. Scavenging and begging on route would have to be resorted to. Any strategy for survival would have to be employed. A few emigrants received small subsidies from landlords as an inducement to leave the land and so allow the consolidation of the estates (Fitzpatrick, 1995). However, we found no evidence of this with Viscount Dillon's tenants.

Most likely, the Halloran party walked the 150 miles to Dublin and almost certainly Thomas and Judy's family went as a unit. There were 7 children. The oldest was James, certainly still only a boy of about 12, and the others even younger: Patrick, Michael, Thomas, Mary, Bridget and Catherine, born during the famine and possibly still her mother's breast. The whole land was destitute and starving. As they trudged along the road to Dublin, there were other hazards apart from hunger. To be fit to emigrate at all must have signalled to other desperate wanderers of the highways that the party may have had cash and resources, making them a possible target for attack and robbery. No doubt the difference in appearance between those with a port destination and those with no destination was small, but tell-tale signs were probably discernible to those eyes made keen with hunger and desperation. It was necessary to travel in groups and be ever watchful, trying to blend in with other destitute travellers who wondered the roads aimlessly, looking for any form of nourishment.

It is noticeable that most of the descriptions of the famine victims were made by people who observed them from relative security. Below, John Mitchel, in *The Last Conquest of Ireland (Perhaps)* (1876), describes the sights he witnessed from his coach window as he travelled towards Galway.

> *In the depth of winter we travelled to Galway, through the very centre of that fertile island, and saw sights that will never wholly leave the eyes that beheld them: – cowering wretches, almost naked in the savage weather, prowling in turnip-fields, and endeavouring to grub up roots which had been left, but running to hide as the mail-coach rolled by – groups and families, sitting or wandering on the high-road, with failing steps and dim, patient eyes, gazing hopelessly into infinite darkness; before them, around them, above them, nothing but darkness and despair: parties of tall, brawny men, once the flower of Meath and Galway, stalking by with a fierce but vacant scowl; as if they knew that all this ought not to be, but knew not whom to blame, saw none whom they could rend in their wrath; for Lord John Russell sat safe in Chesham Place; and Trevelyan, the grand commissioner and factotum of the pauper-system, wove his webs of red tape around them from afar. So cunningly does civilization work!*

This is how the Halloran party would have travelled, scavenging and begging along the way; yet furtive, hiding in shame and fear from the eyes of those who travelled in comfort and security; who belonged to an alien distant world they were not part of, whose very security and prosperity were a threat and source of shame.

We hear little from those who actually experienced great hunger in the Great Famine and from those who were driven to the extremes to ensure their own and their family's existence. This is probably no accident. Few who experience near death by starvation can do so with dignity and integrity. Halloran family folklore consists of stories of places and work, places like Kiltimagh and Ballyhaunis and work on the railways. There is also talk of the rivalry between the Batley and Birstall Irish, even that some Irish were involved as strike-breakers. But the terrible circumstances that drove the community from their homeland to Birstall in the first place have not come down in family folklore. The experience is frequently described as 'unspeakable', and that is the way it was left by most who experienced it. One of Cathal Póirtéir's informants in his study of famine folklore has this to say:

> *Several people would be glad if the famine times were altogether forgotten so the cruel doings of their forebears would never be again renewed and talked about by the neighbours.*

Along with the shame of destitution was the failure to provide for one's family. Survival bought its own guilt as well as grief for those who perished. There was the angry resentment of having been wronged and, in many cases, the shame of having done wrong. People stole and were stolen from; the Great Famine stripped the land of people and freed it for others to take. Food scarcity brought spiralling prices that many could not afford but others profited from. Another of Cathal Porter's informants gives this account heard from his father:

> *When they went to bring the potatoes into the house in the spring, as is still the custom in these parts, they had been all stolen, though the outward appearance of the heap remained undisturbed and the theft must have taken place at night. He said his father told him that they of the household cried out in despair when they discovered the cruel wrong.*

There were more unspeakable things than theft and profiteering. Among the images of famished mothers and their children, many analogous to those of Mary and Christ, there are those more darkly horrifying. In the anonymous poem 'Thanatos' of 1849 we hear of one such mother:

> *The mother-love was warm and true; the want was long withstood –*
> *Strength failed at last. She gorged the flesh; – the off-spring of her love.*

However, the very communal nature of their effort must have been a solace and a source of comfort and strength. Companionship was important, and even the flight from home was marked by snatched periods of cheerfulness despite the pain of want and of leaving. This is how, in a letter to his father, another young emigrant described meeting up with all his friends and embarking on the boat that would take them away from Ireland.

> *We came to the depot. There we met our comrades, and you might think it was out of heaven we came to them. Micheal Greedy, Patt McGrath and Bridget Neylon were as glad as if we gave them a thousand pound for being along with them. I hope we will have luck please God. We had a good friend Neil Armstrong - long may he live. He tried every experiment to have us along with our comrades and it did not fail him. Whatever way the wind blows I was glad to be along with my neighbours. (Quoted in 'Flight from famine' by David Fitzpatrick in 'The Great Irish Famine)*

Chapter 3 – THE HALLORANS WHO LEFT AGHAMORE

As we shall see, this strong sense of kinship and neighbourliness was a key feature of the lives of the Hallorans and their Mayo neighbours when they moved to Birstall. There the Irish families continued to live among and marry into neighbouring families from home. However, they had

Departure of the "nimrod" and 'Athlone' steamers with emigrants on board for Liverpool

fled from a rural nightmare in a pre-industrial age and landed in a new form of hell born of industrialisation. But, the experience probably only strengthened their sense of kinship, which, no doubt, ensured their survival. It is to that survival that we Hallorans and O'Hallorans, the descendants of Judy and Thomas, owe our existence.

Fitzpatrick (1995) comments that the success of the shippers in getting most of the emigrants to their destinations alive, is as astonishing as the networks created to secure such a massive exodus. The passenger trade was rickety and unregulated at best and many steerage passengers experienced disgusting and dangerous conditions, many dying of fever and hunger on route. The Atlantic crossing, especially to Quebec, the destination of the notorious 'coffin ships', was much longer and more dangerous than the passage taken by Thomas and his kith and kin. Nonetheless, it is hard to image how they managed to face theirs children's and their own hunger in the crowded and diseased conditions on board ship, as the families huddled together facing an unknown future.

The road from Mayo to England had been well trod long before the Hallorans (and probably Stensons and others) trudged it during the Great Famine. The first important influx started after the rebellion of 1798. This marked the beginning of an increasing migration into England, which was temporarily reduced by the beginning of mass emigration to America, only to resume during the Great Famine. 403,500 left for the United States alone between 1831 and 1841. The Scots Irish had massed at the American frontiers in the previous century. In the early 1840s, Canada was the chief destination, but often only to use Quebec, Halifax, St John and St. Andrews as staging post for entry into the United States. The passages were cheap. Boats brought cotton from the United States and timber from Canada so the emigrants were used as ballast on the return trip. Fares ranged from 15s in the cheaper cargo vessels to £2.10s on the more expensive steam ships. By 1818, high wages in North America attracted many Irish workers who became a major part of the workforce in the construction of the Erie Canal in New York State and similar projects. At present we do not know if any of Thomas' generation went to the United States, though a number of the later generations did. 'Emigration begets emigration' and many Irish left for 'Americay' encouraged by good reports from earlier emigrants and often their financial help. Today, an estimated 70 million people worldwide claim some Irish descent; among them are 45 million Americans who claim 'Irish' as their primary ethnicity.

Connaughtmen and horned cattle to the far platform

Instruction on vessels sailing between England and Ireland

Britain was less favoured than America because it was the home of the oppressor and the Irish were often received with hostility. Emigration to Britain, however, became increasingly feasible in the pre-famine period. In 1818 the first steam packet, the Rob Roy, linked Belfast and Glasgow. This was soon followed by ferries between Cork and Dublin and Liverpool. Competition brought fares as low as 10d (pence) in steerage and 3d on deck (Swift, 2002). Liverpool was, for many, only a stage before emigrating to North America. In 1846, 280,000 people entered Liverpool from Ireland of whom 106,000 moved abroad. Many of the others, like Thomas' family, moved to other areas of the rapidly industrialising northern England. From the end of 1847, the effects of the Great Famine were felt less and the waves of immigration decreased in number and in size.

Before the Great Famine, it was mainly single young men who had gone to England and Scotland for work, some as navvies, and some as seasonal migrants. Few had settled there permanently. Particularly in the west of Ireland, countless small land holdings had been so subdivided through the generations that many sons could no longer attract wives as their holding, if they had one, could not support a family. Equally, many young women could bring no dowries and were left unmarried. Furthermore, as families and rents grew, many of the men had to travel to England to earn the all-important cash to pay their rents. Survival was the prime motive for those who left home to work.

Seasonal migration to Britain

The proximity of Britain meant it drew a significant number of itinerant seasonal labourers, referred to as 'spalpeens' (from Irish *spailpín*, an itinerant labourer). In Britain, the Irish workers were very poor, prepared to accept lower wages, work longer hours and live in poorer conditions than the locals. They were also sometimes used to break strikes, as we shall see in Batley in 1832. In 1835, there was a drop in the number of Irish immigrants going to England, mainly, it was reported, because of the bad treatment received there. This was about the same time there was a drop in the Irish entering Batley. No

Seasonal migrants

doubt, the fact that the Irish tended to work for lower wages and some of them were used to break strikes exacerbated the situation. This would not, of course, be the first or last time immigrants have had this type of experience. The Irish spoke a strange language and practised an exotic, foreign and threatening religion. As temporary seasonal migrants, they made little or no attempt to integrate themselves into British life.

There is the distinct possibility that Thomas, or members of the party with which he travelled, had already become familiar with the area around Birstall as seasonal labourers or navvies. There is a record in the 1841 census of a Thomas Halloran working as a labourer in Birstall – one of 29 people lodging at the same address. There is no way of knowing if this is the same Thomas, or even a relative, but the birth date (1807) is the same. There was a William Halleron, a bricklayer, recorded, together with wife, Sarah and daughter Mary, in the 1841 census in Holbeck (next to Morley in South Leeds). So certainly some Irish men knew of the Birstall area and the work opportunities it offered.

The seasonal migrants had traditionally gone to earn money to pay their rent. They worked in harvesting corn, digging potatoes, collecting turnips, picking hops and draining land. Generally, these workers were widely dispersed throughout England and Scotland. They followed well-established routes to Britain. Those from Connaught traditionally walked the midland route to Dublin, Holyhead and then set sail to Liverpool. This is probably the route Thomas, Judy and family took with Michael. This continued to relatively recent times. Mary Hudson remembers stories being told of the Irish seasonal agricultural

Chapter 3 – THE HALLORANS WHO LEFT AGHAMORE

workers who walked to Birstall from Liverpool for harvest time, presumably having already walked to Dublin from the west of Ireland.

One Birstall inhabitant told of the regulars who turned up for harvest on his grandparents' farm. His grandmother would bake mutton pies for their arrival and, after a huge meal and home-made ale, they would sleep for over twenty hours before setting to work. Another Birstaller was reputed to walk to Liverpool to find workers and then bring them back. However, this yearly migration began to decline with the mechanisation of farming and by the 1880s, migrant labourers were mainly active in the northern counties of Northumberland, Yorkshire and Cheshire in Scotland.

When the harvesting season was over, they returned to their families in Mayo every year to pay their rent and to support their families; returning to the hardship of life in the West of Ireland and to living again among family and neighbours.

Hugh Dorian gives us an interesting account of the role of the migrant worker as seen by those who stayed at home and depended on his earnings to pay the rent.

There is a deep dependency on the few shillings brought home by some members of the family to complete the amount [for the rent]. These poor creatures, so much welcomed home now, have been at their service since May and put up their time in the wet and cold, before the rising and after the setting sun, late and early and now too glad to get under the old walls, to turn out their earnings, not one penny of which was spent by them, but kept carefully to assist father or widowed mother to stop the gaping mouth of the greedy landlord for a time. So careful would these poor creatures be of their earnings that for days before leaving service they would be thinking of the best and safest way to carry it home without it being lost, and it would defy the art of a London pickpocket to find out where they had it concealed on their persons. And on the journey home if the distance was considerable they had no call to use any of it, for the masters and mistresses were always so kind as to put into their kit as much bread as was enough, and some to take home.

When the whole community was devastated by the horrors of the potato crop failure, the experience they already had of life on the British mainland gave many the option of moving to take up more permanent or long term employment in places like Yorkshire. Though this was no doubt a desperate measure; the alternative was death through disease or hunger. However, relatively few permanent immigrants worked in agriculture.

In order to gain a contemporary view of these workers and a better understanding of them, it is interesting to look at some original documents. The following are extracts from parliamentary papers of 1836, entitled *Report on the state of the Irish in poor Britain*. They are taken from *Irish Migrants in Britain 1815-1914: Document*, by Roger Swift.

We ought not however to overlook the advantage of the demand for labour in England and Scotland being amply and adequately supplied, and at a cheap rate and at very short notice by Irish simply because they are potato-fed and a disorderly population. Their irregular habits and low standards of comfort may be regretted; but it is to be remembered that these Irish have been, and are, most efficient workmen; that they came in the hour of need, and that they afforded the chief part of the animal strength by which the great works of our manufacturing districts have been executed.

Irish harvesters.

It remains to speak of those persons who periodically migrate from Ireland to Great Britain, and after a short absence return to their homes; or of those who leave their country for an uncertain period, but revisit it occasionally, and never altogether lose their connection with it. Irish labourers come in large numbers to England and Scotland for the corn and sometimes the hay harvest, landing for the most part in the ports of Glasgow, Liverpool and Bristol. It is well known that they are for the most part labourers from the western and mountainous counties of Ireland; that they often shut up their houses and leave their wives and children to beg about the country during their absence; and they frequently pay their rent with the money which they earn in England. Their conduct is in general orderly, their habits remarkably frugal and sober, and they appear to give satisfaction to their employers.
Mr George Forwood, Assistant Overseer of the parish of Liverpool [stated] 'the Irish come over from 500 to 700 in a steam packet, principally at harvest time; a considerable number of these have their families with them, and others have their families follow. They have been bought over in numbers for 1s.[shilling] a head, and they never pay more than 5s for the passage to England; the latter is the common price for their passage

back to Ireland, exclusive of provisions. Those who have been over before become ... leaders of gangs. All these are agricultural labourers when they are in England.

John Thomas, [who] has a farm four miles from Birmingham on the Warwick road [stated] 'in harvest time Irish labourers get 12s a week, a quart of beer a day, and are lodged at night in a barn; frequently a dinner is given them on a Sunday, and sometimes also on Thursday. Frequently too many come, and will work for low wages, as low as 8s a week. When they leave us they go to Staffordshire, and get back in time for their own harvest. Most of them have little land. Those that worked for me were extremely frugal; out of seven persons, six were very orderly; the seventh was disorderly, and the others refused to work with him. The English dislike their being employed; the master is forced to protect them from abuse.

The impact of Irish labourers in West Cheshire, 1834

Report on the state of the Irish poor in Britain parliamentary papers 1836, evidence of Henry Potts, clerk of the peace in Cheshire, Feb. 1834.

q. *Would it be advantageous for this town and neighbourhood if the Irish immigration could of a sudden be completely stopped?*

a. *The city of Chester and its immediate neighbourhood would no doubt be benefited by stopping the immigration of Irish labourers; but many persons who have occasion for much labour would give an opposite opinion.*

q. *Could the work in the town be done, or could the harvest in the country be got in without Irish labourers?*

a. *The population of Chester and its immediate neighbourhood is considered abundantly sufficient for the work of the town and county, without the Irish; but I am informed, that in the less populous districts of the county their assistance is important to the harvest, and the expense of getting it in would perhaps be doubled; for the benefit nevertheless of the English labourer.*

q. *Has the Irish competition lowered the general rate of wages in this town and neighbourhood; and if so, in what departments of industry, and to what extent?*

a. *Certainly, more particularly in harvesting hay, corn and potatoes, and in road making to a considerable extent, and to some extent in other departments.*

q. *Has the Irish immigration increased the amount of the poor-rates in this town and neighbourhood?*

a. *Yes, indirectly, in as much as the English labourer used to make his rent during harvest-time, for which he now frequently applies to the parish, and in the case of refusal, probably finds his way into the poor house.*

At Newton (a small town near the shore of the river Dee, ten miles from Chester), two or three years ago, there was a fight between the Irish labourers and the Cheshire, Lancashire and Welsh labourers. I am told the quarrel was provoked chiefly by the English party, who look upon the Irish with much jealousy. There was a similar affair, on a smaller scale, in Chester last week, when a party of Irish road-makers were attacked by Chester labourers, and two of them were much beaten and abused; the offenders have been punished. The following information was furnished by a gentleman on the spot; - 'The native labourers in this part of the country exceed the demand for labour at all times of the year excepting harvest; in the harvest-time some Welsh and a few Irish (but very few) are employed to reap. The Cheshire men are very jealous of the Irish, who under sell them, and use all means to prevent their coming; they beat them, steal their sickles etc. I could not find that any Irish families had settled in the neighbourhood.

The discussion about Cheshire is interesting in that, quite incidentally, it had the highest population of Hallorans in mainland Britain in the 1850s, living mainly in Runcorn and Birkenhead, two towns on the southern side of the Mersey and very close to the disembarkation point of many Irish immigrants. However, the number of births indicates a number of settled families who did not appear on either the 1841 or 1861 censuses, again illustrating the transience of the Irish immigrants and the use of the Liverpool area as a jumping off point to inland Britain or the United States. In 1861, most Hallorans were found in Toxteth Park, Wigan, Manchester, Fulwood, Hulme - all areas of Lancashire. By 1881 they are in Liverpool, Great Crosby, Wardleworth, Toxteth Park, and Everton. By 1891, the Lancashire areas of Great Crosby, Wigan, Liverpool, West Derby and Manchester had the largest populations of Hallorans.

Of course these people could have come from any part of Ireland and no documentary link has been made with them and the Hallorans of the Birstall area, apart from a few examples of Hallorans moving between the towns of Birstall and Wigan and Manchester. The table below is interesting in that it

Chapter 3 – THE HALLORANS WHO LEFT AGHAMORE

illustrates the decline of migrant Irish labourers in more rural parts of Britain and the great increase of permanent migrants in the northern industrial areas and Scotland.

It is not known at present whether the Thomas and his young family made directly for Birstall or if they first stayed in Liverpool for a period. If they spent some time in Liverpool they would have experienced conditions not much better than those in their famished land. In Liverpool it was calculated that in 1847 there were 35000 people, mainly Irish, living in cellars, while some 5341 inhabited cellars described as 'wells of stagnant water'. Typhus, dysentery, cholera and other fevers were endemic. Dr Duncan, the first public health officer appointed in Liverpool, was rapidly overwhelmed by these waves of immigration and estimated that in the town as whole, 60,000 caught the fever and 40,000 contracted dysentery. Liverpool authorities could not cope with this influx of mouths to feed, which crippled and impoverished the city. In June 1847, under the new Poor Law Removal Act, about 15,000 Irish were deported back to Ireland. The description, at the end of this chapter by Engels in 1845 gives some idea of the conditions the family encountered.

	1841		1851		1861		1871		1881		1891	
	pop	bth	pop	bth	pop	bth	pop	bth	pop	bth	pop	bth
Lancashire	5	1	19	6	42	12	43	27	46	16	57	46
Yorkshire					10		28	20	22	13	21	
Midlothian					16	9	22	11	16	12	18	
London							27		38		51	28
Glamorgan					12						37	25
Lanarkshire	5	1							22			16
Devon			6	5			7		13			
Surrey	6	4			12						15	
Cheshire			20	5								
Hampshire				1			12					
Middlesex	10		8									
Lincolnshire				5								
Durham	6	6										

Distribution of Halloran name in Britain from 1841 to 1891[1]

'Pop' indicates the population of Hallorans in the county. 'Bth' indicates the number of Hallorans born in county.

The navvies

In the eighteen century the Irish had gone to England and Scotland to work on the canals. As processes of industrial production and coal mining developed, heavy goods had to be moved around Britain and, in a huge feat of civil engineering, canals were dug and locks constructed linking the natural waterways to allow coal and industrial products access to the new factories and sea ports. These canals were known as 'navigations', or more optimistically, 'eternal navigations', intended to last forever. The workmen, particularly the manual labourers working on these projects, were called navigators. The term was coined in the late 18th century and shortened to 'navvies' soon after. Canal navvies typically worked with shovels, pickaxes and barrows and a huge number of them were Irish. The work allowed them to see much of Britain firsthand and many were quick to respond to the employment opportunities which were opening up either as migrant farm labourers or later in railway construction.

---

1 http://www.reference.com/browse/Navvy

Of course we don't know if Thomas or any of his forebears were among the army of navvies who travelled over from Ireland, but certainly many from county Mayo would have done so. The canal construction companies kept scant records of labourers' names and addresses, much less birthplaces, so the Irish engaged in these nomadic occupations have been consigned to eternal anonymity. From 1830 onwards the construction of canals in Britain was superseded by contracts to construct railway projects and the same term was applied to the workmen employed on building rail tracks, their tunnels, cuttings and embankments[1]. As we have seen, it is part of the Halloran family folk lore that the first Hallorans in Birstall worked in railway construction.

Navvies working on railway projects typically continued to work using hand tools, supplemented with explosives (particularly when tunnelling). Steam-powered mechanical diggers or excavators (initially called 'steam navvies') were available in the 1840s, but were not considered cost effective until much later in the 19th century, especially in Britain and Europe where experienced labourers were easily obtained and comparatively cheap.

The navvies working on the railways in England in the early part of the 19th century lived in squalid temporary accommodation. Those working on the Liverpool and Manchester Railway were paid daily, and their pay was said to go on ale and porter, to the detriment of their health. Thus when the workers were unfit to work, they were not paid in money but meal tokens. These could be handed in at meal caravans for a bowl of soup and a portion of bread. This caused much resentment as the companies profited from these outlets and thus clawed back much of what they paid in wages.

Nick Sullivan, in *Navvyman*[2], describes navvies as 'perpetual outsiders: a people apart. Sub-working class. Sub-the-bottommost-heap of English working society'. He goes on to write of the Irish:

The Irish were cast out even by the outcast navvy: they were the minority within the minority, the outsiders inside the outsiders. Although they made up only ten per cent of the whole, the Irish were the common factor in about a third of navvy riots. The Irish put it down to bigotry. In 1839 the Liverpool Mercury reported that an Irish navvy called Peter McDonough had been defrauded of his wages at Ellesmere Port by a hagman called Isaac Dean. 'After I was employed by Dean,' McDonough told the newspaper, 'it was often hinted to me that I ought to consider myself a fortunate kind of Irish animal because I was not driven from the place with sticks or stones, as many of my countrymen had been before my coming, for no other reason than being Irish. I witnessed a few of these Irishmen hunts since I came. One poor fellow, who got employment, and began work, was attacked in a dreadful manner; he ran, and was pursued by them with stones, etc. from which he received a severe cut on the head; his coat, after taking from it a case of razors and a comb, they rolled up with hot bricks.'[3]

Though many of the navvies lived in obscurity, these men changed the British landscape and industrial infrastructure. Some of these men went on to develop their own construction businesses and employed

---

1 http://www.reference.com/browse/Navvy

2 Nick Sullivan, in Navvyman (2006) A Victorial Web Book

3 http://www.victorianweb.org/history/work/sullivan/1.html

men from home. Today, Irish-owned companies account for one tenth of the almost one hundred billion pound British construction industry.

However, it was not a life for family men. When the Great Famine forced men to leave Ireland with their families, they had to abandon the nomadic life and find settled employment and places for their families to live, no matter how squalid.

Condition of the Working Class in England, by Engels, 1845

These Irishmen who migrate for four-pence to England, on the deck of a steamship on which they are often packed like cattle, insinuate themselves everywhere. The worst dwellings are good enough for them; their clothing causes them little trouble, so long as it holds together by a single thread; shoes they know not; their food consists of potatoes and potatoes only; whatever they earn beyond these needs they spend upon drink. What does such a race want with high wages?

The worst quarters of all the large towns are inhabited by Irishmen. Whenever a district is distinguished for especial filth and especial ruinousness, the explorer may safely count upon meeting chiefly those Celtic faces which one recognises at the first glance as different from the Saxon physiognomy of the native, and the singing, aspirate brogue which the true Irishman never loses. I have occasionally heard the Irish-Celtic language spoken in the most thickly populated parts of Manchester.

The majority of the families who live in cellars are almost everywhere of Irish origin. In short, the Irish have, as Dr. Kay says, discovered the minimum of the necessities of life, and are now making the English workers acquainted with it. Filth and drunkenness, too, they have brought with them. The lack of cleanliness, which is not so injurious in the country, where population is scattered, and which is the Irishman's second nature, becomes terrifying and gravely dangerous through its concentration here in the great cities. ... He builds a pigsty against the house wall as he did at home, and if he is prevented from doing this, he lets the pig sleep in the room with himself. This new and unnatural method of cattle raising in cities is wholly of Irish origin. The Irishman loves his pig as the Arab his horse, with the difference that he sells it when it is fat enough to kill. Otherwise, he eats and sleeps with it, his children play with it, ride upon it, roll in the dirt with it, as any one may see a thousand times repeated in all the great towns of England.

The filth and comfortlessness that prevail in the houses themselves it is impossible to describe. The Irishman is unaccustomed to the presence of furniture; a heap of straw, a few rags, utterly beyond use as clothing, suffice for his nightly couch. A piece of wood, a broken chair, an old chest for a table, more he needs not; a teakettle, a few pots and dishes, equip his kitchen, which is also his sleeping and living room. When he is in want of fuel, everything combustible within his reach, chairs, doorposts, mouldings, flooring, finds its way up the chimney. Moreover, why should he need much room? At home in his mud cabin there was only one room for all domestic purposes; more than one room his family does not need in England. So the custom of crowding many persons into a single room, now so universal, has been chiefly implanted by the Irish immigration. And since the poor devil must have one enjoyment, and society has shut him out of all others, he betakes himself to the drinking of spirits. Drink is the only thing which makes the Irishman's life worth having, drink and his cheery carefree temperament...

With such a competitor the English workingman has to struggle, with a competitor upon the lowest plane possible in a civilised country, who for this very reason requires less wages than any other. Nothing else is therefore possible than that, as Carlyle says, the wages of English workingman should be forced down further and further in every branch in which the Irish compete with him. And these branches are many. All such as demand little or no skill are open to the Irish. For work which requires long training or regular, pertinacious application, the dissolute, unsteady, drunken Irishman is on too low a plane.

CHAPTER 4

The Irish in Batley

Though they only lived a few miles apart, the Irish in Birstall have always viewed themselves as a distinct group from the Irish in Batley. Both groups originally came mainly from Mayo, nonetheless, there was intense rivalry between them, which, though it has dissipated over the generations, sometimes became violent and persisted for many decades. We have established to some extent why these two groups considered themselves distinct and that the original Batley Irish came to the area before the Great Famine, and the Birstall Irish arrived as a direct result of it, and the Hallorans were among the very first of the settled Irish community in Birstall.

Batley

When the Irish arrived in numbers in 1832, Batley was a large village engaged in the manufacture of shoddy and other woollen fabrics. It is situated two miles north of Dewsbury and eight miles south-west of Leeds. It had been a major centre for the manufacture of woollen products for centuries specialising in 'heavy woollens', which were heavy felted cloths of the type used for coats and blankets. Originally, this was a cottage industry, and buildings from that period had large stairs windows to allow in as much light as possible as most of the weaving was done at home. However, the industry was expanding and becoming heavily industrialised, and with the industrialisation came the railways. This brought with it a need for more labour and major industrial disputes. Both these conditions brought in an influx of Irish. It is clear from the English censuses of 1841 that there was already a large Irish community in Batley, whereas there were very few in Birstall. The question therefore arises as to why the Irish from Aghamore settled in Birstall, rather than Batley.

Birstall had coal and woollen mills that were developing rapidly. However, there was probably reluctance on the part of the Mayo newcomers to enter a town already dominated by Mayo men from a different parish. Parochial rivalries were strong in Ireland, and there was a strong sense of affinity with family and neighbours. These rivalries had been greatly exacerbated by the competition for land as the population of Ireland grew in the 18th and early 19th centuries, instilling a suspicion of the stranger. It was a case of looking after one's own.

It has come down through family lore, and been affirmed by Joe Halloran, the grandson of Martin, that the Batley and Birstall Irish always considered themselves quite different groups. He said the Birstall Irish came from the Aghamore, Knock, Killkelly areas of Mayo and the Batley Irish 'came from somewhere called Charlestown' in Mayo, but he did not know exactly where that was. This is most interesting as we saw in chapter 2 that Charlestown is a relatively new town located not far from Aghamore. Significantly, it was established by Charles Strickland, Viscount Dillon's local agent and town planner, in whose honour it was named. Dillon was the landlord of both areas. One wonders whether Dillon and Strickland had connections with the Batley/Birstall area.

An early picture of Batley town centre

Heavy woollens

Vivien E Tomlinson[1], whose family was closely associated with the textile industry in the area, outlines the development of the industry around Batley. The industry had been hampered by the lack of a major river, the local river being a poor source of waterpower. She points out that the development of steam power allowed textile industry to prosper in the town. Before then, there was probably only a mill powered by donkey. This was used only for scribbling and slubbing, processes done to prepare wool for spinning. Several steam-powered mills were built in the district in the 1790s, including one built at Birstall Smithies, which seems to have been roughly contemporary with the first in Batley itself, the Clerk Green Mill.

In 1826, Carlinghow Mills were built by John Nussey of White Lee, while John Burnley, one of those involved in Hick Lane, set up his own business nearby at Hick Well Mill. Other mills very quickly appeared in Batley, including a major one in Havercroft, at first referred to as the Batley Subscription Mill, but by the 1830s called The Old Mill. Other mills were to follow in or near Batley.

Many Irish lived in the streets around these mills according to the 1841 English census. The same census indicates that the biggest part of the Irish community lived in Havercroft. These were 'Company Mills' where groups of clothiers banded together, contributing towards the ventures, and producing a vast output of yarn for individual clothiers to take away and weave.

Shoddy and the Luddites

Benjamin Law, a local mill owner, developed a process of turning recycled old rags mixed with some virgin wool into a material called 'shoddy' around 1813. Michael Sheard and Sons of Hick Lane Mill, at first referred to as Batley New Mill, was said to have been the first built expressly for the purpose of making clothe from shoddy. However the first machines for tearing up the rags were set up by Messrs Joseph Jubb and J. & P. Fox.[2]

This is how the popular Yorkshire commentator, Isaac Binns (1882), described shoddy at the time.

> *Though we have invented a new material, we have also invented a new expression. Shoddy has become a world-wide use as a name denoting want of quality in anything, and that is what we grumble about... But shoddy cloths are made, as a rule, so that the price is no object (and the peasant can afford) to wear cloths made from them. In short, shoddy, we believe, is a great leveller, besides being a great invention to boot; and Batley by its aid, had become known in the markets of the whole world.*

So, Batley was in the lead in the recycling business just as the industrial revolution was taking off.

However, the introduction of new machinery for this process caused enormous problems with the local workers, which resulted in the infamous Luddite riots, some of the worst of which occurred in Gomersal in 1812. These were uprisings of workers protesting against the new power looms. Many of the rioters were injured or killed and the ringleaders executed at York.

This is how Samuel Jubb (1860) described it in *The history of the shoddy-trade: its rise, progress, and present position*:

> *About the year 1812 or 1813, the new machines were coming into use in various places, but they were met by the most determined opposition on the part of the 'croppers', and in many instances, these misguided men proceeded to acts of violence, especially directing their attacks against the machines themselves; in fact they destroyed them wherever they could. At length the 'Luddites,' as they were designated, composed chiefly of 'croppers,' made a strong attack on the premises of Mr. Cartwright, of Rawfolds, near Leeds, who had procured some of the machines; but Mr. C. having had intimation of the intention of the rioters, had taken efficient measures for defending his position; he obtained the aid of a number of soldiers, who were posted in the mill: there was firing on both sides, and several of the rioters were severely wounded, if one or two were not actually killed. The besiegers were signally defeated, a number of them being captured on the spot; but the most striking part of the story remains to be told. No fewer than sixteen or seventeen of the ringleaders*

---

1 http://vivientomlinson.com/batley/ui54.htm

2 Much of the history of Batley that follows comes from Maggie Blanck's family history site.

were hanged at York for their illegal and violent conduct in this affair... We are shocked to hear that so many persons perished on the scaffold for an offence which, though very heinous, would not now be punished near so severely; and we have good reason to congratulate ourselves that the laws now breathe a milder spirit, founded, we trust, on the improved and milder character of the people.

Such was the state of industrial relations the decades before the Irish came into the district.

The 1841 English census - the Irish arrive in Batley

A toll road built in 1832 between Gomersal and Dewsbury included a branch to Batley (the present day Branch Road) which allowed for 'the growing volumes of wool, cloth and coal' to be transported. Until then there had only been foot and cart tracks. People migrated to Batley from other parts of England and, controversially, many Irish arrived. They were among the first to use the new toll road. We get a snapshot of this community from the 1841 English census.

At that time, 107 Irish-born people were living in Batley with a considerable number of locally born children. The family names include: Burns (3 Irish-born members), Carr (3 Irish-born members), Douneley (6 Irish-born members), Downs (5 Irish-born members), Durgan (2 Irish-born members), English (2 Irish-born members), Gragan (2 families, one of 3 Irish-born members and one of 8), Harber (2 Irish-born members), Henney (6 Irish-born members), Hepworth (3 Irish-born members), Hopkinson (2 Irish-born members), Keegan (4 Irish-born members), Kelly (3 Irish-born members), Kirkwin (5 Irish-born members), Lynch (8 Irish-born members), Martin (2 Irish-born members), Murphey (6 Irish-born members), Osburn (4 Irish-born members), Rochford (3 Irish-born members), Tierney (9 Irish-born members), Warren (3 Irish-born members), Welsh (2 Irish-born members) and White (2 Irish-born members). The greatest number lived in and around Havercroft, Chapel Fold and Nottingley Well.

What is noticeable about this group is that most of them started to arrive in the early 1830s but the stream stopped quite abruptly soon after. Of the children of Irish parents born between 1824 and 1835 - that is those of between 6 and 15 years old - 52 were born in Ireland. This suggests their parents had left Ireland no more than 16 years previously and many less than six years. Furthermore very few other Irish were in Batley before them as only three children were born there between those dates. Strikingly, no child under 6 had been born in Ireland - that is after 1835, which suggests the stream temporally halted. In contrast to that, at least 7 were born in Yorkshire during that period. This suggest that the vast bulk of the group started to arrive at the same time in the early 1830s and very few if any came after 1836.

An examination of the work done by these people indicates that they may have been specifically recruited to work in the woollen mills. Of those whose occupation is given, 30 were recorded as woollen labourers, 14 as woollen weavers or spinners, 3 as rag sorters or merchants and 6 in other aspects of wool processing. In contrast, just 3 are recorded as labourers, 2 as servants, 1 as an agricultural labourer and 1 as a miner.

New Street, Batley in the early 1960

We also know that this influx of Irish was not well received by many of the locals. In 1858, Samuel Jubb, a local manufacturer and son of Joseph Jubb, an original member of the Hick Lane Mill, suggests much of the hostility against the Irish may well have resulted from the perception of the Irish as 'strike breakers' and as driving down the already low wages. A strike in 1832 according to Judd (1860):

was instrumental in bringing a considerable number of Irish people into town, to replace the refractory hands: they formed quite a colony at first, and have increased numerically since. For a considerable time, the presence of the Irish was felt to be irksome by the natives, who regarded 'paddy' as an intruder, and looked down upon him as a member of an inferior race.

This strike occurred the same year the toll road was opened in 1832. The initial movement of the Irish into the town, it would appear, was a result of a strike against mechanisation and mass production, not to mention re-cycling, in the woollen industry The dates and manner of their arrival and the nature of their employment suggest that these were the Irish who were recruited to break the strike and that very few, if any of this group appear to have been navvies or working on the railways.

The memory of this strike and the hostile reception the Irish received must have lingered within the Irish community and is reflected later in Betty's memoirs. However, it appears unlikely that the first Hallorans who appeared in Birstall a decade or so later were connected with any of this earlier group of Irish immigrants. This is explored more fully in the next chapter. Nonetheless, in the years that followed many of the Irish who came to Birstall, including many of the Halloran womenfolk, worked in the shoddy trade and it is informative to look at the nature of this industry. Furthermore, the legacy of the role of strike-breakers may well have contributed to the general anti-Irish feelings which affected all the immigrants for a long time, as the following comments by Isaac Binns (1882) indicate:

Higher up the street, which was then known as Up Lane, there is the street called New Street- now chiefly tenanted by the sons of Erin- I could never tell of a new house being built in the street, but yet I suppose it has been new once, and do not care how soon it becomes a new street again- a street with new houses, and especially new tenants. It is but natural that there should be a bad lamb in a flock; and a bad street in a town, and this may fairly claim all the honours which can attach to a dwelling place of a race of people, who, while disdaining to build up charities, are the first to put in a claim to be abusers of them.

So the local people did not particularly welcome the arrival of the Irish. This is how Jubb (1858) describes the relations between the local Yorkshire people and the Irish.

[These] were of a very unfriendly nature; and their serious 'rows' and collisions resulting from their antagonism, which occurred, kept the town in a state of excitement, apprehension, anxiety, and, we may add, of alarm. Time, the great healer of sorrows, however, has softened the asperity of those feelings and reconciled, if not wholly, in a great measure at least, the two bodies. It is not improbable that even the employers themselves would have been glad, after a while, to witness the 'exodus' of the Irish; but once here, they became fixed on the spot, and as matters have turned out, it may have been for the best.

This was written in 1858, suggesting that relationships were on the mend, perhaps because mill workers, English and Irish, felt that they had a common enemy and made common cause. There were 'agitations' and partial strikes of hand loom weavers in Batley in 1851 and 1852. Jubb lists 1825, 1837, 1840 to 1843, 1847 and 1857 as slow years for the shoddy trade. There was a panic in 1857; business was paralyzed for months with the mills only working half time. He says that 'good' years for the shoddy trade were 1836 and 1853.

Slubbers, the men who worked the slubbing machines, had not had an increase in wages for at least 20 years. Slubbing machines, or slubbing billies, created a slight irregularity in yarn by knotting or twisting or by including uneven lengths of fibre in spinning. Jubb looks at this as a positive turn of event and says, 'this class of workmen has enjoyed the steadiest and most uniform wages of any class in the business'. Perhaps they would not have agreed.

So, despite the difficulties and the bad years, the woollen industry flourished. One of Law's nephews figured out a way of incorporating tailors' clippings into the process. This was called 'mungo'. By 1855, 35,000,000 pounds of rag were being sorted and processed into yarn to make mungo and shoddy. In 1860, at the height of Sheard's business success, there are said to have been 130 shoddy manufacturers in the West Riding of Yorkshire, 80 firms employing 550 people to sort the rags and around 7,000 tons of shoddy being manufactured a year. Though probably not among the group of Irish who first worked in the Batley mills, the Hallorans who moved into Birstall became very familiar with shoddy and mungo production in the years that followed.

The success of the shoddy industry quickly put the name of Batley on the world map. The following quotations are given by Vivien E Tomlinson, the great, great, granddaughter of the above Isaac Binns

There are few places in the wide world whose names are more universally known than Batley. Far away from the east to the west, even as far as in each direction as man is clothed to protect himself from the cold, Batley

Chapter 4 – THE IRISH IN BATLEY

is spoken of; the kingdoms of the Old World trade with it; and upon the bright and sunny shores of 'the land of the west' many men find their interests bound up in it. ... [I]ts temples, though many in number and various in degree of merit, are neither the dwelling-place of the gods nor the Hades of a lower race; they are not dedicated to the Muses or to Apollo; they are dedicated to-Rags! Batley was once, and that not long ago, a remote secluded village lost almost to the world. Now as a borough it is a huge commercial maggot that has fattened on vestural corruption.

The following comments were made by Baines (1859):

The manufacture has forced its way, and made Batley, Dewsbury, and the neighbourhood, the most prosperous parts of the woollen districts. There are now in Batley alone fifty rag machines in thirty-five mills, producing no less the 12,000,000 pounds of rag-wool per annum.

There was a 'shoddy king' and a 'shoddy temple', properly known as the Zion Chapel. This imposing building in the town centre was opened in 1870, and reflected the popularity of the Methodist movement in Batley.

Working with shoddy

The following description comes from Vivien E. Tomlinson's Family History

It was a dirty trade, and smoking chimneys and more coal pits to fuel the boilers made Batley a dirtier place. Early rag machines were known as 'devils' with reason, for they spewed out unpleasant dust, and could catch fire. Sorting rags took some skill, but it was an ill paid occupation done by women and children. At first this was often in small family ventures, with all members rallying round, as can be discerned in these pages, but later moved into larger mills. Some scorned this product at first, but later staggering amounts were used.

An interesting if disturbing description of the processes involved in the manufacture of shoddy is given by George Head in his account *A Home Tour through the Manufacturing Districts of England in the Summer of 1835*. He writes:

As I was anxious to see somewhat of the above process, I walked from Dewsbury to the village of Battley Carr, on the river Calder, about a mile distant, where there are several rag mills, and paid a visit to one of them. The rags were ground, as they term it, in the uppermost apartment of the building, by machines, in outward appearance like Cook's agricultural winnowing machine, and each attended by three or four boys and girls... at the top come out at the bottom, to all appearance like coarse short wool. A single glance at the ceremony going forward was quite sufficient to convey a tolerable idea of the business – a single whiff of air from the interior of the apartment almost more than could be endured. ...

some little notion may probably be given by stating, that the boys and girls who attend the mill are not only involved all the time it works in a thick cloud, so as to be hardly visible, but whenever they emerge, appear covered from head to foot with downy particles that entirely obscure their features, and render them in appearance like so many brown moths.

Once the rags had been ground up and processed into yarn, the making of shoddy and mungo was a similar process to the making of woollen and worsted. Rags were collected from two sources, one being old rags from old clothes that were collected by ragmen for a price. The ragmen would then sell them to the rag merchant. The other source was new rags that were bought by the rag merchant as scrap from clothing manufacturers and tailors. We shall see when we examine the 1861 English Census in more detail that Thomas's daughters Mary and Catherine were woollen factory workers, as was their boarder Catherine Convey. From the 1871 census, when they were living in Brownhill, we see that Kate was a rag sorter, Bridget was a fuller and Catherine Convey, who was still with them, was also a rag sorter. In Michael's family at the same time, Mary was a boiler or briler, though what exactly that is so far is unknown.

Many saw shoddy as an adulteration of pure wool. Ministers even preached against it, calling it 'devil dust'. However, the fact that this new material was so cheap resulted in a huge surge in production and need for labour (mainly women), which drew in the huge numbers of labourers, both from the agricultural area of England, but also from famine-stricken Ireland.

Jubb reports there were about 900 boys and girls employed in the mills in 1858. He says that a small portion of these were 'half timers' and attended school. School attendance was mandated for all children aged nine to thirteen under the Factory Act in 1833. The mills were open six days a week. They were closed on Sunday and at 2:00 on Saturday 'affording, as it does nearly half-day holiday'.

Hick Lane, Batley

There was a large wage difference between men and women in the shoddy trade. Female rag sorters received from 6s 6d to 7s per week, while their male foremen received 20s to 25s., a difference of about 300%. It would appear that much of the collecting and sorting was controlled by rag merchants, usually of small capital. Their function was to hold stocks of rags and in some cases to sort them according to colour and grade. Samuel Jubb, writing in 1858 about the cloth industry, gives the following statistics on employment in Batley:

Wages in the Cloth Industry in Batley

Occupation	No. employed	Wage per week
Rag sorters, women	500	6s 6d
Slubbers	220	30s
Piecers, machine attendants	148	6s
Piecers, boys and girls	70/140	1s to 3s
Overlookers	30	35s
Hand loom weavers	1260	18s
Power loom weavers	500	9s
Drawers	70	30s

One would hope that the workers could occasionally afford a treat at a small confectionery shop opened in 1853 by Michael Spedding. This business would expand, moving to larger premises in 1927 and later becoming Fox's Biscuits. Today, along with Tesco, it is one of the two largest employers in the town.

CHAPTER 5

The Irish arrive in Birstall

The Hallorans and their neighbours completed their fearful journey from Aghamore to Birstall on foot in the late 1840s or very early 1850s. Whether they arrived in a series of small groups or in one large group, we do not know. Neither do we know if they stopped off somewhere, perhaps Liverpool or Birkenhead on their way, or whether Aghamore men already working in the area, greeted them on arrival.

We are still not sure why they made Birstall their final destination, or indeed, whether they intended it to be; certainly, some of them, we suspect, did move on shortly after arriving. However, for a considerable number, Birstall became their home for three or four generations, and remains so today.

A very moving and interesting source of material about the Birstall Hallorans is given in Betty Halloran's (née Walsh) account of her own life and times. Betty was born in 1915, and married William (Bill, Willie) Halloran (1913-1972), the youngest son of William Halloran (1876-1925) and Elizabeth (Eliz) née Prendergast (1874-1948). Bill was Tom and John's younger brother, one of the three brothers who reached adulthood and to whom this book is dedicated.

Betty Halloran's daughter, Mary, wrote up this 'autobiography' of her mother based on stories and accounts Mary had heard from her. She wrote it in the first person, as she feels it is her mother's authentic voice. Betty gives this account of family recollections of their first coming to Yorkshire.

> *Birstall was in the 'shoddy' area of the 'Heavy Woollen District' of West Yorkshire. There were already a number of strong religious groups: Congregational, Wesleyan, Temperance before the large contingent of Irish Catholics moved into the area in the latter half of the 19th century. Exiles because of the potato famine, men who had worked on the canals, then the Liverpool-Leeds Railway had eventually worked their way to Yorkshire and had then found work as colliers or in the woollen industry. They mostly came from the same villages in Ireland and were all from Sligo or Mayo.*
>
> *Both my grandparents had come to England as babies, speaking Gaelic. They had established their own immigrant community in this part of Yorkshire, taking over whole areas, like Jewish ghettos. I was once told that many of the men had been employed to break a strike in the mills, but I do not know if that really is true. However, there was a lot of resentment of the Irish community and we were often referred to as 'Mucky - Irish', as if it was a self-evident description.*

Family folklore said that the Hallorans arrived in Birstall after working on the Manchester/Leeds railway (M&LR), having previously worked on various canals. The M&LR was formed in 1836 to connect the two growing industrial cities by rail. It was engineered by George Stephenson himself and was the first trans-Pennine railway. Its name was changed to The Lancashire & Yorkshire Railway in 1847. The line opened in stages with the first section from Manchester to Littleborough opening in July 1839. The second stage was opened by the M&LR in October 1840 between Hebden Bridge and Normanton, where its trains then ran on the rails of the North Midland Railway into Leeds.[1]

---

1 http://southpenninesrail.co.uk/stations/history.html

If Thomas or Michael worked on the Manchester & Leeds Railway, it is probable that they came sometime in the 1830s without their families, as younger migrant workers in their early twenties and teens.

The Manchester & Leeds railway was the first of the Trans-Pennine railways and it opened in 1841, before Thomas settled in Birstall with his family and Michael. Having fled the Great Famine they may have returned to the area as one they already knew and then worked on other railway developments on the Yorkshire and Lancaster Railway. Batley had a train station by 1848 and there was a branch line to Birstall in 1853. The Leeds, Dewsbury and Manchester Railway was completed in 1848 and a short branch to Birstall was completed in 1852.

Hebden Bridge Station on the Manchester & Leeds Railway line

Poor Paddy works on the railway – made popular by the Dubliners

In eighteen hundred and forty one,
Me corduroy breeches I put on,
Me corduroy breeches I put on,
To work upon the railway, the railway.
I'm weary of the railway.
Poor Paddy works on the railway.

In eighteen hundred and forty two,
From Bartley Pool I moved to Crewe,
And I found meself a job to do,
Workin' on the railway.

Chorus

I was wearing corduroy britches,
Digging ditches, pulling switches, dodging hitches,
I was workin' on the railway.

In eighteen hundred and forty three,
I broke me shovel across me knee,
And went to work with the company,
In the Leeds and Selby Railway.

Chorus
In eighteen hundred and forty four
I landed on the Liverpool shore.

Me belly was empty, me hands were soar
With workin' on the railway, the railway.
I'm weary of the railway.
Poor Paddy works on the railway.
Chorus

In eighteen hundred and forty five,
When Daniel O'Connell he was alive,
Daniel O'Connell he was alive,
And workin' on the railway.
Chorus

In eighteen hundred and forty six
I changed me trade from carryin' bricks.
Changed me trade from carryin' bricks
To work upon the railway.
Chorus

In eighteen hundred and forty seven
Poor Paddy was thinkin' of goin' to heaven.
Poor Paddy was thinkin' of goin' to heaven
To work upon the railway, the railway.
I'm weary of the railway.
Poor Paddy works on the railway.
Chorus

These dates coincide with the date 1851, when we know Thomas and Michael first appeared on English records. Two thousand men, mostly Irish navvies and some experienced tunnellers, were employed to excavate the stone lined Morley tunnel, which is 3420 yards long and 24 foot wide. When this was completed in 1847, the long aqueduct with 30 foot spans, was built. It is said that many men, both Irish and English, stayed after the completion of these, including the originator of the Fox Biscuit company.

Thomas and Michael could have been involved in any of this work as both were reported as being labourers in the 1851 census. If they had not had direct experience of working as migrant labourers or navvies before the Great Famine, they knew of men who had, some of whom may have been relatives. So they probably knew such work existed and may have all moved to Birstall at that time.

Chapter 5 – THE IRISH ARRIVE IN BIRSTALL

Birstall

At about the time they settled in Birstall, it was said:

> the parish comprises 13,180 acres, lying between Leeds and Halifax, and Bradford and Dewsbury. It increased its population from 14,667 in 1801 to 29,724 in 1841. Its inhabitants are extensively engaged in the manufacture of blankets, woollen cloth, worsted stuffs, and cards for machinery; and its prolific mine of coal and ironstone, and quarries of building stone, give employment to about 600 men.

The fact that the Irish had moved into an expanding area offering employment opportunities and soon were working in the coal mines and woollen industry meant this small group of displaced Irish could put down roots.

Daniel Defoe had this to say about Birstall when he toured the area in 1723-24:

> ... a little town called Birstall. Here ... they begin to make broadcloth..... This town is famed for dyeing, and they make a sort of cloths here in imitation of the Gloucester white cloths.

In 1738 a survey made of the parish for the Master and Fellows at Trinity College stated:

> This parish by the great increase in trade in the woollen manufacture is become very populous of late and the lands very much improved, by so many houses being build and small parcels of land laid to them, which are thereby brought into good tillage.

In 1812 a similar survey stated,

> The parish is extensive and fertile but as the Clothing and Blanket Manufacturers are carried out in this part of the country, the land is divided into small farms for the convenience of the tradesmen who attend to their trades more than to farming, the consequence of which is that area of the ploughed lands are not well managed and the crops in general not so abundant as in many other parishes where the land is not so good in quality. Part of the parish is also in high situations and the corn late in ripening, which is another disadvantage. There is coal in almost every part of the parish.[1]

In the 1841 census, many Birstall people had been described as 'weavers'. Many old cottages, some even surviving into the 1950s, had the tall upstairs windows needed to give sufficient light for this cottage industry. But, as we noted in Batley, the Industrial Revolution had transformed the area. New methods of producing cheap woollen cloth had been developed. Mills were established in the 1850s providing work for hundreds. By the 1860s, several more mills were being built in Birstall - Carrs Mill in 1861, College Mill and Prospect Mill in 1864 – producing an even greater demand for labour.

A land divided into small farms must have evoked comparisons with their own impoverished holdings and powerful memories of a former rural life for Thomas and family. More importantly, it offered the prospect of employment. Certainly, it was a much more salubrious place than the industrial cities of the north where most Irish immigrants were forced to settle into appalling conditions, which the Hallorans may well have experienced in Liverpool. They must have felt their situation was better than that of many of their countrymen and women who were living in the filthy warrens of dilapidated buildings depicted so vividly by Engels.

However, there own living conditions were as bad as any, and of course, they were not at home; and must have felt alien in terms of language, religion and culture. As Betty remarked in her memoirs, Birstall and the whole of the West Riding were steeped in religious nonconformity, dissenting from the established Church of England. The main denominations were Baptists, Congregationalists, Presbyterians, Quakers and Unitarians. At times when religious tolerance was low, these dissenters moved from one group to another, often meeting together at night in someone's barn in order to avoid the authorities.

Birstall was also a Methodist centre much frequented by John Wesley, the founder of Methodism, and Benjamin Ingham was also 'active in the Parish'[2]. Another famous son of Birstall was a stonemason called John Nelson. He heard John Wesley preach while working in London and converted to Methodism and himself became a great preacher.

---

1 - For history of Birstall we are indebted to http://www.maggieblanck.com/Land/Birstall.html

2 John Nussey, Introduction to the Birstall Parish Register by the Yorkshire Archaeological Society – http://www.maggieblanck.com/Land/Birstall.html

Birstall is most famous as the birthplace of Joseph Priestley, the scientist who discovered Oxygen amongst many other things. Priestley attended Batley Grammar School for Boys. This was founded by the Rev. William Lee in 1612 and is on the same site on Carlinghow Hill, just outside Birstall.

In this very austere, staid, Methodist environment, where the workers were kept firmly in place, the Irish certainly brought attitudes and a life style that challenged Birstall traditions. In Ireland their rhythms were determined by seasons and weather. The change to rigid working hours, together with terrible overcrowded urban conditions, must have been difficult, and contributed to a culture of hard drinking, minor law breaking, and often riotous behaviour.

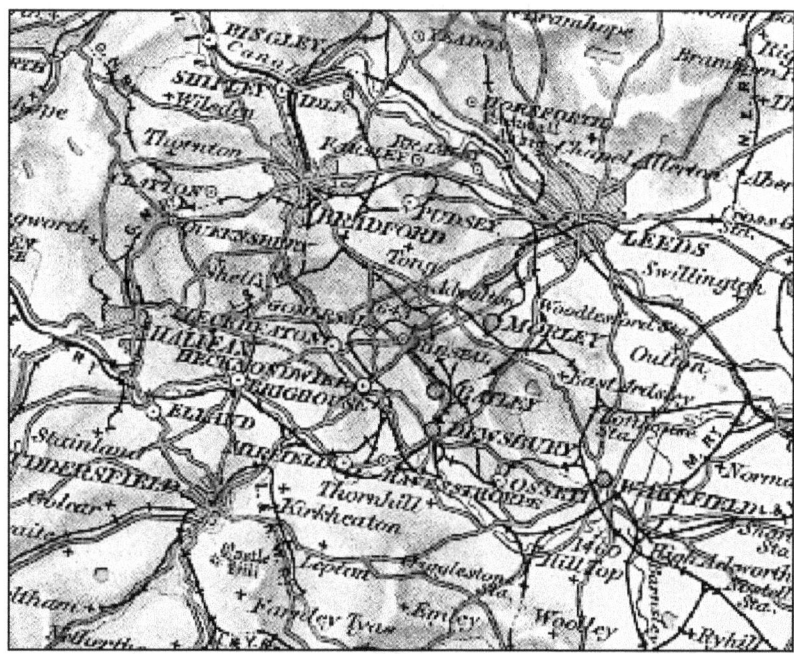

The first generation of Irish

The 1841 English census

Comparisons between the 1841 English census for Batley and Birstall reveal considerable differences between the two Irish communities. We noted that in Batley there was an Irish community of 107 people, including 22 family groups. However, in Birstall there were eight people recorded as born in Ireland. Of the two families, one was a young family of three, named Shar (later entered as Shea, probably O'Shea). No occupation is given. The other is a family of Wallis, where the parents, William and Elizabeth, who were born in Ireland, had eight English-born children, the eldest being 15, indicating that they had left Ireland some time before. There also is a Henry John Smith (35), a clergyman, living in a household of 3 with his English born wife and an Irish woman Mary Sheelin. The other Irish were single people: one young woman, Mary Bahan, living in Likler (?) with a number of elderly people (it seems likely she was a servant) and one agricultural labourer. There is also a Caroline Bennis, a 40-year-old teacher, living in a girl's school.

It should be borne in mind that the census returns may well not have captured the full picture, especially of the Irish immigrants and migrant workers who were by their nature in transit and unsettled. Nonetheless, there is little sense here of an emergent or settled Irish community. Neither are any of these names, strange and perhaps inaccurately written as some of them may be, associated with the Mayo townlands where Thomas Halloran and so many of his neighbours who appeared in Birstall a few years later came from.

The 1851 English census - Low Lane

However, the situation was quite different ten years later. By that time, a considerable number of illiterate Irish cottiers had moved into Birstall. It was a concerted movement of a cohesive group who nearly all came from the remote and famine-stricken parish of Aghamore, County Mayo. According to the 1851 English census, there were 159 Irish-born residents in Birstall. This included 21 families, nearly all of whom came from the same parish in Co. Mayo. Furthermore, there were 20 men and women recorded as lodgers and 25 recorded as visitors. Of the 159 Irish-born, 79 lived in Low Lane. One of the larger families, living in no. 89, was that of Thomas and Judith Halloran and their children.

Chapter 5 – THE IRISH ARRIVE IN BIRSTALL

It is worth looking at the information provided by the census in some detail as it gives us quite a vivid picture of the origins one Irish immigrant community in industrial England. Generally they lived in the poorest dwellings. Although the exact houses on Low Lane cannot be identified, houses here were generally of the 'one up and one down' variety, gathered around a 'yard' with possibly a shared earth closet and a well. There were also small 'cots', small one room cottages, with thatched roofs.

A family of Kellys lived in number 47 Low Lane. John (49) is recorded as head of the family and was a labourer. With him were his wife, Mary (48), and their three children: Catherine (17), Mary (15) and James (12). Also living there were John Dogherty (22), a labourer, and John and Michael Kelly (13) - both nephews, Bridget Kelly (14), a niece, and Peter Waldron (23) and Jordan Henry (18), both described as 'visitors'.

Low Lane in the 1850s

A long-established family of Wallaces lived in number 69. It seems likely that they were not connected with the new wave of immigrants. William (54) was born in Waterford, Ireland, and his wife Eliza, (60) was born in County Down. Both were recorded as being confectioners. Their presence obviously pre-dates the Great Famine as they lived with 5 of their children and 2 grand children, all born in England.

In no. 70 there was a family of Frains. Patrick (25), the head of the family was a labourer, and Bridget (29), his wife. They had two sons: Patrick (14) and John (6), and two daughters: Mary (12) and Winifred (9). Staying with them were three visitors: Thomas Feeny (17) a labourer, Honora Henry (22) and Catherine McLees (30) (probably McCue).

There were also Kellys in no. 72. The head of the household, Laurence (26), was a labourer. Their two children were born in Yorkshire, suggesting that they had been there since at least 1848. Their 3 year old, Anne, appears to have been the first child from this recently arrived Irish community to have been born and survived infancy in Birstall. The only pointer to their exact origin, at this stage, is that the census enumerator gave their place of birth as 'Ireland' and usually as 'Mayo'. There were two visitors in the household: James Giraughtey (22) and Honora Kilkenny (30), a married woman living on her own.

In no. 75 we find a small family headed by John Kilkenny, 23, born in Mayo. This household was unlike most of the other ones in that it does not appear to be unduly overcrowded – though perhaps it was just smaller than the others. Also, his wife Ellinor, 21, was born in Sheffield. Their only child, Michael was a baby and born in Birstall. There is a Bridget Kilkenny (29) born in Mayo, who is a visitor, and another visitor, Patrick Swift (26), also born in Ireland. This unusual family name also appears in Aghamore. Unusually, everyone in the household is recorded as working.

Living next-door to the Hallorans, in no. 89, we find Patrick Frain (40) and his wife Catherine (30) in a household which includes 14 people. Parish records indicate that her maiden name was Halloran and she may well be Thomas and Michael's sister. They had 3 daughters - Mary (13), Bridget (11), Catherine (8) - and one son James, (6). There was also a Mary Higgins (35), a visitor with her three younger daughters, Bridgett (9), Ann (7), and Housusah (4). Mary is recorded as unmarried. There were two young Stinsen (Stenson) girls, Hannah and Judith, aged 14 and 12. They were probably related to Thomas Halloran's wife Judith Stenson. The fact that they were not living within their own family is further evidence of the fragmented nature of the post-famine families and the improvised informal networks of extended family networks and neighbours. Patrick Frain was one of only two earners in this large group. A Michael Quain [Quinn?] (43) also lived with them. He was married and also a labourer.

In No. 90 Low Lane lived Thomas Halloran and family, in a household which is described in detail below.

In house no. 94 we find an Ann Hopkinson (27) who was born in Ireland. She was the wife of Joseph Sharp, a mechanic born in Bradford. They had no children.

Another large Irish group lived in No. 187. Here we see two families, the Kilkennys and the Bretts. Michael Kilkenny (35) is recorded as head of the household. He was a labourer. Bridget (35) was his wife,. They had three daughters: Mary (15), Bridget (12), Catherine (10), and Ann (3). Poignantly, the three older daughters were described as 'beggars', but this had been crossed out by the recorder.

Also in this household were William Brett (40), a labourer, his wife Bridgett (30), and their three daughters: Mary (12), Betty (10), and Bridget (7). This family was described as lodging with the Kilkennys. Ellen Filmby (30) and Patrick Tooke, (10) were recorded as visitors. There appears to be only one earner in the household.

The rest of the street, up to No. 168, is inhabited by local English and a few Scottish families. No doubt the local families felt apprehension, if not annoyance at these large, non-English speaking groups of people who had come directly from diseased and famished areas and who had no idea of town living; many of whom had, no doubt, spent much of their lives in one-room wattle huts shared with pigs and chickens, a lifestyle the Irish became notorious for, even in an English urban setting.

Thomas Halloran (1808/9-1887) and family in 1851

The first evidence of Thomas Halloran (b. 1808) and family reaching England is found in the 1851 English census reproduced below.

This is a remarkable document in the history of the family because it gives us a snapshot of James, Tom, John, Bill and Bernard's great grandfather more or less at the point he and his family arrived in Birstall. The bitter experience of the famine and their flight from it would still be fresh and vivid in their minds, and their fears for those left behind still keen and sharp.

We get a sense of how unfamiliar they were with English life and the English language by the strange spelling of their name. They probably knew little or no English when they left Ireland and were in all likelihood illiterate in both Irish and English. It is reported in the Irish census of 1911, fifty years later, that the older generation of Hallorans who survived to remain in Aghamore were primarily Irish speakers and illiterate. The English census enumerator would have to do as well as he could with the way the name was said as Thomas struggled to give a comprehensible version of the name Ó hAllmhuráin. He probably omitted the initial Ó as was usual in Mayo when Irish speakers anglicised their names for official purposes, and it somehow ended up with 'Haliyon' (or maybe 'Halizon').

Chapter 5 – THE IRISH ARRIVE IN BIRSTALL

Thomas Halloran (b. 1808) and family in the 1851 English census

Obviously, finding the earliest Halloran in Birstall when the name was spelt 'Haliyon' could defy the searches of all but the most assiduous genealogist. Well, Mary Hudson is such a one and she must be credited with finding the last piece of the jigsaw that allowed us to go backwards from the entry for Thomas' brother Michael, where we found the reference to Aghamore in 1871 census, to the Griffith Valuation where we found James Halloran in Carrowbaun.

In 1851 Thomas and family lived in 90 Low Lane, Gomersal. He was 44, his wife Judith (later entered as Judy) was 40. She, later children's baptismal certificates reveal, was a Stenson. Their son James was mistakenly entered a 'Thomas' here. Again, one can sympathise with the poor enumerator trying to make sense of fifteen or sixteen people from assorted families in these tiny houses. James was 14, and a labourer like his father and possibly working along with him. There were also Patrick 'Paterick' (12), Michael (10), Thomas (9), Mary (7), Bridget (5), and Catherine (3). None of these children were recorded as being 'scholars', which was the usual way of referring to children at school.

Michael (23), Thomas' younger brother by 21 years, also lived with them. All the family had been born in Mayo, Ireland - probably in or around Carrowbaun. The sequence of the children's names and the ages of the family members allow us to identify this family as the same Halloran family that appeared in the census of 1861 and forges the direct link to modern times.

If Thomas' family were not enough for one small house, there was another family of five living with them as visitors. These were Thomas (34) and Anne (26) Brenen and their three children, Margaret (11), Patrick (3) and James a few months old. All are recorded as having been born in Ireland. If this is correct, it would mean that they had only just arrived, though it is difficult to imagine undertaking and surviving such a trip when pregnant and with a new born baby. The uncharacteristic gap in the ages of this young family suggests its own disturbing famine story.

What is not recorded here is that Judith Halloran was pregnant at the time, and gave birth to a son, Francis, in August of that year. However, the following year double tragedies were to strike the family. Bridget died and was buried on the 26th August 1852, having survived the famine and the journey to England. She was recorded as being 8 years old. The previous year, in the census, she had been recorded as only 5. It is likely that many of the children's ages were underestimated; their development having been retarded through the ravages of the Great Famine.

Five days later, on August 31st, one-year-old baby Francis was also buried. He had died of smallpox, most likely of the same disease that had killed his sister five days before. He was probably the first member of the Halloran family to be born in England.

No.	When and where died	Name and surname	Sex	Age	Occupation	Cause of death	Signature, description and residence of informant	When registered	Signature of registrar
9	Thirieth August 1852 Birstal	Francis Holoran	Male	1 Year	Son of Tom Holoran Labourer	Small Pox Not Certified	X The mark of Judith Holoran Present at the Death Birstal	Thirty First August 1852	Benj'n Moore Registrar

Certified Copy Pursuant to the Births and Deaths Registration Act 1953. FD 706845. Registration District Dewsbury. 1852. Death in the Sub-district of Gomersal in the County of York.

Francis Halloran's Death Certificate. He was one year old. His sister, Bridget, had died 5 days previously

Most of the evidence about the Irish families in Birstall comes from the English census of 1851, but there are other sources of information. There is evidence that other members of the Halloran family were in Birstall around this time. Batley parish records (which included the residents of Birstall) show that a Patrick Halloran married Bridget McNamara in 1853 and that three children, Mary, Julia and Michael, were born in 1854, 1855 and 1857 respectively, before that family moved away. Another Patrick Halloran married a Sarah O'Brian and lived in neighbouring Heckmondwike, before they moved to Wigan. The records also show an Ann Halloran married a Pat McNamara in 1852. However, we have no evidence of their presence in Birstall after that. Other Hallorans included William, Joseph, Bridget and Mary, all of whom were recorded between 1851 and 1854 as being godparents in St Paulinus parish baptismal records.

This means the total number of known adult Hallorans in and around Birstall in the early 1850s was nine. As well as Thomas (1808-64) and Michael (1827-77), there were Catherine Frain (neé Halloran b. 1821), the two Patricks, Ann, William, Joseph, Bridget and Mary. We know Thomas and Michael were brothers. It is likely that Catherine was their sister. The fact that there were two Patricks in the same generation indicates Hallorans from two families emigrated around the same time. Apart from Patrick and his family who went to Wigan, it is likely that other members of the family moved on elsewhere in Britain or maybe to the United States, perhaps via Canada.

Other Irish in Birstall

Though the bulk of the Irish lived in Low Lane, many of the single Irish probably lived very unsettled lives, living here and there, while those with families settled into what permanent, if overcrowded accommodation they could. This may be why Ann and Patrick do not turn up on the census returns. Or perhaps they arrived in England later. However, areas like the Market place and the Smithies, near Low Lane, also contained a number of Irish families, many of whom probably came from the same part of County Mayo.

Chapter 5 – THE IRISH ARRIVE IN BIRSTALL

1851 English census for showing Irish neighbours in Low Lane

Market Place

In no. 132 is the family of Charles (68) and Bridget (34) Cahalin [Callaghan?]. Charles is a labourer. They have five daughters and a son: Mary (15), Hannah (13) and Rosa (11) are all described as labourer's lasses, perhaps working to their father. There are also Sarah (9), Marieta (6) and Thomas (4). The younger children are not recorded as being in school.

- Visiting them is another family of Frains: John (30), a labourer, and his wife, Margaret (28) and baby son James (6 months).
- There is also an Ann Carron (20), a servant to a Benjamin Shaw English family and
- John O'Connor (48), a widower and labourer staying in a lodging house.

Smithies

Lodging in the Smithies is a Peter Waters (24), a labourer.

There is also a family of Sheas [O'Shea]. James (46), the head of the household, was a slubber. He and his family are described as born in Ireland as British Subjects, perhaps to distinguish themselves from the rabble of Irish speakers who had just arrived. His wife is Jane (44), described as a slubber's wife. His son is James (18). This is one of the few families also recorded in the 1841 census. There they were entered as 'Shar'.

Birstall Lo St,

Here we find Mickal (26) and Margaret (27) Cain [possibly Kane or O'Kane]. Martin is a labourer. They have 2 sons John (4) and Thomas (1), both born in Birstall.

Lodging with them are:

- Denis Didger (32), no occupation; Thomas Gallagher (21), a labourer; and John Hain (31), also a labourer.
- Bridget (20), Michael (26) and Ann (31) Lions (Lyons).
- John Hain (31) and Margaret Haire (31) [possibly Hare or O'Hare]. He is a labourer.
- Ann Charlesworth, born in Bagnal, Co Carlow, the wife of an Englishman with children at school. With the family is a John Ross (33), a widow from Sligo.

Bottoms

Margaret Hopkinson (18) is a servant to an English family called Sharp.

At no 37 is Ann Purcill (32), born in Queens County. She is the wife of a Scottish timber yard labourer. They have 2 sons, William (12), a coal miner, and Joseph (5). Both were born in Queens County.

Cobbler Hill

In no. 57 is the family of Andrew (40) and Mary (40) Dain? Elsewhere in the census form they are called 'Cain', possibly being Kane or O'Kane.

Unusually, they have two daughters in employment, Mary (16), a rag picker and Catherine (14), a woollen factory hand.

- Staying with the Kanes is a married couple, their name spelled 'Horkan' in the Ancestry.com transcription, though 'Hocalian' is the name written on the census form and this is a name which appears in the townland of Carrowneden in Aghamore. They are James (25), a farm labourer, and Bridget Hocalian (24), his wife. However, the proximity of the sound of the name to O'Halloran is interesting.

Chapter 5 – THE IRISH ARRIVE IN BIRSTALL

Field Head (Over Highlands)

The Linskey (transcribed Glinsky) family of John (40), and Mary (40), lived in 64 Field Lane. He was a stone mason's labourer. They had seven children at the time, Thomas (20) and John (12), both miners, Michael, (14), described as a beggar, as were his sisters Bridget (10), Margaret (8), Ann (6). Their youngest son Patrick was 2.

Also living there were the Cunningham family, Henry (35), an agricultural labourer, his wife Anne (32) and son Anthony (6), who was at school.

Top Birstall

The Lyons family was written 'Sions' in the Ancestry.uk.com transcription but 'Lions' on the census form itself. In Top Birstall we find William (34), a labourer, his wife Mary (32), daughter Ann (13), and son John (1).

Gelderd Road

Here we find the Waldron family. They were reported as born in CA Mayo, Ireland. There was Austin (50), recorded as a farm labourer, his wife Bridget (48), their son Patrick (17), also a farm labourer, and their daughter Bridget (11).

There are also records of three Irish women who had married local men:

- Ann (63) married John Dalton of New Street, Gomersal,
- Henicha (29) married Thomas Hanson of Spa Hill, Gomersal. They had 4 children.
- Mary (66) married John Lees, a retired dyer and Chelsea pensioner (someone receiving a pension for service in the British army) of Great Gomersal.

Also

- Joseph Woodlead (44) of Great Gomersal married a Yorkshire woman, Jane, and they had no children.

Four Irish men were in lodgings with non-Irish families:

- Gerrard Dalton (56), a Chelsea Pensioner lodged in New Street, Gomersal
- Mannie Moloney (40) lodged in Wickumber, Gomersal, with William Barslow's family.
- Michl Smith Daly, lodged in Spen, Gomersal, with the Kitchen family.
- John Thornton (18) a collier who lodged in Whitehall, Gomersal, with William Hacking.

A number of Irish were in service i.e. were domestic servants:

- Margaret Kenedy (19) was a servant to a Highland family in Warrens Lane, Gomersal.
- James Maryck (45) was a servant in Castlehill house, Gomersal.
- Elizabeth Mulvany (18) was a servant on a farm, Mu[?]any, Gomersal.
- Henry Philips (34), was a farm labourer in Popeley Farm, Gomersal.
- John McDonald (66) was a servant to a cloth draper, George Taylor, in Throstle Nest, Gomersal..

And finally:

- William Allott (22), a coal miner of School House Lane, was born in Birchfield, Mayo, Ireland, though the rest of the family, including his brother, were born in England.
- Jessie Cooper, only one year old, was born in Belfast. Her parents were both comedians and lived in Lane End, Gomersal.

It is interesting that very few, if any, of the names of the single men and women in Birstall can be traced back to Aghamore. However, the names of those living in families, either as relatives, lodgers or guests, almost invariably can be. It appears these single people were not part of the concerted movement of people from Aghamore and they appear not to be such an integrated part of this community of immigrant families. It also suggests that the famine-induced flight from Aghamore was a massive collaborative effort among neighbours to save a number of families from an entire community. No doubt fewer would have survived had it depended on uncoordinated individual effort.

Family names in Aghamore Parish, Co. Mayo

What is remarkable is that so many of the names of the Irish families which appear in the 1851 English census at this time also appear in Aghamore parish, Co. Mayo. This is illustrated in the table below.

Surname	Townland
Brenan	Barnagurry, Carrowneden Aghamore, Mountaincommon, Crossard, Derryclaha, Rath, Carrowneden
Frain	Rath
Feeny	Falleighter, Mountaincommon, Tooreen
Giraughty	Falleighter
Halloran	Carrowbaun
Henry	Cappagh, Crossard, Corhawnagh, Scardaun, Cloongawnagh
Higgins	Caher, Rath, Cloongawnagh, Casheltourly
Kilkenny	Falleighter, Addergoole, Ballyhine, Scregg, Caher, Carton, North Falleighter, Liscosker, Liscat, Lismeegaun
Kelly	Carrowbaun, Derrycoosh, Derrynarud, Derrycashel, Liscat, Cloonturk, Rinn, Addergoole, Derryclaha, Meeltran, Derrynaned, Doogary
Linskey	Cappagh, Aghamore, Scardaun, Aghataharn, Carrowbaun, Carrowscoltia, Crossard
McCue	Caher
McNamara	Annagh, Cloongawnagh, Coogue, South, Carton, Liscat
Stenson	Carrowbaun, Falleighter, Arderry, Carrowscoltia
Swift	Meeltran, Carrowscoltia
Waldron	Rath, Mountaincommon, Aghamore, Caher

Irish family names from Birstall in 1851 that appear in Aghamore Parish, Co. Mayo (Griffith's Primary Evaluation)

Furthermore, we know from parish records in Birstall that an Ann Halloran and a Patrick Halloran both married McNamaras, a name that does not turn up in the English census but is found in Aghamore.

The family-based nature of the migration is evident from the fact that the Irish-born community in Birstall included 33 children of ten years old or under, only one of whom was at school – Anthony Cunningham from a family that did not appear to be part of the exodus from Aghamore. How recently some of the families had arrived is apparent from how young some of the babies born in Ireland were: James Frain, son of John and Margaret, was 6 months old; and James, son of Thomas and Ann, was 7 months old. These children were either born on the journey from Mayo or immediately before their mothers started out.

We notice that the Linskey children, (transcribed 'Glinsky' in the census) Michael, (14), and his sisters Bridget (10), Margaret (8), Ann (6) were described as 'beggars'. The youngest children of one of the Kilkenny families were similarly described, but 'beggar' had been crossed out. This may be because the column on the form only asks for rank, profession or occupation, and the term 'beggar' did not seem appropriate. However, it does reveal sensitivity to the description that might disguise the fact that many

Chapter 5 – THE IRISH ARRIVE IN BIRSTALL

of the children of the newly arrived families in fact begged for a living. No doubt the famine years had removed any qualms they may have had about this.

Unlike the Irish who had entered Batley a decade or so previously, those who came to Birstall were not drawn by the prospect of ready employment. In Batley, it was obvious that the Irish were attracted by employment in the woollen mills, where 58 Irish-born out of a group of 107 were employed. Only 3 of the group are recorded as labourers, 2 as servants, and 1 as an agricultural labourer and there was only 1 miner. In Birstall, by contrast, labourers were by far the largest group, 32 in all, including 3 labourers' lasses.

The fact that so many of the newcomers were labourers and that so few actually had work, points to the Birstall group having very different origins to the Irish in Batley. In Birstall, of those over ten years old, 61 were recorded as having no occupation. Unlike the Irish who came earlier, they did not take up existing jobs; rather they simply turned up, perhaps because many of the men knew the area as migratory labourers or from previously working on railway construction, and hoped for work. In a word, it appears the Irish were 'pulled' into Batley by the prospect of work, but 'pushed' into Birstall by the Great Famine.

The vast bulk of the families had come from Aghamore parish, County Mayo, possibly walking together for weeks if not months, carrying small children and even babies much of the way. They had to get food as they travelled. It is unlikely that the Kilkenny and Glinsky children were the only ones who begged. They arrived with virtually no belongings. The cottages they rented were tiny, completely overcrowded and unfurnished. The likelihood was that they slept on straw. However, the Irish men were obviously in demand as 'labourers' and they found employment quickly. The women, with the exception of a couple who were also recorded as 'labourers', were not employed in 1851. Similarly, none of the children were at school; illiteracy was obviously the norm. There were also 7 farm labourers. However, there were only 6 miners and only 5 involved in the woollen or shoddy industry, none of whom were from the Aghamore family groups clustered around Low Lane and the Market Place. This is in stark contrast to the Irish in Batley - only a few miles away - who were overwhelmingly involved in work in the woollen mills. We can only assume that these conditions were preferable to the hell they must have left behind in Ireland. Now, at least, they could have food, shelter and the support of friends and families.

This small cluster of Irish families clearly reflects the displaced clachan settlements from which they came. What is striking is the broken but mutually supporting nature of the famine-scattered kith and kin. The families were large but uncharacteristically young. There are a number of children and young adults, male and female, who appear to be neither working nor at school; this is in contrast to later censuses where the young Irish men seem to be almost invariably working in the mines and the women frequently in the woollen trade, and where all children under twelve were at school. This is a glimpse of a nascent community. These are the ones selected by survival and the extended families at home to flee the Great Famine. They had given up the meagre opportunities offered by the land in East Mayo for a life of the unknown in an English industrial town. In some cases there may have been hard decisions about who should go and who should stay. In such cases those who left represented the families' main hope of survival and their flight had probably eaten into the families already pitiful resources. They were, in all likelihood, also seen as a lifeline for other members of the family who hoped to follow them out if money arrived – an expectation that must have filled the families with a sense of guilt at their own survival and responsibility to those who remained.

The imperative behind this huge effort was survival itself. Though probably none or very few of these people could read or write, they were no doubt receiving messages like these sent from a more literate man who wished to flee the socially indiscriminate diseases and hunger that accompanied the famine.

Dear brother, if you send anything, no matter what part of the year it is with the help of God nothing will stop me going to you. For the honour of our lord Jasus christ and his blessed mother hurry and take us out of this. If you don't endeavour to take us out of it, it is the first news you will hear by some friend of me and my little family to be lost by hunger. (Quotation from 'Flight from Famine', Fitzpatrick, D. (1995))

The Great Famine and its aftermath led to a huge and coordinated operation of mutual help to ensure the survival of families and young people. This reflected patterns of cooperation manifest in the family-based clachan and rundale systems in the townlands of rural Ireland. However, during the Great Famine the struggle was not about cooperating in working the land on whose produce the family depended - this system had failed - but about how to maintain the family itself, and to do this they drew on the support of kith and kin from their own parishes and townlands, just as they had done at home.

What we see here in Birstall is a microcosm of a huge and highly organised though informal system which spread into the United States, Canada, Australia, mainland Britain and even Latin America. Initially it was a flight by young men and families, but soon even the aversion to emigration of young girls was overcome, and we see examples of young girls with no parents in Low Lane. Indeed, from the Great Famine onwards, male and female emigrants were evenly balanced. For all, it was a migratory flight, which, according to Fitzpatrick (1995), was unprecedented in recorded history; a million people left the country between 1846 and 1850 and the numbers were even greater in the next five years. Networks of settlers had been developed with astonishing rapidity in earlier years providing some protection and assistance to future immigrants and changing the demography of the English speaking world.

That the largely illiterate and starving of Ireland could pull off such a massive evacuation is quite remarkable. Fitzpatrick (1995) calls it a 'miracle of private ingenuity and determination'. Very few secured official subsidies or help as these were usually given only to tenants of crown and very large estates. Most were left to their own devises - however, these proved amazingly resourceful and efficient.

Thomas Halloran (1808/9-1887) and family 1861 onwards

Ten years after the first census where we first discovered that Thomas (b. 1808) and Judy (b. 1809) and family had not been *lost by hunger*, they had moved to 101 Common Lane, Batley. This is now just near the intersection roundabout of the M62 and the M1. Thomas was described as an agricultural worker, taking work he would have been familiar with at home. The younger members of the household were Patrick (b. 1837), Michael (b. 1839) and Thomas (b. 1841), who were now coal miners. Mary (b. 1843) and Catherine (b. 1847), who were 18 and 14 respectively, worked in the woollen mills. As noted earlier, young Bridget had died, having survived the Great Famine and the journey to England. However, we find another wee Bridget aged 7, born three years after the previous census, and two years after the death of one-year-old Francis. She was the first of the family to have been born in England to survive infancy and was at school.

They also had a Catherine (Kate) Convey staying with them as a boarder. She was 24 at the time and had been born in Co. Mayo. She stayed with them for some time but by the 1891 census was, by coincidence, lodging with Thomas Kelly, Mary Hudson's great-grandfather on her mother's side. The surnames MacConaway (Mac)Conway, (O)Conway, Conboy and Convey are anglicised variations of the same Irish surname. The sept of *O Conmhachain* is found in Co. Mayo. It was first anglicized as O'Conoghan and later Kavaghan, but has been corrupted to Conway and sometimes Convey. Mayo accounts for about twenty-five per cent of all the Conway births registered in Ireland[1]. A Catherine Conace?, aged 30 appears as a visitor with the family in the census of 1871, ten years later. Is this the same woman, allowing a little licence with her age?

There appears to have been a mistake in the 1851 census as two sons named Thomas were entered. It is likely that James Halloran (b. 1835), who was living in 21 Gelderd Road, Gomersal, according to the 1861 English, is Thomas and Judy's eldest son; his date of birth makes this quite possible. He and his family are discussed in the section on the second generation.

At this stage the younger men were working in the mines. Generally miners started as children hurriers and this is probably why neither Thomas nor Michael worked in the mines, though their sons did. As we have seen, it is also possible that Thomas or Michael were already familiar with the area, having worked as migrant labourers previously. Migrant Irish labourers usually worked on the harvest and we can note that Thomas was an agricultural labourer in 1861.

---

1 http://www.goireland.com/genealogy/family.htm?FamilyID=56

Chapter 5 – THE IRISH ARRIVE IN BIRSTALL

The English Census returns for 1861, showing Thomas Halloran's (b. 1804) family

1871

By 1871 there had been changes as older family members moved out and a young family seemed to have moved in. The family had also changed address, now living in 184 Brownhill, Batley, a few hundred yards from where Thomas' son, James, lived with his wife Bridget. Thomas was reported as being 63, though he was probably 67, and was now a hawker. 'Judey' was reported as being 61, which is consistent with the 1861 census and was classified as 'wife'. Catherine, now Kate, was 23 and a 'rag sorter', a job always done by women and girls. Bridget was 17 and a 'fuller'[1]. Also in the household and recorded as 'visitors' were Catherine Convey (30), a rag sorter; Michael Mallon (22), a labourer; and Thomas Prendergast (20), also a labourer.

The English Census returns for 1871, showing Thomas Halloran (b. 1808)'s family

There were also three young children, James (b. 1868), Patrick (b. 1869) and Mary, aged 3, 2 and 2 months, respectively. They are recorded as 'visitors'. These children, it appears are Catherine's (b. 1847), Thomas and Judy's second daughter. She married Thomas Moran in 1866, and the children should have been entered as surnamed Moran. Catherine had four more children in the 1970s but died aged only 33 in 1880, having given birth to 7 children. It seems that Thomas Moran then married Honora Halloran but died in 1886. In the 1901 census, one of his sons is found living in Chandler's Alley supporting two younger sisters.

Coach Lane, Brownhill – an Irish ghetto?

Incomes were low and rents were relatively high. However, Thomas and Judy and the rest of the Irish community did not have the luxury of much choice, as most of the housing was not available to the Irish. It is reported in Malcolm Clegg (1994), that the Irish moved into housing which had been emptied by epidemics. They lived in overcrowded, low-rent housing, sharing the cost with others. The Irish quarters were distinguished by appalling health conditions, as evidenced by high disease mortality from fevers and tuberculosis, high infant death rates, absence of clean water, a lack of facilities for disposing of human

---

1 Fulling involves two processes in wool cleaning —scouring and milling (thickening). These are followed by stretching the cloth on great frames known as tenters and held onto those frames by tenterhooks -

and household waste, and a high crime rate. In the grossly over-crowded conditions, large families occupied single rooms. Very often they shared these with adult lodgers who were not members of the same family. In some areas it was necessary to sub-let beds on a 'shift basis' because so many people occupied the house.

It is reported that in the Bradford area, (BBC Local History) ethnic concentrations of Irish, like those in Coach Lane, Brownhill, persisted until the end of the century[1]. Where the Irish dominated particular streets, however, they were not shut off from the native population. In both above censuses, we see that many of their neighbours had English names and were born locally. Essentially, though gathering close to kin, the Irish lived and worked alongside their poor English neighbours.

The Typical cottages, Brownhill where Thomas and Judy lived

The area boarded by Coach Lane and the Huddersfield Road is known as Brownhill, which is also referred to as 'Birstall Without' because it was just outside Birstall. A map of the area is found at the end of this chapter. Though officially part of Batley, its people identified more closely with Birstall. As noted above, the Birstall and Batley Irish communities had separate origins and developed separately. The Irish of Brownhill were more closely connected to their compatriots in Birstall and Gomersal; indeed were largely members of the same group. However, we also note from the frequent changes of address and the fact that some members of the family cannot be located in the area again, that these predominantly Irish communities were not stable, and many sectors of the immigrant communities were notoriously transient.

In some areas the Irish were excluded from skilled jobs by lack of education, prejudice and Orangeism (particularly in Glasgow and Liverpool). The craft unions also guarded their traditional membership and were reluctant to take in the Irish. The Irish response to this sometimes came by way of a song, one of the versions of which, *No Irish Need Apply,* is given below.

---

1 http://www.bbc.co.uk/bradford/content/articles/2006/05/12/bradford_irish_katie_feature.shtml

Chapter 5 – THE IRISH ARRIVE IN BIRSTALL

NO IRISH NEED APPLY
I'm a decent boy just landed from the town of Ballyfad;
I want a situation, yes, and want it very bad.
I have seen employment advertised, it's just the thing," says I.
But the dirty spalpeen ended with, "No Irish Need Apply".

"Whoa", says I, "that's an insult", but to get the place I'll try,
So I went to see the blackguard with his "No Irish Need Apply".
Some do count it a misfortune be christened Pat or Dan,
But to me it is an honour to be born an Irishman.

I started out to find the house, I got it mighty soon.
There I found the old chap seated, he was reading the Tribune.
I told him what I came for, when he in a rage did fly,
"No!" he says, "You are a Paddy, and no Irish need apply".

Then I gets my dander rising and I'd like to black his eye
To tell an Irish gentleman, "No Irish Need Apply".
Some do count it a misfortune to be christened Pat or Dan,
But to me it is an honour to be born an Irishman.

I couldn't stand it longer, so a hold of him I took,
And gave him such a welting as he'd get at Donnybrook.
He hollered, "Militia murther", and to get away did try,
And swore he'd never write again, "No Irish Need Apply".

Well he made a big apology, I told him then goodbye,
Saying, "When next you want a beating, write "No Irish Need Apply".
Some do count it a misfortune to be christened Pat or Dan,
But to me it is an honour to be born an Irishman

However, there was great variability. As we see in Batley, and as shown by many of the mill areas, where there was expansion, advancement was possible. In this regard the Halloran women were important. Working in the woollen mills they were entering a workforce in its infancy and at the point of considerable expansion. Being a new industry, its workforce was not tied to traditional craft unions.

This was less the case with the coalmines. Though jobs were obviously available, advancement was limited. But what is noticeable is that the Irish in Batley and Birstall at the time depended less on Irish community than the economic infrastructure of the area for employment. Though being a member of the Irish community obviously helped the immigrants in terms of support through family and kinship and a sense of cultural and religious solidarity, it did not get them jobs. In this way they were unlike later Irish immigrants who could rely on the success of previous Irish immigrants, particularly in the building trade where there were large Irish owned companies.

Michael Halloran (1827-77), born in Oughamore (Aghamore) and family

1861

In the 1861 census we discover another family of Hallorans, mistakenly entered as 'Allen'. They were living in 14 Gelderd Rd, Birstall. Michael aged 33 (b. 1827), was the head of the family and a farm labourer. Michael is almost certainly Thomas' (b. 1808) much younger brother whom we first saw in the 1851 census living with him. Hannah/Honora Stenson/Stinchin, his wife, was 28 (b, 1833). It is likely that they met in Mayo or knew each other from childhood. They would certainly both have experienced the Great Famine. Records show that they had married in 1851, though according to the census of 1851 she would have been under age, born in 1837 (or perhaps 1833 according to the 71 census). They already had four children: Mary (b. 1854) aged 7; Thomas (b. 1855) aged 5; .Patrick (b. 1858) aged 3 and John (b. 1861) 6 months old.

THE HALLORANS FROM BIRSTALL AND AGHAMORE

The English Census returns for 1861, showing Michael Halloran (Allen) (b. 1827)'s family

Anthony Stenson, a widower aged 55 is a visitor, and no doubt a relative of Hannah and Judith, though we know he is not their father. He was called John according to their marriage record. Another visitor is Michael Kenny (20). Both are farm labourers like Michael. Catherine Gallagher (64) is a lodger.

As already noted, we know from Michael's marriage certificate that his father's name was also Michael, and he was described as a labourer, but whether in Ireland or England, we are not sure.

As with his brother ten years previously, the English enumerators were still struggling with anglicised versions of Irish names. Then it was 'Haliyon', this time it is 'Allen'. This suggests that the family is still illiterate. However, his elder brother Thomas' family is recorded as 'Halloran' in 1861. This may well be because his children are older and received this standardised form of spelling from school, or perhaps from the mining company or mill in which they worked. There was probably little or no paper work involved in being a farm labourer so no official name was required. Perhaps Michael was simply known as 'Allen' where he worked. Birth records show more standardised spellings of 'Halloran' as the parish priests would be more familiar with anglicised forms of Irish names. Later, many Irish anglicised their names to avoid the stigma of being Irish. However, with Michael there was no prospect of disguising the fact.

1871

By the 1871 census, the name was settled as 'Halloran', which is one of the standard anglicised forms of Ó hAllmhuráin which also emerged in the parish records in Aghamore, though Holleran and other similar forms were also used.

In 1871, Michael and Hannah are found in 31 Church Street, Birstall, near Low Lane, with a much larger family. Michael aged 44 (b. 1827), was recorded as the head of the family and a labourer, Hannah/Honora Stenson/Stinchin, his wife, was 38 (b. 1833).

Mary their daughter was aged 17 (b. 1854) and was a burler[1], Thomas was 15 (b. 1855) and was a coal miner, as was his younger brother Patt, aged 13 (b. 1858). John, aged 10 (b, 1860) and James, aged 8 (b, 1862), were 'scholars'. There were also Anne, 3 (b. 1867) and Bridget, 1 (b, 1869). Baptism records confirm James', Catherine's and Anne's birth around these times. However, another child, also Ann, is born in 1872, four months before Michael died. However, tragedy was to strike in April 1873 when Michael died, age 47, leaving Hannah with very young children – including the 4-month-old little Ann.

What is significant about these entries is that they tell us Michael and Hannah were born in Co. Mayo, Michael in Oughamore (Aghamore) in 1827 and Hannah in Clamfullough (Cloonfallagh?) in 1833. We are very fortunate in this, as it is a very rare example of reference to a specific birthplace. Usually the place of birth is given simply as 'Ireland' or 'Mayo'. It was this information which gave us the direct link to James Halloran in Carrowbaun. However, this particular enumerator entered many specific birth places and helps us understand how close the family ties in the community were. They include Cambrack, Coongownagh, Kilkelly and Mirconghtt.

---

1 one who removes little burs, knots, or extraneous matter, from wool

Chapter 5 – THE IRISH ARRIVE IN BIRSTALL

The English Census returns for 1871, showing Michael Halloran (b. 1827)'s family

What is noticeable about this snapshot of the family is that in contrast to the 1851 census, the young people were at work and the children at school. What is more, there was one family to one household. Certainly we see in other cases that visitors and relatives of one sort or another frequently lived with various families; the cases were not as extreme as in 1851, nor were the households so crowded. Life seems much more settled and families nearer the nuclear model. Also the number of wage packets coming in was greater. The pattern is more urban and there is more indication of integration, through work in particular, into the wider English community.

Michael, we know, married in England and it is interesting to speculate about how matrimonial arrangements were made and how this differed from their homeland. Even before they left Ireland, traditional marital patterns and family life had undergone a profound change among the peasantry of Connaught. Traditionally marriage had been seen as a pact between families to secure the inheritance of family land holdings. Matches were made through the medium of the local matchmaker or *Babhdóir* who usually received a bottle of whiskey for his trouble. They would be arranged in the parlour of a pub. Much consideration would have been given to what land or tenancies the man would inherit. Young women would come with dowries that had been carefully negotiated between the two families and were frequently measured in acres of land and cattle; the young people themselves had little to do with the arrangements. The more prosperous the family, the greater the dowry, which in turn gave greater control to the parents. Daughters with no dowries and sons with no or very small portions of land often did not find marriage partners.

Over-population, poverty and the Great Famine had combined to make this system redundant for many, as they possessed no land. Irish women could and did escape the dowry system through emigration, which gave them improved marriage opportunities and a chance of a better social position through paid employment. This proved to be a strong 'pull factor' in female migration which increased throughout the nineteenth century.

However, the Irish that came from Aghamore had come from an area which itself had only relatively recently been heavily populated. The massive increase in the rural population in Ireland from the mid 1750s onwards was due largely to the fact that surplus populations in the areas of pastoral farming moved to the more mountainous areas and bog lands where they could eke out a living thanks to the potato. The spread of this crop meant people could survive in areas previously largely uninhabited. Often, rather than wait to inherit their small portion of existing family land, sons would venture into new bog lands where they could grow and live on potatoes. Landlords encouraged this as it meant more land was cultivated and new rents could be collected. This led to even sharper increases in the population, further fuelled by the fact that fewer restraints on marriage led to many marrying earlier. This trend would possibly have developed further in Birstall where securing farmland was of no significance. Young people were freer to marry as they saw fit. But in Birstall they still belonged to a small tightly-knit community and informal family pacts were still important in the new urban environment. Perhaps the services of the matchmaker were retained as negotiations were still needed. New immigrants were indebted to neighbours and relatives in all sorts of ways: for accommodation, money, and for advice on jobs and how to live in their new world. In short, the emigrants depended on each other. Dependency required some sort of reciprocity and acknowledgement. Informal pacts were probably entered into for the benefit of both families. Help was given to others when times were hard in the knowledge that help would be required in turn.

THE HALLORANS FROM BIRSTALL AND AGHAMORE

Very few of the Irish group who came from Aghamore seem to have married outside this group for a number of generations. This was the spirit of the clachan and rundale system which underpinned community life at home in Mayo. The sense of common interest in fleeing the famine together and settling into a new environment were no doubt reflected and strengthened through marriages between the families. Certainly, the first generations would have been cut off from the local population by poverty and barriers of language and religion. Newly arrived in a new country, by 1851 they found themselves in a new situation, Michael and his nephew James marry girls from the house next-door, probably as they would have done in Ireland.

1981

By the following census in 1981, Hannah had moved to live at 5 Coach Lane; James and Bridget were at 8 Coach Lane, typically supported by the extended family. Thomas (b 1856), their son, who was about 17 when his father died, appears to turn up on the 1881 census, when he was in his early 20s. His address was 107 Brownhill, where he was entered as a boarder with Mike and Catherine Henry, (born in Ireland) and their family, and with a Margaret Kelly aged 17, and also a boarder.

1901

In the 1901 English census we find James Halloran (b. 1863). He was married to Ellen (b. 1866). They lived in 3 Partington Sq. He is entered as being a 'coal hewer (below ground)'. They had 6 children: John (b. 1889) aged 12, Willie (b. 1891) aged 10, Mary (b. 1893) aged 8, Ann (b. 1894) aged 7, Margaret (b. 1899) aged 2, and James (b. 1900) aged 2 months.

At present we have no records of Mary, Patt (b. 1858), John, Anne or Bridget and know little about the decedents of Michael and Hannah.

Roman Catholicism in England

At that time Catholicism was viewed with general hostility in Britain. As discussed in chapter 1, the Penal Laws, had been designed to suppress Catholicism in Britain and Ireland, however, the Catholic Church and its clergy were held in the highest esteem by the Irish peasantry. In the face of government oppression and landlord indifference, the Catholic clergy had tried to bring education and some form of relief and advancement to the starving in Ireland. The ordinary Irish family entrusted the rituals that surrounding birth, marriage and death to them. The feast days of the Catholic Church marked passing of the seasons. It also played a dominant role in providing political and social leadership to the thousands of Irish who entered North Yorkshire in the nineteenth century. Much of the work in securing fundamental legal rights for the Irish Catholic immigrants fleeing from poverty and political unrest was done by men like Canon Harrison, who did much to improve the lot of the inmates of the Union Workhouse[1].

The Roman Catholicism that the Irish bought with them had little or no pre-existing place in Birstall, yet it became a defining feature of their identity in England. Only one Roman Catholic family are known to have lived in Birstall prior to the Irish influx. Mary Pirrot had married Joseph Clapham early in the ninetieth century. They had three sons who had property interests in public houses, residential accommodation, and coalmines. They did not operate the usual 'no Irish need apply' policy and were probably responsible for getting a number of Irish started in the coalmines. Mary's daughter, Annabella, was the mother of Miss Mortimer, who had a pawnbroker business in Cross Street and was a great benefactor of St Patrick's Church (Clegg 1994).

However, the lifting of penal laws against Catholics took place over a number of years, beginning in 1778 and culminated in the repeal of the Test and Corporation Acts in 1828 and the granting of Emancipation in 1829. The reestablishment of an Episcopal hierarchy in 1850 signalled the Second Spring of the Catholic Church in England, preached by Cardinal Newman. This enabled the recently appointed Bishops to provide churches for their flock. The Catholics of the area built their first church, St. Mary's, in 1824-

---

1 http://www.bbc.co.uk/bradford/content/articles/2006/05/12/bradford_irish_katie_feature.shtml

Chapter 5 – THE IRISH ARRIVE IN BIRSTALL

25 in Bradford and this was followed by St. Patrick's. In 1841, Bishop Briggs sent Father O'Leary to Dewsbury, where, in a rented room, he said the first Mass for some 300 Catholics[1].

Urban living

Clegg, in the *History of Birstall* (1994), describes how the Irish had gained a reputation for a lack of hygiene and riotous living. The lack of cleanliness was a major issue as health problems were a constant risk. The housing was damp, lacking in ventilation, congested and overcrowded. The Irish, who had little idea of healthy living, continued to house friends and relations for decades. They used damp cellars as further habitation, to add to their general overcrowding, and kept dogs, hens and pigs with them. Latrines were shared by numerous families, usually a pit against the wall of a house, draining under the foundations, and only occasionally emptied. Urine was collected from tubs scattered around the houses and used as a scouring agent in the woollen processing. Vermin thrived on the rotting waste left in the streets and shared yards. Throughout the Heavy Woollen District, rows of poor quality back-to-back houses were hurriedly built to house the growing population, with only shared basic sanitation.

By 1878, Batley municipal authority recognised the problems these created and banned further building of back-to-backs, though continued to allow the square blocks of four houses. Diseases and epidemics, such as typhoid, scarletina, diphtheria and smallpox were common, and especially virulent amongst the overcrowded Irish. Even as late as 1874, twelve children died from scarlet fever in one month – Irish children were most at risk. In 1859, of 136 deaths, 52 were of children under one year and 35 of children between one and five years old - constituting almost two thirds of the deaths. Diarrhoea, a major cause of infant death, resulted from milk being contaminated by dirt or flies (Clegg 1994). This terrible spate of infant deaths, as we have seen, affected Thomas and Judy' family. Two of their children died of small pox within 5 days of each other. Their next-door neighbour, Euphenesia Sucksmith, was buried the next day and 4 year-old Anne Kelly, two days later. Their infant cousin James, son of Michael and Honoria, died 3 months after that, though the cause of his death was not recorded[2].

Puerperal fever caused the deaths of many mothers, but was remedied in later years simply by the washing of hands, especially by the midwife. The need for improved public health was the main reason given for establishing Birstall as a separate township from Batley and Gomersal, and, in July 1863, it became a municipal authority in its own right (Clegg 1994).

Another reason the Irish were often not welcome was their unruly behaviour, generally resulting from drinking. They tended to keep to their own pubs: The Horse and Jockey was close to Low Lane, where many of the Irish lived. The Coach and Six, an ancient coaching inn, and The Blacksmith's Arms were at the Gelderd Road, and Coach Lane (the lower part of Leeds Road) junction. Just down the road at the entrance to Brownhill was The Vaults. There were also pubs that have disappeared, such as Flemings Hotel in Low Lane, better known as 'The Irish pub', and with a name that suggests an attempt at integration - The Rose and Shamrock.

In the late 1860s, a group of twenty drunken Irishmen walked into the Vaults late at night, and having created a major disturbance, threw large stones through the windows as they left. However, after another fight there, the Irish were treated with sympathy due to the 'provocative playing of 'Boyne Water'. On Easter Monday, after a crowd of Irish had drunk heavily at the 'Horse and Jockey', they moved back to Coach Lane where a great battle broke out, with men women and children joining in until sufficient injuries quietened it down. However, fines ensued. After a battle outside the Coach and Six, on another occasion, the magistrate said that one man's name was familiar as a regular offender and that 'the Bench must put down that system of civil war which was going on in Birstall. However, it appears that most of the fighting was between the Irish themselves or running battles with the Batley Irish (Clegg 1994). We have seen how these two Irish groups had had separate origins and networks of connections. The Irish obviously brought the intensity of local rivalries with them to Yorkshire.

---

1 Much of the following comes from St Patrick's website: http://birstallstpatrick.org.uk/history.htm

2 Birstall Parish records of burials at this time give ages (apart from infants), the names of fathers, their employment, and the name of spouses. Batley parish records only give ages at time of death.

THE HALLORANS FROM BIRSTALL AND AGHAMORE

The Coach and Six, Gelderd Road. Thought to be 300 years old when demolished in 1955

After a spate of burglaries, six policemen had been appointed for Birstall in 1854 in and the first uniformed policeman had been appointed in 1862. There was a 'lock-up', where offenders were kept before being sent to the police cells in Dewsbury, and by 1866, police cells were being built in Birstall (Clegg 1994). It seemed that the police were much involved in the brawls around Coach Land, and also at Mount Top (not the Irish here!), so perhaps the Halloran brothers were well acquainted with them.

The following is a tongue-in-cheek (non-PC) story placed on the Aghamore Discussion Board, and gives a flavour of the lives and stories of *Achadh Mór* men in Yorkshire

> *The story of Achadh Mór's (Aghamore's) entry into world historical annals goes something like this. A bunch of hardy Achadh Mór men were enjoying a week-end 'get together' in a pub in Yorkshire - -some historians insist that New York's Bronx was the location. Suddenly the amiable chatter was interrupted, when apparently the courage and manliness of the East Mayo men was called into question and by implication the good name and reputation of their area was sullied.*
>
> *As a result battle lines were swiftly drawn up, a section of bar stools was catapulted to one side by brawny calloused working hands. In one sweep the counter was cleared of glasses, clearly to prevent the other side from playing dirty by deploying shards of glass, but also to ensure a free counter top from which to launch the occasional polecat assault. Surprised patrons or neutral bystanders all stood well back or at least as far back as they could when the blood curdling shouts of "Up Achadh Mór", signalled the beginning of exchanges. As the battle progressed it became clear that yet again the famous men of Achadh Mór were gaining the upper hand. Before long another fearsome battle cry, "Come on Achadh Mór" prefaced the final heave. Just at that point, one of the neutral 'hurlers on the ditch' leaped forward. Though perhaps 'hurler' is not the most appropriate nomenclature in this case, since according to one eyewitness account "he was as black as the ace of spades", and therefore hardly likely to have been a patron of our ancient game. Anyway, fearful for his own safety it seems, as the neutral ground began to shrink, this black man is alleged to have waded in on the local side with fists flying, shouting the immortal lines "Me an Achí Mór Man too"!*

Could this battle, or one like it, have taken place in the Blacksmith's Arms. Was this an account of an heroic encounter between the Swinford men of Batley and the Aghamore men of Birstall. We will never know, but it is likely that occasions like this, with those self same combatants, perhaps without the dusky bystander, did take place among the Irish in Birstall, and less frequently, between the Irish and some of their English neighbours.

Chapter 5 – THE IRISH ARRIVE IN BIRSTALL

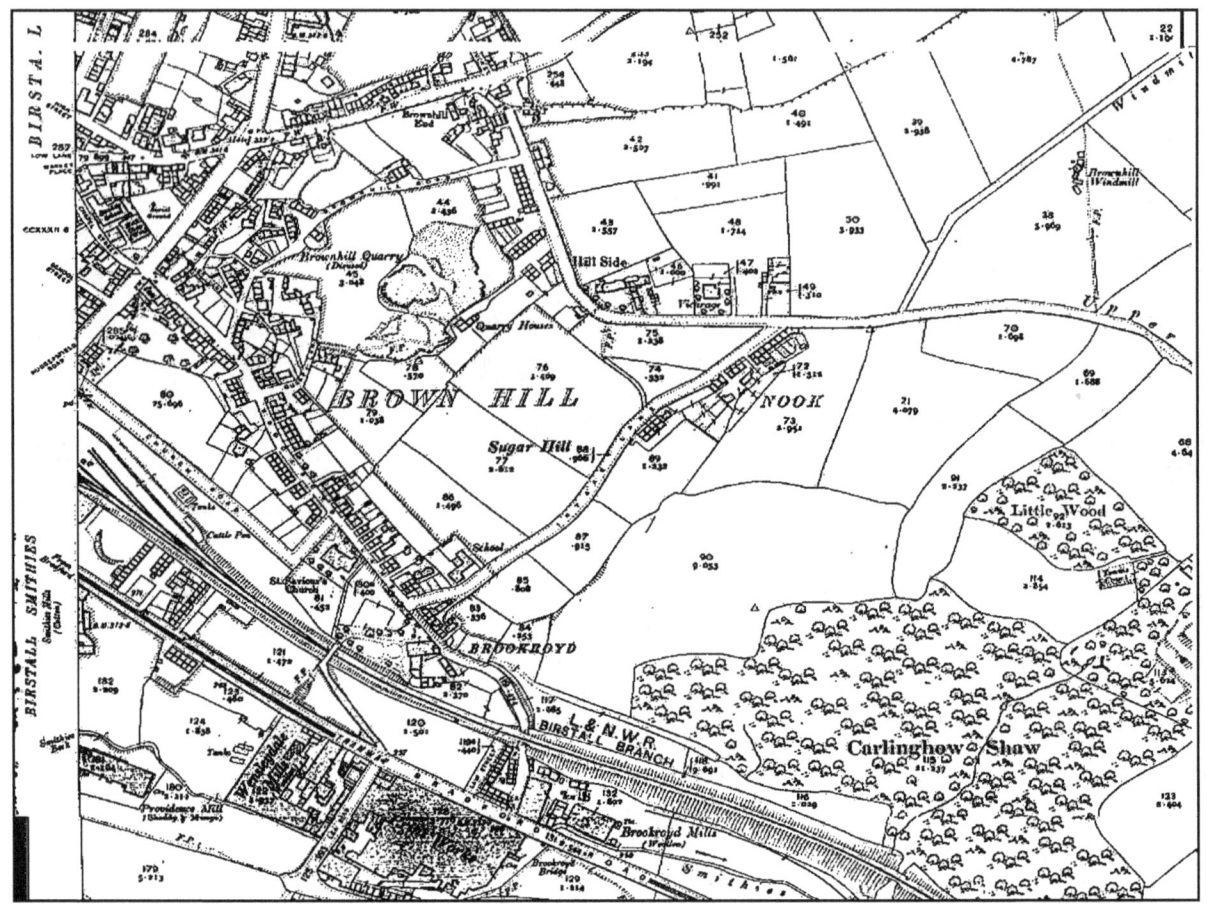

Brownhill, OS Map, revised 1905

CHAPTER 6

The second generation - Birstall

Going down the mines

The area around Birstall was still quite rural when Thomas and family arrived there; however, coal and the woollen industry both proved to be explosive engines of change throughout northern England, especially in altering work patterns and working conditions for most ordinary people. With the building of the railways there was a greater demand for coal, partly to service the railways but mainly because of the increase in business for the mills with the development of the 'shoddy' process in the area. Coalmining made woollen clothing affordable for everyone, and not only for the rich, as it powered the new mills which, enabling mass production, and transported the raw materials and the finished products in ways never possible before. The demand for wool grew rapidly; the railway meant that distribution was easier and allowed used woollen cloth to be purchased from all over Britain and eventually throughout Europe. Therefore, by the 1850s the demand for miners and factory workers ensured employment for as many Irish as could get there and find a place to live. In 1851, a group of Batley mill owners even placed a notice in the Manchester Guardian appealing for families to move to the town (Clegg 1994).

At that time, the normal route to becoming a miner was to enter the pits as a child. Very few, if any of the males who left Ireland as adults became miners; yet we know that Thomas and Judy's sons, James (b. 1835) Patrick (b. 1837), Michael (b. 1839) and Thomas (b. 1841), all did. The girls, however, all worked in the woollen mills. The children of the Irish newcomers could be considered fortunate in one respect. The Mines Act of 1842 prohibited the employment of women and girls and all boys under the age of ten down mines. Later this was extended to boys under 12. This, however, was resisted by many, as some of the local mine shafts were so narrow that only small children could work them and people found ways around the law. We have the example of John Walsh, aged 10 weeks in the 1861 census, but ten years later recorded as a miner aged 12.

The argument for child labour was spelt out in this is a collier's testimony to the *Children's Employment Commission of 1842*. This useful source of conditions in south Yorkshire has proved particularly interesting and is the source of the testimony that follows.

> *I am sure if boys are prevented from coming to these pits when they are 10, they will be too big and too stiff to learn the work and that if they come younger it naturally keeps them down and prevents their getting too big. We cannot learn them at 10 either. Girls ought not to remain longer than 13 because there are things which make it improper afterwards. It is wrong work for girls to come among naked folk after that. Sometimes I leave the boy to fill a corve or two after I get out of the pit. I think 10 hours plenty for lads or men to be in the pit. We could not do to change lads for relays. Children could not go to school after they come out of the pit. There isn't half as much pains taken with the Sunday Schools as there was. Children generally don't get near enough education here.*

Mining in South Yorkshire

Most youngsters entering the mines would have had a family history of such work and would have followed their fathers and were probably working for them. So, Thomas and Judy's two eldest sons, James' (b. 1837) and Michael's (b. 1837) first experience of the coalmines must have been terrifying, never having encountered such work before. Being teenagers, they would have entered the mines as hurriers, working to strange men, as there were no family members to take them on and introduce them to pit life.

We get a feel of what hurrier did in the following extracts from the Children's Employment Commission of 1842. These and all following extracts pertain to South Yorkshire. In the first we see that the usual introduction to the coalmine for a child and the first step to becoming a coal miner was to work as a hurrier, a job done by James Halloran and many of the young men in his family. Prior to the Mines Act, very young children, possibly only 5 or 6 years old, would have worked as 'trappers'. Their job was to

Chapter 6 – THE SECOND GENERATION

open the self-closing trap doors to allow the corves (coal wagons) to pass. It was also an important job in controlling the ventilation, yet it was left to small children. As using children this young had been prohibited, it may have been that trapping was done by young boys like James and Michael, as a way of introducing them to pit life.

Hurriers

The chief employment of children and young persons as I [author of report] have stated, is that of conveying the coal from the bank faces to the shaft, where there are no horses and to the horses, where there are any. They do this by propelling the corves before them and in some very thin coal beds, in crawling and pulling them after them. These cases occur in small pits only. The corves are oblong wagons, on small wheels of 9 or 12 inches in diameter running on railways, which are laid down in nearly all the gates of every colliery. These corves vary greatly in size carrying from 2 or 10 cwt. of coal but the commonest size in the thicker beds of coal are made to hold 6 cwt. of coal and weighing about 2 or 2.5 cwt. themselves, making a weight of about 8 cwt. in all.

The operation of propelling these corves is called hurrying, and in some places, tramming. It is done by placing both hands on the top rail of the back of the corve and pushing it forward running as fast as the inclination of the road or the strength of the hurrier will permit. The hurriers are generally paid and employed by the colliers themselves, each collier undertaking, either by himself or in conjunction with another, not only to 'get', that is to hew out an allotted bank of coal, but to deliver it at the horse gate, or at the shaft as the case may be. The work of the hurrier is not, therefore, as may be readily supposed, confined merely to the hurrying of the corves backwards and forwards along the gates. When the hurrier arrives with his or her empty corve at the bank face, it has to be filled, and in the north part of my district all the small part of the coal must be riddled (i.e. sieved) also. In these operations the hurriers almost invariably assist.

Hurriers are usually employed by the workmen they assist and these, as we have seen, from a very large proportion of the whole body of the children. The remainder are hired by the master; children in no case make these contracts themselves. They are made by their parents, for whom indeed in many cases they work. In many cases the children do not know what they earn. I have no reason to think that the manner in which the engagements are made tend anywise to injure the children...

The labour of hurrying in many of these pits is very great. Not so much because the gates are low but in nine cases out of ten, because less pains are taken to keep the rails in repair and to drain the roads... There is something very oppressive at first sight in the employment of children hurrying all day in passages under 30 inches in height.

Hurrying on all fours

Where the coal is very thin children not infrequently hurry on all fours in the following manner: A broad belt is buckled round their waist to the front to which the chain is fastened which, when they go down on all fours, is passed between their legs and attached to the corve, which they draw after them, thus harnessed to it like animals. This is extremely hard work[1].

Getting, trappers

Sometimes when the collier has not got sufficient coal by the time the hurrier returns, the hurrier takes the pick with which the coal is hewn and helps to 'get'. By this means the art of getting is learnt and the hurrier by degrees becomes a collier, and at 18 or 19 finally leaves off hurrying altogether.

---

1 The Children's Employment Commission 1842, For Inquiring into the Employment and Condition of Children in Mines and Manufactories

Dr Thomas Rayner, a Birstall surgeon, had unwittingly been instrumental in opening up employment opportunities for the Irish labourers due to his contribution to the Report on the Condition in Mines. The Factory Act of 1833 prevented children below the age of nine from working in the woollen mills and limited the hours of those under thirteen. There was no such legislation for the mines, so in 1833 many children were transferred to work in the pits in even worse conditions than the mills. Children, as young as five (often 'bought' from the poorhouse by the miners), worked as 'trappers', opening the doors to allow the corves, the small wagons which carried the coal, to pass through. By about seven they graduated to 'hurrying' the corves back and forth (one to pull, wearing reins, and one to push using head and shoulders).

Dr Rayner' reported on the resultant deformities which included flattened skulls, protruding chests, inwardly curving backs, knees flexed outwards. He also reported on the sexual vices and illegitimacy resulting from women working alongside men at the coal face. As a result, children were prevented from working in the pits and women were restricted to working above ground. The result of these changes was to open opportunities for the Irish to fill the vacancies. However, the mines in this part of Yorkshire had narrow seams, perhaps only 14', so conditions were horrendous for the thirteen, fourteen-year olds who had even greater difficulties negotiating the narrow openings than the smaller children.

The local mines

Around Birstall, there were old mines at Howley, between Brownhill and Morley, Howden Clough, two near Upper Batley Low Lane (the Boggard or Windmill pits), one at White Lee and another at Gomersal. The first four were within a mile of where James and Thomas and their families lived but there were many other 'day oils', i.e. shallow pits, in the Batley Low Lane and surrounding area. This might account for the move across Birstall to the Gelderd Road, Coach Lane area which is close by. Several of the pits were owned by the Clapham family, an old English Catholic family. The three brothers owned large areas of land and several pubs as well as owning and tenanting several pits. They were notoriously wild and made regular appearances in court because of their drunken behaviour. The fact that they were Roman Catholics, and given to unconventional behaviour, may have meant they were sympathetic in employing the newly arrived Irish youngsters.

Many shallow pits, known locally as 'day 'oils' even in living memory, were found at Staincliffe, Healey, Carlinghow, Upper Batley, Brownhill. It is possible Thomas' sons may have worked in Brownhill or the Boggard pit, as it was the closest to where they lived.

Working shallow mines

These local mines were located in positions to the northwest of the great Barnsley Seam, which was the most important seam in the coalfield, and delivered 50% of the coalfield's output. It was generally 3m thick. The seams consistency varied from top to bottom. The upper portion was a bright soft coal, the middle portion a hard dull coal known as the 'hards', and the lower portion another band of bright soft coal. The hards were used in locomotives and steam ships. The soft coals were mixed with other coals for coke making. Being on the periphery of the seam, the Gomersal or Birkenshaw mines were known as thin mines, the depth of coal often being no more than 18', and they used children to crawl through the narrow passageways.

Chapter 6 – THE SECOND GENERATION

Testimony of Joseph Ellison, Esq., of Birkenshaw, near Birstall

I have been practically acquainted with collieries nearly all my life. On the Low Moor, the Bowling and Bierley Mines the bed will not average more than 18 inches. The main gates will be about a yard but the bank gates not above 32 feet. They consequently employ very young children. They generally go to work as early as 6 years old and remain as hurriers till 12 or 13. ... The average time they work will be from 6 in the morning till 4 in the evening. They make Saturday a short day and on Monday they often don't work at all. It is called Collier Monday here. The employment of children decidedly stunts their growth and renders them unfit for any other occupation.

There are few girls about here in the pits. It is an exception now since the mills became plentiful but formerly there were as many as boys. It is cruel and highly improper. I know a case of a girl being employed as a hurrier having been attempted to be ravished frequently by her father-in-law till at length she could not go down the pit. Where girls are employed the immoralities practised are scandalous.

I believe that the gates in the thin coal pits might easily be made high enough to admit of the employment of mules. It would be a little more expense to the masters and perhaps the price would be raised a little of the coal but I do not believe it is at all impracticable to do without the labour of children till they are 12 years old in the pits.

The average distance the hurriers have to drag the corves is 150 yards each way and in most pits they are kept so hard at it that if there is the least cessation in their work, down they drop and fall asleep immediately. Sometimes the younger ones get severely beaten by the colliers when they cannot breed children enough themselves for the hurriers they want and are forced to apply to the Poor Law Guardians for pauper children. I am a Guardian myself and know it to be a fact. ... Parents prefer any other sort of employment for their children.

Take the colliers as a body and I will undertake to say there is not a more ignorant class in the whole of Yorkshire. The children are only sent to Sunday Schools and a great many of them are not even sent there. ... I know it is a fact that a collier now living has taken a child of his own, who was only 3 years old, into a pit to hurry and when the child was exhausted it was carried home, stripped and put to bed... The colliers about here are considered the very lowest in civilisation of all other classes. There are about 6000 colliers ironstone getters in a circle of three miles round this place who will employ 8000 hurriers. They employ these themselves and pay them themselves.

Extracts from children's interviews

The nature of this work and much else about the mines of South Yorkshire are graphically presented in *The Children's Employment Commission 1842*, For Inquiring into the Employment and Condition of Children in Mines and Manufactories. The following are responses to the questions asked by the commission's researchers. As the interviewer was trying to establish something of the children's education, the interviews ended with a few short questions on general knowledge and arithmetic.

Testimony of a boy James Leather aged 13 years examined at Flockton

I have been working four years in the pit. I have been hurrying all the time. I have hurried all the time myself. I go down to the pit generally at 6 but sometimes at 4 and often at half past 4. It is a roller that lets us down. We come out at 4, sometimes later, and sometimes sooner. We stop in general at nine or ten. Sometimes we don't stop at all for dinner. Sometimes we find it hard work and sometimes easy. We are generally tired at night.

A. The gates are not higher than a yard.
A. I can read and write.
A. I go to Sunday school. We come to evening school on Mondays.
A. They teach us to read and write at Sunday School,
A. They teach us religion a little.
A. I have never heard tell of Christ. I don't know what happened to him.
A. They pray in the morning but they don't teach us to pray.
A. I don't know whose book the Bible is.
A. I know there is a place called heaven, which is a good place.

Testimony of a girl Hannah Vaux, aged 12, examined at Flockton.

> A. I have been working two or three years at a pit. I have been to Sunday school all the time.
> A. I read in the Bible and the Irish class books.
> A. It is the Sunday School at Mr. Stansfield's house.
> A. Jesus Christ came to save us from sin and was reviled by men, nailed to the cross, and he rose again. He is in heaven now.
> A. My father and mother never teach me anything and all I learn is at the evening school, once a week, and on Sundays.
> [Spells indifferently and knows very little of arithmetic but has a fair knowledge of geography].

The reference to 'Irish class books' is very interesting. Is it a reference to classes for Irish children? The Sunday school at Mr. Stansfield house illustrates that there was, on this occasion at least, a close involvement between the mine owners, in this case Messrs Stansfield & Briggs of the Flockton mine, and the children who worked the mines. Certainly the mine owners would not run schools with Irish books.

Testimony of a girl Bessy Bailey at Flockton

> I shall be 15 next Tuesday. I hurry in the pit you was in this morning. I have been in a year and never in any pit before. I like it very well. I hurry with my brother. It does not tire me very much. I always work naked down to the waist and with trousers on and all the girls I know hurry in the same way, except two. I have been three years at a Sunday school. I cannot read much. I have not been at Sunday school for a year because I have to work at home to help my father to get the dinner and to wash the pots up. I go out to walk a bit in the afternoons. I go to the Methodist Chapel every Sunday evening. I think it is the best place on Sunday nights.
> A. Jesus Christ died for his son to be saved.
> A. I know who the apostles were.
> A. 22 pence is 3 shillings and 4 pence.
> A. I don't know how many weeks there are in a year.
> A. I don't know what Ireland is, whether it is a town or a country.

Testimony of a boy, Joseph Whetley, aged 13 years at Flockton

> I have been in the pit for five years. I don't find it very hard work. I hurry. I go to a Sunday school [He cannot read.] I go to the Chapel on Sundays. I don't know who Jesus Christ was. I don't know who made the world. I have heard of God and he is in Heaven, if not, to fire and brimstone. I don't know which is the largest town in England but I know Wakefield and Leeds. I have heard of Ireland. My mother was born there but I don't know whether it is a country or not. Sometimes I play on Sundays and sometimes I sit at home.

Testimony of James Cargill examined March 19th.

> I am turned 11. I work as a trapper at Messrs. Day and Turbell's pit. I went to pit about four years ago and then I hurried. I go to all pits where my brother goes. I go at seven in the morning and I come out at half past five. They use me very well. They don't lace me because I have got my brother in the pit.
> A. I go to Sunday school sometimes.
> A. God made the world.

Chapter 6 – THE SECOND GENERATION

A. It's about a year since I went into the Catholic Chapel.

A. I sit quietly at home on Sundays. I am quite sure that I never heard anything about Jesus Christ coming on earth to save sinners.

A. I don't know how many weeks there are in the year. There are 12 months.

A. Ireland is a town but I don't know what Scotland is.

Testimony of a boy, William Beaver at Flockton

I am going 16. I hurry in Mr. Porter's Pit. It is hard where I work. We hurry at the far end with my brother. Sometimes we hurry 15 and sometimes 20 corves a day. There used to be girls there but not now, because the pit is nearly worked out. I have been at a Sunday school. I can read 'Reading Made Easy.'

A. The Lord made the world. He sent Adam and Eve on earth to save sinners. I heard my grandfather tell about it. He's a great reader but he can't see.

A. I have heard of the Saviour. He was a good man, but he did not die here. He is in Heaven. We must pray to be saved. There is but one God and he does not die like men.

A. Jesus Christ was nailed on a cross but that is all I have heard about it.

A. I have not begun to learn to write.

A. I get bread to eat or dinner and we get to sup out of the beer bottles when the men let us. There is water but there is ochre among it. We get potatoes and meat, and a bit of bread when we come out of the pit. We get as much as we can eat. I am never poorly.

A. London is the largest town in England. I never heard mention of France. I never heard mention of Wales or of Scotland but I know people that come from Ireland. I think Ireland is a town as big as Barnsley where there is plenty of potatoes, and lots of bullocks.

A. 20 pence is 1 shilling and 8 pence, 32 pence is 2 shillings and 8 pence, 7 times 3 is 32, no it's 22.

A. I have learnt the Lord's Prayer.

[Though this child can repeat the Lord's Prayer he has no comprehension what it means.]

One of the questions asked by the interviewer must have been, 'where is Ireland?' and these are the few reference to Ireland in the South Yorkshire report, suggesting that in the late 1830s, early1840s when the interviews were being carried out, there were a few Irish working in the coal mines and we know many came in the 1830s to work in the strike-bound woollen mills. However, there must have been very little communication with adults.

There is quite a lot of evidence that the miners were a local, settled, and quite established, if hidden part of the community at that time. However, changes were taking place in the work force as the Irish started to come into the area, many of whom worked in the modernised woollen mills that were springing up in the district.

Extract from the report on the use of girls in coal pits

The practise of employing females in coal pits is flagrantly disgraceful to a Christian as well as to a civilised country. On descending Messrs. Hopwood's pit, at Barnsley, I found assembled round the fire a group of men, boys and girls, some of whom were of the age of puberty, the girls as well as the boys stark naked down to the waist, their hair bound up in a tight cap and trousers supported by their hips. (At Silkstone and at Flockton they work in their shifts and trousers.) Their sex was recognisable only by their breasts and some little difficulty arose in pointing out to me which were girls and which were boys, and which caused a good deal of laughing and joking.

In the Flockton and Thornhill pits the system is even more indecent, for though the girls are clothed, at least three fourths of the men for whom they hurry work stark naked, or with a flannel waistcoat only, and in this state they assist one another to fill corves 10 or 20 times a day. I have seen this done myself not once or twice but frequently. Neither do the girls or the men attempt to gainsay the fact, as you will perceive by the evidence of witnesses.

Testimony of a young woman, Elizabeth Day, aged 17 working in the Messrs Hopwood's Pit in Barnsley.

I have been nearly nine years in the pit. I trapped for two years when I first went in and have hurried ever since. I have hurried for my father until a year ago. ... I have hurried by myself going fast on three years.

Before then, I had my sister to hurry with me. I have to hurry up hill with the loaded corves, quite as much as down but not many have to hurry up hill with the loaded corve.

We always hurry in trousers as you saw us today when you were in the pit. Generally I work naked down to the waist like the rest. I had my shift on today when I saw you, because I had to wait and was cold but generally the girls hurry naked down to the waist. It is very hard work for us all. It is harder work than we ought to do.

I have been lamed in my ankle and strained my back. It caused a great lump to rise on my ankle bone once. The men behave well to us and never insult or ill use us, I am sure of that. We go to work between five and six but we begin to hurry when we get down. We stop an hour for dinner at 12. We generally have bread and a bit of fat for dinner and some of them have a sup of beer, that's all. We have a whole hour for dinner and we get out from four to five in the evening so that will be 11 hours before we get out. We drink the water that runs through the pit. I am not paid wages myself. The man who employs me pays my father but I don't know how much it is.

I have never been at school I had to begin to work when I ought to have been at school. I don't go to Sunday school. The truth is, we are confined bad enough on weekdays and want to walk about on Sundays but I go to Chapel on Sunday night. I can't read at all.

A. Jesus Christ was Adam's son and they nailed him to a tree but I don't rightly understand these things.

Prostitution in pits

When it is remembered that these girls hurry chiefly for men who are not their parents, that they go from 15 to 20 times a day into a dark chamber (the bank face), which is often 50 yards apart from any one, to a man working naked, or next to naked, it is not to be supposed but that where opportunity thus prevails sexual vices are of common occurrence.

Add to this the free intercourse and the rendezvous at the shaft or bullstake where the corves are brought and consider the language to which the young ear is habituated, the absence of religious instruction, at the early age at which contamination begins and you will have before you in the coal pits, where females are employed, the picture of a nursery for juvenile vice which you will go far and wide above ground to equal.

The evidence of Mr. Berry, the clerk to the Board of Guardians, No.198, attests the number of cases of bastardy which occur from these pits. It is, however, well known that bastardy is by no means a proportionate index to the amount of unchastity and that the most profligate women are the least likely to bear children. It is but due however to the character of the colliers to state that a very general practice prevails among them of marrying the girls they seduce.

The masters sincerely desire to get rid of this grievous system but they are powerless and the excuse among the men who keep up the practice is, that they cannot afford to lose the wages of the girls, and can find 'nought else for them to do.' It is highly probable that girls, once initiated into the moral schooling of a coal pit, do find it difficult to obtain respectable employment afterwards. But, as respects their inability to keep their daughters out of the pits, I would beg to refer you especially to the evidence of the iron stone getter. The colliers of Silkstone, who make the greatest practice of sending their girls into the pit, can earn 24s. a week themselves, without counting the earnings of their sons.

Colliers' lives out of sight.

It cannot be too constantly remembered that the mining population, owing to the early age at which they begin work, owing to their spending the daylight out of sight, and owing to their need of fresh air and light on Sundays, are a class, the great bulk of whom mostly live out of sight of the rest of the community and almost wholly out of its ken. They are reached by none of the institutions. Sabbath schools form the chief link, but of these the efficiency, except for the rudiments of reading, and the mere beginnings of the machinery of instruction, is next to none. As means of informing the mind, or improving the heart, they are wholly ineffective and a mere mockery, as far as religious instruction is concerned, in five cases out of six.

'I know of no old colliers' - Testimony of Thomas Rayner, surgeon of Birstall May 26th 1841

Collier children are liable to rickets. Those who are scrofulous have a protrusion of the chest, the back curved inwards and the knees flexed forwards. They are taken in at 5 years, both boys and girls, because they cannot be taken to the mills till they are 13. It is decidedly injurious to their health.

I have had 27 years practice and I know of no old colliers. Their extreme term of life is from 56 to 60 years of age, I account for the stunted growth from the stooping position which makes them grow latterly and

Chapter 6 – THE SECOND GENERATION

prevents the cartilaginous substance from expanding. The privation for light also tends to prevent the healthy action of the skin.

The Board of Guardians at Batley apprentice children without due care to ascertain their age. The boy Thomas Townsend, aged 5 years, would not have been brought back to the workhouse had not the grandfather interfered and demanded it. We threatened to acquaint Mr. Chadwick and the Commissioners with it. The colliers and children decidedly work 12 hours a day if the work is plentiful. I think 8 full working hours would be sufficient and a child not under 9 years of age would bear this number of hours very well.

It was fairly common for miners to cut coal while naked; an illustration from the 1842 Children's Employment commission for Yorkshire

Testimony of John Ibbetson aged 53, examined at Birkenshaw, near Birstall.

I have been 45 years in the pits. I am the father of the children you have examined at Mr. Harrison's pit. I have had three ribs of one side and two on the other broken and my collarbone and my leg skinned. My reason for taking the girls into the pits is that I can get nought else for them to do. I can't get enough wages to dress the boys for going to school I get 5s. 6d. for the girls and I and my two sons earn 17s. 6d. on a average a week. I am done up. I can't addle much. The eldest girl does nothing at all. We get potatoes and a bit if meat or bacon when they come out of the pit. I knew a man, called Joseph Cawthrey who sent a child in at 4 years old and there are many who go thrust behind at that time and many go at 5 and 6 but it is soon enough for them to go at 9 or 10. The sooner they go in the sooner their constitution is mashed up. I have been 13 hours in a pit since I have been here but 8 hours is plenty. The children went with us and came back with us. They worked as long as we did, The colliers and the children about here will be 12 hours from the time they go away till they come home. They could not addle a living if they were stinted to work 8 hours at present ages. The children don't get schooling as they ought to have. I cannot deny it. I cannot get the means. I have suffered from asthma and am regularly knocked up. A collier cannot stand the work regularly. We must stop now and then, or he would be mashed up before any time. We cannot afford to keep Collier Monday as we used to do.

Testimony of a collier, examined near Batley, 1841 in the Dewsbury Union

If Government keeps children out of the pits, they ought to provide something else for them to do. A child can't be made a collier of who doesn't begin before he is 13. It is not the age hurt them; it's the long irregular hours they work.

Accident at Messrs. Travis and Horsfalls, Barnsley

A loss of two lives occurred still more recently at Barnsley. Board gates ought to be always stopped up with puncheons. and notwithstanding the warning given to the children, the blame in this case attaches in my opinion, distinctly to the under steward for not at once, putting up puncheons, and for trusting even for one hour to a mere verbal warning, which every one acquainted with the heedlessness of collier children knows to be no precaution at all.

Accidents may be caused by the breaking of ropes. A month before the inspectors came to this area one of the ropes at Mr. Micklethwaite's colliery at Ardsley, near Barnsley, broke as two men were ascending, both were killed.

Testimony of John Micklethwaite, Esq., proprietor of the Oaks Colliery, Ardsley, near Barnsley, examined March 15th.

I entrust the entire management of the pit to an agent and I merely come and ride over here as an amusement and do not interfere with the pit at all. The coroner's inquest will give the best information about the rope being broken when two men were killed about 6th January. It is impossible to take any precaution against such accidents. There is not a doubt the rope broke through frost and there is no doubt the rope was sufficiently strong. I've never been in the pit and never will go. We have no children under eight or nine years as far as I know. I don't know whether there are lasses or not working in the pit but I must refer you for all information to the underground steward.

Wages

Wages were paid on a weekly basis, the wages of the men varying greatly with their industry and strength. For young able bodied men the average will be perhaps 20s. a week, but many make 25s. In the thin coal pits wages will be from 10 to 20 per cent less.

Education

With regard to the fruits of education and with respect even to the common truths of Christianity and facts of Scripture, I am confident that the majority are in a state of Heathen ignorance. The evidence of the children exhibits a picture of moral and mental darkness which must excite horror and grief in every Christian mind... Some are indeed better instructed but of those who work in collieries there is not above one out of three or, at most, two out of five, who can answer the commonest questions relative either to scriptural or secular knowledge. I unhesitatingly affirm that mining children, as a body, are growing up in a state of absolute and appalling ignorance... That their moral condition is not equally bad I attribute to the hard work they are subjected to, to their close confinement when at work, and to the weariness when work is over, and which often renders rest the greatest luxury. At the same time, as regards morals, there is a fearful amount of swearing and indecent language prevalent in coal pits.

Schools

The statistics of education, though they exhibit the meagreness of its extent, convey no adequate idea of its deficiency in quality. In nineteen out of twenty instances, the mind of the child is as much uninformed even after a couple of year's tuition as before it went to school. The notion is inveterately implanted in the mind of the great majority of the schoolmasters and schoolmistresses, that comprehension is no necessary part of instruction and others seem to imagine it a matter of intuition and are astonished that a child has not learned what it has never had the means of understanding. 'Have I not been preaching justification by faith, by the law of Moses, and setting forth the essence of the Godhead, this very morning?' exclaimed a Calvinist preacher and schoolmaster in a paroxysm of amazement of finding that a group of scholars could not explain who or what Christ was! The chances against a child are very great, first, there are the chances that the teacher does not, or cannot, put himself in the position of a child, to feel its ignorance and supply them, then, there is the chance that where apt instruction is given, the child's attention is not gained, and which the elliptical system of questioning is so admirably adapted to secure. It therefore follows that in the vast majority of cases child and teacher jog on in the established ruts, so ingeniously devised to avoid the exercise of mind and everything in the shape of instruction, save the mere mechanism of memory. From the tale of day schools, it appears that, according even to the return of the schoolmasters themselves, out of 1891 children at a school in different villages, not near one half can read the Testament and little above one third can write.

Chapter 6 – THE SECOND GENERATION

James Halloran (b. 1839) and Bridget Higgins 1842-1884/7 and family

By 1861, it would appear, Thomas and Judy's eldest son, James, now aged 26 (misnamed Thomas in the 1851 census) had married 'the girl next door', Bridget Higgins, aged 18 and born in Co. Mayo in 1842. They had married in late 1859 and he was down as head of family and working as a coal miner. This couple are Tom, John and Bill's grandparents, and the great grandparents of the authors. They had a baby boy, Thomas Halloran, aged 2 months, born in 1861 in Birstall. In the 1851 census we see Bridget had lived with her mother, Mary, as well as sisters and brother, with the Frain family in No. 89 Low Lane.

The English Census returns for 1861, showing James Halloran's family

They had set up house in Birstall, part of Gomersal township. The 1861 English Census indicates that they were living in 20 Gelderd Road (now part of the A62), a couple of miles from the Gomersal Colliery, Birstall, but close to the Boggard Pit, Upper Batley Lane. With a reputation for unsanitary conditions and the scene of so many epidemics, including typhus in 1842, cholera in 1849 and 1859, Gelderd Road should have been an area to avoid. However, this was to be the Irish 'ghetto' for some years to come. At least they now had some space. His parents, and younger brothers and sisters, were living nearby in Brownhill, officially part of Batley but close to the centre of Birstall and always seen as a part of Birstall. From the 159 Irish in 1851, there were now 378, of which 158 lived in the Gelderd Road area. Together with the 149 English who remained, over 300 were now living in the same accommodation that had housed 101 in 1841.

The 'nuisances', the shared dry toilets, and general unsanitary conditions were blamed for the high incidence of disease; some of these houses were still without sinks in 1905, many had dry 'privies' in 1911. Moves to improve the sanitation of Birstall were begun in June 1854. In 1863, Birstall was given autonomy to create its own water and sewerage systems with the local doctor instigating the changes. Dr Thomas Rayner was an extraordinary individual, instrumental in many changes in both sanitation and working conditions and later to become the Medical Health Officer for the area. We have already seen some of his evidence to the Children's Employment Commission of 1842. However it was ten years before a piped water system was built and much longer before the 'fearful death rate' in Birstall was improved with a decent sewerage system. Even in the 1950s, many houses still shared neighbourhood toilets.

James' sister Bridget, born in 1846, had died by 1861 but his mother had had another daughter in 1854 and given her the name Bridget, something that seemed to be a general tendency in the community. Although it was made compulsory to register births and deaths in 1837, it was not until fines were introduced in 1875 that it became universal and it is impossible to find out what happened to the first Bridget, or the many other registered and unregistered births and deaths at the time.

The 1871 census shows the family was at the same address at 20 Gelderd Road, but that James had not spent *all* his time mining or brawling! By now his family has grown and he has seven children, four boys and three girls. James was still a miner, but there were 4 children at school: Thomas (b. 1861) aged 11, James (b. 1863) aged 9, John (b. 1864) aged 7, and Michael (b. 1866) aged 5. Mary (b. 1867) aged 4, Ann (b. 1869) aged 2, and Catherine (3 months) were at home. As if that wasn't enough, there are also two lodgers: John Naifsy (30) a labourer and Thomas Stinton (20), a mason's labourer, the latter perhaps a relative of Hannah.

There was no Catholic school in Birstall at this time, but St. Mary's in Batley was opened in 1868 and the Birstall Catholics went there for schooling and church. There was a school somewhere in the Brownhill area and many 'Dame' schools existed though these are not clearly recorded. Other schools were denominational: the National School, built in 1818 and enlarged in 1848, was the main school in Birstall. A Wesleyan school was built in 1861 but it is not likely that these were used by the Catholic community.

THE HALLORANS FROM BIRSTALL AND AGHAMORE

Thomas probably did not start school until he was seven when he could go to Batley. Until the 1890s, school cost 1d per week.

The English Census returns for 1871, showing James Halloran's family

By the time St Mary's school was built, there was insufficient room for the Birstall children and land was owned by the community in Low Lane, so St Patrick's school was started in 1876, with a procession involving 1000 people and two brass bands; an obvious display of commitment and pride. The first inspection in 1878 reported an excellent start. By then there were 122 pupils with space for fifty more. The school doubled as a chapel initially, as the church was not built for another thirty years. There had been a Catholic priest in Batley since 1853 and eventually St Mary's was built in 1870. For a couple more generations, the Birstall Catholics walked to Batley for Mass and social activities until 1905 when the Bishop of Leeds decided that Birstall should be a separate parish, and St Patrick's church was built together with extensions to the school. A major benefactor was Miss Mortimer, the great-great granddaughter of the only post-reformation Catholic living in Birstall at 'The New Inn' in 1790. Her family, the Claphams who had owned pits in the Upper Batley Land area, were wealthy and Miss Mortimer ran a pawnshop in Cross Street (another growing Catholic area) and was the church organist.

Counterfeit coinage

However, all was certainly not education and religion in the family. The Criminal Registers of 1791-1892 for England & Wales, County of Yorkshire, West Riding in its return of all persons committed to appear for trial, indicates that James Halloran was convicted at Sheffield of 'Uttering counterfeit coin' and imprisoned for 12 months.

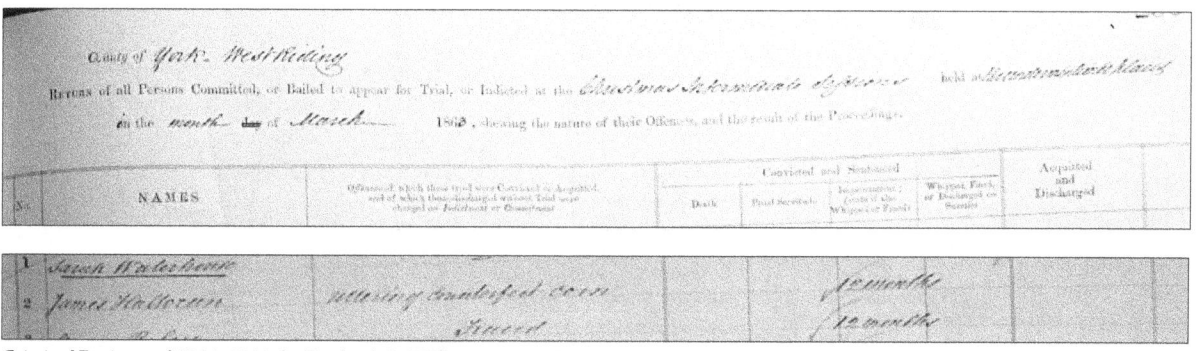

Criminal Registers of 1891-1892 for England & Wales

It is not clear why he was tried in Sheffield, as normally it would have been a case for Leeds or York magistrates. Perhaps the crime had been committed in Sheffield. The trial took place at the Christmas Sessions, in the month of March, 1863. He was about 28 at the time and his oldest son was a toddler and his son James was born that year, perhaps when he was in prison. John was born the following year. The offence of 'uttering counterfeit' coins can be distinguished from producing or diminishing coinage, the former involved forgery the latter involved filing, milling or colouring coins to create more coins or to sell the metal. Uttering coins involved putting them into circulation, usually knowingly. The relative leniency of the punishment suggests that he might have been a small player in a bigger operation. This idea is supported by the conviction of John Cuddy within three days at the court at York for 'feloniously

Chapter 6 – THE SECOND GENERATION

Halloran marriages and children of the second generation

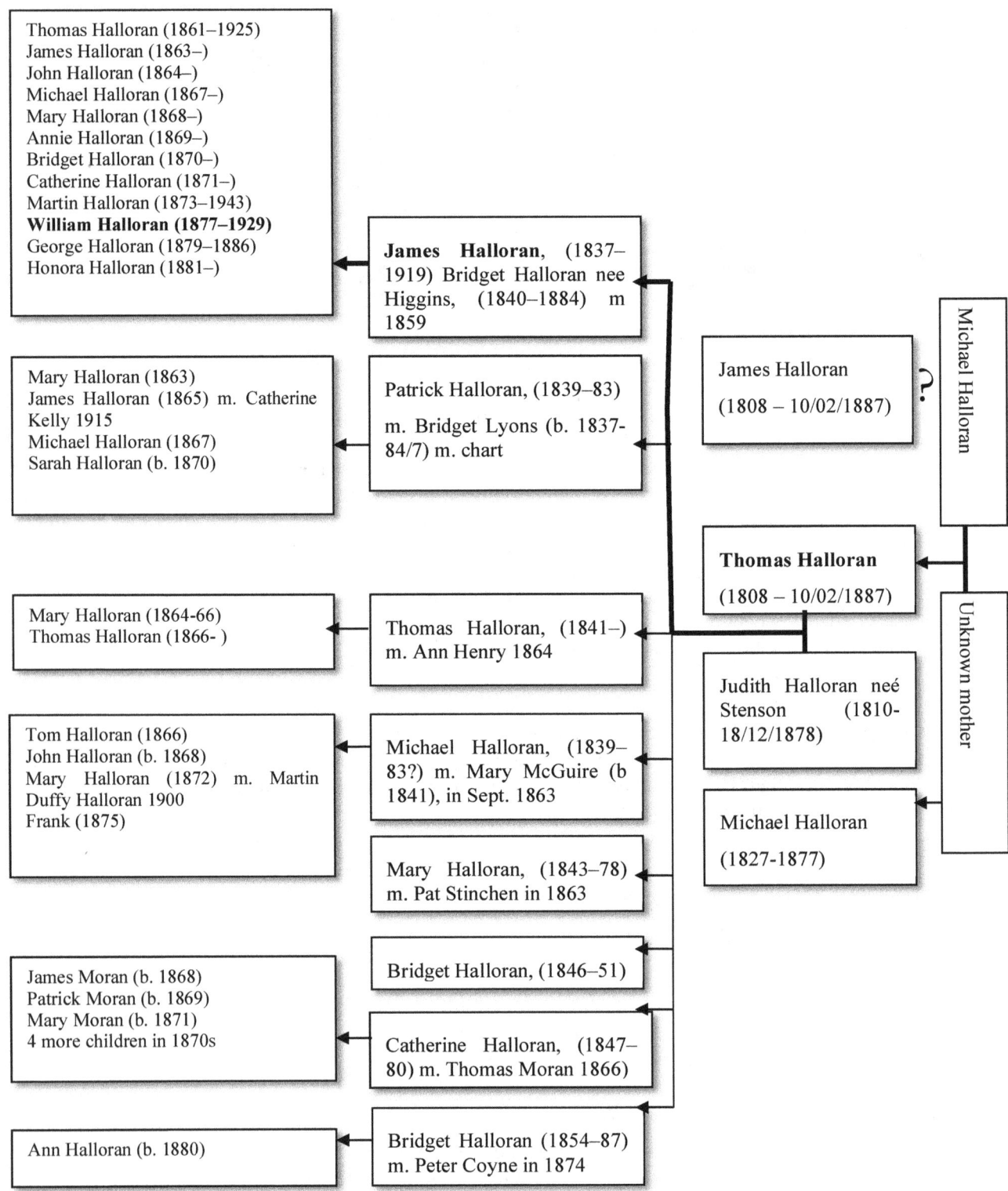

uttering counterfeit coin after a previous conviction for uttering counterfeit coin: also larceny'. His sentence was:

> 1st offence, 18 months hard labour. 2nd offence 2 months hard labour to commence on expiration of first imprisonment'.

He, presumably, was the father of Ellen who later married James's second son, James. Mary Hudson recalls Maggie and Nell, two of the Industrial Avenue aunts referring to their grandfather with a shudder: 'a dreadful man, a dreadful man!'

However James seemed to have no problem in resuming work as a miner after his year in prison; perhaps he did work for the Clapham family! By the 1881 census he was 44, and still a miner and the family had moved to Coach Lane. By this time Thomas 20 (b. 1861) was a miner too and James 18 (b. 1863), John 16 and Michael 15 were all coal hurriers. Mary 13, Annie 12, Catherine 10 and Martin 8 were at school. William 4 and George 2 were at home. By this time they had given up on lodgers, or perhaps the other way around!

The English Census returns for 1881, showing James Halloran's family

Their neighbour at No. 5 Coach Lane was a Hannah Holleran (b. 1841). She was the head of the house and aged 40. Her children were James, Hannah and Bridget. This would appear to be Michael Halloran's (b. 1827) widow. He had been among the original group who escaped the Great Famine with his elder brother Thomas and family. He had died at the age of 50, and the fact that she was James and Bridget's neighbour is presumably the family support system at work. Many of the men died young and the cause of death is not known. The 'Halloran heart' might be suspected but other diseases were rampant and the mining conditions resulted in a numbers of fatal accidents. There is no record of the family in the 1891 census.

1901

By 1901, James had moved to 113 Leeds Road. He was now 65, an age consistent with the 1861 census. He had left the mines and was a general labourer. Bridget had died in 1883, aged around 43, two years after having her eleventh child, which perhaps answers the question why she died young. Also living there were three of their sons: John (36); Michael (34), and William (24). All three were recorded as coal hewers. Also there was their youngest daughter, Honoria (Anorah), aged 20, who was a dressmaker and is recorded as working on her own account.

Mary had married Martin Duffy, another miner, and they had Anthony and Mary Ann and then Norah Theresa and Veronica after the turn of the century. Annie married Thomas Higgins, a miner, at the end of 1899 and Agnes and John were born to them by 1901.

Catherine (Kate) married Charles McCarthy. He also was a miner but his family, who had emigrated from Ireland to the US, returned when his brother, Eugene, was drowned and his mother could no longer cope without family support. They also lived in Farrah's Buildings, and their first children, Mary and Thomas, were born by 1901 whilst Annie, who married David Tully, and John were born in the 1900s. Martin

Chapter 6 – THE SECOND GENERATION

married Norah Sheridan in 1894 and had Katy (later Gavaghan who lived on Cambridge Road), George and Bridget. Annie was a great mate of the authors' Uncle Tom.

Patrick and Bridget Halloran (b. 1837) and family

Patrick, Thomas and Judy's second son, had also become a miner by 1871. He had travelled over from Ireland with his parents, having been about ten when the Great Famine started to devastate his homeland. The famine itself, the horrendous trip walking to Dublin and his parents' quest for work when they arrived in England must have ensured that his education, such as it was, had been thoroughly disrupted. He too married an Irish girl, Bridget Lyons (b. 1835), two years his junior. In 1871, they had four children before he died in 1883, age 46. These were Mary (b. 1863) aged 8, James (b. 1865) aged 6, Michael (b. 1867) aged 4, and Sarah (b. 1870) aged 1. They lived in Chandler Alley, near Partick's uncle Michael's family in Church St. Their nearest neighbours were the Duffys and Prendergasts from Mayo and the Walkers who were born locally.

Despite having four very young children, Bridget was reported as being a mill operative. Also, all the children, but Sarah, were 'scholars', so presumably at school.

The English Census returns for 1871, showing Patrick Halloran's family

Michael and Mary Halloran (b. 1839) and family

In 1871, Michael, the forth son of Thomas and Judy and James' younger brother, was already married to Mary McGuire, also born in Ireland, and had two young sons - Tom (b. 1866) aged 5, and John (b. 1868), aged 3. Michael was a miner and Mary a 'birler' (i.e. 'burler'), that is she removed burls or small knots from finished cloth. Interestingly, Tom at 5 was at school. This family also lived in Brownhill, at number 181. Michael also died young, probably in 1883 - Mary is described as a widow on the 1891 census.

The English Census returns for 1871, showing Michael Halloran's family

THE HALLORANS FROM BIRSTALL AND AGHAMORE

The English Census returns for 1881, showing Michael Halloran's family

In 1881 Michael and his family had moved to 108 Crop Street, Gomersal. Their first daughter, Mary had been born in 1872 and another son Frank in 1875. Thomas and John, now 16 and 13 respectively, were horse drivers in a coal pit.

Their neighbours were Murphys and the parents were born in Ireland. There was a household of Irish lodgers; however, there was also a Bennet from Derby and the Walshs. We notice that, though the Irish predominate in the area, it is not exclusively Irish, though the Irish households are the most crowded.

This family had a number of cousins, children of Michael and Mary McGuire: There were Thomas, John and then Mary and Frank, born in the early 1870s. Mary later married Martin Duffy and perhaps this is the link with the Bradford Duffy family who were close to Tom, John and William in the 20th century.

Of James' (1839-1919) other brothers and sisters we have only sketchy records. Thomas (1841–?) married Ann Henley 1864. They had Mary in 1865, but she seems to have died in March 1866. Their son, Thomas was born later in the same year, but we have no further record of him.

Rag pickers at the turn of the century, Bridget Kelly, Betty Halloran's mother, front, second from left

Work, health and accidents

By the 1871 and 1881 censuses, more Irish workers had flocked to Birstall, no doubt informed by Mayo relatives and previous neighbours of the employment opportunities. The 1871 census reflects the growing population. Many families on this census had children born in the 1850s, in Ireland, but most of those of the 1860s were born in Birstall.

In 1872, Briar Mill opened, followed by the Providence Mill and then Printworks and many of the Irish worked in these. The women were almost all employed as 'rag-pickers', sorting out the huge amounts of rags arriving from all over Europe, for reprocessing.

There were pit accidents to add to the death toll from diseases. Disaster funds were set up following major, newsworthy disasters. However, individual accidents usually attracted little outside attention. Following a disaster, collections in churches, donations from mine owners and major donations from local miners created a fund from which a widow and children would receive starvation wages. The nearest hospital was the Infirmary in Leeds. However, local women practised as midwives and an herbalist worked from his house on Low Lane. In 1877 in Batley, Michael Spedding took over from his father-in-law, Joseph Fox, as a bone setter. Most working families could not or would not pay for a doctor. When a roof fall occurred in a pit, they would 'send for the Batley bonesetter'. Meanwhile his wife and daughter

Chapter 6 – THE SECOND GENERATION

were producing biscuits and brandy snaps to develop Fox's Biscuits, which was eventually to supersede the mills as Batley's biggest employer. In 1786 a new hospital had been built in Dewsbury, mostly run by local doctors. A cottage hospital followed in Batley in 1883.

Transport had improved with the building of the tramway from Dewsbury to Birstall, which opened in July 1874. The trams were horse drawn but five years later a fleet of thirteen 'steamers' were operating in the area, though at first a man with a red flag *and* a horse drawn tram had to lead the way. Eventually, the passengers, paying money into a small wooden box, could make the round trip to Dewsbury in one and a half hours. At the turn of the century these were replaced by electric trams.

When money was plentiful, people of Birstall were able to take advantage of the improved railway routes and visit the seaside. A line connected Birstall to Batley and another was reached by climbing the 70 steps on Gelderd Road, or getting to Mount Top, to Upper Birstall Station. Some of the mills organised a day's outing for all their employees, setting off at 5:30 and returning late at night.

The Birstall 'feast' was celebrated towards the end of August. Every town in the area had weekend when the mills closed. This soon lengthened to include Mondays and Tuesdays. Fairground rides and stalls would appear in the ancient fairground. There were hoopla stalls offering china and cheap glassware as prizes. Toffee apples were a great attraction and young men would demonstrate their strength by pulling swing ropes, hoisting their screaming girlfriends into the air. Families got together for birthdays and even wakes, using any excuse for a party, to which people, of course, brought their own cups and plates.

The Morley pit mine disaster

There were many pit accidents over this period, and as nearly all the Halloran men were miners, these must have impacted greatly of the families. The mining conditions in Yorkshire were particularly bad with inflammable gas and poor ventilation being common hazards. As the seams were less than 30 inches high, miners often had to work lying down. Mining was a constant battle to survive. Some mines would only pay for minimum sized lumps of coal, the rest not being counted in pay calculations. Pay was particularly bad in Yorkshire as it was assumed that wives could find work in the mills. With miners being paid only for the coal produced and not for the time they worked, there were inevitably cuts in safety. Pillars of coal had to be left to bear the roof, but the safer the pillar, the smaller the pay! There were many deaths and injuries from roof falls or being crushed by 'corves' of dug coal. The risk of fire was high, as early miners needed candles for light. Even after the introduction of the safety lamp, fire was needed below shafts to create airflow. Even when naked flames were banned, controlled explosions were used to blast down coal. There was no compensation for accidents or loss of life. The pit owner who paid for the funerals of his employees in the Thornhill disaster at Dewsbury was seen as a great benefactor.

Headline story in the London Illustrated News

However, such disasters evoked a great community response, especially among the families of coalminers. A striking example was the explosion at Morley Main Colliery that took place on Monday the 7th of October 1872. The mine itself had been opened in 1855. Two shafts had been sunk to depths of 120 and 150 yards. Thirty-four miners lost their lives during this disaster, which made front-page news on national weekly newspapers. The inquest took place at the Royal Hotel and it was brought to the notice of the coroner that the miners had almost certainly been smoking during their shifts. Apparently, this was a normal occurrence and one of the deceased miners had an empty packet of matches in his hand.

This disaster resulted in a great upsurge of community support. Volunteers worked in hazardous conditions to bring up the bodies. The majority of the miners had died of suffocation, as the explosion had destroyed the ventilation system in that part of the mine, hampering the work of bringing the bodies to the surface. The disaster left 26 widows and 40 fatherless children. Neighbours and those from surrounding districts helped raise money and supported the families. The pit head was at the side of Albert Road and close to the Miners Arms. The colliery was last worked on 23rd of July 1909[1].

The Cooperative Society was a major donor to the Morley Fund. The widows were awarded a weekly 5 shillings and plus 6d per child from the disaster fund. One widow was given £5 to allow her to return to Ireland. With rents of around 3 shillings per week, bread at 1 penny for a large loaf and butter at 1 shilling 9 pennies per pound, eggs at 1 shilling per dozen, bacon at 1 shilling per pound, cheese at 11 pence per pound, their life styles must have been most frugal. The owners, William Ackroyd & Brothers of Birkenshaw, also gave support.

During the 1870s and 1880s, with an increase in union support, owners began to agree to miners' demands for a reduction in the working day to eight hours, subsidising coal to miners' families and eventually to increases of pay to 15 shillings per ton of coal dug.

In 1882, another accident occurred in Bruntcliffe. In 1879 and 1892 there were accidents in Dewsbury and in 1893 there was an explosion in Thornhill, which resulted in the deaths of 139 miners. More accidents occurred around Wakefield (eight miles away) at this time, notably in Stanley, Middleton and Lofthouse. However, many small incidents were left unrecorded, though these involved, in total, thousands more deaths and maiming accidents. From 1840 to 1970 200,000 miners died, the vast majority before the turn of the century. Between 1881 and 1909, 3300 men died in Yorkshire mines alone. With the extra hazards from inhaling coal dust, as well as Yorkshire having a reputation for pits being 'gasometers, the fieriest in England', it is not surprising that there were 'no old miners in Yorkshire'.

Women in the mills

For the women, working in the mills offered the chance to make some money to contribute to household expenses and gave them some independence. However, the women in the Halloran families and throughout the Irish community were often 'rag sorters', as described in the census returns, but 'rag pickers' in their own terms. Rags were brought to the local rail stations from around the world. At a time when nothing was wasted, nothing discarded, the state of the filthy, verminous, flea infected rags can hardly be imagined. As the huge bundles were brought in, unwanted items were removed. Then each individual piece was felt by the women, who could identify every type of cloth and type of weave and sort them for the most appropriate process. For this, a weekly wage of 6/- was paid, in the 1860s, though male weavers could earn £1:2:0.

Nonetheless, the development of factories, especially in the textile industry where the vast majority of workers were women, was the start of the great process of transformation of women's place in society, giving them a role valued, if exploited, in the in the developing industrial economy.

Sorting rags

---

1 http://www.wakefieldfhs.org.uk/morleyfhg/Morleymining%20disaster.htm

Chapter 7 – THE THIRD GENERATION

The third generation - Birstall

The usual practice among new Irish immigrants to Britain was to disembark from the ship, move to an Irish ghetto and then to disperse to other areas. However, a surprising number of the Irish immigrants remained and established a stable, clearly defined community in Birstall. The 1860s and 1870s saw the emergence of the third generation of the Irish community that had originated in Aghamore. The stable employment offered by the coalmines and woollen mills was no doubt responsible for this.

Thomas Halloran (1861-1925) m. Ann Brennan (1867-1932)
- John Halloran (1889-1921)
- Mary Halloran (1892-1916)
- Phelim Halloran (1892-1960)
- Anne Halloran (1894-94)
- Ellen Halloran (1896-1971)
- Ann Halloran (1900-1966)
- Thomas Halloran (1902-1969)
- Francis Halloran (1906-1969)
- Honora Halloran (1909-1979)

James Halloran (1863-1911) m. Ellen Cuddy
- John Halloran (1888-)
- William Halloran (1891-1940)
- Mary Halloran (1893-1954)
- Ann Halloran (1894-1953)
- Thomas (1895 -95)
- Margaret Halloran (1898-1967)
- James Halloran (1901-1962)
- Ellen Halloran (1904-1969)
- Henry 1905-05
- Joseph Halloran (1907-1975)

John Halloran (1865) m. Mary Gillespie 1909?

Michael Halloran (1866) m. Mary Duffy 1901

Mary Halloran (1867) m. Martin Duffy 1901

Annie Halloran (1869) m. Thomas Higgins

Catherine Halloran (1871) m. Charles McCarthy
- John McCarthy (1905-1969)
- Annie McCarthy (1902 1969)

Martin Halloran (1872-1943) m. Norah Sheridan (1875) in 1894
- Catherine Halloran (1895–1979)
- George Halloran (1896–)
- Bridget Halloran (1899–)

William Halloran (1876-1925) m. Elizabeth neé Prendergast (1866-1948)
- **James Halloran (1905–1905)**
- **Thomas Halloran, (1908–1975)**
- **John Halloran, (1911–1990)**
- **William Halloran, (1913–1972)**
- **Bernard Halloran, (1916–1922)**

George Halloran (1879-86)

Honorah Halloran (1881-?) m. Stephen Frain
- Mary Frain

Parents: James Halloran (1839-1919) and Bridget Halloran neé Higgins (1842-1884)

THE HALLORANS FROM BIRSTALL AND AGHAMORE

The security of regular employment for adults and children appears to have perpetuated the practice of early marriage and large families, practices that their land-starved cousins in Aghamore had to abandon. We know James and Bridget had a family of eleven children and their history will be traced in this chapter. We will try to outline what is known about them, including their ninth child, William. He and his sons Tom, John and Bill's father will be the subject of chapter 8.

By the 1880s, money must have been easier as sons James, John and Patrick were miners alongside their father, the first two at the coalface and the younger two as hurriers. It was the practice of all children at to pass their wages to their parents until they left home.

However, the family must have been completely devastated in 1884 when Bridget died, aged 45, leaving Honora, 3, George, 5, William, 7, Martin, 11 and the girls Catherine, Annie and Mary in their early teens. Bridget must have been an extraordinary woman. She gave birth to eleven children in twenty years and, unlike in previous generations and the experience of many of the contemporary neighbouring families, all seem to have survived. However, her death was followed two years later by that of her youngest son, George, at the age of about 7. William would have been about 10 at the time. His experience of the death of a younger brother was mirrored in the following generation when his three sons, Tom, John and Bill experienced the death of their young brother, Bernard, when he was only six.

It is difficult to imagine how these early deaths were coped with. The support of a community of relations and friends was undoubtedly essential. It seems likely that Thomas and Judy, living nearby in Brownhill in 1871, were a source of support. However, they were 63 and 61 respectively at that time. Judy was to die on December 18th 1878, aged 68. Thomas outlived her by eight years – his death is recorded as on 7th February, 1887 when he must have been 79.

Thomas, unusually for that time, left a will, with James as sole executor. Amazingly, after a lifetime as a labourer, agricultural labourer or 'hawker', he had managed to leave £125, equivalent to £9000 in today's money. It is difficult to imagine how Thomas could leave any money at a time when a miner, considered well paid, was perhaps able to earn £1:10:0 per week. Thomas earned considerably less than this as an agricultural labourer, and made a living simply 'hawking' for perhaps twenty years. Could there be a connection between the charges in 1863 against James and John Cuddy of 'Uttering Counterfeit Coin'? Perhaps! However, it is not untypical, that where there has been great poverty - and James would have remembered the Great Famine and known great want as a child – the need to save becomes a great imperative. It is often the only way to lessen the risk of an early death or destitution.

Thomas was the son of a subsistence farmer who had experience the failure of the land to support his family. He had seen his neighbours and perhaps members of his family die of starvation, not because of lack of food but because of the lack of the means to purchase it. It is little wonder therefore that a determined man, mindful of his family's welfare, would put his faith in accumulating cash while his contemporaries in Ireland strove for their rights as tenants and particularly the right to own the land they worked.

1890s: hard times

However, the 1890s saw a slump in the mining industry. The fact that all six of James' sons were miners, - as were his three sons-in-law - meant they were very dependent on the coal mines and were probably not in a position to help each other out. However, most of the family (with the exceptions of Thomas, James and Martin) did not marry until the later 1890s, towards their thirties and after the mining slump. Therefore without children they avoided, perhaps by necessity, the worst problems of that time.

As in Ireland, the only alternative to support within families was the 'workhouse'. There had been a workhouse in Birstall since the late 1700s but an Act of Parliament in 1834 cut money for occasional outdoor relief and made the conditions and discipline of the workhouse such that they would be 'a terror to the poor and prevent them from entering'. This same legislation had had a profound effect in Ireland at the time of the Great Famine, as we saw in chapter 2. There was huge opposition to this legislation, led by Feargus O'Connor, a Leeds journalist, with a protest rally of 200,000 people, leading ultimately to the Chartist movement. Nevertheless, a new workhouse Union for the Dewsbury area was built. Typically, its procedures were draconian, including separating families by sending the men to Dewsbury, the women to Birstall and children to Batley. Cold showers were enforced on entry, whatever the weather. Men were

Chapter 7 – THE THIRD GENERATION

forced to walk to and from Birstall to register in Dewsbury, and only then were they allowed entry to the Birstall workhouse.

Instead of building fever hospitals, the ratepayers of Birstall voted to keep those sick from disease, 'isolated' in the workhouse, posing, of course a risk to others there. The offer was: 'aired water and bread for breakfast, bread water and ½ oz. of cheese for dinner and more bread and water for tea before being sent to bed (a plank) at 6'clock'. There was no alternative outside help, and so there was no possibility of parish help, especially for the Irish. We have already seen how the workhouse had been a last resort for the starving during the Great Famine. Many could not face the shame involved, the way it split up families and the fact that it was often the source of disease and death.

The family members must have supported each other. Though there were many charities set up in Birstall these were mostly run by religious organisations and involved Church of England attendance. The St Vincent de Paul was, of course, a possibility for Catholic families, but stories handed down seem to point to the Halloran family being proudly self-contained. There was a union, which was mostly a mutual insurance for injured miners. In 1874, soon after the Morley disaster, a branch of the West Yorkshire Miners Association was set up at the Horse and Jockey. Union members could get sick-and-accident pay of 10 shillings per week and widows would receive 4 shillings a week with 1 shilling for children under 12. Strike pay was also available, and hopefully the miners in the Halloran family were members, as accidents were regular and disputes were to arise some years later.

Picking for coal in Morley

Early in the 1890s, there was a slow-down in the economy and the miners were asked to take a 25% pay cut. The mine owners, had, of course, discouraged unions almost as much as they resisted safety measures, and some even paid less to union members. There were no national agreements until the next century and pay varied from area to area and mine to mine. Often after an agreement on the pay for a corf of coal, the owner would increase the size of the corves. The unions began to employ 'weighmen' in collieries and this substantially increased wages, by up to 25%. But owners got together to impose a large pay cut when demand was low. The miners had asked for an eight-hour day and payment of a 'living wage' rather than one based on fluctuating coal prices. The miners refused to accept the 25% cut and were eventually 'locked out'. Months of great hardship followed, often the only meals coming from soup kitchens and meals for children in schools, and no coal supply for the gas works or the mills, all of which had to close. Families were reduced to searching for coal to warm their homes.

Union members had some union support but a total lock-out meant that all suffered. Things became bitter at White Lea Pit and at Bruntcliffe, which was at this stage the nearest to the Halloran homes. In one incident in Morley, 5,000 miners marched to the pit on being told that deputies were drawing coal and caused a considerable amount of damage when the manager drew a gun. This particular dispute was the greatest in Britain with 300,000 miners from Yorkshire and the Midlands refusing to accept the 25% cut. It was to last for 17 weeks before hunger, cold and 'the highest infant mortality rate ever recorded' drove them back to work with few concessions and without having secured the principle of 'a living wage'.

Despite the hardship experienced by the miners and their families, there was a gradual increase in prosperity. Birstall had several small shops in Gelderd Road and Coach Lane but most were in the centre of the town, then the lower Middlegate area, stretching from the Coach and Six up to Cross Street. A market had been held where Middlegate widened out and another outside the New Inn at Cross Street. In the 1890s, plans were made to develop a new centre at the part of Low Lane below Middlegate and Cross Street. With the rise of the 'Co-op' movement, six smaller shops had been built around Birstall, with a large one to follow in the centre.

By this stage many of the Irish families were living in Cross Street and Back Cross Street, with still the same pattern of small 'cots' – one-bedroom houses built around an earth yard with a shared earth toilet or midden. Other houses had been built in terraces, often 'back-to-backs', or 'one-up-and-one-downs'. These usually had a 'ginnel' in the middle of the terrace so that the back yards could be accessed. The front houses, in back-to-backs, or the fronts of bigger homes, were close to the road, possibly with a tiny front garden. Life happened in the back yards though, with their outdoor privies and washing lines - areas where children played and families chatted. Chandler's Hill and Chandler's Alley were in a poor area, close to Cross Street.

The Catholic Church

From having virtually no presence in the area in the mid-nineteenth century, the Catholic Church grew steadily throughout the second half of the nineteen century and became firmly established. The repeal of penal laws against Catholics had started in 1778 and this had culminated in the repeal of the Test and Corporation Acts in 1828 and the granting of Emancipation in 1829, largely due to Daniel O'Connell's political campaigning in Ireland. The Episcopal hierarchy was re-established in 1850 with the establishment of bishoprics and parishes as well as the building of churches and schools; a necessary consequence of the arrival of so many Irish Catholics. Stories have been passed down among the Irish community of how, in the early days of their arrival, the Irish walked to Leeds or Wakefield on Sundays to the nearest Catholic churches.

In 1841, a priest was appointed for the parish of St Paulinus, in Dewsbury, and the first mass was celebrated in a rented room with 300 in attendance. In 1853, St Mary's parish was established in Batley when the first resident priest arrived[1]. It was the 4th parish established in the area. For the next 17 years services the priests and people struggled to find the means to build a church. Although land was bought in 1861, it was not until late in 1869 that Batley's first Roman Catholic Church, St Mary of the Angels, was completed. It was opened on December 15th 1870 by Archbishop, later Cardinal Manning. This church is still in existence[2].

In the Bishop's visitation to Batley of 1870, the records state that the Church also owned land at Birstall on which there was a shop and house and four cottages. Documents held at the diocesan archive, dated 7th December 1870, describe the land as 'all that messuage or dwelling house and shop site at Low Lane End in Birstall with garden, yard and land ... and also 4 cottages or dwelling houses situated in Birstall.' It further stated 'that this land was to be held in trust for the premises built there to be used as the site of the Church, Chapel or place of religious worship, a site for a school and dwelling house and for any other purpose which the Trustees might think fit for the benefit of the RC congregation[3].'

The bulk of the flock, consisting mainly of Irish immigrants and their descendants, resided in Batley and Birstall. In fact, as we have seen, Thomas and his family lived in 90 Low Lane in 1851. Although the Parish covered Batley, Birstall, West Ardsley, Morley, Gildersome, Gomersal and White Lee, all of the parishioners were within four miles of the church.

---

1 http://www.stmarybatley.co.uk/about%20us.html

2 http://en.wikipedia.org/wiki/Batley

3 http://www.birstallstpatrick.org.uk/history.htm

Chapter 7 – THE THIRD GENERATION

Low Lane, Birstall 1910

Ordinance Survey Map of 1882 – 1892

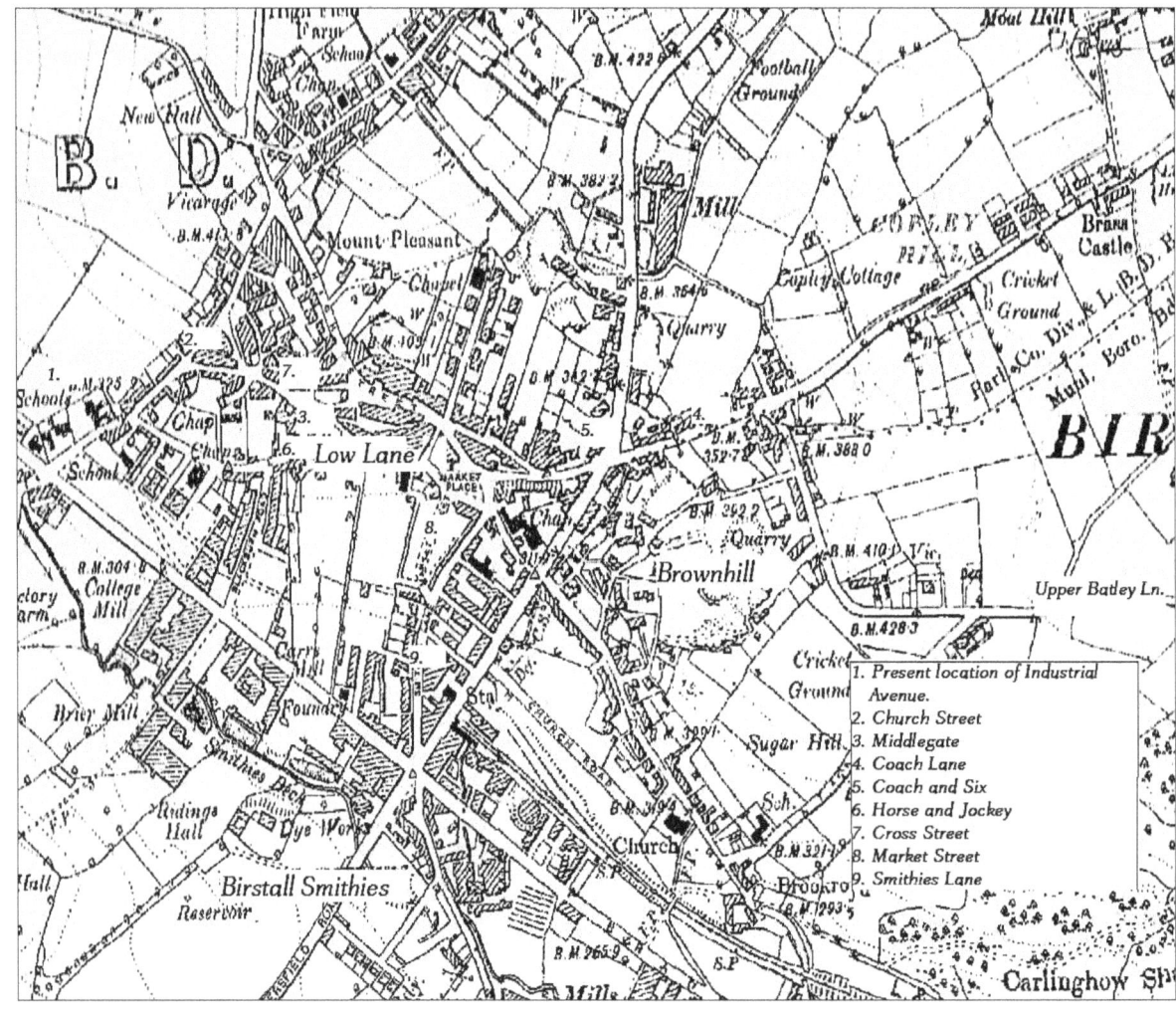

1. Present location of Industrial Avenue.
2. Church Street
3. Middlegate
4. Coach Lane
5. Coach and Six
6. Horse and Jockey
7. Cross Street
8. Market Street
9. Smithies Lane

THE HALLORANS FROM BIRSTALL AND AGHAMORE

Thomas Halloran (1861-1925) and Ann Brennan (1867-1932) and family

In 1887, Thomas, James' eldest son, married Ann Brennan (1867-1932), who was born in Staffordshire, of Irish parents. He had moved to Morley to work, no doubt at the largest Morley Main pit, where earlier disaster had struck in 1872. They had nine children, creating another branch of the family in Morley.

It is reported that Thomas, though born in Birstall, had a strong Irish accent throughout his life. At some point he went to Chicago, and looked at the possibilities of staying, but returned to the wonders of Morley. Perhaps he had joined other members of the family who had emigrated to Chicago, as some had disappeared from Birstall over the years.

Thomas' eldest son, John, died in tragic circumstances in 1921, aged 32, leaving seven young children, the twins Margaret and Thomas being only a few months old. It appears that Mary, his 5-year-old daughter, was nearly adopted by his younger brother William (1876-1925) and Lizzy, his wife, as a sister for Tom, John and Bill – a story discussed in the next chapter.

In traditional Halloran fashion, his widowed wife Ann and children went to live with Thomas and Ann and their son Phelim. Phelim apparently was the family hope; alone in the family, he had been educated in Batley Grammar School and had a good job as an accountant. One of Thomas' grandsons, John, son of Francis, was to become the Medical Officer of Health in Bradford. The rest of the family included the usual collection of successfully educated teachers.

Thomas Halloran and son Francis taken about 1917

James Halloran (1862/3-1911) and Ellen Cuddy and family

1891 English census returns for James Halloran (1863-1911) and family

1891

James was William's second eldest brother. We find him living at 223 Partington Square, Birstall, in 1891. This was a slum area between Bradford Road and the town centre on Low Lane. He was married to Ellen Cuddy (b. 1866) and they had two children at this stage: John (b. 1889) aged 2 and Willie (b. 1891) who was only seven months. He and his boarder, Patrick Cuddy (Ellen's elder brother by five years), were both coal miners. Patrick had been born in Ireland.

Typically of this tight, closely-knit community, Ellen's father, John, lived next door at 225. He seems to have had a string of minor convictions over previous years, including the escapade involving counterfeit coinage mentioned in the previous chapter. With him were Margaret and Ellen, 22-year old twins. He had been widowed for many years by this time; he was recorded in the 1871 census with five children, the twin girls being only two at that time.

Chapter 7 – THE THIRD GENERATION

1901

By the time of the 1901 English census, James and Ellen were still living in 3 Partington Square with six children: John (b. 1889) aged 12, Willie (b. 1891) aged 10, Mary (b. 1902/3) aged 8, Ann (b. 1903/4) aged 7, Margaret (b. 1908/9) aged 2, and James (b. 1910) aged 10 months. James was described as a 'coal hewer - below ground'. Ellen presumably worked at home and the children would all have been at school. Margaret, referred to as Maggie, was remembered as physically disabled.

1901 English census returns for James Halloran (1863-1911) and family

The family continued to grow with the birth of Nell in 1902, Henry in 1905 and Joe in 1909. Sadly Henry died as a baby.

They moved to 11 Industrial Avenue, a terrace near St Patrick's. Tragically, Ellen died soon after Joe was born, in 1909, and then James died in 1911 leaving eight orphaned children. Ellen's two sisters moved in to bring up the family, one going out to work and one staying at home. Maggie, the crippled daughter, rarely left the house but remembered her aunt looking out of the window at the view of White Lea and saying how she would love to see what it was like up there, so far away – though in fact it was only two miles away! From a modern perspective, this seems to be an amazing sacrifice but it was just accepted by all concerned. The rest of the family, especially William, Tom, John and Bill's father, helped support the family of cousins. At this stage, two of the sons, John and Willy, were already mining. When Willy married, he lived in the house next door at 9 Industrial Avenue and had one son James. He married but had no descendent

John married Gertrude Walker in 1918 and had a daughter Eileen, who was later the sister-in-charge of children's department in St James' Hospital, Leeds. Sadly aged 19, during a bout of flu, Eileen had an argument with her fiancé, Tony Dagnall. She remained unmarried until they met again when they were 57, a meeting that led to their marriage. She died 9 years later.

Eileen is one of the first examples of a member of this family of immigrants achieving a successful career outside the narrow confines of the pits and mills. She had been an assistant in Woolworths until opportunities were thrown open for young women by World War One when she went into nursing.

Their second son, Willy, went on to marry May Clifford. They had a boy, James, born on the 30 April 1927. Considered the founder of British Mass Communications Research, he had a brilliant academic career, finishing his days as Emeritus Professor in Leicester University. He died on 16 May 2007 and one of his many obituaries is reproduced on the following page.

Michael Halloran (1866-25) and John (b. 1865)

There are no records found of marriages for James' sons, Michael or John. They were still at home with James on the 1891 census, as 34 and 36-year old bachelors. There are marriage records of Michael and John Halloran, however these are attributed to other branches of the family. We know a Michael married Mary Ann Gillespie in 1909 but whether this is James' son is very uncertain.

Similarly, we can find no definite marriage records of Mary and Ann. However, there are possible death records.

In memoriam James D. Halloran (1927-2007)[1] David E. Morrison (edited)

Professor James Dermot Halloran's death on 16 May 2007 sees the departure of a remarkable man. He was, without doubt, the founding father of British Mass Communications Research, a position secured through his establishment of the Centre for Mass Communications Research at the University of Leicester.

James, or Jim as everybody knew him, was born into a strongly Catholic working class family in 1927 in West Yorkshire. His father was a trade union official, and all his relatives worked, when they were in employment that is, in the mines and factories. To be brought up in such circumstances, and at such a time, was to breathe the air of trade unionism and the politics of organised labour.

Debate with his father over socialist issues was common; indeed, often heated. He informed me that in youthful righteousness he had once called his father, 'a bosses' man'. What is for sure is that the poverty that he witnessed in the recession years of the thirties was formative on the critical stance that he took to social and communicative questions. Although poor he was always quick to point out that everyone in his area was, and that his family was never desperately poor as in the case of some of his school friends...

To understand the social and political circumstances of his early life is to understand much about Jim's no-nonsense approach to social questions... He was often scathing of cultural and media studies scholars with what he saw as their involvement with the trivia of social arrangements, and their often glorification of working class life. Had he not been an academic, Jim could have been a hard bitten union official... Indeed, he was a 'fixer', or to put it somewhat more politely, a good political operator...

Jim had gained a BSC in Sociology and Economics from the University of Hull in 1951, and had briefly been a school teacher and a prison tutor when he joined the University of Leicester in 1958 as Senior Tutor in the Department of Adult Education. ... He was persuaded to write up his lecture notes by the editor of a radical Catholic Journal, *Doctrine and Life*, whom he had met by chance. Published in Dublin, he wrote around eight articles, which were then taken up by a left wing radical publisher in England, Sheed and Ward, and produced as *Control or Consent: A Study of the Challenge of Mass Communications* in 1963.

He [Jim] saw to it that an appropriate institutional structure for the study of mass communications was created, namely, by developing the Leicester Centre for Mass Communications Research..[O]ne might consider that the newness of the venture attracted a certain type of individual ready to commit to this emerging academic field – it was many years before there were any university posts in mass communications, and hence somewhat of a risk for those who, so to speak, signed up with Jim…

On the International scene his legacy lives on in the thriving and important International Association of Mass Communications Research (IAMCR).

Jim died in hospital surrounded by his family... [W]e remember him as a great figure in mass communications research, and as a man who had an enormous zest for life.

On my last visit to him in hospital he recounted how as a schoolboy in Leeds he had at the cricket nets faced up to one of the all time great English fast bowlers, Fred Trueman. Jim was no match. One of Trueman's hurled balls hit him and broke his toe. It was with massive pride that Jim said: 'Freddie Trueman broke my toe'.

David E. Morrison, Professor of Communications Research, University of Leeds. Editor's note: Jim Halloran was a colleague of WACC in the 1970s and 1980s. In particular he advised on two research projects - an exploratory survey of media and its developmental role in Indonesia and Zambia, and later a study of mass media and village life in India. Ever sharply critical, he could always be relied upon to separate the wheat from the chaff. But his apparently blunt exterior concealed a warmth, generosity and conviviality that readily emerged under the influence of a good malt whiskey.

---

1 WACC, http://www.waccglobal.org/en/20073-media-and-terror/458-In-memoriam-James-D-Halloran-1927-2007.html

Chapter 7 – THE THIRD GENERATION

Nonetheless, in searching for records of Michael, an interesting link with Ireland was discovered. In 1891 a Michael Halloran was lodging in Birstall with Martin Lyons and family. Michael married Mary McCarthy in 1892. His marriage record gives his father's name as "Patrick". Baptism records show that they had five children in rapid succession: Margaret, Thomas, James, John and Mary. However, by the 1901 census, only Michael, by that time a widower, and two sons, James and John were living with the Lyons families. This census gives his place of birth as "Raith, Ireland". It is highly likely that this is Patrick Halloran and Catherine Tigue Halloran's son, Michael who was baptised on 13th Dec 1868 in Aghamore, Co. Mayo, and who lived in Raith (Rath) (see chapter 10). However the death of a Michael Halloran is recorded in 1925 in the Batley Workhouse. These records indicate the date of birth as around 1867, which strongly suggests this is the same Michael who left Aghamore in quest of a better life, only to die alone and in poverty in England.

Interestingly, his son John must be the John who tried to enlist into the British army in 1916, in Galway and was discharged a little later for falsifying his age.

The First World War made a huge difference to the Industrial Avenue family. Willy, John and James were called up, though Willy was discharged in 1816 due to a gunshot wound to his hand which resulted in 30% disablement. He also had problems with his eyes.

The sisters talks of 'lost loves' during the war, too, and most remained unmarried, except for Mary who married in 1921 and had two children, James and Ellen, in 1922 and 1925. However both these children died within a few weeks of birth; it is not surprising, therefore, that she is found in photos sitting on a deck-chair with Betty Halloran on Mothers' Union day sea-side trips, watching young Mary and Bernard play in the sand.

Martin Halloran (1872-1943) and Norah Sheridan (1875) and family

By the 1901 census, Martin was aged 28 and married to Nora née Sheridan (b 1875) who was 26. They had three children, Catherine (b. 1895) aged 6, George (b. 1897) aged 4, and Bridget (b. 1899) aged 2. They lived in 98 Cross Street. Martin also worked in the mines and was recorded as a coal hewer.

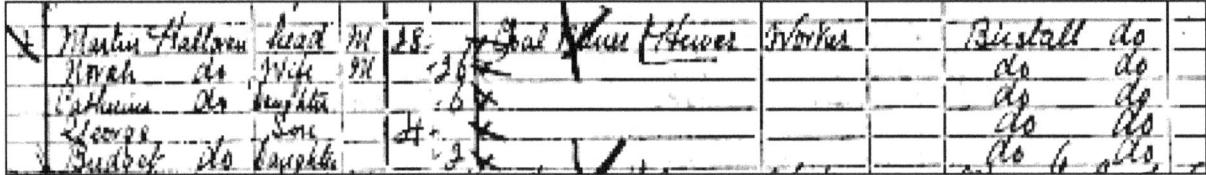

English census returns of 1901 for Martin Halloran (1872-1943) and family

Martin's eldest daughter, Katie, married James Gavaghan and they had four children: Nora, Mary, James, and Ellen. These were first cousins of Tom, John and Bill, with whom they were close. Mary kept in touch with Tom and Bill from Omaha, Nabraska, after she married an American G.I. Ellen used to baby-sit Bill's children in 11 King's Drive, Birstall, before starting a large family of her own.

Martin's son, George, had six children: George, Kathleen, Norah, May, Joe and Anne. Mary Hudson (neé Halloran), in researching this book, recently met Joe and Anne, the last two remaining members of this family in the 'Irish Nash' in Batley, where Tom Halloran, her uncle and the oldest of the brothers, played the piano for many years. Joe had never married, but Anne had a large family: four daughters, nine grandchildren, and eight great-grandchildren. This branch of the family produced a number of teachers and a young man who went on for the priesthood.

"Nanna from Knock"

Also when conducting research for this book, Seán was contacted by Paula Ashton, who was born in Batley but now lives in Sligo She was in mourning for her great friend Joan Halloran, born in Birstall in 1950 but who spent her final years in Donegal where, sadly, she recently died of cancer. Paula and Joan had worked together on both of their family trees, and she felt it would be a fitting tribute to Joan to pass on to us what information they had gathered. As it happens, one of their informants was the self-same Joe Halloran who had been so helpful to Mary in 'Irish Nash' in Batley. He was in fact Joan's uncle. It is thanks to this connection that we are able to clarify what had been for us a very imprecise idea of the

THE HALLORANS FROM BIRSTALL AND AGHAMORE

family's exact connection was with one of the witnesses of the apparition in Knock. She gave us a piece from the *Yorkshire Post* which tells the story and is included at the end of this chapter.

The family connection with "Nanna" from Knock

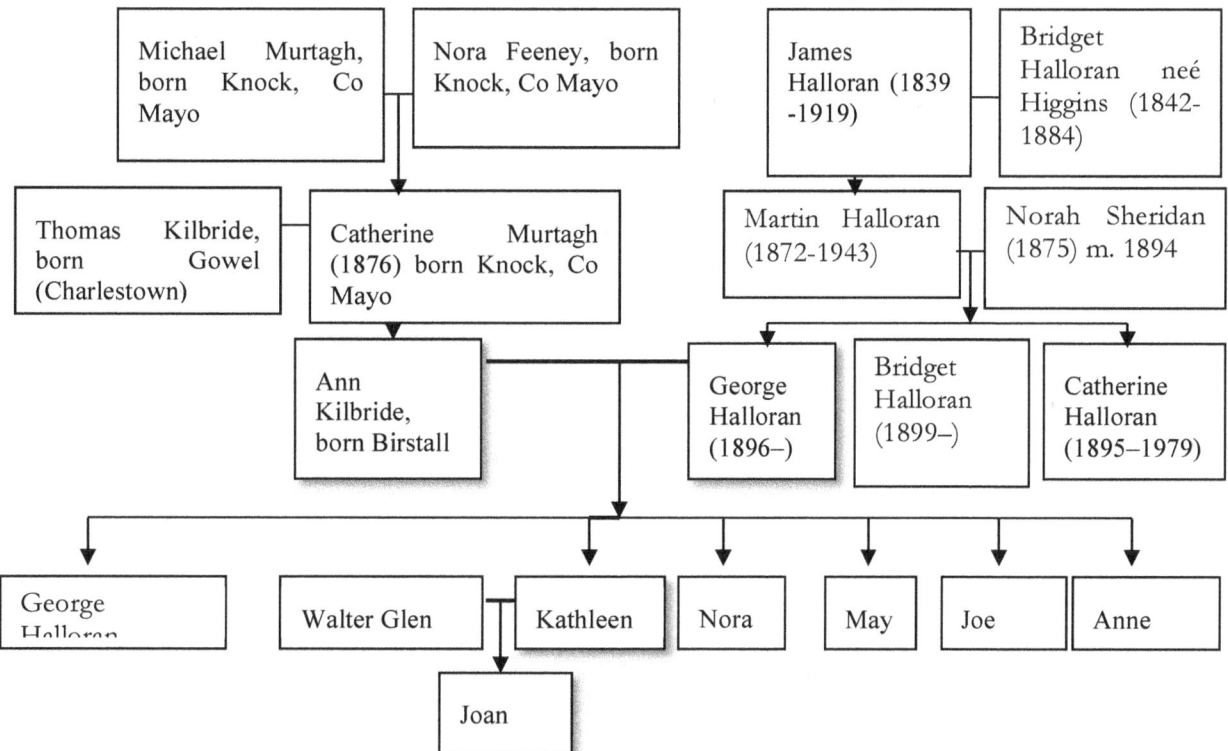

The newspaper article reproduced on the next page gives their story.

William Halloran (1876-1929), Elizabeth Prendergast (1874-1948) and family

The 1901 English census shows William, aged 24, still living with his father, James (b. 1836), his brothers John (b. 1865) aged 36, and Michael (1867) aged 34 and his sister Anorah (b. 1881) aged 20. He was the ninth of eleven children, and the grandfather of the two authors of this book.

The 1901 English census for James Halloran (b. 1836) family

The two older brothers had looked set for bachelorhood, but William married Elizabeth (Lizzie) Prendergast (1874-1948) towards the end of 1904 and they had five sons, three of whom survived to adulthood - Tom, John and Bill. John is the father of Seán O'Halloran and Bill of Mary Hudson, the two authors of this family history. Their story appears in the next chapter.

Honorah Halloran (1881-) m. Stephen Frain

Honora married Stephen Frain in 1906 and their eldest daughter, Mary, was a great friend of Willy (Bill) Halloran (1913-72) in later life. She married John Madden and they had a son Christopher.

Chapter 7 – THE THIRD GENERATION

WITNESS OF APPARITION

Batley Woman's Claim

"Yorkshire Observer" Special

June 1936, Dewsbury, Monday

TO-DAY I had a chat with Mrs. Catherine Kilbride, of Holland Street, Caledonia Road, Batley, who claims to have been a witness of a supposed apparition of Our Lady, St Joseph and St John the Evangelist, at Knock, a little village in County Mayo, Ireland, some 57 years ago.

The Knock Shrine is visited by many thousands of pilgrims every year, and many cures are claimed to have taken place there.

Interest has been stimulated by the announcement that an Ecclesiastical commission is being appointed to make an inquiry ordered by the Holy See, into the events of 57 years ago, and as a result it is hoped that Knock will be sanctioned as a privileged shrine of Our Lady. Witnesses of the supposed apparition are to be examined by the commission, one being Mrs Mary O'Connell, an 87 year-old lady in Ireland.

A LOVELY LIGHT

Mrs Kilbride, who will be seventy next month, is a native of Knock, her maiden name being Murtagh.

She came to England when a girl, residing for some years in Birstall before going on to Batley.

Her husband, the late Mr Thomas Kilbride, and his brother the late Mr. Dominic Kilbride, were well-known Batley footballers.

So convinced is Mrs Kilbride that she witnessed the apparition that she remarked, "I wish I was as sure of heaven."

There had been stories of several apparitions, she said, before the parish priest of Knock believed them.

A boy then told the priest that a lot of people were outside the church, and when the priest asked what they were doing there he replied, "Our Blessed Lady is there."

The priest said, "Nonsense." The boy replied the St. Joseph and St. John were also there".

Mrs Kilbride said that when the priest went out "he saw for himself, and believed it – but not before he thought it was a rumour that was going about."

Afterwards she said, the church was in darkness, when all at once it was lit with a lovely light.

Describing the supposed apparition, Mrs Kilbride said Our Lady was in white, like a statue she has in her home, an St Joseph and St John were in a kind of brown.

Our Lady's feet she said, were near the ground at the gable end of the church, and when a lot of people ran to kiss Her feet She disappeared.

CURES PILGRIMS.

Mrs Kilbride recalled the first cures claimed at Knock.

A day or two after the parish priest had witnessed the apparition, she said, a man who had worn an iron shoe owing to a disability, was able to jump a wall outside the church without it.

Rich and poor alike made pilgrimage and for some time the church was open all night long.

"It was once fairly late," she said, "when an old man who was at the altar rails began screaming and shouting. Nobody knew what was happening, but the old man, who had not seen for years, walked out of the church with his sight restored.

Cripples who were cured left their sticks and crutches, and pilgrims took away cement from the gable wall where the apparition was supposed to have occurred, some being brought to England by Mrs. Kilbride.

Mrs. Bridget McLaughlin, an older sister of Mrs. Kilbride, still lives near Knock.

CHAPTER 8

The fourth generation – Tom, John and Bill

1910s: some good times

In this chapter we deal with the family and early life of the parents of the writers of this book - John (1911- 1990), Seán's father, and Bill (1913-1972), Mary's father, as well as their older brother and our uncle, Tom (1908-1974). We have seen in the 1901 English census that William (1876-1925), aged 24, was living at home with his father, James (b. 1836), and his two brothers John and Michael and his sister Anorah. William Halloran, not long after that, married Elizabeth (Lizzy) neé Prendergast (1866-1948). In fact, the first baptism in the new parish of St Patrick's is of James Halloran, born to William and Elizabeth Prendergast, on 7th December 1905. Sadly, he died within his first month. Thomas was born on 27th February 1908 and then John on 17th April 1911. William followed on 28th December 1913 and Bernard on 17th May 1916. Though James would have been an uncle of ours, none of our generation knew of his existence; and we wonder whether his surviving brothers did.

The family lived in a 'back-to-back' at Farrah's Buildings, off Upper Batley lane, in Birstall, surrounded by other relatives and close friends. This was somewhat better housing and, unusually, their landlord accepted the Irish, many of whom were now a bit better off, as tenants, though the 'No Irish need apply' rule often still applied, both for housing many jobs.

Certainly, life was changing. The Irish Catholic community was becoming more firmly established by the day. St Patrick's church had been completed and could seat 400. There were signs of prosperity. Cooperative Society shops were opening, and there was a department store on Low Lane and five smaller branches further from the town centre; a boon to the housewife who had to shop every day. In Batley, an impressive building, appropriate to the booming town, was opened. The town and many homes were lit by gas supplied by the Bradford Road gas works. However, coal fires were used for domestic heating.

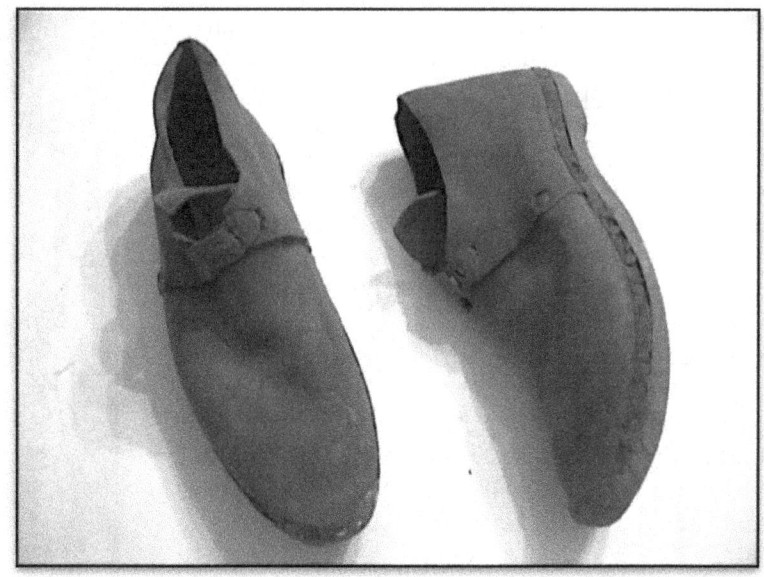

William's pit boots

Amongst the usual tradesmen, Birstall had boot and shoemakers, herbalists, wheelwrights, dry-salters, watch and clock makers, stocking knitters, pawnbrokers and cloggers. A horse-drawn tramline had been built along the Bradford road. This must have helped some travellers, though most people continued to walk, as it was quicker. The introduction of steam-driven trams caused much consternation at the turn of the century but the Red Flag Act kept things to a walking pace. Eventually electric trams were brought in by 1905 and several accidents followed, but there were no major casualties.

Health was improving. A new hospital was built in Batley and a large additional 62-bed hospital for infectious diseases was built at Oakwell, in Birstall, with an additional building to take up to 16 Smallpox patients.

There were three doctors in Birstall, of whom Dr Ogilvy was known to accept creative payments from the poor and was a great supporter of the schools. Visiting St Patrick's regularly, he was impressed by the

Chapter 8 – THE FORTH GENERATION – TOM, JOHN AND BILL

voice of Annie McCarthy, daughter of Catherine, William's sister and a neighbour in Wooler's Place. He offered to pay for singing lessons to develop her talent but the family turned this down, as they did not want her to 'lose her soul' if she got on the stage! She retained her excellent voice, nonetheless and was a good friend to Tom in later years, as he shared her love of music.

William, Lizzie and family life

Apparently, Lizzy and William despite having four sons would have loved a daughter. Lizzie was sure that she had miscarried a girl, a misfortune brought on by her turning a heavy flock mattress. In 1921, William's older brother John, from Morley, died leaving a very young family, including eight-month old twins. The other children were looked after by family: John, two year old at the time, was brought up by his uncle Phelim. Mary, aged about five, came to live with William and Lizzie and the boys were thrilled that they might have a sister. New clothes were bought including a beautiful coat with velvet collar. However Mary wanted her mother and after a time went back home. The cousins at Industrial Avenue remained very close, almost part of the same family and always remembered Lizzie as the kindest lady.

In 1922 Bernard died aged seven. It was said to be of scarlet fever, though Lizzie blamed it on a dirty old dog that belonged to an elderly neighbour.

The family was well fed by their mother who was an excellent cook and baker. She contributed to the family budget in hard times by providing food for the Irish Democratic League Club. There was always a side of ham hanging from the roof smoking over the fire. William always claimed that it tasted at its best when maggots were crawling all over it. The boys were not so certain.

They were always well dressed, though Thomas had deformed feet because of wearing 'passed-down' shoes. There appeared to be a strong sense of order and routine in the household. Cleaning was thorough and the doorstep scrubbed every week and carpets beaten outside regularly. Washing took place on Mondays, and the baking was done every Thursday. John used to talk of how he knew the day of the week from the smell coming out of the house. At the time when William was still a miner, a galvanised bath was set up every evening in the living room for him to have a good scrub. For the rest of the family, Friday night was bath night, with Bill, the youngest, getting into the water first and the others having to make do with the water being 'topped up' from the kettle.

William Halloran and his son John

There *were* some hard times: Bill (also known as Willy) wanted a pet rabbit and saved up the 6d by doing jobs for neighbours. Shortly afterwards, his rabbit went missing and, sitting down to a dinner of rabbit stew, he realised where it had gone. Sadness was overcome at the thought of the effort of saving 6d and he expressed his outrage. His father gave him 6d but then charged him 6d for his dinner and took it back. One cannot be too not sure if this was a warped sense of humour or done to cover over the embarrassment of not having money for food.

There was a green field site close to Industrial Avenue where the boys played. One Sunday after mass, when dressed in their best, the boys dared each other to jump across the lime pit. Of course Willy had to try, but he fell in. His friends dragged him out and rushed him to his Uncle James home in Industrial Avenue where he was stripped of what remained of his new suit and put in a bath. He was not too badly burned but his clothes were ruined. Fortunately for him, his mother said nothing. She was just glad he had survived!

People began to have time for recreation. Older children travelled to Batley to the heady attractions of the shops, the roller-skating rink, or the Park. This was opened between Birstall and Batley in 1920 and had a boating lake, bowling greens and tea rooms. The family managed to afford holidays to the seaside, especially to Blackpool, and once to the Isle of Man. Perhaps the Isle of Man trip was to the famous Isle of Man TT motorcycle races. The first one was held in May 1907. When getting off the ferry, Lizzie hesitated with fear on the gangplank, embarrassing the lads, but her fear turned to amusement when William shouted down from the boat, 'Come on Lizzie, it won't sink because you're on it!'

Well-dressed children in the 1920s

Bill, also known as Willy *Bill, protected by big brother Tom* *John*

William gave up mining early in life, or perhaps it had given him up. He was a huge man. Betty Halloran recalled having to step off the pavement to get around him when she was a girl. He hated the mines and with few other opportunities open to him he set up, quite successfully, as a 'bookie'. At that time taking 'ready money' (cash) for bets was illegal, so he had to take 'back payments' after the event, which often proved difficult, especially from those who had lost.

However, he proved to be imaginative in organising betting opportunities even outside of horseracing, taking bets, even on the donkeys, to pay for the trip to the seaside. He regularly took his son, Willy, out of school to various sporting events. Willy was lifted over the heads in the crowds to get a good view of cricket matches while his dad called, 'who fancies this batsman to get 10 runs?' Apparently very few batsmen made more than 10 runs, though if they did, they scored *considerably* more. So those less skilled at working out odds than William overestimated how many batsmen made ten runs, making it a good bet for the bookies.

He was very direct in getting back money owed to him. His sons were regularly embarrassed when walking down the street with him as he would point and call out loudly, 'See that feller over there, lad! He owes your father two pounds!'

Perhaps because he made some money, William made another career change and became a publican, a licensee of the Blacksmith's Arms near the Coach and Six. This was an ideal location for his Irish clientele as it was at the junction of Leeds Road and Gelderd Road, just where a footpath cut down from Upper Batley Lane and the Farrah's building/Woolers Place area. As young boys, Tom and John were

Chapter 8 – THE FORTH GENERATION – TOM, JOHN AND BILL

sometimes taken by their father down to the pub to sing for the customers. They would have used the small path leading from their house to the steps next to the pub, just a couple of minutes away

Naturally, the repertoire of songs that went down well in the pub was not the usual repertoire of a small boy. Tom told the story of how he got into trouble as an infant in Sister Clarice's class when asked to sing a nursery rhyme. He broke into 'Who were you with last night, out in the pale moonlight?' while theatrically pointing at the explosive nun! She was not amused, though he did not know why. Everyone had enjoyed it in his father's pub when he and John sang it.

The Coach and Six at the bottom of Coach Lane/ Leeds Road The Blacksmith's Arms was just off the right of picture

Tom was artistic and musical and an obvious irritation to his father, a keen sportsman who would push him out of doors to 'play with the other lads'. Tom simply sat on the step until his mother got him back indoors. He was sent for piano lessons but these only lasted a few weeks, thanks to the vagaries of the betting trade! William seemed to have some progressive ideas for the times but he also had a strange sense of humour. He was doing well as a bookie and had had a phone installed, one of the first in Batley (in the Tel. Directory he was,- Wm Halloran, Commission Agent, Batley 370). Unfortunately the phone had to be upstairs, not the best place for a man of his size. Lizzie's sister, his sister-in-law, had a habit of ringing up at mealtimes. William would rush up stairs, assuming it was a punter, but on discovering who it was would say 'Oh, we're not in!' and put the phone down!

William was keen on music and had one of the first wireless sets but would become irritated as he delicately tried to find a signal. He loved sentimental Victorian songs and taught many of these to the boys. Both Tom and John were musical. John, like his father, loved singing with his family, especially when driving on long journeys in Kenya. He passed on some of the songs he learned from his dad, including the music hall numbers that he had learned from him, two of which are reproduced here. John would sing at parties at the drop of a hat. He had a wide repertoire of humorous songs, as well as opera and a range of Irish ballads. He had a good tenor voice and was often called on to sing at weddings.

Tom and John used this small path next to the pub when called on to sing

Tom was a very talented and dedicated musician. Fortunately for his musical development, a customer with a huge accumulated debt handed over his piano to William in lieu of payment. William decided this would be an ideal opportunity for Tom so wrote the name of the notes on the keys and let Tom teach himself. Thereafter, he spent all his spare time absorbed in his music and became a brilliant pianist.

Although he mostly enjoyed classical music, he was able to earn some money, first playing at the local cinema for the silent movies and later in pubs and clubs.

Songs William sang with his sons

A boy and a maiden once stood

A boy and a maiden once stood
On a pathway that led to a wood.
Said the youth to the maid with a sigh,
'There's something, I can't tell you why.
Dear you must try to forget,
And fancy that we'd never met,
You'll soon find a lover that's true
Who will cherish you all your life through'.

'I want no one else', said the maid,
Just listen to what I've to say,
You wish me to forget you,
You say 'tis best we part.
When all my life I've loved you,
In return you'll break my heart.
Men were deceivers ever,
I've oft times heard folks say.
But believe me when I tell you dear,
You'll want me back some day'.

What I want is a proper cup of coffee

A sultan sat on his oriental mat
In his harem in downtown Persia.
He took a sip of coffee, just a drip,
And he said to his servant Kersia,
'Oh curse ya', curse ya', curse ya',
That's the worse cup of coffee in Persia, 'cause

Chorus

All I want is a proper cup of coffee,
Made in a proper copper coffee pot.
I may be off my dot,
But I want a proper coffee made in a copper coffee pot.
Iron coffee pots, and tin coffee pots, there no use to me.
If I can't have a proper cup of coffee,
In a proper copper coffee pot,
I'll have a cup of tea

Religion and education

An interesting insight into how Roman Catholicism played a major role in the life of the Irish community and was an elemental part of their identity and family is given in Betty's memoirs.

Family voices – Betty Halloran's childhood

My life story has been dominated by several intrinsic features: the influence of the Catholic Church, struggling to live in industrial Yorkshire, and the family's role before the advent of the welfare state.

The Roman Catholic population grew in leaps and bounds throughout the nineteenth century as Irish Catholics surged into the area's rapidly expanding industrial base of woollen mills and coal mining. It was no longer considered sufficient to send small children down mines or into mills, as it had been when at the time of the first Irish immigrants. Second generation immigrants looked to the Catholic Church for their education and much of their welfare, and this was recognised as a priority, especially as there was little government financial help for voluntary schools and costs had to be met through parish collections. The Visitation papers of 1870, found that there was sufficient school provision for the children of Batley but not for the children of Birstall. By the mid 1870s, a day school existed somewhere in the Brownhill/Brookroyd, but a more permanent school (since demolished) was erected in Birstall in 1876, supervised by the parish priest of Batley, Father Gordon, in 1876. Malcolm Clegg's *A History of Birstall* records that on Whit Tuesday 1876 two brass bands and over 1000 adults and children processed along Low Lane for the laying of the school's foundation stone. Mass was celebrated in this school on an improvised alter until the Church was built.

From 1881 till 1894, the Sisters of Charity of St Paul ran St. Patrick's School. Nuns from this order are still a part of St Patrick's parish community. A new St Patrick's school is now in Nova Lane, built in 1965 and extended three times.

In 1905, St Patrick's was established as a separate parish in Birstall. Various families donated the interior furnishings of the church - perhaps the greatest benefactress was Miss M. A. Mortimer. Mary Hudson tells of hearing how some families donated the wedding rings of deceased mothers on which to hang the curtains of the tabernacle. One can only wonder what became of these.

This is how Betty continued her story.

Chapter 8 – THE FORTH GENERATION – TOM, JOHN AND BILL

Family voices – Betty Halloran's childhood

I was born on the 9th January 1915, in my grandmother's cottage on Back Cross Street, in Birstall, in the West Riding of Yorkshire. My birth rather symbolised the rest of my life, a long bitter struggle ending in sadness.

After many hours of labour, my mother's relatives realised that medical help was needed. In spite of their poverty, they sent for the doctor, somehow money would be raised for the fees. However, Dr. Dick (yes, that was his name!) was out at dinner. Eventually he was found, entreated to come, but refused to come until the dinner party was over! When he finally arrived some hours later, my mother was near death. He was much the worse for drink but must have managed something as I was eventually born. I was told that I was small enough 'to fit into a pint pot', and there were no expectations that I should live. However, my grandmother gave me to my mother, Bridget, to hold, even though she could no longer see. Her last words were 'Oh, Mother, I wish I could see her!'

My mother had married over a year previously, when pregnant with twins. Unfortunately, she lost both of these before losing her own life giving birth to me. My father could not look after this tiny baby but when he remarried; his new wife did not want to take on a baby so my grandmother had to keep me[1]. *This rejection has always stayed with me, even though I know that my grandmother loved me dearly. I always lived with an expectation that I would die, especially panicking about having my own children and being quite phobic about hospitals. Needing to be in hospital months before my second child was born, I wrote long letters to my husband asking him to always take care of our daughter in case I died.*

Betty remembers living with her grandmother

Against all odds, I survived and was named after my mother and brought up by my grandmother. She must have been quite an expert as she had had at least eight children, herself, my mother being the third youngest.

It wasn't the first time that she had taken in relatives. When her sister died, she had taken her eight-year-old son, Tommy, for a few years. Eventually he went back to his family but returned to live in Birstall when he retired as he remembered the time with my grandmother as the happiest of his life, and her as the kindest person he had known. She spoiled me dreadfully, buying me sweets and a new 'Whitsun' dress every year and whatever she could afford in the way of making up for my lack of parents. After coping with her vast family, she must have felt quite well off with a husband and a son both in work. Unfortunately, I suffered for years with terrible rotten teeth, as a result!

She was very house-proud and the whole of the flagstone kitchen floor was scrubbed, on hands and knees, every day. We lived in a 'two-up and two-down' house; the main room downstairs was the big kitchen but we also had a parlour with better pieces of furniture but it was cold and very rarely used. Hung on the wall was a big photograph of my mother with dark eyes that seemed to follow me round the room. If I felt lonely I would walk around in front of the picture and know that she was watching over me! The families of the group of houses in our part of Back Cross Street shared a lavatory in the yard but

---

[1] Interestingly enough, we discovered his new wife was Catherine Prendergast, though Petty was not aware of this irony at the time.

there was a pot under the bed for night-time. In our cottage we were lucky to have a stone sink and a tap. Many of the houses had to share one of those in the yard, too.

None of the houses had a garden and they were grouped around a dirt yard, which gave a good sense of neighbourhood. Only the main roads had a hard surface.

I slept upstairs when I was older, in my own room, and Uncle Jack had the other, the rest of the family having left home. My grandparents slept downstairs in a 'shut up' bed that was put away every day as it took up much of the room. In front of the fireplace, upon which grandmother did much of the cooking, was a large 'rag rug'. We made a new one out of old rags, and put it down after the whole house was cleaned out, every Christmas Eve.

My grandmother had most of her family and their children for a party on Christmas Eve. They, of course, all brought their own cup and plate as was normal in those days. My grandmother had enough for Auntie Katie's family as they did not possess any and drank out of jam jars at their house. (Their father was a 'boozer' and they had lots of children, so were very poor).

Every Christmas Eve my Uncle Mark would appear. We did not know where he lived or with whom or what he did, but he was made welcome and, as far as I know, no questions were asked. We would get no letters and hear nothing from him until the next Christmas Eve, but there he would always be!

Sometimes my grandfather's sister and family would come over from Saltaire, near Bradford. They were lucky enough to have one of the cottages belonging to the Salts Mill but I did not like going to their house because they had blazing rows. My grandfather's sister was terrible to look at because once she had hit her husband and he had thrown an oil lamp back at her. It had broken; oil landed all over her and caught fire, burning one side of her face. We occasionally visited them on a Sunday afternoon.

Another of my grandfather's brothers, Uncle Lawrence, had gone to live in Durham as a collier. We visited him when I was seven (and also visited the seaside for the first time whilst we were at his house) and he came back to Birstall a few times. He had had lots of sons, most of whom had been killed in World War One, but I can't remember how many. Relatives were spread far and wide. Some had gone to America and my grandmother kept in touch with them all, somehow. Presents were sent and my most treasured was a nightdress-case (never used, of course) in the form of a doll. (Last year I saw a similar one on The Antiques Roadshow, by the same maker.) However, I wasn't given my first book until I was twelve, - The Girl Guide's Annual.

My grandfather was known as 'Crafty Kelly' and I never heard him given any other name though I'm not sure why he was given it. Apparently he was a good storyteller and had a great sense of humour and so was in great demand at 'wakes'. In those days, it was important to stay awake to keep the rats away from the corpse and so there was quite a party to keep all the mourners awake, especially the night before the funeral. Whisky was offered to all those who helped keep awake to watch over the corpse. Unfortunately, my grandfather was very keen on whisky and every so often, he would go on a 'blinder' and drink himself stupid for three or four days. After that he would be perfectly sober for perhaps six months before he felt the need to escape again. He was a collier and although he had been injured in a pit accident years before, he was a strong man and reputed to be a good worker: he must have been an excellent worker not to lose his job after these drinking bouts!

Chapter 8 – THE FORTH GENERATION – TOM, JOHN AND BILL

My grandmother was always kindness and sweetness to me. Once when she was brushing my waist-length hair, the brush caught and snagged and I turned and hit her. She looked at me sadly and said simply 'Thank-you', the worst reproach I have ever had!

When I was nine, my grandfather was taken very ill and was at home in the 'put-up bed' for quite a long time until he died. Before he died he told my aunts that he had seen a lot whilst he was ill and my grandmother was not coping as well as everyone thought.

After his death we had no real income and were much poorer and my grandmother began to age rapidly, becoming more and more confused. She had always taken complete care of me, never asking me to help with cooking or shopping. Now I had no idea how to look after myself, let alone look after her.

I remember one occasion when I was going to have my photograph taken, as requested by the American relatives. I put on my best white dress but was unable to find my best white shoes. My only other footwear was a pair of long laced black boots, which were worn through in places. In the end I had to wear the boots for the photo but felt humiliated and I cut off the bottom bit of the photos when they arrived.

Uncle James was still at home and had some money but was used to spending most of it on himself and had a reputation to keep up as a 'snappy dresser'. As a man in those days, he had no idea how to cook or organise a home, either. He would often give me some money to go and buy a dozen buns (and I ate the thirteenth on the way back) but there was often no other food in the house as my grandmother sometimes shopped but often forgot.

Suddenly, from being pampered and taken care of, I had to look after myself, a house, and a confused old lady.

Parish matters

The school, built in the 1870s, had a temporary chapel but Birstall was part of the Batley parish and St Patrick's was establishing some independence. A football club had been organised in 1893 and later a cricket club too. Birstall Catholics were keen to have their own church but this was against the wishes of the Batley priests. Parish rivalries ensued, and in 1900, the Batley priests denied the Whit procession access to the school where it was to begin. It went ahead nonetheless, as the organisers found other premises for the 1000 strong procession to assemble.

In 1901, the first Irish Democratic League Club (IDLC) was established in Cross Street. Naturally, it was seen as an ideal venue for social events, and alcohol was introduced in 1903. The club's first 'supper' was held in the New Inn in 1905, though later it moved to larger premises across from the 'Horse and Jockey' club, where billiard tables were installed both upstairs and down. This introduced issues related to 'decency and drink', issues close to Father Peter Russell's heart. He was the curate at St. Mary's and very strict on such matters. He had organised an anti-drink campaign, especially aimed at the Irish clubs in Batley and Birstall. He is also reported to have stood at the church door declaiming and sending home anyone indecently dressed, that is who showed any arm or ankle, or skin below the upper neck. At the Whit Monday open-air gala, organised by the Irish Democratic League Club (ILDC) in 1903, drink was sold, against his wishes. As he felt that some people were 'under the influence' he ordered mixed dancing to stop, remonstrating with one man, a non-Catholic, who refused to do as told, so the priest stopped the band and the whole proceedings. The ensuing row went on all summer as the IDLC felt that he had no business to interfere in their affairs.

The move for a separate parish grew, in part because the school needed to expand. Finally a new church, presbytery and school buildings were proposed at a cost of £3000 to £4000, Miss Mortimer, of the Clapham family being a major benefactor. The new priest, appointed by the bishop of Leeds, was none other than Father Russell himself. He continued to declaim against sinners and loose morality from the pulpit whilst encouraging the children to learn surprisingly bloodthirsty Irish Rebel songs. Auntie Nell shuddered at the songs she sang as a little girl.

Irish Democratic League Club

St Patrick's soon became the centre of life for the Irish Catholic community. Outings, teas for special occasions, and an enormous May procession were all organised on a parish basis. The non-conformist churches had these occasions and the Catholics were not to be outdone. Many of the events involved pageants and dressing up. There was the May Queen, with her white clothed attendants, as well as all sorts of other costumes, which were homemade and passed on to new children every year. Willy was an Irish Forester one year whilst Bridget Walsh got to be 'The Maid of Erin'!

Betty Halloran remembers the Church

When I was younger we had to go to Batley to church, as we had no church yet in Birstall in spite of such a large Catholic population. It was quite good to meet up as so many people were related anyway. When we got our own priest, Father Scannell, he often came into school and taught some catechism classes. He was Irish and very anti-English and taught us terrible rebel and patriotic (Irish) songs to sing for the St. Patrick's Day show that we put on at school. We were all scared of him and terrified that he would pick on us for dressing 'immodestly' when he inspected us as we came into church for Sunday mass.

Schooling

In 1905, there was controversy when the County Council insisted that the Brownhill Catholics should be attending school in Batley, so as to fit the growing numbers of non-conformist children into the two Birstall church schools (St Patrick's and St Peter's, Church of England). The boundaries between Birstall and Batley were quite arbitrary and Brownhill flowed naturally into Birstall. Most of Upper Batley Lane, Brownhill, one side of Leeds Road, one side of Coach Lane, Woolers Place, and Farrar's Buildings were all within half a mile of St Patrick's but several miles from St. Mary's in Batley. Whilst Birstall Catholics were happy for adults to walk to the social club at St. Mary's, it was quite another thing for children to walk five miles a day to school. St Patrick's was ordered to expel 19 Brownhill children. A similar request was not, however, made to the Church of England School. Being part of the Birstall community and having neighbours across the road entitled children to go to Birstall. There was much protest from the Catholics but fortunately Councillor Flynn intervened and went to see the Minister for Education and the West Riding County Council order was overturned.

In Birstall, relative prosperity meant that the school, enlarged in 1907, had almost 200 pupils. The school was run by Sister Mary, a wonderful teacher and much loved by the children, into whose lives she instilled a sense of worth and hope. She was thought to have been from a wealthy, upper-class family and she insisted on good manners, cleanliness and decorum, at a time when the usual epithet for the community

Chapter 8 – THE FORTH GENERATION – TOM, JOHN AND BILL

was 'Mucky Irish', which persisted for many more years, even as the ghetto areas broke down and equality of opportunity allowed them to move out of the mines and mills.

Bridget Walsh (Betty) as The Maid of Erin *Willy as an Irish Forester*

Here we get a view of schooling as seen through the eyes of Betty as a child.

Family voices – Betty Halloran remembers her schooling

From the age of four I had gone to St. Patrick's school. In the first few years we had a lovely teacher called Sister Clariss. Later teachers were less popular and I remember one boy hitting one teacher when she had mocked him. Usually, children did not tell their parents if they had been punished, as that would have earned an even worse punishment for shaming their parents by behaving badly. However, I remember one mother running into school, and chasing the teacher all round the classroom before other people came to the rescue. I have no idea what had caused the anger! For my last few years, I was in the headmistress' class.

She was a nun called Sister Mary. We all had the greatest respect for her and she certainly deserved it. She was obviously from a wealthy background and tried to pass on her social graces in an attempt to get rid of any excuse for discrimination. We girls, especially, were taught to be 'ladylike', to sit demurely, to dress modestly, and speak well, 'You can always tell a lady by her finger nails!' etc. We all had to polish our shoes (if we had them!), show respect to our elders, and support those less well off than us.

Twice a year, we had processions through the town, to show how proud we were of our faith and our Irish background. The men carried huge banners for different aspects of Catholicism: - the Papal banner, the Corpus Christie banner, etc. In May, a statue of the Virgin Mary was carried and crowned in church by the May Queen. These were major events in our lives. One year I was chosen to dress as the 'Maid of Erin' and was very proud of myself, leading a section of the procession.

On reflection, I must have been quite clever and I knew that I was good at 'sums' and spelling as I was always in demand as someone to sit next to (in the double desks, my partner could copy my work). I loved reading and read every book that I could find. My best friend in Back Cross Street was Josephine Stenson and her mother owned most of the houses there. She had lots of books and I read everything that she owned. School friends, who I had done the work for but who had wealthier parents, later became teachers but of course, I did not sit the 'scholarship', as I could not have afforded the uniform or the bus-fare to the Grammar school.

Knowing, what was happening at home, Sister Mary had always been extremely kind to me. Many a morning she sent me to a lady next door to the school, (Mrs Phillips) who gave me a warm drink and something to eat. Eventually, I started going home every playtime, morning and afternoon, and of course everyone went home for dinner. I had to check that my grandmother was still at home, or go hunting for her. However many times I asked her to 'Stay here until I get back', she would forget and go in search of something that she straightaway forgot! I remember one day being very frightened when I could not find her at playtime, the neighbours had not seen her leave the house and I searched all over for her. I finally saw her right at the other end of the market place and chased after her only to find that it was another woman who had an identical shawl.

As for the Halloran boys, both Tom and John did well at school but young Willy saw himself as the class entertainer. Betty remembered him 'winding up' his friend Willy McLaughlin like a tingalarie man (travelling organ grinder) until the class could no longer sing for the giggles. He always had difficulties with spelling, though his learning problems were not helped by regular absences from school when he went with his father to horse races and sports venues. It is highly likely the real source of his difficulties was dyslexia.

Tom was sent off to St. Bede's Grammar School in Bradford. Not many had the ability, and few from the area could afford the fares and uniforms or the loss of the child's income when he or she reached working age. However, he did well enough to win a scholarship, and the family were obviously in a position to afford it. Tom especially enjoyed Latin and literature and one day when reading a book whilst walking to school, he walked out in the road and was knocked down by a horse and cart that drove right over him. Being quick thinking he managed to roll into the middle and avoid the wheels and continued to school, not telling anyone.

Two years later, John also won a scholarship to St Bede's grammar school and it was decided Tom would leave, as the family must have been hard pushed to afford the fees for more than one child there. No doubt the expense of a new uniform was saved as all clothes were 'passed down'. John, however, did exceptionally well at St Bede's, both academically and in sports so it was decided that he should continue. He was Willy's hero - head boy and games captain, winning the Senior *Victor Ludorum*. However, gaining a scholarship to St Bede's was a traumatic event in John's life. Later he talked of a school cap being put on his head and a blazer on his back and being sent off on a long bus journey to a different world. Being a scholarship boy, he never felt he was really part of the world inhabited by the grammar school boys of Bradford, but that cap and blazer also set him apart from the other boys in Birstall.

There are stories of their social life from around this time. Much of this engaged the entire family, with William, the father, playing a dominant role. William was a sponsor of the local cricket team, as John, Joe, (their cousin from Industrial Ave) and young Bill were keen sportsmen. However, on one occasion, Joe

Chapter 8 – THE FORTH GENERATION – TOM, JOHN AND BILL

was not selected for an important match so William, being who he was, sent him to tell the captain that if he didn't play, 'there'd be no more teas' - though no doubt Lizzie, rather than William, actually prepared them.

One evening John came home late and knocked on the locked door. His father opened the bedroom window and called, 'Who's that?', 'It's John', came the reply. Firmly shutting the window, his father said, 'No, it can't be! Our John wouldn't be out at this time of night'. The door remained locked!

Betty's life with Auntie Mary

Betty's life, however, remained unsettled.

> *Eventually the family must have decided that this could go on no longer [Betty having to look after her aging grandmother alone]. Aunts Norah and Katy lived in Birstall but had huge families and could hardly afford to look after their own children. My youngest aunt was Mary. She also lived in Birstall but was married to a 'non-Catholic'. This had caused many problems, as both sides of the family hated the religion of the other side. Cook, her husband, was a few years younger than her and they had 'had to get married' when he was only seventeen. Both sides of the family had had my cousin christened in their own churches; there was much animosity between the families. Cook had run off to join the navy for a few years and Auntie Mary had come back to live with us. However, they only had one daughter and she and I were quite close, being only children, even though she was four years younger than I was. Both Auntie Mary and Uncle Cook worked in the mills so they were comparatively well off. If I had been given a choice, I certainly would have chosen to live with them! My other cousins always seemed dirty only having jam jars to drink out of and Auntie Katy's husband had once frightened me to death - even though I did not really know what he was doing.*
>
> *It was finally decided, and my grandmother, Uncle James and I were moved from our cottage to a live with Aunt Mary and Uncle Cook. I was now ten. The house was overcrowded with my cousin, Ellen, and myself sharing a bed and my grandmother in another bed in our room. There were more problems as several mills had to sack workers, this being the late 1920's. First Uncle James lost his job but found a job selling insurance if Cook could be persuaded to be his indemnifier, if that is the right word. It meant that Cook would be responsible for any debts and would lose £50 if James were to abscond. Finding the £50 was obviously difficult but they felt that James could soon pay back the money. Less than a year after we had moved to live with them, my grandmother died and I was left feeling lost and unloved, imposed on relatives again but this time I knew I was unwanted. Not long after this Cook also lost his job! That left Auntie Mary as the only real breadwinner, not good for the male morale, especially in the 1920's! She had a wonderful contralto voice and worked in the evenings to earn extra money. She billed herself as 'Madame Hinchliffe' and sung from opera, operetta, and popular songs like 'Ave Maria', 'Bless this House', etc. She was in great demand and out often.*
>
> *Soon afterwards, Uncle James gave up trying to sell insurance to a population fast becoming unemployed and disappeared, leaving Cook with his debts. Cook became majorly depressed.*

Entering the world of work

The 1930s proved to be difficult times for all. On October 26th 1929, at age 52, William had a heart attack and died; life had to change for them all. At the time Tom was about 21, John was 18 and Bill, 16. His death coincided with a general economic depression. Coal miners and mill workers, alike, were out of work throughout the 1930s. Many of the mills were closed and others were on 'short time'. Probate records show that William left £260:18:0 so there was money to tide them over until income began to come in. Things, however, had improved for the community over the years. In 1911, 211 out of every thousand children died, but by 1932 this had fallen to 58 per thousand. People generally could afford better hygiene and health care. As a group, they remained frugal and self-sufficient. With the horrors of their history behind them, they must have been better able to cope with the Depression than might our generation. Soup kitchens again opened and children had basic meals provided in schools.

In the early 1930s, William Keenan, husband of Lizzie's sister, died. So a sensible solution was for Lizzie and the boys to move to live with her in Heckmondwike.

Family voices – Betty Halloran - the boys leave school

When he [Bill/Willy] left school he had been apprenticed, unpaid, as a joiner. But his father had died so he had to change his apprenticeship to one, which earned some money, and so he worked as a hairdresser. His older brother was at grammar school and doing well so the rest of the family had to make sacrifices to help him; there was no state help, of course. Willie, after six years as an apprentice had started up his own shop and employed Phyllis to do 'ladies hair styling' upstairs while he and his friend John Daley (until he was called up) did the men's downstairs.

Tom worked with his father in the upstairs office which he had, by 1926, in Birstall High Street. However the two had regular rows and one punter remembered entering the door to be met by Tom racing downstairs with his father chasing him and saying, 'Yon young bugger's just told me to shite!'

Tom's real talent was as a musician. However, with his fine ear, he could not abide the mistakes of the less talented. He organised concerts at St Patrick's, shouting at singers who missed a note and walking off in rages if he was not taken seriously. When George Formby was 'all the rage' John bought a banjo and tried to learn how to play a popular tune. Tom listened for as long as he could and then simply took the instrument out of John's hands and smashed it over his head! Apparently, Lizzie took all this with calm and a dry sense of humour. John, however, continued to enjoy George Formby, and would later sing his songs while driving, to the delight of his own children.

With none of the boys working, and indeed John's indenture as an architect and Willy's apprenticeship costing money, Lizzie's sandwich and bread making would certainly not support them. Tom had a spell working as a booking clerk at Birstall Station but that came to a rapid end when Tom, shouted at for making tea, threw the teapot at the Station Manager and was promptly sacked.

Market Place, Birstall, c, 1910

Willy had to give up his apprenticeship and got a job as a 'bob-a-week-lather-lad' at Collinson's Hairdresser's in Birstall, where he could learn a trade but without the expense involved in many apprenticeship schemes. He eventually became a hairdresser in his own right and worked at that most of his life. Willy asked for a pay rise but, in spite of thinking of Willy as heir to the business, Mr Collinson felt he could not afford this. A shop next to the cinema was up for rent so Willy, encouraged by John, took over the rent and went to Leeds where, one Sunday, they ordered all the fittings for a hairdresser's shop, at a cost of £101:9:6 and set up a barbers shop for men.

Chapter 8 – THE FORTH GENERATION – TOM, JOHN AND BILL

1920s Social change and moving out of the ghetto

In the previous chapter we saw how the First World War impacted on William's older brother James Halloran's family in Industrial Avenue family, where the sons Willy, John and James were called up. William and his family, though, were not too seriously affected. Most of the men in the district were miners, and were classed as having reserved occupations. However, stories were passed on of the horrors of war, which left a strong impression on the boys.

Family voices – Betty Halloran remembers growing up and starting work

We struggled on for another year or so, and as I was to be leaving school at thirteen, I began to look for a job myself. Nothing turned up, and I left school. From the day I left school, I got up every morning for seven o'clock, and walked the five miles or so down the road towards Dewsbury, stopping at every one of the dozens of mills on one side of the road to ask if there was a job. I then walked back, stopping at the mills on the other side with the same enquiry. I also felt it was prudent to change my name, as 'Bridget' was so obviously Irish which meant that there was even less chance of me getting a job. I became 'Betty', which was close, and much more English sounding. My surname, Walsh, was not such an obvious problem.

After about four months I finally found a job. The pay was poor (I think 12/6 a week) but they could obviously offer less to a thirteen year old than they could to an adult, so I stood a better chance than did Uncle Cook. I gladly paid my weekly wages to Auntie Mary and was given 6d a week in spending money, out of which I had to save to buy my 'best' clothes. Most of my clothes were cast offs from my younger cousin (I was very small, still!) though when I asked if I could have some money for a bra, my aunt gave me one of hers to 'take-in',- she being about size 40E whilst I must have been nearing 32A. If I wanted an apple or orange to eat, I had to pay extra for that! I felt myself to be quite a Cinderella figure, but at least I did not feel so indebted to everyone!

My colouring was very dark and I felt that this was very ugly. I must have had ancestors from the wrecked Spanish Armada, off the West Coast of Ireland. I was once told of a grandmother on my father's side who was very dark, wore some foreign national costume, and did not speak English. She had been brought back as a bride from a foreign war but I do not know which. My cousin Ellen was fair and this made it even worse as I felt I compared very badly with her, even though we began to speak of ourselves as sisters. Someone once referred to us as 'Like night and day' and I was mortified by the comparison.

Cook remained out of work for several more years but my job improved. I moved to 'Printworks' where I was promoted several times and given the responsibility of ordering precise amounts of matched colours for new runs of prints. At fifteen, I was invited to take an office job. However this would have meant a very small cut in pay until I was trained and Auntie Mary refused to let me accept. Later she heard of an opportunity for me to take a weaving job which was slightly better paid though was much harder and more boring but it did not occur to me to question her decision so I had to leave Printworks where I had been very happy and was a respected employee. I had made many life-long friends there, the first time I had had friends outside the Catholic community. Vera Dudfield was a good friend all through the war and for years afterwards too.

By now we had been able to move into one of the new council houses in Birstall. It was a wonderful house with a bathroom and a back boiler so we could get hot water without having to boil pans on the stove and fire. We also had a toilet of our own which was in an entrance by the back door so you didn't even have to go outside at night in the cold!

Uncle Cook's stepbrother came to live with us for a while as he was crippled and needed care, but he died after a year or so. He was a lovely, gentle man.

Each time my pay rose I asked for a little more spending money as my clothes were laughed at, at work, and I was beginning to resent the fact that my cousin was so much better dressed than I. However, I was accused of 'not appreciating what had been done for me', and threatened with having to 'pay for my keep' so I looked for other ideas.

I went to evening classes to learn how to sew as this would help with my clothing problems. The first thing I made was a pair of cami-knickers with a buttoned waistband, which I thought were wonderful

Despite financially difficult times, John's indenture at an architect's firm in Ilkley, with additional expense for rail fares and appropriate clothing, was seen as sacred! Tom joined the religious order of 'Saint John of God', an order that specialised in nursing, and went to Ireland for a period, but did not stay.

Though the young people of the fourth generation of the Birstall Irish were establishing themselves in a variety of different walks of life for the first time, connections still existed with Aghamore. Tartanne, Lizzie's sister, so named after Tom's pronunciation of 'Aunt Margaret Ann' as a baby, had visited some relations in Ballyhaunis, in Mayo. Horror stories came back, typified by the comment, 'Oh you don't wanta be usin' tem durty tings', when she rushed to use the railway toilets on her way home. Who exactly she had visited is not known but there was still regular contact with relatives in Aghamore. As we saw in the chapter 7, William's brother, Martin Halloran (1872-1943), married Norah Sheridan (b. 1875) who had recently arrived from Mayo, and whose grandmother, it was reported, was a witness of the apparition in Knock.

Family voices –Betty neé Halloran meets Bill (Willie) Halloran

My group of friends were mostly from St. Patricks. By now a church had been built in Birstall and we did not have to walk to Batley to St. Mary's to mass every Sunday. There was a spare room under the church which was made into a 'Young Men's Club' and we started to have socials there now. There was a billiard table installed which took up most of the room but it was somewhere to go which cost us nothing. We put on shows, many written by Tom Halloran, two or three times a year. We made all our own costumes and they were great fun, with singing, dancing, around the central story line. At regular intervals, Tom would lose his temper because we were being silly or just incompetent. He would show us girls how to do the dances and direct the actors and sing the parts for those who could not sing, as well as playing the piano for the whole show. When he became frustrated with us he would explode with anger and storm off and it would take ages to pacify him and persuade him to come back.

In my group of friends was Willie Halloran, Tom's younger brother, and the same age as me. We had often been in the same class at school even though he was a year older. He was much quieter than Tom though he had tended to entertain the class when the teacher was not looking. He had missed school often when he was younger as his father had been a book-maker and had taken Willie with him when he went to Horse Racing, sports events, etc. About this time, Uncle Cook applied for a position as a publican and we moved to 'The Saw', at Batley. At first I hated it, embarrassed to live in a pub and mortified to have to help serving customers so I mostly did the washing up.

I gradually saw more of Willie Halloran although we did not go out on out own for years. He was a good dancer and we both went to Stivvies too. Once when we were late walking back from a dance, I was locked out of the house, even though I was twenty two, at the time. I had to sleep overnight in Willie's shop and was in serious trouble in the morning. Willy spent lots of his time at St Patrick's 'Young Men's Club' where he was a good

Chapter 8 – THE FORTH GENERATION – TOM, JOHN AND BILL

snooker and billiards player, winning several matches. Once, having learned little from the lime pit incident, he accepted a dare to put a billiard ball into his mouth, learning too late that you can stretch your mouth open but the muscle tire rapidly. It was some time and a lot of panic before his friends forced his mouth open and retrieved the ball. He was very involved in life around St Patrick's. The cinema was extremely popular, usually showing two films every week. He also enjoyed dancing and regularly went to 'Stivvies' at Gomersal as well as at St Mary's, where there was a good social club with regular dances. He regularly partnered Bridget Walsh (Betty), whilst trying to get work in the 1930s Depression, but a whole group of school friends spent time together.

With Willy working in Birstall and the fact that the family's friends and social life were there, they wanted to move back from Heckmondwike. Members of the family caste their eyes on new housing being built on King's Drive, across Middlegate from Chandler's Hill. However, it was only possible to get a mortgage with a professional job in those days, so John, at that time a Borough Surveyor in Preston, secured the mortgage and was the nominal owner and dealt with the transaction by post. Lizzie had cash for expenses and a deposit and eventually the property, costing £435 with a £390 mortgage (with £2:10/- monthly payments) was completed in February 1935. John thought they should buy no. 11, which had been used as the builders' store but Lizzie preferred no. 6, clean and with a south facing garden: they bought no. 11. The Adams family became their neighbours at no. 6, Lees at no. 8 and Lynches at 10. The Irish were moving out of the ghetto after three generations!

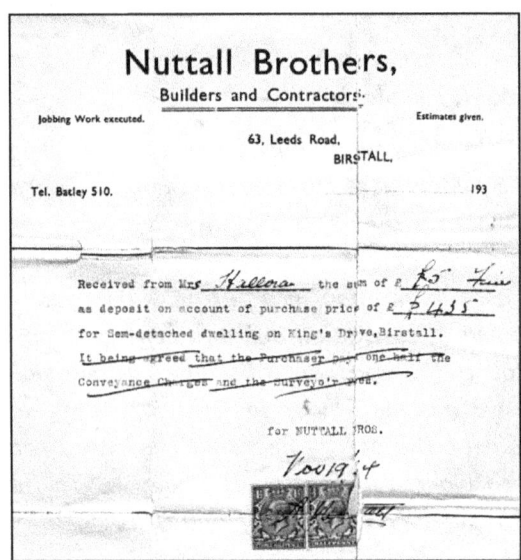

Receipt for deposit on 11 King's Drive and the house itself

Courtship and marriages

In Heckmondwike, John met Eileen Sheehan, a young teacher from Co. Cork. She was teaching at the local Catholic primary school and they started 'courting'. Their courtship consisted of long walks between Heckmondwike and Birstall. These lasted seven years before they felt they could afford to get married. When John qualified he got a job in Borough Surveyor's Office in Preston. He was delighted when he got the job as he had applied for many, only to be constantly turned down. However, his self-esteem was dented one day shortly after starting work when his boss asked him if he knew why he had been selected for the job. About to reply something to the effect of being the best candidate, he was sharply pulled up when his boss quickly answered the question himself, 'it was because you had been out of work the longest.'

John married Eileen Sheehan, in Dun Laoghaire on 9th August 1938, a location halfway between Yorkshire and County Cork, where Eileen came from. On their honeymoon they visited Glendalough, an ancient monastic site and seat of learning in County Wicklow where the famous holy man St Kevin confronted his demons. This always remained a special spot for them and they later named one of their sons Kevin.

1940s: the War Years

On their return from their honeymoon in Ireland, John and Eileen lived in Leeds but their newly married life was disrupted a year later by the outbreak of war. John was called up to the Air Ministry where he was a civilian civil engineer. At first they were posted to Evanton, in Ross and Cromarty in the far North West of Scotland where their first daughter, Maureen, was born on 13th January 1940, apparently in a disused police station. Michael was born there, too, in April 1942. Maureen remembers the huge lions that guarded the entrance. Bill was called up a few years later.

Family voices – Betty Halloran remembers the onset of war

For me the war meant freedom. I had to join the Fire service and had a marvellous time there. I did secretarial work and accounting and was rapidly promoted. I became much more confident and could organise other people well. We all lived life to the full and enjoyed every evening and weekend.

Though always called 'Willy' by the older generation in Birstall, Betty had persuaded him to be called Bill. He had asked Betty to live at his home in Kings Drive. She found it strange to live with Willy's family but felt that his mother was delighted to have her there, even if Tartanne was less welcoming. Betty was in the Fire Service and worked long hours but managed to have a great time, still going out dancing with friends, to the pictures with Tom and even on trips to Blackpool. She saw that time as 'the best days of her life' and was always amazed that Willy's mother never commented on her life style. As an orphan, she felt that at last she had found a loving mother figure. She always appreciated that Lizzie never interfered in her life, then or even after the war when she was a young mother.

Tom in his fireman's uniform

Tom was also in the Fire Brigade. He was Tartanne's favourite nephew and benefited from extra rations from his mother and aunt. Half an egg a week was not considered sufficient for Tom. Once when the fire tender arrived to collect him as Batley Brigade had to go off to support the bombed cities, Tartanne called out, 'Watch out for them fires, Tom', much to the amusement of the other firemen. Betty heard regular stories of Tom's bravery, going into dangerous buildings and rescuing many people, but he never talked about it. He spent a long time in Liverpool which was heavily bombed during the blitz, and it was probably his duties there which made him miss Bill and Betty's wedding.

The family seemed to laugh at their traumatic experiences during the war: Tartanne *always* forgot her handbag with the insurance certificates when they rushed for the air raid shelter. There was much amusement in recounting how the Sisters of Mercy's home was damaged whilst the Fire Brigade, not so familiar with the names of the orders of Catholic nuns, searched for 'Murphy's house'. On another occasion, during the blackout, absent-minded Tom walked into a neighbour's house, and sat for some time wondering why his mother had changed the furniture!

Betty remembers

In 1941 Willie was eventually called up and so closed down the men's department and left the upstairs to Phyllis.

Willy and I had never considered getting married, as he had to support his mother and her older sister who had come to live with them when her husband died. His mother was

Chapter 8 – THE FORTH GENERATION – TOM, JOHN AND BILL

a lovely lady. She was very straight-faced but would help anyone although expecting no thanks or gratitude. She was a marvellous cook and kept the family going through all the problems of her husband's job (you could not accept money for bets, legally, in those days, so punters often refused to pay after the event: unless, of course they had won!) She had always baked and sold bread and cakes to neighbours to make some extra money. After his death she expanded the business, though her and her sister still sold from the house.

Willie still handed his entire shop takings over to his mother and she gave him some spending money. As his brother was now an architect and so deemed to have a safe enough job to get a mortgage, the family had bought a house. ...

Meanwhile, Uncle Cook had joined the Merchant Navy so it was more peaceful at home. Ellen had been in love with a teacher but his family thought she was beneath him and that had fallen through. However she met a customer called Cyril Fenton, a lovely man and they planned to get married. We left the pub and Auntie Mary worked back in the mill as a weaver again. She and I got on better, now that life was not so difficult.

Willy appears to have delayed proposing because he felt that he already had too many responsibilities to get married but after a brief respite, because of his business, he was called up in 1941. At interview, he had volunteered for coalmines or the air force but when his papers came he was sent to the army. He often brought lads back to be 'fed up' by his mother, when on weekend leaves, much to Betty's irritation.

Betty remembers

Willie did his basic training mostly in Lancashire. I once went to see him when he was in Blackpool and the soldiers did their marching down the promenade. We otherwise saw little of each other as he usually brought some poor, lonely, ill-fed chap back with him, if he had a 'leave', so that they could be cheered up by his mother's cooking. Then one day in 1942, he rang me up at work to tell me that he was 'as sick as a parrot'. He then suggested, romantically, that as he had been given a week's 'Embarkation leave' in June, 'We might as well get married. What do you think?'

I managed to organise the wedding for the Tuesday of that week. We even managed to get a dress made in time. The biggest problem seemed to be that the name I had called myself all my life: Walsh, was not the name I found on my birth certificate. Here it was spelled as 'Welsh'. In the end I had to go and find my father to find out which was correct. He hardly seemed aware of my existence but I did meet and then got to know a whole set of new brothers and sisters though I did not want to know his wife. However I only felt anger towards him.

As it was mid-week, not many people could come to the wedding and afterwards, we just had a few close relations for sandwiches, as a reception. The cake was a wartime iced cardboard cover with a tiny sponge cake hidden underneath, just about enough for a taste each. Willie's brother, John, was his Best Man, Ellen was my Maid-of-honour, Auntie Mary, Willie's mother and Aunt came and the only other person was his younger cousin, James. Tom was in the Fire Service and unable to change his shifts.

Afterwards we went on a two day honeymoon to Ilkley and it rained all the time. The following week I moved in to live in his home with his brother, mother and aunt, he went off to North Africa and I did not see him again for five years!

After rapid organisation and borrowing of clothing and food coupons, the two were married on 26th June '41 complete with an iced cardboard cover over a tiny sponge cake. Money did not 'run to the price of a suit' so Willy was married in uniform. Tom, because of his fire fighting duties, could not attend and Cook was in the navy and somewhere in the North Atlantic.

The embarkation leave allowed for a week-end honeymoon in a boarding house in Ilkley when it rained every day, and then Willy set off for Liverpool and the desert in North Africa. He spent the next four years away from home, which he found devastating. He often told stories about the frustrating and amusing incidents but was permanently scarred by the horrors. When Bernard was born, he tried to find a way not to register his birth so that in the event of another war, the authorities would not be able to 'call him up'! He was content to be back home with his family, wanted to travel no further than Leeds, delighted in his children, had no ambition except for his children and would help out anyone.

Elizabeth Halloran, neé Prendergast *Anne (Tartann) Halloran (1894-94)*

Shortly afterwards, John was posted to Halton, RAF station in Aylesbury. The family moved in 1942 when Michael was still a baby. Later John was posted to Heliopolis in Cairo. There he received word of the death of his young son Kevin early in 1946. Everything about the circumstances was most tragic. John was in the process of being demobbed and was refused permission to go home to the funeral. However, he defied orders and returned to Aylesbury in any case. Kevin's mother Eileen, no doubt absolutely distraught, was ill and in hospital. The result is that neither of them was at the funeral. Fortunately, Tantanne, Grand ma Lizzie and Aunt Mary managed to make it down from Birstall. The two older children, Maureen and Michael were taken to Birstall, while Eileen, who was a babe in arms, remained with her mother in hospital.

Kevin had swallowed a penny, the removal of which required surgery. However, he subsequently died of paralysis of the intestine. There was much additional grief as it was felt this was a result of the surgical procedures taking too long. There was talk of suing. Once John was finally demobbed, John and Eileen packed up their family and went to Kenya to start a new life.

It was always a regret of theirs that Lizzie died shortly after they had left. She died at home after a long spell of illness with heart failure age 74: a traumatic time for her family. Bill and Betty's daughter, Mary, was six months old. Shortly afterwards, Tartanne had a stroke but battled on with dementia and loss of movement but a determination to cope until another stroke killed her in 1949, age 84.

At present reckoning, Tom, John, and Bill have at least 39 first cousins on the Halloran side, quite an empire for the grandfather, James. Many of this generation are great achievers, academically. But the next generation, bringing numbers into the hundreds, with the possibilities opened by the Education system, have the world at their feet. There are dozens of teachers, doctors and nurses, journalists and artists – quite a legacy for the illiterate couple, Thomas and Judy, who escaped starvation and misery 150 years earlier.

Chapter 8 – THE FORTH GENERATION – TOM, JOHN AND BILL

	John Halloran (Best Man)		Young James Halloran	
Tartann,		Willy,	Betty.	Ellen (Matron of Honour)
	Lizzie		Auntie Mary	

CHAPTER 9

The Hallorans who remained - Carrowbaun

Introduction

Chapters 9 and 10 will try to outline the lives of the Halloran Families who remained in Aghamore. Unlike the account of the Hallorans who went to Birstall, it will not take a chronological approach, but will rather discuss the four families according to the townlands in which they resided. This chapter deals with Martin Halloran's family in the townland of Carrowbaun, while Chapter 10 deals with the Hallorans of Raith, Cornageaghta and Cahir.

What we can learn of the Halloran families who remained is limited, not only because of the events being shrouded through time, but also by the fact that many Irish records, like the Irish people themselves, were devastated over the years by political violence and disease. During the civil war in 1922, the IRA irregulars destroyed the Public Records Office in Dublin, resulting in the loss of most of the nineteenth century census records. Further records were shredded by the British during WW1. Disaster also struck at the local level; in 1866 the Aghamore parish priest died of typhoid, resulting in everything in his house being burned in a effort to stop the spread of disease. Aghamore parish records (APR) of birth, marriage and death records are only available from 1864 onwards.

However, it is clear the Famine inaugurated a period of population decline that saw the population of Mayo drop by 51% between 1841 and 1901, the highest declines being between 1841 and 51, where there was a 29.41% decline, and 1881-91, where the decline was 10.68% (Vaughan & Fitzpatrick, 1978:p.17). But the situation was quite complex. Aghamore experienced a 15-24% decline between 1841 and 1851, and a 17% to 36% increase between 1851 and 1881. S.H. Cousens accounts for this by the availability of wasteland in the Swinford Union (which includes the parish of Aghamore) drawing in some of those displaced by the massive clearances, especially by eviction, in the fertile lowlands where the number of small farms was significantly reduced at a time when the population of Aghamore increased. It may be surprising but it is a fact that a great swath of wasteland in East Mayo was reclaimed through the drainage of mountains and bogs during the Great Famine. It is likely that some of this work in Mountain Common, Raith and Cahir was done by Hallorans, brothers or sons, cousins or nephews of James.

The Aghamore graveyard and former parish church

As we have seen in chapter 1, a James Halloran is recorded in Griffith's Valuation as a tenant farmer in Carrowbaun in the parish of Aghamore. This is the only Halloran entry in the parish. He is likely to have been born around 1807, maybe the year before Thomas, who went with his family to England during the Great Famine. James may have been the eldest son, and may have taken over the family holding, which had been unable to support the family. This can only be speculation, but the name 'James', though

Chapter 9 – THE HALLORANS WHO REMAINED IN AGHAMORE

common, had obvious significance. Thomas' eldest son, who was born in Ireland before the Famine, was christened James. One of Michael's sons was also named James.

Outhouses in Carrowbaun, probably remnants of the townland clachan where the Hallorans lived. Siobhan, Aibhne, Helen and Seán O'Halloran

The exact relationship between Thomas and Michael, the two brothers, and James is not clear. A source of doubt is the fact that the name 'Aghamore', given by Michael in the English census of 1871 as his place of birth, refers both to the parish and a townland within it. We cannot be certain whether he was referring to Aghamore, the parish, or Aghamore, the townland. If he meant the parish, it is possible the three men came from Carrowbaun. If, however, he was referring to Aghamore, the townland adjacent to Carrowbaun, they could possibly be less closely related, perhaps cousins. We know that Halloran families were also found in the townlands of Raith, Cahir and Mountaincommon after the Famine. Michael's wife Honoria was recorded in the same census as born in Cloonfallagh.

James himself died in Ballinaclocha (an alternative name for Carrowbaun) on 11th May 1882, aged approximately 75. His son, Tom of Cornageaghta, recorded the death. Tom was born in 1839, and would have remembered the Famine and his uncles Thomas and Michael setting off to England with their family and neighbours.

We also know from Michael's marriage certificate, as discussed in chapter 1, that Michael's - and therefore Thomas' - father was also Michael and that he was designated as a 'labourer'. Michael's marriage to Honoria Stinshin [Stenson] took place in Dewsbury, Yorkshire, on 13th November 1851. Michael's wife was Judith Stenson, born in Cloonfallagh. As we saw in Chapter 1, there was a Michael and an Owen Stenson living in Carrowbaun in 1856. We also noted there that a George Stenson and Co. had leased land from the Dillons in Carrowbeg /Carnbeg in 1801. Also in Aghamore, according to Griffith Valuation, we find a Patrick, Peter and Philip Stenson in Arderry and a John Stenson in Falleighter, near Carrowbaun. Extraordinarily, we know that the three Halloran men, James, Thomas and Michael, all married Stenson girls. Phil Reilly told us that her grandfather Martin told her his grandfather (James) had married a Stenson. We also know Thomas married Judy Stenson and Michael married Hannah (Honoria) Stenson.

Nonetheless, Michael's birth in Aghamore means there were Hallorans in the parish in 1827, the approximate date of his birth. However, the earliest reference to Hallorans in Aghamore that we could find is to a Thomas Halloran and Co. which appears in the Tithe Applotment book for the area of 'Caltragh' around 1832. Could this be the Thomas (b. 1807) who went to Birstall, or perhaps his father or uncle? If it were he, he was about 25 years old at the time. The modern spelling for this word is 'Caldragh', which means a graveyard for unbaptised children. These were usually located on the site of an ancient but disused church. In the *Notes on the Parish of Aghamore* by John P. Jordan[1], there is reference to a *caldragh* in Ballinaclough (Ballinacloy). Jordan remarks that if there had been a church on that site, there is now no trace of it. However, Ordinance Survey maps show there is a Fort Caldragh in Ballinaclocha just south of southern boundary of Carrowbaun, where Martin Halloran grazes cattle to this day (see map of Carrowbaun that follows). This fort may well have housed a chapel. This location strongly suggests that these fields have been worked by the Halloran family since at least that time. There is also a Lough Caldragh adjoining Rath townland (see map of Rath) where Hallorans are found in the following generations. Rath also adjoins Carrowbaun, where James Halloran had a holding in 1856.

The 'and Co.' mentioned in the applotment book simply means that Thomas Halloran was the man responsible for handing over the tithes, which he would have been responsible for gathering from others in the area. It probably does not imply any particular status.

In order to find out about the descendants of these shadowy figures, we have to rely on the post-1864 Aghamore Parish records of births[2] and marriages[3] and the Irish Census of 1901.

Hallorans in Aghamore parish in the 1901 Irish census

Looking first at the 1901 Irish census we find records of four Halloran households in four townlands in the Parish of Aghamore. We know that three of them - Martin of Carrowbaun, Patrick of Cahir and Thomas of Cornageaghta - were sons of James[4]. There is also a record of a Patrick of Rath, born about 1866, who married a Catherine Morley (31) b. about 1870. His father is unknown, but his age and the name Patrick indicate he was not James' son.

Townland	Head of household			Other occupants
	Father	Given name	Occupation	
Cornageaghta	James Halloran	Thomas (62) b. abt 1840 married Sarah in 1867	shepherd	Sarah **Coyne** (59) b. abt 1841, wife Michael (20) b. abt 1881, son Thomas (15) b. abt 1886, son
Caher	James Halloran	Patrick Halloran (57) b. abt 1845 married to Winnifrid (56) in 1865	farmer/listed as married	Martin (24) b. abt 1877, son Sarah (18) b. abt 1883, daughter
Carrowbaun	James Halloran	Martin (50) b. abt 1851	farmer	Winnie **Ruane** (46) b. abt 1855, wife Mary (17) b. abt 1883, daughter Winnie (15) b. abt 1885, daughter Bridget (14) b. abt 1886, daughter Martin (9) b. abt 1891 Bridget (55) sister/not married, b. abt 1845
Rath	Halloran	Patrick (35) b. abt 1866	farmer	Catherine **Morley** (31) b. abt 1870 Bridget (8), b. abt 1893, daughter Catherine (6), b. abt 1895, daughter Mary (4) b. abt 1897, daughter James (2) b. abt 1899, daughter Patrick (1mo.) b. abt 1901, son Catherine (72) mother/widow b. abt 18 Bridget Lavan (18) visitor/seamstress

The complete records of Hallorans who appear in the Aghamore parish records of baptisms (1864 to 1903) and marriages (Sept. 1st 1864 -June 24th 1882) appear in the appendices.

---

1 http://www.aghamoreireland.com/history/overview.htm

2 Births - http://www.eastmayo.org/Aghamore_1864_1883_and_Knock_1869_1905_Baptisms.htm

3 Marriages - http://eastmayo.org/Aghamore_Marriages_1864_1882.htm

4 Information from records in the South Mayo Family Research Centre, supplied by Ger Delaney

Chapter 9 – THE HALLORANS WHO REMAINED IN AGHAMORE

Possible Aghamore family tree with dates of birth

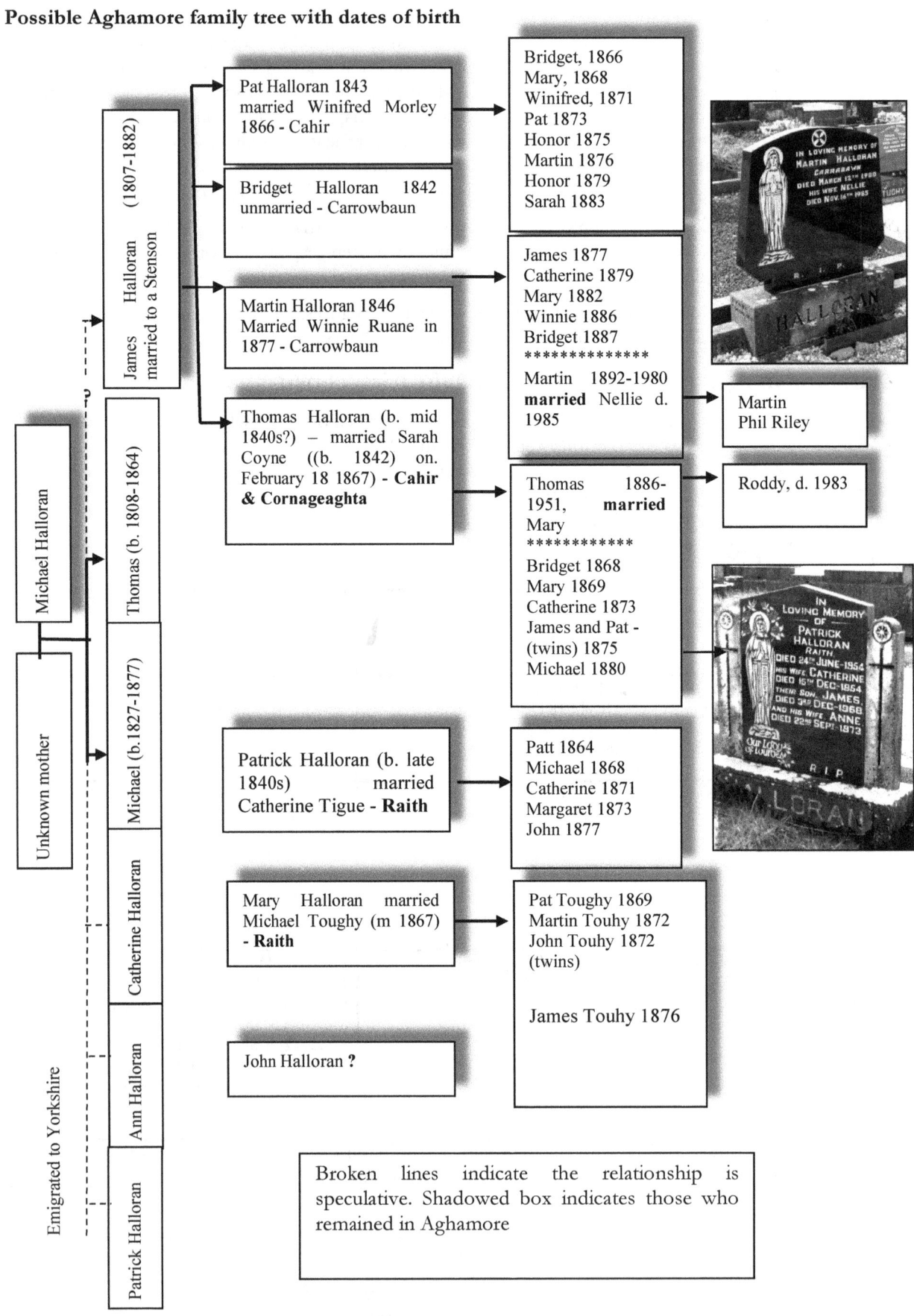

Broken lines indicate the relationship is speculative. Shadowed box indicates those who remained in Aghamore

THE HALLORANS FROM BIRSTALL AND AGHAMORE

Carrowbaun

The details for Carrowbaun in 1856, as found in Griffith's valuation, have been outlined and discussed in chapter 1. Records in Yorkshire reveal the presence there of the brothers, Thomas and Michael, as well as Catherine Halloran (b. 1821), wife of Patrick Frain, whose family were living next-door to Thomas Halloran and family in Low Lane, Birstall, immediately after the Great Famine. Also closely related were Anne Halloran and Patrick Halloran, who, as discussed in chapter 5, married in Birstall in 1852 and 1853 respectively.

Aghamore parish records

In the Aghamore Parish Records, we find evidence of a Martin (b. abt. 1851) Halloran's marriage taking place to Winnie (Una) Ruane (b. abt. 1855) in January 10, 1877.

In these records we also learn of the birth of older children not recorded as living at home in the 1911 census. They are:

- James baptised Dec. 23rd 1877 and recorded as from Ballinaclocha. His sponsors were James and Catherine Halleran from Ballinaclocha. It is unlikely that his grandparents would be his Godparents, so this may be another Halloran family, not recorded in the census. We were told by Martin Joe Halloran of Swinford and his sister Phil Reilly, direct descendants from this family, that James tragically died at five years of age, having bled to death due to a foot injury.

- Catherine, baptised 19th Oct. 1879, is recorded as from Ballinaclocha. Her sponsors were Patrick Ruane and Mary (surname indecipherable).

- Mary, baptised Sept 10th 1882, is recorded as from Ballinaclocha. Her sponsors were James Ruane and Bridget Kelly - Ballinaclocha-. She was reported as being 17 in the 1901 census but must have been a year or so older.

We get some impression about the people and the improving conditions on the Dillon estates during this period from Coulter (1862).

> *The progress of the people in industrial knowledge is slow, but it is plainly perceptible. Some years ago the sowing of turnips and grass seeds was unknown in this locality, but now they are sown in increasing quantities every year, and the people cultivate their land more carefully, though they have yet much to learn in this respect. They are allowed to sell the good-will of their holdings, and even an outgoing tenant is liberally paid for any real improvement that he may have made on his land.*

Irish census of 1901

In the Irish census of 1901, we find Martin Halloran (b abt. 1851) aged 50, and wife and family in Carrowbaun. He was recorded as head of the household and a farmer.

Winnie (b. abt. 1855) aged 46, is his wife. Also in the household are Martin (b. abt. 1892), aged 9 and at school. Mary, reported as aged 17, (b. abt. 1884 though her probable baptism is recorded as Sept. 10th 1882, making her about 19 in 1901). She and her sister Bridget (b. abt. 1887), aged 14 are both seamstresses. Winnie (b. abt. 1886) aged 15, is at school. Also living with them is Bridget (b. abt. 1846), aged 55 - Martin's elder sister and not married. Phil Reilly told us that she made a living by spinning and weaving.

Martin Halloran and family in the Irish Census of 1901

Chapter 9 – THE HALLORANS WHO REMAINED IN AGHAMORE

Their dwelling was classified as 3rd class. That is, it had solid walls, probably stone, its roof was perishable, probably thatch, and it had between 2 to 4 rooms but only two windows on the front wall.

There were 2 outhouses: a stable and a barn. 10 of the 14 families in the townland also had barns, probably to keep hay for winter feed, but 9 families had additional cow houses, 8 had piggeries and 4 had sheds. This places Martin's family quite low down the scale in terms of farming resources. No doubt, they had a pig, but no piggery; it probably lived in the house with them, as had been the practice with poor cottiers for generations. No one in the townland, apparently, had a fowl house, though they appeared in great number later, largely as a result of improvements brought about by the Congested District Board.

Martin Halloran's family is one of 13 family households in Carrowbaun. There are 38 males and 44 females in the townland, making a total population of 82.

However, a radical change had taken place since 1856, the date of the Griffith Valuation - Martin is the landholder of the property in which he and his family lived. Not only that, but every household in Carrowbaun was owner-occupied by the turn of the century.

Irish census of 1911

Martin Halloran and family in the Irish Census of 1911

Moving forward ten years to the 1911 Irish Census, we find Martin Halloran now claiming to be aged 65 – one year older than his wife, so born about 1846, (though estimated to have been born about 1851 according to the 1901 census). Also recorded is Winey (Una), his wife, now amazingly 18 years older at 64, (though estimated to have been born about 1855 according to the 1901 census). Bridget, Martin's sister, is still with them and is recorded as aged 69, though recorded as 55 in the 1901 census. Perhaps she was still spinning and weaving. If it was a case of you're as young as you feel, life must have been hard for the older members of the family, especially the women, who record their ages a substantially older than the passing of ten years.

- Catherine, (b. 1879), known as Kate, had left home by this stage. She married Matt Duffy in Kilmovee and had 3 children. One of their daughters still lives in London.

- Mary (b. abt. 1884), aged 26 (though her baptism is recorded as Sept 10th 1882 making her about 29 in 1911), had health problems and never married. She was still at home, as was Martin (b. abt. 1889), now 19. However, she died relatively young

- Winnie (b. abt. 1886) married a local man, Pat Hunt of Falleighter. They had 9 children, all of whom have passed away.

- Bridget (b. abt. 1887) also emigrated to America, but died of TB shortly after her arrival. On the New York Passenger Lists for 1820-1957, there is a record of a Bridget Halloran, born about 1887 sailing from Queenstown to New York on 23 Apr 1909. This may be her.

- Martin (b. abt. 1890) was a young man of 19 at this time; the youngest of the family and the only surviving male. He stayed on in the home place and married Nellie Regan. They had two children, Martin Joe, now of Swinford but who still grazes the land in Carrowbaun, and Phil

- Reilly, a retired school teacher. These are the two members of the Hallorans of Aghamore that we, the authors of this book, met in the summer of 2010 and who have contributed much to these chapters.

- Annie, who does not appear on either census or in any parish records or parish record, also emigrated to America and settled in New York, where she never married and lived to a ripe old age.

Added to the household, however, is Michael Ruane, aged 5, a nephew. Martin Joe Halloran told us that Michael Ruane was taken in by the family as his own family, relatives of Winnie Ruane, was very large. This was not unusual at the time. Martin's grandfather Martin and Michael were like brothers and remained firm friends all their lives. Michael emigrated to the United States, but returned occasionally to visit the family.

We can notice by this stage that the younger members of the family are all entered as English speakers and as able to read and write, so presumably attending the National School. The older members are recorded as speakers of Irish and English but unable to read and write; a clear indicator of the association of Irish speaking with illiteracy among poorer farmers. All family members are recorded as Roman Catholic. There can be no reason to doubt that the younger members of the family also spoke Irish, as it was the language of the parents. However, it appears that the ability to speak English made it unnecessary to record the fact that the person also spoke the stigmatised Irish language. It was sometime before pride in the language was restored, largely through the Gaelic League.

In a separate entry on the census, we also have a description of their dwelling. It had stone walls, a thatched roof, 2/4 rooms and 3 widows in the front; one more than in 1901, suggesting a room had either been added or made more habitable since 1901, by the addition of a window. Also recorded in the census are out-houses. These include a cow house, calf house, a piggery and a barn - clearly suggesting grazing and mixed farming. The outhouses for cattle, calves and pigs had been acquired since the previous census. However, in 1901 they had a stable, which they no longer possess, which is surprising as ten of the thirteen farms recorded in the townland had stables. It could of course mean that horses were stabled with neighbouring relatives.

Griffith's Evaluation 1856	Head of household 1901	Head of household 1911
	Brennan, Mary	Brennan, Mary
Cox, James	Cox, James	Cox, James
Fahy, Patrick	Fahey, Pat	Fahey, Pat
Galvey, Timothy		
Halloran, James	Halloran, Martin	Halloran, Martin
Keane, Owen	Keene, Pat	Keene, Patk
Kelly, Bridget	Kelly, Thomas	Kelly, Thomas
	Leonard, Pat	Leonard, Pat
Linskey, Owen		Linskey, Mary
Prendergast, Thomas	Prendergast, Thomas	Prendergast, Thomas
Regan, Thomas	Regan, Martin	Regan, Martin
Stenson, Michael	Stenson, Thomas	Thomas Stenson
Stenson, Owen		John Stenson
Tigue, James	Tigue, Julia	Tigue, Julia
	Waldron, Catherine	Waldron, James
	Leonard, Pat	Leonard, Pat

Families in Carrowbaun according to Griffith's Valuation (1856), the 1901 Census and the 1911 census

Chapter 9 – THE HALLORANS WHO REMAINED IN AGHAMORE

The table above is interesting as it shows us who were the Halloran's neighbours in Carrowbaun at the three points at which we have information, namely: Griffith's Valuation (1856), the 1901 Census and the 1911 census. It demonstrates that within the fifty-five years between the Griffith Valuation and the 1911 census there was a remarkable continuity of tenure, which is in marked contrast to the pre-Famine period where we saw much agitation about the shortness of land leases and land clearances. This new stability came about for two reasons: one was to do with the dramatic drop in population due to the Great Famine and its continued reduction afterwards; the other was the impact of land reform legislation, which resulted in the destruction of the Landlord system and the acquisition of the land they had worked on so long by the Irish cottiers and small land holders.

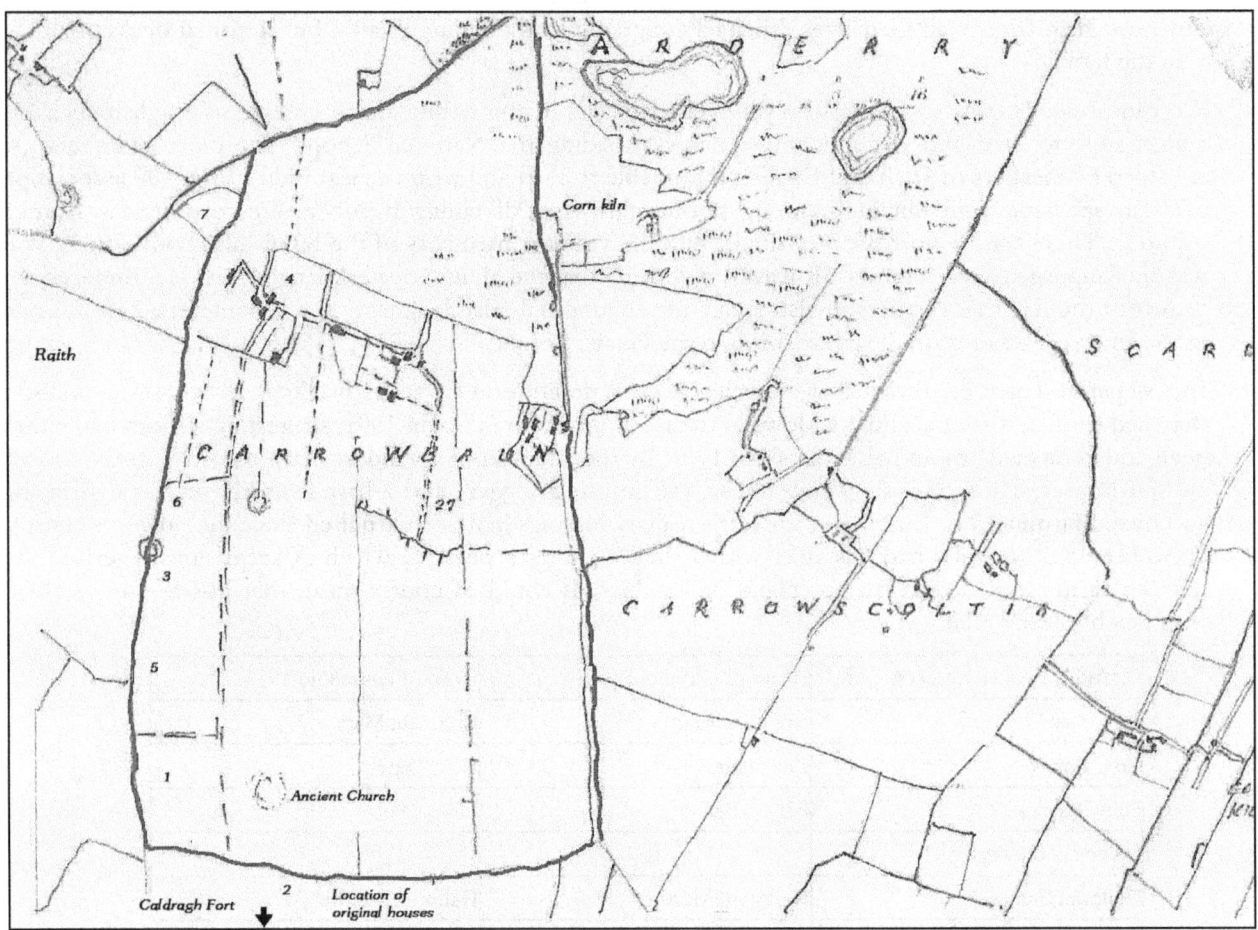

Derived from Ordinance Survey maps of 1838. Numbering indicates names of fields, as indicated below. Just off map is Caldragh Fort, reported as a burial ground for children.

Name of fields

1. *Cnoc a t-Seagail* - hill of the rye
2. *Cnoc na Míoltóg* - hill of the flies
3. *Machaire Charraigin* or *Harraigín*
4. *Long Garbh / Oileán Garbh* - rough or wild island
5. *Móinín, Páirc a' Chruinneacht*
6. *Páirc a' leasa*
7. *Sraith*

Phil Reilly (neé Halloran), whose family worked these fields for at least three generations, remembered the names of the fields used by her father. She vividly recalled some of her experiences over the years, which were published in *Glór Achadh Mór* in 2002 and has kindly consented we could use much of this in this chapter. Phil wrote this account when she retired from teaching at *Tuaidn* Primary School after over forty years service.

Family voices - Phil Reilly neé Halloran

All of the fields had Irish or Gaelic names. We had Cnoc a t-Seagail, the hill of the rye. We also had Cnoc na Míoltóg the hill of the flies. Rye of course was believed to be the best source of straw for roof thatching. Those were hills of sand. It was from Cnoc a t-Seagail that my father drew the sand for our house and from where he got most of the stone for it also. He had to dig out the sand and stones with a pickaxe and shovel and transport it by horse and cart down to the building site.

Another group of fields was called Machaire Charraigin or Harraigín. It's difficult to know if this referred to the flat place of the small rock or Harrigan's meadow, as in the surname.

We had a field that was called Long Garbh but my dad explained that the old Gaelic name in full was Oileán Garbh or the rough or wild island. It was at the lower end of our land across the road and was indeed surrounded by water at least on three sides.

Our neighbours had fields called Móinin, Páirc a' Chruinneacht, Páirc a' leasa and one called Sraith which was a boggy or marshy area near the river. Their sraith was in fact corresponding to our Oileán Garbh.

The names of these fields, alone, suggest that the land was originally boggy and marginal as far as farming was concerned, supporting the belief that only the more desperate would have sought to work it. Also of interest is the proximity of Caldragh Fort to where the Hallorans lived and worked. We noted in chapter 1 that the earliest Halloran we have a record of in the district was a Thomas Halloran and Co. recorded in the Tithe Applotment book in for around 1832 who paid tithes for the area of 'Caltragh'.

Before looking at the Halloran families of Cahir, Rath and Cornageaghta, it is worth examining the immense struggle which took place all over Ireland, and nowhere more than in Mayo, which resulted in the Irish small farmers reclaiming the land they worked.

Michael Davitt and the Land League

On the 25th of March 1846, in Straide, Co. Mayo, a small village about twenty miles from Aghamore, a baby boy called Michael was is born to Martin and Catherine Davitt. The Davitts were small holders whose lives must have been very similar to the Hallorans in Aghamore. Michael was born in the first full year of the Famine, the second of four children born in Ireland. At the age of four, in September 1850, his family were evicted for non-payment of rent. Their landlord was Knox, who, by the early 19th century, held an estate of more than 10,000 acres in the barony of Gallen, County Mayo, situated mainly in the parishes of Templemore, Kilconduff and Killedan. It was a member of this family, Laurence E. Knox, who founded the "Irish Times" newspaper in 1859. They sold the land to Henry Joynt, who, by the time of Griffith's Valuation, held 7 townlands in the parish of Templemore, barony of Gallen[1].

The Davitts, however, were forced to enter a local workhouse. Michael's mother, on discovering that male children over three were separated from their mothers, would have none of it, and decided the family should try to make it to England. Like the Hallorans, they set off with friends on the long journey to England with four small children, at least one of whom was still being breast-fed.

Michael's father, Martin, had been to a hedge school and was literate in both Irish and English. They settled in Lancashire, where Michael started work in a cotton mill as a very small boy. Later, aged eleven, he lost an arm in a factory accident but was refused compensation on the grounds that a boy of his age should not have been working on the machine in the first place. However, a local benefactor, John Dean, recognising his undoubted talents, sponsored him on courses at Wesleyan Mechanics' Hall and he became a typesetter. He was a smart boy and soon learnt French and Italian as well as Irish. He became interested in Irish history and the contemporary problems in Ireland and was greatly influenced by Ernest Charles

---

1 http://www.landedestates.ie/LandedEstates/jsp/estate-list.

Chapter 9 – THE HALLORANS WHO REMAINED IN AGHAMORE

Jones, the veteran English radical and Chartist leader. He was one of the first Irishmen to be radicalized in England.

From the Chartists, perhaps the first working class movement for political and social reform in the world, he developed radical views on land nationalization and Irish independence. He went on to become a journalist and was involved with the Irish Republican Brotherhood. This resulted in his participation in a raid on Chester Castle on 11th February 1867 and gun-running, which in turn led to his arrest and subsequent imprisonment as a Fenian. Unlike many Irish radicals, he was prepared to enter Westminster and challenge the nature of British rule from there, haranguing the British government and the landlords of Ireland in his broad Lancashire accent, which remained with him until the day he died.

The Land War

The year 1870 saw the beginning of a ne2 and highly effective phase of agrarian agitation in rural Ireland aimed at improving the rights of tenant farmers and ultimately achieving their ownership of the land. Davitt returned to Ireland and became a major political force, insisting that, 'the land question can be definitely settled only by making the cultivators of the soil proprietors'. He was soon recognized as a leading spokesman in radical Irish politics and he founded the Land League of Mayo and inaugurated the Land War by establishing the Irish National Land League in 1879, with the support of Devoy and Parnell. It was not actually a "war", but rather a prolonged period of civil unrest, resulting in a number of violent incidents and some deaths. Its aims can be summed up in the 'three Fs': Fair Rent, Fixity of Tenure and Free Sale.

When Parnell became President, the Land League became a major political force. As a result of the escalating protest it became obvious to members of the British Government that the 'Irish problem' could not be ignored, especially as there was such a startling disparity between the way in which Britain and Ireland were governed.

Irishtown Tenants Defence Meeting[1] *26th April 1879, Connaught Telegraph*

One of the greatest public demonstrations ever witnessed in the West of Ireland took place on Sunday last at Irishtown. The object of the meeting was to advocate for the protection of the small tenant farmers against the iniquitous extortion of some landlords, ... and to demand an abatement of the present rent in proportion to the great reduction that has taken place in the value of produce, stock, etc., ... which has placed several thousand tenant-farmers indebted to a degree that they cannot till their lands, pay their rents or support their families; hence the cause of so many ejectments for non-payment of rent that have taken place at the different quarter sessions held in the county.

Since the days of O'Connell, a larger public demonstration has not been witnessed than that of Sunday last ... At 11 0' clock a monster contingent of tenant-farmers on horseback drew up in front of Hughes's Hotel ... Next followed a train of carriages, brakes, cars, etc. .... taking Messrs J. 1. Louden, J. Daly, O'Connor Power M.P., and Thomas Brennan.

At 2 0' clock the meeting began, and was addressed by James Daly, (Connaught Telegraph), Thomas Brennan, John Ferguson (Glasgow), John 1. Louden, John O'Connor-Power, M.R, and Matthew Harris, in the presence of 13,000 tenant-farmers.

Landlord and Tenant Act (1870)

One of their first legislative successes was the Landlord and Tenant Act (1870). The tenant farmers of Carrowbaun had few rights compared to those in England, where there was a right to compensation for improvement made to the property. For the likes of Martin, any improvements usually resulted in an increase in rent, resulting in a complete lack of incentive to improve either their standard of living or methods of farming. The Landlord and Tenant Act was an attempt to remedy this by extending the tenant-right that prevailed in Ulster, where there had been improvements in agriculture. However, the Act did not have the effect the reformers wanted, but it did suit the landlords. By providing compensation for improvements made by the tenant, and by granting compensation for giving up the land, evictions were

---

1 Extracts from Kiltimagh: Our Life and Times, Eds. Peter Sobolewski & Betty Solan, Kiltimagh Historic Society.

made easier. The Act actually facilitated land clearances and did not address the main concern of the tenants, which was security of tenure rather than compensation after eviction. However, even the right to compensation was often thwarted. Some landlords continued to increase rent, forcing tenants into arrears and then claimed the arrears against any improvements. Land shortages meant that there were enough needy tenants ready to pay the increased rents. An aggrieved tenant could take the matter to court, but all he could hope for was monetary compensation; he was compelled to surrender the land regardless.

By the late 1870s, the economy of Mayo was in crisis. Pressure for reform increased as famine again threatened the countryside. Incessant rain and bad harvests meant yields were down, rents could not be paid and evictions increased. These conditions hardly changed throughout the decade and, for many, were as bad as during the Great Famine. Though the horrors of the Great Famine have given it great prominence in Irish history, it was not a catastrophic aberration. For many of the ordinary rural population of Connaught, it was simply a particularly intense and prolonged period of hardship and hunger, conditions which visited them frequently over the course of their lives. The Table of Distress contained in the *Reports on the Condition of the Peasantry of the County of Mayo, during the Famine Crisis of 1880* reveals the extent of that hardship in the 1880s. There is an entry for Aghamore.

TABLE OF DISTRESS

District	No. of persons in distress. First local estimate.	Latest returns on number in distress. March 1st	Extracts from appeals of local committees, duly authenticated
Aughermore	3000	1,800	People actually starving; bad harvest and no employment.
Ballyhaunis	1,000	11,550	Small farmers, total failure of crops.
Bekan	3,000	2789	Fifty families in state of starvation, the others almost as bad.
Bohhola	2500	2685	Eating seed potatoes; pawning every available article.
Charlestown	5000	4136	Unless generous assistance forthcoming, the scenes of '47 will be repeated.
Claremorris	1000	3560	Distress widespread and severe. The poor entirely depending on charity.
Foxford	3500	Increasing every day	Entirely depending on Mansion House committee; terrible destitution.
Knock	2000	2500	Terrible destitution. People half-starved.
Killasser	3000	3330	Failure of crops caused general and deep distress.
Kiltymagh	2500	Increasing every day	Unless permanent relief be established, starvation will be general.
Swinford	3000	3000	Destitution due to failure of crops and want of usual earnings in England.
Strade	2800	2800	Struggling poor people, now destitute owing to failure of potato crop.

The Dempsey Eviction

An illustration of how the Land League was adapting a more radical approach in its challenge of landlord power is the case of the Dempsey eviction. The Dempseys lived thirty miles from Aghamore in Loona More, a townland near Balla. Just one month after the foundation of the Land League, the family of Anthony Dempsey was evicted by Sir Robert Blosse Lynch. In 1877 and 1878 the crops were bad and by May 1879 Anthony owed £26, and Sir Robert Blosse Lynch issued a decree against him. Despite being told the circumstances, he still decided to go ahead with the eviction. The Dempsey family were struck down with fever and measles and the sheriff, on seeing the plight of the family decided to postpone the eviction.

Land League activists from Balla posted notices of a rally on the Dempsey property. On the day of the proposed eviction a large gathering of reporters from throughout Ireland and England arrived. The rally, which was led by the Fenian leader, P.W. Nally from Balla, consisted of a large body of men all armed with sticks. Charles Stuart Parnell was also sent for and Michael Davitt arrived by train in Balla. As the

Chapter 9 – THE HALLORANS WHO REMAINED IN AGHAMORE

column of men approached the Dempsey residence they were met by the R.I.C. who challenged them with pointed rifles. Parnell ordered the Land Leaguers to fall back1.

According to the report of R.I.C. Inspector Wise, the rally was large. It was chaired by John J. Loudin and a number of resolutions supporting the aims of the League were passed. However, after the glare of the media attention had died down the eviction went ahead. The Land League realised that mere rallies would not be sufficient to stop the evictions and if news of the Dempsey eviction spread it would not augur well for the movement. Therefore it was decided to pay the £26 rent out of League funds. Following the payment the Dempsey family was allowed back into their cottage.

This climb-down convinced those agitating for land reform that much more radical, united action was needed. Davitt had been greatly influenced by the working class radicalism of English socialists and trades unionist who found strength in solidarity. This combined with the traditions of the Whiteboys and Ribbonmen, who frequently menaced traders who overcharged and landlords who pushed up rents and evicted their tenants, transformed the nature of Irish protest and agitation to great effect.

Charles Stewart Parnell

The Plan of Campaign

The Plan of Campaign was thus launched by members of the Irish Parliamentary Party, including Timothy Healy, Timothy Harrington, secretary of the Irish National League, William O'Brien and John Dillon. The plan was to secure a reduction of rents where tenants could not pay them because the poor harvest created new famine conditions. If a landlord refused to reduce the rent, the rest of the tenants, even those who could afford it, would refuse to pay any rent at all. As it was, rents were frequently pushed beyond the value of the holdings determined by the Poor Rates. To strengthen their hand and undermine the Land League, the British Government prevailed on Pope Leo XIII to issue a rescript condemning the Plan of Campaign and the practice of boycotting, warning the clergy to stay clear of such activities. However, this had little effect on some members of the clergy who were often deeply involved in the campaign.

Martin and his family were almost certainly caught up in the agitation surrounding this campaign. The Dillon Estate in Mayo, then probably owned by Arthur Edmund Denis Dillon (1812-1892), the 16th Viscount Dillon, attracted much notoriety, and questions about high rents were asked in Westminster. Mr Daniel Crilly, Westminster MP for Mayo North, had visited the Dillon estates and made speeches to the tenants supporting the Plan of Campaign, and, as incitement to withhold rent was a punishable offences, he and others, were in the process of being prosecuted when he made the following speech in the House of Commons on the 2nd February 1887:

> *Not very long ago the rental of that [Dillon's] estate was £5,000; but, owing to the ceaseless industry of the tenants, it had increased to £25,000. Yet the tenants of that estate never saw their landlord, and never received from him one single penny to improve the condition of their wretched homes. Today there was standing near the avenue leading to the mansion of Lord Dillon, at Loughglynn, a village of hovels that would simply disgrace a Zulu kraal. A Zulu kraal would be comfort and magnificence compared with the village of Loughglynn ... Lord Dillon was asked to give 25 per cent reduction .... not 20 per cent of the tenants could pay their rents from the produce of the soil. The other 80 per cent of the tenants paid their rents from their earnings in the harvest fields of England; but, during the last two or three years, that source of income having failed owing to the agricultural depression which prevailed, the tenants were not able to*

---

1 Brian Hoban - http://towns.mayo-ireland.ie/WebX?14@195.LsDgehPp3vR.0@.2cb63f00

pay their full rents, and when they asked for the moderate reduction of 25 per cent their request was insolently refused. Lord Dillon, so the story ran, declared that he would rather go into the workhouse for two years than grant one single penny of abatement[1].

The tenants joined the Plan of Campaign, and the result was that, though the pressure of the Government brought by the Chief Secretary failed to induce Lord Dillon to give one penny of reduction on rents, the Plan of Campaign induced Lord Dillon to give 20 per cent reduction, pay all law costs, and reinstate evicted tenants.

The defeat of Lord Dillon was a momentous event in the lives of the Hallorans of Carrowbaun. We don't know to what extent Martin Halloran was involved in the agitation, or whether he was part of the 20% who could not afford to pay the rent, or part of the 80% who could. The fact is the tenants won.

Unaffordable rents were not the only problem. The law and its enforcement still lay in the hands of the landed gentry. The full force of the law continued to be applied to members of the Irish Parliamentary Party, yet landlords like Viscount Dillon and their agents were frequently guilty of abusing it.

John Dillon MP for Mayo, East, was a firm believer in constitutional reform. His grandfather and great grandfather, Luke, were tenants on the Dillon estates in Lissians[2], less than 20 miles from Carrowbaun. Luke was evicted for non-payment of rents, even though, it appears, he was an impoverished descendent of the Viscount Dillons. As a member of parliament, John Dillon MP asked the Chief Secretary to the Lord Lieutenant of Ireland to answer a series of questions about a case of serious assault. He asked:

whether, at Ballaghaderreen, County May, at the Petty Sessions on Monday the 25th July, a prosecution was brought by Patrick Shryane against Thomas Casey and John Brennan for assault?

whether the former [Thomas Casey] is a process server who served several ejectments for Lord Dillon, and the latter [John Brennan] an employee of Lord Dillon's under agent?

whether the only magistrate present was Lord Dillon's agent, Mr. Hussey?

whether, in the course of complainant's evidence, Mr. Hussey asked his [Shryane's] solicitor if he intended to call any witnesses, and, on being answered in the affirmative, immediately remarked that he should consider their evidence worthless, and without any application ordered all Shryane's witnesses out of Court? ...

whether Brennan called no witnesses in his defence, and, notwithstanding this, Mr. Hussey dismissed the case?; and/

if the above facts be true/ whether he will direct the attention of the Lord Chancellor to the conduct of Mr. Hussey in trying cases in which he is personally interested?[3]

The issues raised by Crilly and Dillon suggest a new, more ruthless and high-handed approach to tenants in the Dillon estates, and that the Dillon agent, Hussey, took a very different approach to Charles Strickland. John Dillon's questions clearly suggest the degree of collusion between Dillon's agent, as a magistrate, and his bailiffs, and the powerlessness of the ordinary people in the face of such collusion. Whereas such men could act with impunity, the law was applied assiduously to those who sought reform. However, the growing strength of the Irish Parliamentary Party combined with more forceful and strategic agitation in the countryside began to have an effect.

In October 1880, at a mass meeting of the Land League in Loughglynn, the residence of Viscount Dillon, the idea of ostracising ordinary Irish farmers as well as the landlords' bailiffs and agents was proposed. James Grogan declared:

The man who takes a farm from which another has been evicted is worse than the man who evicts, is a powerful weapon in the lands of the landlord. He is a traitor to our country and an enemy to our cause, and should be denied the recognition of every man. No man should buy from him, no man should lend to him, no man should speak to him on the highway or byway, at Mass or at meeting. Everyman's hand should be against him, his life should be made miserable, until he is obliged to surrender his ill-gotten prey.

---

1 Westminster Orders of the Day: http://yourdemocracy.newstatesman.com/parliament/orders-of-the-day /HAN1 030300 S

2 Máire McDonnell-Garvey states it was the De Freyne estate.

3 http://yourdemocracy.newstatesman.com/parliament/questions/HAN1071946

Chapter 9 – THE HALLORANS WHO REMAINED IN AGHAMORE

Brennan declared:

> *We have prospects of a golden harvest this year and the question will come to be decided whether you will quietly surrender that harvest in order that a few idlers may enjoy the usual quantity of champagne. (Quoted, McDonell-Garvey, 1995, p: 128)*

> **Extracts from, Reports on the Condition of the Peasantry of the County of Mayo, during the Famine Crisis of 1880. Drawn up by J. A. Fox, a member of the Mansion House Committee**
>
> *At Ballaghaderreen ... Typhus fever had broken out, and had extended to some ten or twelve families altogether already. Here, as elsewhere, the people were stricken with terror at the proximity of a disease, accompanied by delirium in some of its stages, which might have the effect of depriving them of the consolations of religion at the hour of death. ... The Poor Law system provides in theory that no man shall die of starvation, while it will be my painful duty now to report, on unimpeachable authority, that many thousands of human beings would have died of starvation during the past few months except for the relief doled out by the various charitable committees throughout North Mayo during that period; and what the fate of this destitute population must be, should our funds fail before the gathering of the harvest, will be abundantly shown by my subsequent observations. Many thousands of persons - men, women and children - are wholly supported by the charity of these committees throughout the wide area.*
>
> *I do not believe that tongue, or pen, however, eloquent, could truly depict the awful destitution of some of those hovels. The children are often nearly naked. Bedding there is none, everything of that kind having long since gone to the pawn-office, as proved to me by numerous tickets placed in my hands for inspection in well-nigh every hovel. A layer of old straw, covered by dirty sacks which conveyed the seed potatoes and artificial manure in the spring, is the sole provision of thousands - with this exception, that little babies in wooden boxes are occasionally indulged with a bit of thin, old flannel stitched on the sacking. Sometimes even charity itself had failed, and the mother of the tender young family was found absent, begging for the loan of some Indian meal from other recipients of charitable relief - the father being in almost every instance away in England labouring to make out some provision for the coming winter.*
>
> *Men, women, and children sleep under a roof and within walls dripping with wet, while the floor is saturated with damp, not uncommonly oozing out of it in little pools. The construction and dimensions of their hovels are, as abodes of human beings, probably unique. On the uplands they are mostly built of common stone walls without plaster, and are often totally devoid of the ordinary means of exit for the smoke, as it may also be almost said they are devoid of anything in the shape of furniture. On the low-laying lands on the other hand, they may be briefly described as bog holes, though by a merciful dispensation of the architect, these are undoubtedly rendered somewhat warmer out of their very construction out of solidified peat and mud. Their dimensions are even more extraordinary still, varying from 12 feet to 15 feet, down to half that limited space, yet all of them are inhabited by large families of children, members of whom sleep on a little straw spread on the bare ground, with nothing to cover them except the rags and tatters worn during the day. I invariable found them on the occasion of my visits crouched around the semblance of a fire, lighted on the open hearth. And this at mid-summer, showing how terribly low must be the vitality among them ...*
>
> *It was only when I was accompanied by a Catholic priest could I get an insight into their appalling character ... Everywhere the condition of the children was dreadful, having nothing but Indian corn, badly cooked, to live upon, and the parents only too glad if the charitable funds provided the family with half enough even of that. Sometimes there was a miserable cow about the premises, ... and this cow was supplying milk, principally gratis, to a small number of children other than the owner's, to mix with the Indian corn ... At other times cabbage, without a morsel of condiment, save salt was found where there was no meal, and in some instances, one was found mixed with the other. But, in numerous cases, there was neither milk, meal or cabbage about the premises, and in those I gave some temporary relief ... Yet in the most destitute cases hardly a word of complaint was uttered on the subject, it being a habit with, if not the nature of, the Mayo peasant submissively to ascribe his lot in times of scarcity as well as plenty to the 'will of providence'.*

THE HALLORANS FROM BIRSTALL AND AGHAMORE

Boycotting

The tenant farmers felt a new courage and sense of empowerment. Rents were withheld; agents, bailiffs, and process servers were boycotted. Even those who supplied these men goods and services were in danger of visits at night and threatened, as well as being boycotted themselves. No doubt, in many cases, injustices were done and innocent family members suffered; however, as a form of protest, such measures were so widespread and difficult to combat, that the pressure on the British government became insurmountable and the positions of many landlords untenable. Gradually, the demands of the Land League were met and reforms like the Land Law (Ireland) Act (1881) were enacted. These are discussed in detail in chapter 10, as is the impact of the Act on the Hallorans of Rath, Cahir and Mountain townlands.

The power of this political ostracism is well illustrated in this account by Bernard H. Becker, described as a Special Commissioner of the *Daily News*, in *Disturbed Ireland: Being the Letters Written during the Winter of 1880-81*. In this extract, he describes trying to find out the whereabouts of a 'lister', that is person on the list of those to be ostracised. He had wanted to meet this man and had enquired about him in Westport, but to no avail.

> *As a resident on Lough Mask for seven years, and agent to Lord Erne, he seemed to be a man concerning whose movements the country side would probably be well informed. But nobody knew anything at all about him… In one of the larger stores I saw that the mention of his name drew every eye upon me, and that the bystanders were greatly exercised as to my identity and my business.*

The man he was enquiring about was Captain Boycott. Becker, however, was not deterred by the lack of information, he set off to find him. He describes this chance encounter on the road.

> *Beyond a turn in the road was a flock of sheep, in front of which stood a shepherdess heading them back, while a shepherd, clad in a leather shooting-jacket and aided by a bull terrier, was driving them through a gate into an adjacent field. Despite her white woollen shawl and the work she was engaged upon, it was quite evident, from her voice and manner, that the shepherdess was of the educated class, and the shepherd, albeit dressed in a leather jacket, carried himself with the true military air. Both were obviously amateurs at sheep-driving, and the smart, intelligent bull terrier was as much an amateur as either of them, for shepherd, shepherdess and dog were only doing what a good collie would achieve alone and unaided.*
>
> *Behind the shepherd were two tall members of the Royal Irish Constabulary in full uniform and with carbines loaded. As the shepherd entered the field the constables followed him everywhere at a distance of a few yards. All his backings and fillings, turnings and doublings, were followed by the armed policemen. This combination of the most proverbially peaceful of pursuits with carbines and buckshot was irresistibly striking, and the effect of the picture was not diminished by the remarks of Mr. and Mrs. Boycott, for the shepherd and shepherdess were no other than these…*
>
> *It will be recollected that about a month ago a process-server and his escort retreated on Lough Mask House, followed by a mob, and that on the following day all the farm servants were ordered to leave Mr. Boycott's employment… For seven years he has farmed at Lough Mask, acting also as Lord Erne's agent. He has on his own account had a few difficulties with his workpeople; but these were tided over by concessions on his part, and all went smoothly till the serving of notices upon Lord Erne's tenants. All the weight of the tenants' vengeance has fallen upon the unfortunate agent, whom the irritated people declare they will "hunt out of the country." … Personally attended by an armed escort everywhere, he has a garrison of ten constables on his premises, some established in a hut, and the rest in that part of Lough Mask House adjacent to the old castle. Garrisoned at home and escorted abroad, Mr. Boycott and his family are now reduced to one female domestic. Everybody else has gone away, protesting sorrow, but alleging that the power brought to bear upon them was greater than they could resist. Farm labourers, workmen, herds-men, stablemen, all went long ago, leaving the corn standing, the horses in the stable, the sheep in the field, the turnips, swedes, carrots, and potatoes in the ground, where I saw them yesterday. Last Tuesday the laundress refused to wash for the family any longer; the baker at Ballinrobe is afraid to supply them with bread, and the butcher fears to send them meat. The state of siege is perfect…*
>
> *There remains in the ground at least five hundred pounds worth of potatoes and other root crops, and the owner has no possible means of doing anything with them. Nor, I am assured on trustworthy authority, would any human being buy them at any price.*

Here we see the operation of the 'boycott'; the most powerful weapon in the peasants' armoury. We also see the coinage of a new term 'to boycott' that resulted from the widespread reportage of this hapless military gentleman.

Chapter 9 – THE HALLORANS WHO REMAINED IN AGHAMORE

Although a train load of Orangemen were brought down from Ulster to save the harvest, the result was a shambles. The great landlords were increasingly forced to grant concessions and the politicians in Westminster began to address the grievances of the small land holders on their estates.

The Congested Districts Board

The Congested Districts Board was established in 1891 to alleviate poverty and "congested" living conditions in the west of Ireland. In Mayo, the initial funds were used largely in making loans to factories set up by the Sisters of Charity in Foxford and Ballaghaderreen (McDonnell-Garvey, 1995). It also supported other public works, such as building piers to assist fishing, modernising farming methods and sponsoring local factories to increase employment and stem the flow of emigration. Though cynics saw it as a ploy to 'kill Home Rule with kindness', it did much to improve the prospects of those who lived in the most congested and poverty-ridden parts of Ireland. Some of its most significant work was done after 1909, when it was granted powers to make compulsory purchase of estates and began redistributing over 1,000 of them.

However, many major estates were purchased prior to the acquisition of these powers. Martin Halloran was about 50 when he came into possession of the land he, his father, and probably Michael, his grandfather, had worked for at least three generation. In 1899, the Dillon estate, consisting of 87,669 acres, was bought by the Congested Districts Board for £29.000 and the land divided equally among the tenantry, who were given loans, transforming their lives. Not that there weren't delays. McDonnell-Garvey (1995) reports that up to 1904 there were problems apportioning turbary rights to the 2,500 tenants, and, by the end of March, £20,689 had been spent by the board on drainage. On 23rd January 1902, in a debate on the Irish Land Question, John Redmond, MP for Waterford and the leader of the Home Rule Party, spoke of the improved condition of the small farmers on what had been the Dillon Estate.

> *The Congested Districts Board recently purchased in County Roscommon a large estate belonging to Lord Dillon. On the estate were thousands of wretched tenants trying to eke out a living on poor patches of land. The Board are not only selling these holdings to the occupiers, but are also dividing amongst them the large grass lands on the estate, so that in the future the occupiers may have sufficient land to enable them to live. Under that operation these tenants are getting an immediate reduction in their annual payments of about one-third of the rent. That is a most beneficent transaction. It is about the best and holiest work upon which man could be engaged in Ireland.*

By 1902, Martin Halloran (b. 1846) could feel secure that his son, also Martin (b. 1892), would inherit the farm. Thus, the small holders' and Parnell's dream, of 'peasant propriety' was being realised. Michael Davitt, however, was disappointed. His hope for the massive nationalisation of land was never realised. This had a profound impact on the nature of rural Ireland and meant that in turn Martin (b. 1892) could leave his land to his son, Martin, whom we met, and was still grazing cattle on his own land in 2010.

Family voices – Phil Halloran O'Reilly, Carrowbaun/Muimin

The Regan's of Cúighiú

My mother Nellie Regan (1900-1985) was the eldest of a family of nine from Aughtaboy, Cúighiú (Coogue). My grandfather and grandmother were Tom Regan (1872-1959) and Julia Kneafsey (1873-1951) of Cúighiú.

My mother attended Cúighiú primary school and did one year at the convent in Coillte Mach (Kiltamagh). She had an Uncle, Michael Kneafsey in Coillte Mach at the time and stayed with him and went to school to the nuns.

My mother went to America when she was sixteen. She went over to an Aunt, Margaret Regan, and the intention was that she would go on to night school or whatever over there and further her education. However, once over there she got a job and the education plans were set aside. She was earning and of course some of the dollars had to be sent home to help support the family. Eventually the passage was paid for the next sister or brother to go out to the States in turn. This was done until in the end six of the Regan family had emigrated to the US. The family was made up of Nellie (my mother), Celia, Rose, Mary, Tom, John, Tony, Paddy and Frank. Mary, who was Rose's twin, died at the age of three.

The Hallorans and Stensons of Carrowbaun

My dad was a quiet, gentle type of man. He was noted locally for being fairly handy. He often repaired all kinds of things for people. Though he had no particular trade, he'd have a go at fixing carts and bicycles and building sheds and walls. He did this work out of enjoyment and glad to do a good turn for someone but he often said that the thanks that he usually received was, "Well aren't you lucky you're so blessed, so handy". He used to laugh about that.

His father had died when he was quite young and dad so took over the farm from an early age and more or less had to run it himself.

The Stensons

My father was also a good folklorist and he had many of the genealogies of local people and a lot of local history. For example he was related to the local families of Stensons - his grandmother was a Stenson.

He used to talk of seven Stenson brothers who left Co. Leitrim and came to Achadh Mór and settled in the area, between Fal Íochtar (Falleighter), Ceathnú Bán and Ceapach (Cappagh). They had come apparently as herds to work on the grazing farms in the later half of the 1800s[1]. Three adjacent townlands of Ballyine and part of Screig and Buailí were made up mostly of large grazing farms, but whether it was to those farms that the Stensons first came as herdsmen I'm not sure. It's interesting also that a branch of the Hallorans were also herdsmen in Cathair farm near Woodfield and in Corr na gCéachta (Cornageaghta) farm near Achadh Mór and they were related to us.

There was a family of Stensons beside Fal Íochtar (Falleighter) school, (Jackie's) Philip Stensons were over the village in Ard Doire (Arderry) and other Stensons farmed in Ceapach (Cappagh), Ceathrú Scoillte (Carrowscoltia) and in Cluain Gamhnach (Cloongoonagh).

The family next door to us were Tom and Ellen Stenson, Uncle and Aunt of the late Maisie Fox, the local primary teacher, who came to live with them. …

Ellen, I considered a great friend, even as a young child. My brother Martin and I would drop into her house a few times a day, to share any little news. If we got new shoes or clothes or even a new ribbon it was important to go out and show it to Ellen. She'd always admire it and assure us we were great. We were always treated to sweets or biscuits or a fistful of raisins. She was a warm-hearted generous person, even the itinerants knew that because whenever they called to look for charity they left Ellen with bread, heads of cabbage and whatever she could give. It was a house we loved to call to.

Ellen died when I was in first year in secondary school and I really missed her. …She always wore the traditional style black clothes. In fact all the old women at that time wore black I'm not sure at what age they decided to wear black but they had a full

---

1 Records indicate it was earlier than that. See chapter 1.

length black skirt, black blouse and cardigan. My grandmother always was in black and so was the old lady next door, Anne Tighe. Anne died around the same time also...

My father didn't learn Irish formally at school but he had lots of gaeilge and could actually follow the Irish news on radio and television in later years and get the gist of it. His grandmother was an Irish speaker and he had lots of old sayings in Gaelic.

The older generation were very self-sufficient. They grew their own vegetables, potatoes, oats and had their own milk. I think they would be amazed to find that despite a productive land and a mild climate and modern machinery most people are buying vegetables and potatoes and milk today. But what would really astound them I think is that we are actually buying water, which in some cases is dearer than milk.

There were always eggs, milk and butter available and even if somebody arrived unexpectedly, a substantial meal could be put down, with home produced chickens and bacon or whatever.

My mother had a wonderful way of creating simple delicacies also. She'd whip up a batter with flour and have a scone or pancake ready for the table in a half an hour with homemade butter and jam ready. She had herbs and spices in store always, cinnamon, nutmeg and cloves.

Farming

We got a tractor fairly early on - I think Martin my brother was only seventeen when they decided to invest in a tractor. It was a grey Massey Ferguson and Martin did hire work in it. In spring he'd do ploughing, harrowing and drilling. And in the summer he would be very busy with the hay. At home, even before the arrival of the tractor, we did a lot of tillage, oats, barley, even wheat a few times, a good deal of potatoes, mangolds, turnips and all the vegetables. My mother was big into vegetables also. As well as the usual carrots and parsnips she'd have spinach and all types of onions, parsley, beetroot, radishes, peas, and broad and French beans. We were put to the weeding as soon as we knew what a weed was and there was plenty of work involved. But yet there was great variety for the dinner table and everything was fresh. We'd just go out to the garden, pick some peas for example come in and shell them at the table. Being so fresh they cooked in a short time and there is no doubt that really fresh produce has a special flavour.

Radio, Football and Politics

There was a radio and a gramophone in our house since my parents got married and people used to come to the house for broadcasts of football matches and particularly at election time to listen to the political speeches and see how the various candidates were faring. There was particular interest and excitement when Clann na Talún (the Farmers' Party) fielded candidates in Mayo and elsewhere. I think my dad supported Clann na Talún. He was related in some way to Domnick Cafferky from Cill Móibhí (Kilmovee), a prominent T.D. in the Clann and a gifted speaker. Of course, people used to get very involved in politics at that time and occasionally "hot under the collar" when debate got serious. Sometimes families even mightn't be talking to one another if they were voting in different directions.

People often visited and played cards in our house in winter and my father himself would go visiting to Owen Keane's in Baile na Cleithe (Ballynacloy) or he'd go up to Rath na gCupán (Rath) to Tommie Cassidy, another great friend of his or to Willie Walsh's. The women went visiting occasionally too. I often went with my mother to Hunt's in Fál Íochtar (Falleighter), our relations or to Tarpey's in Árd Doire (Arderry) because Mrs. Tarpey was also a cousin of ours, through the Ruanes. And we would also go to Pa Ruane's and Griffin's in Fal Íochtar , (Falleighter) other relations. We'd call to Tighe's of course next door and to Stenson's on the other side. On Sunday afternoons, I would go to Waldron's to play with the girls.

Primary School in Fal Íochtar (Falleighter)

I went to primary school in Fal Íochtar (Falleighter), which was just down the road from us. My brother Martin and I started school together and were always in the same class.

My two teachers were Tom Nolan, who was principal, and Mrs Cunnane from Kilgarrif, Cúigiú, who was the assistant. She started there when I began school and in fact she stayed or boarded in our house.

There were no cars at the time and it was a long distance to travel each morning and evening so she stayed with us. Her husband Pat would bring her down Sunday evening and collect her again in the pony and trap on Friday evenings. She had seven children so it was only in later years I realised how difficult it must have been for her to be away during the week, because her youngest child was only four, the same age as myself...

Everybody walked to school. As soon as we went out our gate in the morning we would stand and look to our right and all the crowd would be coming over the road from Ceathrú Bán (Carrowbaun), Tighes, Waldrons (Mary Waldron was my friend), Regans, Keanes, Leonards, Coxes and the families from Árd Doire (Arderry) and Carrowscoltia. Then as we went down past Hunt's house, we'd meet the crowd from Rath na gCupán (Rath) who had come down across the river, the Duffys, Harringtons, Cassidys, Freynes, Boyles and Prendergasts. Finally when we reached the school we met up with those from Fal Íochtar (Falleighter) itself, Caol Doire , Áthán Buí and even a few families from Cloch Bhuaillí at various times.

On summer days especially coming home from school, we'd take off our shoes at the Trimóg River and very often walk under the bridge at the road though often warned of the danger of that. We could spend a half hour there at the river looking for líbíns as we called them, or watching a stick float under the bridge.

We had the open fire in the school, which the boys put down in the morning. Water was drawn from the well. Anything that was needed for the school was got from Jackie Stenson who lived next door. For example if the fire didn't kindle up you went down to Jackie's and he gave you a few coals to help get it started.

School Games

We played catch, hide and seek and hopscotch which was a great favourite with the girls. We'd spend ages with our polished stones and our squares drawn out on the yard as we hopped up and down. We also played "thread the needle", rhyming games with a handball and a game called" draw, draw, bucket of water".

The boys played a game called "spanning buttons". There was a period of really keen competition when they'd have buttons pulled of their clothes, so eager were they to participate. You hit a button off the wall and then the second person threw a second button and if you could span the two buttons with your hand both of them were yours. Whoever ended up with the greatest number of buttons was the winner. Of course buttons began to disappear off coats in the hall from time to time!

Chapter 9 – THE HALLORANS WHO REMAINED IN AGHAMORE

> *The boys also played handball against the school gable.*

Phil went on to get a county scholarship to St Louis Convent, Kiltimagh, from where she went to Teacher Training College in Blackrock, Dublin. She retired from teaching at Tuaidn Primary School after over forty years service. More of her early experiences can be found in *Retirement Reminiscences*, published in *Glór Achadh Mór* in *2002*.

We can leave the last word to her:

> *I loved growing up in Carrowbaun. It was a simple but happy life and we never wanted for anything. We got an opportunity for education that our grandparents never had.*

Opportunities that the famished generations before her never had either. Our forebears had seen their children go hungry. Some, like her great grandfather, James (1807-1882), survived the Great Famine on the land that they later had to struggle hard to possess. Other's like Mary and Seán's great, great grandfather, Thomas (1808-1864) fled the Great Famine with family and neighbours, and settled among the coalmines and woollen mills of Yorkshire, forging out very different lives from their parents and cousins. We owe them our existence, even though it is almost impossible to imagine theirs.

CHAPTER 10

The Hallorans of Rath, Cahir and Cornageaghta

Post-famine Mayo

By the end of the century, the four Halloran families in Aghamore were 'peasant proprietors', working their own land. There was still much hardship, and emigration was the only option for many, but they were no longer at the mercy of landlords and their agents. They still paid large sums annually for the land, but now it was to pay off loans acquired for its purchase, not rent to work it. In this chapter we hope to give a partial account of how that came about.

Apart from James' holding in Carrowbaun in 1856, we do not know the size of the Halloran holdings in Raith, Cahir or Cornageaghta, or indeed if they had holdings in these townlands at that time. If they did, their holdings were very small, as land with a rateable value under £3 in 1856, was below the threshold for valuation by Griffith's Valuation. However, it appears that Hallorans in Aghamore may had benefited from the famine depopulation and land clearances and gained or consolidated their holdings around that time. After the Great Famine there was still great hardship, but there were growing prospects. With the enlarged and more prosperous British population, the demand for beef increased, reflected in better livestock prices, accelerating the move away from tillage farming and giving the advantage to larger farms, though this trend was slower and less marked in Mayo than other parts of Ireland (Jordan, 1996). Nonetheless, it is obvious from the census returns that people from these townlands were focussing more on grazing cattle. When we met Joe Byrne of Aghamore we discussed the changes taking place at the beginning of the nineteenth century. He pointed out that the Hallorans and Stenson, and indeed many of the farmers in the area, had become herdsmen.

Also there was less pressure on land. As we see in the accompanying table, the population had dropped dramatically. Hunger, disease and emigration had cleared much of the land. The landlords accelerated the process, and evictions were used to clear farmland for grazing to capitalise on the rise in livestock prices though this trend was more marked in the larger farms of central Mayo (Jordan, 2000). Emigration was highest during the famine in the more prosperous central plans of Mayo but by the 1870 it was the poorer regions, like Swinford, where emigration was highest.

	Carrowbaun		Cahir		Rath		Cornageaghta		Mountain	
Year	Pop	Houses	Pop.	Houses	Pop.	Houses	Pop.	Houses	Pop.	Houses
1841	107	17	220	38	245	53	13	3	476	91
1851	95	15	197	35	193	46	0	0	357	66
1861	100	14	169	30	202	43	0	0	290	44
1871	89	14	280	49	282	60	5	1	294	43
1881	99	14	262	46	323	59	7	1	276	43
1891	94	13	206	37	295	55	8	1	278	51
1901	86	14	205	39	234	51	4	1	272	42
1911	82	13	185	35	240	52	2	1	237	43

Population figures for the townlands of Carrowbaun, Cahir, Rath, Cornageaghta, Mountain

Aghamore was in a middling position: the best land around Kilmoremoy was valued at about 37shillings per acre, in the western parishes, including Kilcommon and Crossmolina and Boorishoole it was valued at up to 3.9 shillings and acre and in Aghamore between 4 to 7 shillings and acre (Jordan, 2000). So, there

Chapter 10 - THE HALLORANS OF RATH, CAHIR AND CORNAGEATHTA

were opportunities for expansion and consolidation of holdings and the Hallorans seemed to have grasped them. Before looking at these Halloran families in more detail, it is worth looking at aspects of the social life that were changing.

Marriage and family post famine

The gradual collapse of the rundale system and an increase in farm size in Mayo led to a decrease in family size and fewer early marriages. Furthermore, landlords became increasingly unwilling to countenance further subdivision. The disaster of the famine led people to be more cautious and parents increasingly looked to the commercial possibilities in marriage. Those who had acquired a bit of land became concerned to leave the farm intact to a single heir and provide a dowry to allow at least one daughter to marry well (Jordan, 2000). The privilege of marriage fell to the heir, not necessarily the eldest son. Even this was often delayed until the father's death or old age.

Hugh Dorian (2000) gives accounts of ways 'of bringing around the sacred bonds of wedlock', and some of them are quite surprising. He writes of contract marriages, abduction and runaway. His accounts of these appear on the following page.

Regarding the first, those with a bit of land would engage in 'contract marriages', which were probably more typical of the emerging type of farmer. Often in such cases, the other sons emigrated or remained bachelors; marriage for them being unlikely. Much the same applied to daughters, the one selected or prepared for marriage had the dowry, while her sisters emigrated or remained local spinsters. The couples often had little say while parents went into protracted negotiations, looking for assurances about what and when the groom would inherit the land, and the nature of the bride's dowry in terms of how much cash or stock was involved. The inevitable result was an increase in bachelors and spinsters and the persistence of emigration; the proportion of women who could marry fell, and the number who emigrated grew.

However, as Dorian's account illustrates, the matters of the heart were not always arranged in so practical a manner, especially among those with less to lose or gain, and who did not relish a life of celibacy. He gives us accounts of runaway elopements and even abductions. The latter ware probably possible because of the high cost of weddings and dowries, and the family pride involved. As only one family member would inherit land, the others were left with little chance of making a living.

Dorian's accounts of abductions is supported by the *First Report Inquiring into the Condition of the Poorer Classes in Ireland*, (1835), where it was claimed that, though the custom was in decline, it was farmers' daughters 'from their possessing fortunes', who were more exposed to the danger of abduction.

With time, the proportion of young men and women fell in County Mayo while the percentage of unmarried older people rose (Fitzpatrick 1985). Within forty years, between 1871 and 1901, Mayo was transformed from a region with high marriage and fertility rates to one with low marriage levels but continued high fertility, as farmers attempted to secure a higher living standard by reducing he pressure on the land. We see this in the four Halloran families in Aghamore, where a number of members simply disappear from the area, presumably having emigrated. Also, families are smaller than in Birstall, where there is also evidence of emigration but also the persistence of early marriages and large families.

We will now return to our exploration of the Hallorans in Aghamore, and examine the family in the townland of Rath, Caher and Cornageaghta.

Contract Marriages

Those belonging to the higher sphere of worldly life ... could ride in saddles and pillions to public places,..., and signalled the same by bombastic shows, though it did not necessarily follow that their engagements proved more happy... [T]he intended spouses often had never seen each other before, and as a consequence were each ignorant of the faults and frailties and temper of the other. Negotiations were carried on by the friends on either side and when an agreement was come to, the young man was told to prepare and visit his intended father-in-law. Soon he, all blushing, was on the road with a few friends, well supplied with the native beverage to spend a pleasant evening.

Abductions

The abduction case: – It was not surprising to hear in the morning that such a man's daughter was taken. This was usually owing to a disparity between the families in some respect generally in regard to pecuniary inequality. Here the would-be groom might fear a rejection of his claim if he went straight forward and proposed. Or it might be that he had not the necessary courage to do so. His usual resort in such a case was to consult his friends about the prospect of his plot and work accordingly. Lo! In the dead of night the old man's house is surrounded, there is an entrance, and the prize is carried off. In such cases every precaution is taken that no one be harshly treated. The maiden was especially well cared for, and the old father was offered what was considered the gift of gifts, ... a bottle of the best five and two[1] was also presented, to not forget the old woman... [T]he young woman ... in the meantime ... is borne away on the arms of strong men ... soon to be introduced to a young man whom she never saw, ...

Next morning the news spread rapidly that Biddy or Kate So and So "was stolen", ... but no person would think of obstructing the marriage, for when it was once known that this took place, the young woman in question would find it difficult to get a match again, and the young bachelor was in as awkward a position, slighted and neglected and jeered at by the girls. ...

By the influence of arguments, promises, or if necessary threats, the old fellow was forced to give in, to encroach upon the results of his hitherto hard life's toil, and to promise such terms in cash and chattels as would relieve his daughter for the present in bondage.

Nor was there such a thing unknown as "stealing the stolen". The young girl, not feeling at ease, would find means of communicating with her chosen friends, and they by a bold manoeuvre and her willingness they carried her off. There was then the commotion among the friends of the abandoned one who wished to have him settled at once before the story got circulation. I have known a man in his bachelorhood thus left desolate [whereupon] his friends hawked him about during the night, opened and solicited three doors [i.e. families] before they got a welcome admission. The girl in the fourth took pity on him where he did not expect it, and next day there were hastily celebrated two marriages and the whole affair hushed up.

Runaway marriages

Runaway marriages were of more frequent occurrence and ... were more to be enjoyed than the former [abduction]. They took place in nearly every case at the fair or market. .... This was considered the best opportunity; no suspicion was raised for they were dressed of course for the fair. They could thus spend the day with their friends till darkness set in when their escape became easy. They now eloped with two or three confidants to a friend's house somewhat about.

Next morning they quietly got married. Then proceeded the outbursts of displeasure and dissatisfaction among the relatives on both sides. One party would say, "it is no match", neither giving any "face" or inlet to the new member of the family. The other priding themselves on their honour and dignity would say, "it is well known that one of our family never demeaned themselves by joining such people or their stock" ... These paltry objections arose more than anything from the fact that the friends wished to save themselves the expense of celebrating the wedding, and still more to keep free from promising anything by way of a 'portion[2]'

... the young couple had to make the best of a bad matter, or a good one we hope, and start in life for themselves. When a beginning was made and things going on well they were not so neglected, for all of a sudden they who were so bitterly opposed match at first relented and began to assist the happy pair...

---

1 Presumably premium legal whiskey.

2 Dowry

Chapter 10 - THE HALLORANS OF RATH, CAHIR AND CORNAGEATHTA

Rath (Raith)

Despite their being no evidence of Halloran landholders in Rath (also Raith) at the time of the Griffith Valuation, the family of Patrick Halloran is found living in Rath in the Aghamore Parish Records of Births and Marriages. However, it must be remembered that by the time valuations were made in Aghamore - probably around 1856 - houses of a rateable value under £3 had been excluded from the valuation and they may well have been living in the townland at that time, perhaps as cottiers or landless agricultural labourers.

Griffiths Valuation

Reference to map	Name		Description of tenants	Area	Rateable Annual Valuation		Total Annual Valuation
	Townlands occupiers	Immediate Lessors			Land	Buildings	

Ref	Townlands occupiers	Immediate Lessors	Description	Area (A. R. P.)	Land (£ s. d.)	Buildings (£ s. d.)	Total (£ s. d.)
	RATH. (Ord. S. 81 & 82.)						
1	—	The Immediate Lessor.	Black Lough (part of).	1 2 20	—	—	—
2	—	Same.	Lough Coldragh (pt. of).	5 2 22	—	—	—
	a. Thomas Frain,	Same.	Land and house,		2 5 0	0 5 0	2 10 0
3	b. John Frain,	Same.	Land, house, & office,	43 1 3	2 5 0	0 5 0	2 10 0
	c. Thomas Frain (weaver),	Same.	Land, house, & office,		2 5 0	0 5 0	2 10 0
	a. Henry Waldren,	Same.	Land, house, & office,	42 3 16	2 10 0	0 5 0	2 15 0
4	b. Patrick Morelly. (See lot 7.)	Same.	Land and house.		5 0 0	0 5 0	5 5 0
	a. Michael McDonnell,	Same.	Land, house, & office,		3 10 0	0 5 0	3 15 0
5	b. Dominick Nowlan,	Same.	Land, house, & office,	30 3 4	1 15 0	0 5 0	2 0 0
	c. Edmond Higgins,	Same.	Land and house.		1 15 0	0 5 0	2 0 0
	d. John Gauley,	Michael McDonnell & Dominick Nowlan.	Garden and house.	0 3 10	0 5 0	0 3 0	0 8 0
	a. Michael Conway,	The Immediate Lessor.	Land, house, & offices,		5 0 0	0 10 0	5 10 0
	b. Owen Conway,	Same.	Land, house, & office,		5 0 0	0 10 0	5 14 0
6	c.	Same.	One cottage,	83 0 2	—	0 4 0	
	d. Patrick Conway,	Same.	Land and house,		2 10 0	0 6 0	2 16 0
	e. Hugh Boyle,	Same.	Land and house,		2 10 0	0 5 0	2 15 0
	a. Michl. Conway (James), (See lot 8.)	Same.	Land, house, & office,		4 5 0	0 10 0	4 15 0
7	b. James Morrelly. (See lot 8.)	Same.	Land, house, & office,	37 1 4	4 5 0	0 10 0	4 15 0
	c. John Walsh, (See lot 8.)	Same.	Land, house, & office,		4 5 0	0 10 0	4 15 0
	— Patrick Morelly,	Same.	Land,		3 0 0	0 10 0	3 10 0
8	a, b. Michl. Conway (James),	Same.	Land and cottages,	48 3 18	3 0 0	0 10 0	3 10 0
	c, d. James Morelly,	Same.	Land and cottages,		3 0 0	0 5 0	3 5 0
	e. John Walsh,	Same.	Land and cottage,				
9	a. Michael Judge,	Same.	Land, house, office, corn-mill (gig), & kiln,	21 3 14	6 0 0	1 0 0	7 0 0
				61 0 33	28 0 0	—	28 0 0
10	Edward P. McDonnell,	Same.	Land,	14 0 29	4 15 0	—	5 4 0
11	a. Thomas Walsh,	Same.	Land and house,			0 5 0	
	b, c.	Same.	Two cottages,			0 4 0	0 4 0
12	a. Michael Bones,	Same.	Land, house, & offices,	50 0 22	7 10 0	0 10 0	8 0 0
	b. Patrick Byrne,	Same.	Land, house, & office,		2 10 0	0 5 0	2 15 0
	a. Francis Common,	Same.	Land and house,		3 15 0	0 5 0	4 0 0
	b.	Same.	Land and house,		3 15 0	0 5 0	4 5 0
13	c. Patrick Regan,	Same.	Two cottages,	51 2 19		0 5 0	
	d. Charles Jordan,	Same.	Land, house, & office,		3 15 0	0 5 0	4 0 0
	e. Patrick Lafferty,	Same.	Land and house,		1 17 0	0 3 0	2 0 0
	f. Honoria Jordan,	Same.	Land, house, & office,		0 7 0	0 8 0	0 15 0
14	a. Martin Knavesy,	Same.	Land, house, & office,	42 0 30	3 15 0	0 5 0	4 0 0
	b. James Gleeson,	Same.	Land and house,		5 0 0	0 5 0	5 5 0
	a. James Doyle,	Same.	Land, house, & office,		5 0 0	0 5 0	5 5 0
15	b. John Byrne,	Same.	Land and house,	59 0 23	5 0 0	0 5 0	5 5 0
	c. Owen Brennan,	Same.	Land and house,		5 0 0	0 5 0	5 5 0
	d. Mary Duffy,	Same.	House,		—	0 3 0	0 3 0
	e. Michael Walsh,	Same.	Land and house,	60 0 25	11 4 0	0 8 0	11 10 0
6	a. Owen Brennan,	Same.	Land,		8 16 0	—	8 16 0
	b. Michael Jennings,	Michael Walsh and Owen Brennan.	School-house,		—	0 5 0	0 5 0
7			Lough Crunnan (pt. of).	4 3 0	—	—	—
			Total,	659 1 14	177 9 0	12 8 0	189 17 0

Griffiths Valuation record of the townland of Rath

In chapter 9, we discussed a reference to 'Thomas Halloran and Co.' that appears in the Tithe Applotment book for the area of 'Caltragh' around 1832. There is a Lough Caldragh adjoining Rath townland and this strongly suggests there were Hallorans in the area at least 30 years before Griffiths Valuation. There was more than one family. We also know that the Patrick Halloran of Rath (b. abt 1866) was not a son of James who we found in Griffith's Valuation in Carrowbaun in 1856. He had a son called Patrick who was born earlier. This Patrick was born well after James' children and may well have been a nephew.

Rath, like Cahir and unlike Carrowbaun, was more than a scattering of small farms clustered around a *clachan* or *stráid*. At the time of Griffith's Valuation, it contained a corn mill and a kiln, as well as a schoolhouse. There were 24 houses and 8 cottages. The landholders in Rath were nearly all the recorded as 'immediate lessors', which often meant the occupier (lessee) owned the land or was a representative of the landlord. However, in this case we have learned that the landlord was Taaffe. It appears that, at the time, the landholders may not have known who the landlord was, as the property may have been in the hands of the Landed Estates' Court set up to facilitate the sales under the Encumbered Estates Act. This is discussed later in the chapter.

The farms here were larger than in Carrowbaun. Normally the italicized 'a' indicates the principal tenant and those marked 'b', 'c', 'd' etc. sub-tenants, probably holding land sub-divided according to the rundale system. As the same family names reoccur, it is probable the holdings represent a complex network of family connections. Where the holder is not marked as the immediate lessor, the tenant is an immediate neighbour, as in the case of Michael Jennings, a schoolmaster renting a school room from Michael Walsh and Owen Brennan. There is also the case of John Gowley?, who rents a very small plot, a garden and a house from Michael McDonnell.

Rath

Aghamore Parish Records (APR)

For more information about the second half of the nineteenth century we can turn to Aghamore parish records and find the following information about Hallorans in Cahir. We know that a Patrick Halloran married Catherine Tigue, date unknown. There are records of the baptism five children.

- Patt was baptised on 4th Dec 1864 and sponsored by Pat and Judith Tigue. According to information from records in the South Mayo Family Research Centre, supplied by Ger Delaney, a Patrick of Rath was father of Patrick who married Catherine Forkan in 1892 and of Martin of Caher who married Maria Kenny in 1906.
- Michael was baptised on 13th Dec 1868 and sponsored by Tim Kelly and Bridget Stenson.
- Catherine was baptised 15th Jan 1871 and sponsored by John Halloran and Margaret Snee. Perhaps this same John Halloran sponsored Martin on 30th October 1876. We know little of him otherwise.
- John was baptised on 9th December 1877 and sponsored by Thomas Holleran and Mary Feeley.

Chapter 10 - THE HALLORANS OF RATH, CAHIR AND CORNAGEATHTA

- Margaret Halloran was baptised on 3rd August 1873 and sponsored by Thomas and Bridget Halloran.

As we discussed in chapter 7, a Michael Halloran was lodging in Birstall with Martin Lyons and family in 1891. Martin Lyons was married to Bridget Halloran, recorded as born in Raith, whose baptism would have taken place prior to 1864, the date of the destruction of the earlier parish records. It seems likely that this is the Michael listed here, as the census gives his place of birth as 'Raith, Ireland'. His marriage record gives his father's name as Patrick, which is also consistent with him being a member of this family. He had married Mary McCarthy in 1892 in England, and had 5 children. His wife died soon after the birth of their fifth child. In 1901 he is recorded as still living with the Lyons family but with only two of his sons. One of these sons, John, joined the British army in 1916, but was dismissed the following year as he was found to be under-aged. He had joined up in Galway and given his father's address in Birstall, which strongly suggests there was still a lot of come-and-go between Mayo and Yorkshire at the time. A death record of a Michael Halloran, John's father, indicates that he possibly died in the Batley Workhouse in 1925.

The Workhouse record is of a man born around 1867/8, which strongly suggests the same Michael we see here. Why he died in poverty and alone despite having had 5 children and living close to relatives and neighbours from his homeland, is not known. But it does illustrate how the hopes offered by emigration and a new life were sometimes dashed.

In Raith also we learn Michael Touhy and Mary Halloran were married on 13 Jan 1867, and they were sponsored by Thomas Lyons and Mary Stenson. They had 4 children baptised in the 1870s.

- Martin Touhy (twin of John), baptised on 16 Oct 1872 sponsored by John and Bridget Halloran.
- John Touhy (twin of Martin), baptised on sponsored by James and Catherine Halloran.
- Pat Toughy baptised on 16 Oct 1872 sponsored by Martin Halloran, Bridget Stenson.
- James Touhy baptised on 14 Feb 1869 sponsored by Thomas and Bridget Lyons.

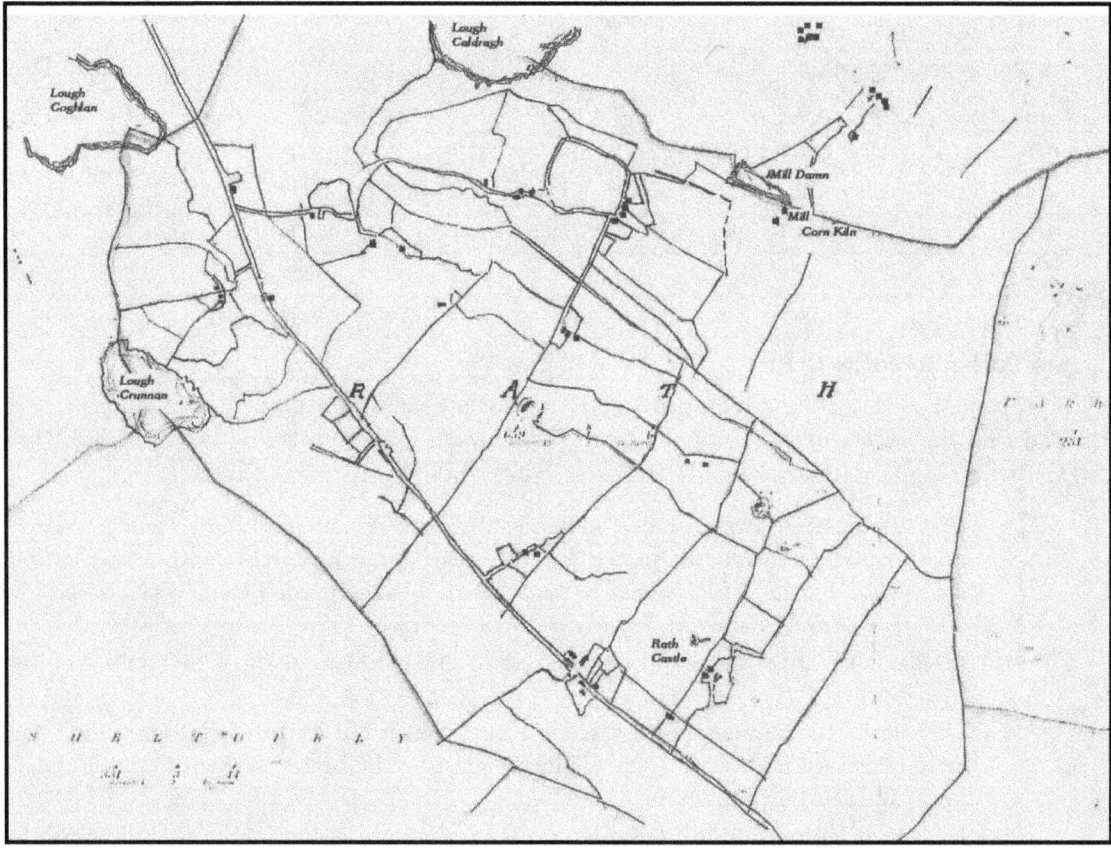

Townland of Rath based on the Ordinance Survey map of 1838. Notice Lough Caldragh to the north. Caldragh is the name of the area where Thomas Halloran had to pay Church of Ireland tithes for around 1834.

THE HALLORANS FROM BIRSTALL AND AGHAMORE

The Taaffs

As we have seen, the landlords of Rath were the Taaffes. There were at least three families of landowning Taaffes[1] in the Mayo/Roscommon region. At this point we are not sure which ones were landlords of Rath, as they are not always referred to as separate estates.

The Taaffes of Killedan leased church land as well as other lands held by the Knox family of Castlerea, near Killala townland, parish of Killedan, barony of Gallen, county Mayo.

The Taaffes of Woodfield held an estate of 9030 acres at Woodfield, near Kilkelly, in the parish of Aghamore, barony of Costello, county Mayo.

The Taaffes of Foxborough held estates in Roscommon and Mayo in the mid 19th century. The Mayo estates were in the barony of Costello while the Roscommon lands were in the barony of Frenchpark.

Both the Woodfield and Killedan Taaffes were descended from James Taaffe of Greyfield, county Mayo and his wife Mary, granddaughter of Terence MacDonagh, an important Catholic lawyer.

These estate contained lands in the parishes of Bekan, Kilmovee, Annagh and Aghamore, barony of Costello, county Mayo and in the parish of Templetogher, barony of Ballymoe, county Galway. Over 600 acres in county Mayo and over 1000 acres in county Roscommon were advertised for sale in the Encumbered Estates' Court in 1854 by Joanna and Julia Taaffe. The county Mayo part was purchased 'in trust' by Mr W. Thomas of Galway. It is possible that this Mr W. Thomas was the new landlord in Rath. The fact that they were in the process of sale through the Encumbered Estate Court might account for the fact that the landlord's name was omitted in the Griffith Valuation in 1856.

They were apparently a junior branch of the Taaffes of Smarmore Castle, County Louth. They had formerly been an influential family in the area but had lost their inheritance thorough maintaining a lavish lifestyle. Their County Louth forebears, however, were a very powerful Norman family and among the most prominent families in Ireland from the 13th century. Branches of the family held the title Earls of Carlingford and Sheriff of Louth for several generations. The second Viscount Taaffe, took a prominent part in the loyalist cause in the English Civil War and was killed at the Battle of the Boyne fighting for King James II against King William III.

Notwithstanding this, King William III confirmed the Taaffes in their titles, mainly because of the position held by the family at the court of the Holy Roman Emperor, William's most important ally. From the 18th century, the Viscounts Taaffe also held the title Count Taaffe in the Holy Roman Empire. A later Count inherited property in the Austrian dominions and was naturalised in Bohemia, giving the avoidance of the Penal Laws, and his fear that his descendants would be exposed to the temptation of becoming Protestants, as the reason for this step.

Notwithstanding their perhaps remote connections with this august defender of Roman Catholicism, some of the Taaffes of Connaught did not prove to be sympathetic landlords of their tenants, as this record from Hansard makes clear[2].

Landlord And Tenant (Ireland) – The Taaffe Estate, Co. Mayo.
HC Deb 09 July 1888 vol. 328 cc723-4
MR. J. F. X. O'Brien (MP representing the Irish Nationalist Party for Mayo, S.) asked the Chief Secretary to the Lord Lieutenant of Ireland, if he is aware that before the appointment of Mr. P. J. Hughes, of Kiltimagh, as receiver over the Taaffe Estate in the County of Mayo, 95 per cent of the tenants signed a Memorial and sent it to Mr. Justice Monroe protesting against the appointment; whether John Daly, of Ballyhaunis, was engaged for five days – namely, the 22nd, 23rd, 24th, 25th, and 26th of May, in serving notices on the tenants over whom Mr. Hughes is the receiver, and was protected by a force of 40 police and a District Inspector; and can he state at what cost those notices were served on the tenants, about 300 in number?
The Chief Secretary (Mr. A. J. Balfour, MP for Manchester, East replied:

---

1 http://www.landedestates.ie/LandedEstates/jsp/family

2 http://hansard.millbanksystems.com/commons/1888/jul/09/landlord-and-tenant-ireland-the-taaffe

Chapter 10 - THE HALLORANS OF RATH, CAHIR AND CORNAGEATHTA

I cannot undertake to make any statement on the subject of the first paragraph, which relates to the action of a Judge in his judicial capacity, and of which the Executive Government have no cognizance. The reply to the inquiry in the second paragraph is in the affirmative. The cost of the detachment of police is about £84 7s

Here again we see evidence of the relentless efforts of many of the landlords to clear their estates of tenants in order to turn the land over to grazing or make it easier to sell. By this time there must have been a strong suspicion in their minds that the compulsory purchase of estates was a distinct possibility.

Irish census 1901

By 1901 the Hallorans were themselves proprietors of their own land. According to the 1901 census, in Rath we find Patrick Halloran (b. abt. 1866), a farmer, aged 35 and the eldest son, recorded as head of the household and a farmer. He was married to Catherine (b. abt. 1870) aged 31. Patrick is in all probability son of the Patrick Halloran married Catherine Tigue, though his baptism is not recorded. This would make him the brother of Michael who went to Birstall. Patrick and Catherine's young family include:

- Bridget (b. abt. 1893 aged 8),
- Catherine (b. abt. 1895) aged 6,
- Mary (b. abt. 1895) aged 4,
- James (b. abt. 1897) aged 2,
- Patrick (b. abt. 1901) aged 1 month.

Also in the household is Catherine Halloran (b. abt. 1829), Martin's mother aged 72. She is a widow. Bridget Lavan (b. abt. 1883) aged 18 is recorded as a visitor and a seamstress.

Irish census of 1901, Halloran family, Rath

They are all recorded as Roman Catholics. The adults can read and write and speak English and Irish. The children are recorded as English speakers, suggesting perhaps that Irish is no longer used as the main language in the household.

Form B1 on the census reveals Patrick is the landholder, and this is true of virtually all of the inhabitants of Raith. The family is recorded as having 9 members, suggesting that Bridget Lavan is part of the family. We see that the house had stone, brick or concrete walls - probably stone, and a non-permanent roof - probably thatch. It had between 3 or 4 rooms, 3 of which are occupied by the family, and it is classified as 3rd class, as are most in the townland, though there are some 2nd and 4th class dwellings.

Each dwelling was occupied by one nuclear family, though older parents and other relatives may have lived with them. There were 51 families in all. The population included 81 males and 89 females; again indicating a predominance of females, as it was mainly males who emigrated or were working temporarily in England. The entire population is 170.

Their neighbours include Boyles, Brennans, Byrnes, Cassidys, Caufields, Commons, Connors, Conways, Doyles, Duffys, Feeneys, Finns, Frains, Freemans, Harrisons, Harringtons, Higgins, Hynes, Jordans,

THE HALLORANS FROM BIRSTALL AND AGHAMORE

Kennys, Kellys, Kilkennys Lynskeys, Malloys, Muldowneys, Murphys, Nolans, O'Brians, O'Dowds, Snees, Spellmans, Stensons, Tighes, Toweys (probably Touhy in the baptismal records) and Walshes.

Remarkably, of these 35 family names, 27 of them are names of families that are still part of the Irish community in Birstall, Yorkshire.

Between the families they owned 2 stables, 30 cowhouses, 3 calve houses, 31 piggeries, 18 fowl houses and 8 barns. Cattle grazing was clearly the main form of agriculture.

Irish census 1911

By 1911, the family had grown. Patrick aged 47, (b. abt. 1864), a farmer, and Catherine aged 46. (b. abt. 1865) were recorded as married for 19 years. Catherine, Martin's mother, aged 78 (though recorded as 72 10 years earlier) is still living with them. They were 8 children at home:

Catherine (16, b. abt. 1895) - no occupation is indicated; Mary (14, b. abt. 1897), James (12, b. abt. 1899), Patrick (10, b. abt. 1901), and Maggie (8, b. abt. 1903), were at school. There were also Ellen (6, b. abt. 1905), Annie (4, b. abt. 1907), and Michael (2, b. abt. 1909). It was reported that there were 9 children born and 9 children living. It appears the eldest, Bridget, had left home.

Irish census of 1911, Halloran family, Raith

The dwelling itself was similar to the house as described in the 1901 census.

There were 51 families in the townland, including 121 males and 119 females; bring the total to 240 inhabitants. This is a remarkable increase by 50 inhabitants in 10 years at a time when the population of Connaught was falling. Furthermore, there is not the same significant imbalance between the male and female populations that was evident in the 1901 census. The entire population was still Roman Catholic, and the vast majority of the townland were owners of their own dwellings

Patrick is reported as only having one outhouse - a piggery. This appears to suggest he was a smaller farmer than most in the townland, as there were 13 stables, 37 cow houses, 22 piggeries, 3 fowl houses and 26 barns; making a total of 100 animal outhouses. The number of stables had increases from 2 to 13, indicating a huge increase in the ownership of horses since 1901. There had also been a dramatic reduction in the number of fowl houses - from 18 to 3. We do not know the size of these outhouses. They may of course be much bigger and the figures may reflect a greater degree in specialisation.

Joe Byrne pointed out that the Hallorans and Stenson, and indeed many of the farmers in the area, had become herdsmen. This is reflected in the censuses of four townlands here, all of which had a large number of cowsheds. He further pointed out that the emergence of the herdsman was accompanied by a massive fall-off of the ploughman, as patterns of farming changed in response to changes in the market, especially the emergence of new consumers in Britain, as more and more people's standard of living improved, and more and more beef was eaten.

There are no Hallorans in Rath now. We understand that some of them now live in Manchester, and we would be happy to hear from them.

Chapter 10 - THE HALLORANS OF RATH, CAHIR AND CORNAGEATHTA

Earlier landlords

The townland had once been the stronghold of the *clann* of MacJordan, and the smaller *clann* of MacPhilip. The MacJordans were descendants of the de Angulos or Costellos and Rath Castle was theirs. They kept possession of it after the Dillons took possession of much of the Costello estate in Elizabethan times and through the later Cromwellian settlement. The ruins show it to have been a large structure[1].

The descendants of the family still retained a small holding about the Castle ruins and a Charles and Honoria Jordan appear in Griffith Valuation. The Castle was known as *Rath-na-gCupan,* tradition says it got its name from the number of silver drinking cups.

The story goes that when a detachment of Cromwellian soldiers were passing by, they decided to set fire to the castle. The leader, hearing of the cups, offered to spare the castle if a cup of wine was given to each of his soldiers. The cups were brought, filled with wine, and there was one for each and one more. Thus the castle was spared for the time. However, when the soldiers returned to plunder the place, a maid from the castle carried the silver away when she saw the soldiers coming and buried it somewhere in the neighbourhood and it was never found since.

Rath Castle

Cahir (Caher)

Reference to map	Name		Description of tenants	Area	Rateable Annual Valuation		Total Annual Valuation
	Townlands occupiers	Immediate Lessors			Land	Buildings	
1 a	Murtagh Coyne,	Francis R. O'Grady,	Land, ho., off., & forge,	18 2 3	3 5 0	0 5 0	3 10 0
– b	Murtagh Coyne,	Same,	Corn-mill and kiln,	—	—	2 0 0	1 0 0
	Michael Flaherty,	Same,					1 0 0
2 a	Michael Flaherty,	Same,	Land and house,	11 1 35	2 0 0	0 5 0	2 10 0
– b			One cottage,			0 5 0	
3 a	Mary M'Donagh,	Same,	Land and house,	12 0 15	1 0 0	0 5 0	1 5 0
b	Bryan M'Donagh,	Same,	Land and house,		1 0 0	0 5 0	1 5 0
4 a	John Daly,	Same,	Land and house,	17 0 12	1 0 0	0 4 0	1 4 0
5 —	Michael Nowlan,	Same,	Land,	1 1 20	—	—	—
– —	Dominick Connolly,	Same,	Land,	0 0 20	—	—	—
6 —	Robert Dillon,	Same,	Land,	0 1 20	—	—	—
7 —	Michael Connolly,	Same,	Land,	11 3 25	1 0 0	—	1 0 0
– a—	Robert Dillon,	Same,	Land,	0 1 10	0 1 0	—	0 1 0
8 a	Michael Connolly,	Same,	Land and house,	26 1 0	2 14 0	0 6 0	3 0 0
b	Thomas Walsh,	Same,	Land and house,		1 6 0	0 4 0	1 10 0
9 a	Mary Costello,	Same,	Land, house, and office,	24 1 37	2 10 0	0 5 0	2 18 0
– b			One cottage,		—	0 3 0	
10 a	Thomas Costello,	Same,	Land and house,	15 2 25	1 15 0	0 5 0	2 0 0
– b	Mary French,	Same,	Garden and house,	0 1 10	0 5 0	0 3 0	0 8 0
11 a	Catherine Casey,	Arthur R. Costello,	Land and house,	16 3 31	3 5 0	0 5 0	3 10 0
12 a	Owen M'Cue,	Same,	Land, house, and office,	25 0 10	2 15 0	0 5 0	3 0 0
13 a	Patrick Costello,	Same,	Land, house, & office,	16 1 35	2 10 0	0 5 0	2 15 0
b	Thomas Fristil,	Same,	Land and house,		2 10 0	0 5 0	2 15 0
14				5 0 8	0 2 0		
15 a	Patrick Waldron,	Same,	Land, house, & office,	32 0 9	10 8 0	0 10 0	6 10 0
– b	Michael Waldron,	Same,	Land, house, & office,			0 10 0	6 10 0
– c	Thomas Waldron,	Same,	Land, house, & office,			0 10 0	6 10 0
16				26 2 20	7 10 0		
17 a	Timothy Flaherty,	Same,	Land and house,	16 2 30	3 0 0	0 10 0	3 10 0
b	John Murphy,	Same,	Land, house, & office,		3 0 0	0 10 0	3 10 0
18 a	Patrick Flaherty,	Same,	Land and house,	13 3 28	4 8 0	0 6 0	4 14 0
19 a	Patrick Connell,	Same,	Land and house,	22 3 7	3 0 0	0 5 0	3 5 0
b	Thomas Egan,	Same,	Land,		4 10 0	—	4 10 0

Griffiths Valuation record of the townland of Caher

---

1 http://www.nanglemedieval.com/BaronyCostello.pdf

THE HALLORANS FROM BIRSTALL AND AGHAMORE

Griffiths Valuation

At the time of the Griffith Valuation we find no record of Halloran in Cahir though there are records of them in the townland soon after. Though, as explained at the beginning of the section on Rath, this does not exclude the possibility of their presence in Cahir and that they were immediate relatives of James, Thomas and Michael but living in the poorest dwellings. Nonetheless, a record of who lived in Cahir at the time is of interest, especially in regards to family names which turn up in Birstall.

Aghamore parish records (APR)

However, we find a Patrick Hallorans in Cahir. He, according to records in South Mayo Family Research Centre, supplied by Ger Delaney was also a son of James Halloran of Carrowbaun. He married Winifred Morley (Morally) and thee are records of the following baptisms:

- Bridget, who was baptised on 27th January 1866, and was sponsored by Thomas and Bridget Mulkeen of 'Auher', (probably Cahir).

- Mary was baptised on 16th February 1868, and was sponsored by Martin Grogan and Bridget Halloran (Martin's sister?).

- Winifred was baptised on 18th May 1871, and was sponsored by Michael Hunt and Mary Morley

- Pat was baptised on 25th July 1873, and was sponsored by John and Winny Egan (Thomas Egan had land in Cahir).

- Honor was baptised on 2nd July 1875, and was sponsored by Austin Waldron and Mary. Honor probably died as child as another Honor is baptised four years later.

- Martin was baptised on 30th October 1876, and was sponsored by John and Catherine Halloran. Martin died Feb. 25th 1901 and his grave lies in Aghamore parish cemetery. Who John and Catherine Halloran are and how they fit in the picture is unknown.

- Honor was baptised on 23rd February 1879, and was sponsored by Thomas Halleran and Catherine Nolan.

Also, according to information from records in the South Mayo Family Research Centre, Michael, a widower, son of Pat Holleran and Winifred Morley married Bridget Halleron, of Caher, daughter of Thomas Halleron and Bridget Kilkenny in 1893.

We also find in the APR a Thomas Halloran and Sally Coyne who married 18th Feb 1867, witnessed by James Hopkins (?) Mary Stenson. We have records of the baptism of two children:

- Bridget Halloran, baptised on 25th January 1868, and was sponsored by Martin Halloran, Mary Stenson.

- Mary Halloran, baptised on 29th May 1869, and was sponsored by Ned and Mary Adams.

This may be the same couple who later appear in Cornageaghta as Thomas Halloran and Sarah Kyne.

Irish census 1901

By the 1901 Irish census we find Winnifrid Halloran, neé Morley (Morally) (b. abt. 1845) aged 56, recorded as head of the household and a farmer, though she is listed as married. She is also recorded as the landholder. We do not know what had happened to her husband Pat, though the fact that Winnifred is not recorded as widowed suggests he was still alive. We also find Martin (b. abt. 1877) aged 24, and Sarah (b. abt. 1883) aged 18. All are recorded as speaking Irish and English. There is no sign of Bridget, Mary, Winifred, Pat or Honor, who may have emigrated. Sarah would appear to be the youngest member of the family was still at home, though we found no evidence of her baptism.

The house was built of stone, brick or concrete - probably stone; and has a non-permanent roof - probably thatch. It had 3 or 4 rooms, 3 of which were occupied by the family and it has 3 front windows. It is classified as 2nd class, as are many in the townland, though most are recorded as 3rd class and two as 4th class dwellings.

Chapter 10 - THE HALLORANS OF RATH, CAHIR AND CORNAGEATHTA

1	Winnifred Halloran	Head of family	Roman Cath	Cannot read	56	F	Farmer	Married	Co Mayo	Irish & English
2	Martin Halloran	Son	Do	Read & write	24	M	Farmers Son	Not married	Do	Irish & English
3	Sarah Halloran	Daughter	Do	Read & write	18	F	Farmers Daughter	Not married	Do	Irish & English

1901 Irish census of the townland of Caher

In all, there are 38 dwellings in Cahir, occupied by 38 families. There were 90 males and 111 females, giving a total population of 201. Again we notice the preponderance of females. The townland also contained 23 stables, 2 coach houses, 1 harness room, 24 cow houses, 9 calf houses, 2 dairies, 23 piggeries, 5 foul houses, 1 boiling house and 19 barns.

Thomas Dillon-Leetch lived in the townland. He was the owner of the only 1st class dwelling, and kept coaches. He may well be the founder of T. Dillon-Leetch & Sons, a legal firm set up in 1889. The firm has passed from one generation to another and maintains its centre of practice at Ballyhaunis, Co Mayo.

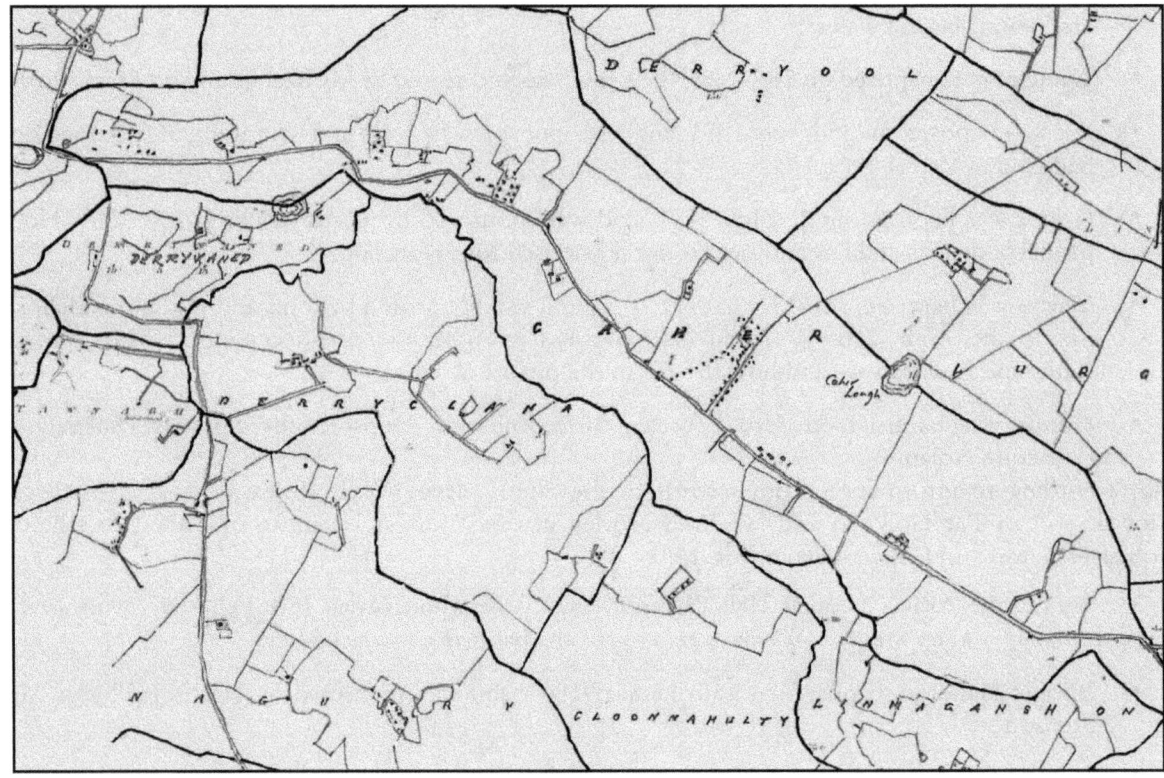

The townland of Caher (Cahir) circa 1837

Irish census 1911

Ten years later, Martin had taken over as head of the household and had been married 6 years. His elderly mother, Winefred lived with them and is recorded as aged 72, that is, 16 years older than at the previous census. However, she has not given over the reins entirely, and remains the owner of the farm.

	Christian Name	Surname				Males	Females			one	born alive	living
	1.	2.	3.	4.	5.	6.	7.	8.	9.	10.	11.	12.
1	Martin	Halloran	Head of family	Roman Catholic	Read & write	40	-	Farmer		Married		-	-
2	Maria	Halloran	Wife	Roman Catholic	Read & write	-	36			Married	6	none	-
3	Wineford	Halloran	Mother	Roman Catholic	Cannot read & write	-	72			Widow		-	-
4													

1911 Irish census of the townland of Caher

Their dwelling is much as it was in 1901 – a thatched, three-room cottage.

Other neighbours in the townland included: Cafferkeys, Connells, Costellos, Cuddys, Dalys, Duffys. Egans, Flaherteys, Frestrels, Gormanleys, Kennys, McHughs, McLaughlins, Murphys, Nixons, Tarpeys, Walshes and Waldrens; 35 families inhabiting 35 dwellings. The total population was 185, including 91 males and 94 females, a drop of 8% since the previous census, though the disparity between males and females had evened out. Thomas Dillon Leetch had moved out of the townland and rented his large property to John J. Cuddy, but he does not keep coach houses and harness rooms.

Altogether, there were 12 stables, 33 cow houses, 17 calf houses, 3 dairies, 26 piggeries, 10 foul houses, and 24 barns.

The landlords

In 1856, the time of Griffith's Valuation, Cahir was split between two landlords, Richard O'Grady and Arthur Robert Costello. There is a record of the Costellos owning Little Cahir, though what part of Cahir this was we do not know at present. These two men were from families of very different origin and this difference reflects the enormous changes that were taking place in land ownership in Ireland.

The Costellos were an ancient family of Cambro (Welsh)-Norman descent. The barony of Costello, in which we find the parish of Aghamore, had been their barony and was named after them. The Costello family had participated in the Norman invasion of Ireland, (1167-1172 AD), with Richard de Clare (Strongbow). In 1235, they engaged in the Norman invasion of Connaught, along with the de Burgos, (Burkes), and the de Lacys, and established the Barony of *MacOisdeaibh*, later MacCostello, in eastern Mayo and western Roscommon. In pre-Norman times, the area had been called *Sliebh Lugha* and was ruled by the *Ó Gadhra* dynasty. In the 12th century, Milo de Angelo removed the *O'Gadhra* seat from *Airtech Mór* to Costello and built a castle there, known as Castlemore.

The Costellos were the first of the great Norman families in Ireland to use the "Mac" (Son of) prefix to their name. Like many other Cambro-Norman families they became "more Irish than the Irish themselves". The name remains very common in Mayo.[1].

The Costellos were settled at Castlemore (*Castle Mór),* from at least the early 16th century. Eventually, they lost most of their wealth and power to the Dillons, whose Mayo estates included the townland of Carrowbaun. The 1st Viscount Dillon was a loyal supporter of Elizabeth I of England in her Irish wars. He was made Collector-General in the reconquest of Connaught and used his position to transfer lands held by the Costello's to himself, through the legal process of 'Surrender and Regrant'. This was designed to enable the transfer of land ownership from the Irish Brehan system to the English feudal system, but the Viscount failed on the 'regrant' part, so becoming the 'legal' landowner of much Costello land in the process. This led to conflict between Dudley (or *Dubhaltach Caoch*) Costello and the Dillons in the seventeenth century. It is claimed that Tomas Laidir MacCostello, was murdered by the Dillons.

The Costellos were one of the many Irish families that, during the seventeenth century destruction of everything Gaelic, produced repartees who fought against Oliver Cromwell and the parliamentarians, with the result that they did particularly badly out the Cromwellian settlement. This settlement involved the forced transfer of ownership of vast tracts of land all over Ireland. In order to repay Commonwealth soldiers and adventurers who were considered loyal to him, Cromwell granted them the lands of his opponents, who were in turn banished to lands in Mayo, Galway, Roscommon and Clare, ('To Hell or Connaught'). This 'transplantation to Connaught also involved transplantation within Connaught, as existing landowners west of the Shannon, like the Costellos, had to make way for the new arrivals and were given estates elsewhere in the Province, resulting in many Connaught estates being broken up. Dudley (or *Dubhaltach*) Costello became an officer in the army of the Confederate Catholics in 1642, and later became a colonel in the Spanish army. After the Restoration he returned to Ireland and devoted the rest of his life to wreaking vengeance on the new Cromwellian proprietors.

Both the Dillons and Costellos fought for the Catholic cause against William of Orange, but Dillon acquired most of MacJordan rights also, as we find him in the 17th century owning all the castles of the

---

1 http://towns.mayo-ireland.ie/

Chapter 10 - THE HALLORANS OF RATH, CAHIR AND CORNAGEATHTA

county except for the MacJordan Castle at Rath, as discussed in the previous section. The *clann* of MacJordan, and the smaller one of MacPhilip, were descendants of the de Angulos or Costellos.

Despite always being on the losing side, the Costello's were not turned out of all their estates but retained the northern portion of the Barony and moved in the early 19th century to the main family residence to Edmondstown House. They held on to English tenures and paid a fixed rent (McDonnell-Garvey, 1995). Most of the Costello estate was in the parishes of Aghamore and Kilcolman, including one townland in the barony of Frenchpark.

During the Great Famine, high poor law rates and loss of rental income forced many landlords into insolvency. Encumbered Estates Acts of 1848 and 1849 instituted the Landed Estates' Court to facilitate the sale of bankrupt estates. This allowed for the repayment of debts to be set against returns from the sale of the land, giving clean title for the new owner. The Costellos appear to have used this to purchase some land and sell other. In 1851, Martin P. Costello bought Lot 3, Cloghansmore and Knockroe, parish of Kilmainemore, barony of Kilmaine, county Mayo, from the sale of the Lewin estate in the Encumbered Estates' Court. In 1862 Arthur Robert Costello advertised the sale of about 1100 acres in the baronies of Gallen and Costello, county Mayo, through the Landed Estates' Court, and about 1050 acres in the parish of St Johns, barony of Athlone, county Roscommon. Perhaps they used this money to redeem, for £5,000, a large section of their estate that had previously been mortgaged to Francis Moore of Summerset, England. It was this part of the estate which included Little Cahir, however, at present, we are not certain that it was in that part of Cahir that Martin Halloran's family lived. In the 1870s however Arthur Robert Costello still owned 7513 acres in county Mayo and 1,038 acres in county Roscommon. The total value of these estates was £1,779.

Edmondstown House, seat of the Costellos. Now residence of the Roman Catholic Bishop of Achonry

The Encumbered Estates Acts where designed to reassert the interests of property by facilitating the transfer of ownership of land. They did little to improve the rights of the tenants. Over 3,000 estates (five million acres) changed hands by 1859, and the new landlords were mostly Irish. The sad reality was that many of them soon started evicting tenants.

Arthur Robert George Costello built a new house in 1864 close to Edmondstown House on the style of a Scottish Manor. Locals called it 'the palace' because of its pretentious design. However, Arthur Robert had to borrow heavily to complete it. As a result he died in poverty on his way to Dublin[1]. The house was bought by the Catholic Church for the Diocese of Achonry from the Costellos and is, today, the residence of the Bishop of Achonry[2].

In 1878 Charles Costello of Kilfree, Gurteen, county Sligo owned 174 acres in county Mayo and 1330 acres in county Sligo. Most of this property was in the barony of Coolavin.

Even to the end of the landlord era, life remained difficult for the tenants, and the contempt of many landlords unabated. Moiré McDonnell-Garvey reports hearing of how many older people of Cahir talked of Captain Costello and his agent, Mr Forbes. Forbes collected rent on horseback and was known to cut down and trample on freshly washed clothes as he made his way to the doors. A garden in Tallaghmore is still known today as Forbe's garden. Perhaps it should be renamed!

The O'Gradys, on the other hand, seem to have been 'new money'. At present we know little of O'Grady's origins. In the mid 1850s, at the time of Griffith's Valuation, Francis O'Grady was leasing a property at Barnaboy, barony of Frenchpark, valued at £4 15s together with 179 acres of land from William Longfield's estate. Later, they owned an estate mainly located in the parish of Aghamore, barony of Costello, but also containing lands in the parishes of Annagh, Bekan, Knock, Kilbeagh and Kilmovee in the same barony and across the county border in county Galway, and in Frenchpark, county Roscommon. Francis Richard O'Grady, like many other Irish men, however, benefited in the long term from the bankruptcy of other landlords, as he had purchased much of his estate in the Encumbered Estates' Court. Whether he purchased Cahir at this time, and from whom, we at present don't know.

Francis R. O'Grady was not an absentee-landlord and was active in local politics and community work. In May 1846, during the first full year of the famine, he was appointed by the Gallen and Costello Relief Committee as Chairman of the Sub-Committee for Aghamore in which capacity he was to write a report on 'the state of destitution in their districts' (Swords, 1999). In October of the same year, as Chairman of the Kilkelly Relief Committee, he wrote asking for meal depots in Ballyhaunis and Kilkelly, 'because of the high price of meal at market, and thus we will be able to keep the already starving poor from outrage,' (Swords, 1999). Later, in September of 1847, as Chairman of the Finance Committee of the Swinford Union he wrote a letter of gratitude to the Lord Lieutenant of Ireland, George William Frederick Villiers. He went on to say:

> In this Union the prejudice of the population to the poorhouse were so deep and inveterate, that the house was a long time open before one pauper could be induced to enter it. Famine, however, came on with such unrelenting severity that in a short time the house was filled with the number (700) it was intended for. On the dreadful month of November 120 were admitted beyond the regulated number, hundreds were refused admission for want of room. Some unhappy beings perished on the high roads and in the fields. Influenced by terror and dismay, leaving entire districts almost deserted, the better class of farmers in numbers sold their property at any sacrifice and took flight for America, and the humbler classes left the country in masses hoping to find a happier doom in any other region. This awful state of things continued in the winter and spring in a greater or lesser degree.

No doubt, some of these joined up with neighbours and found their 'happier doom' in Birstall.

O'Grady also held a number of public offices after the famine. The first meeting of the committee of management in 1852, he was chosen as Chairman of the Board of the Charlestown Dispensary District, of which Charles Strickland was a member[3]. In 1857, he was on the list of Grand Jurors for county Mayo[4], also along with Charles Strickland. He was appointed to Office of High Sheriff for Mayo on November 7th 1856 (The Edinburgh Gazette, November 11, 1856).

---

1 The Costello Heritage: http://skehana.homestead.com/newsletter.html

2 The Costello Heritage: http://skehana.homestead.com/newsletter.html

3 Henry, Cathal, Charlestown Dispensary District - Minute Book 1852 -1894.1, http://towns.mayo-ireland.ie/Web

4 *The Irish-American* - York City newspaper http://www.irishinnyc.freeservers.com/photo2.html

Chapter 10 - THE HALLORANS OF RATH, CAHIR AND CORNAGEAHTA

At present we have no evidence that Richard O'Grady enforced evictions, though no doubt many of his tenants, like those all over Mayo, left the land and emigrated over the following decades. This family appear to belong to a new class of native Irish landlords who came about as an unintended result of the Encumbered Estates Acts of 1848 and 1849. By 1878 George Francis O'Grady held 1342 acres in county Mayo, 654 acres in county Galway and 1099 acres in county Roscommon. His estates were advertised for sale in 1879. At present we don't know who the purchaser of the estates were and would be interested in further information.

The home of the O'Grady family in the 19th century was Tavraun, which is still lived in and well maintained. Their family vault is in Urlaur Abbey[1].

Land Law (Ireland) Act (1881)

Finally, in 1881, opposition to the Land War crumbled and the Land Act finally granted the Land Leagues demand of the 'three Fs' - Fair Rent, Fixity of Tenure and Free Sale. The Irish Land Commission was established to arbitrate a fair rent between the landlord and the tenant. Its decisions were legally binding for 15 years and the free sale of their interest in their holding was conceded to the tenants, subject to the landlord's entitlement to first call as purchaser. There was a belief that the wholesale transfer of land from landlords to tenants would help resolve unrest in Ireland, kill off the Home Rule movement, and create peace and stability. Initially the act was a success; about 75% of eligible tenants took advantage of its provisions, resulting in rents being reduced by about 20%. Excluded from the provisions of the act were a large number of tenants who held an acre, about 150,000 leaseholders throughout the land, and a further 130,000 tenants in rent arrears. The former group had their rents fixed by the Land Law Act (1887).

The Land Commission assumed the land purchase functions previously carried out by the Board of Works under the 1870 Landlord and Tenant Act. The proportion advanced was increased from two thirds to three quarters and the deposit required was reduced from one third to one quarter but the term of 35 years at 5% interest remained unchanged. Under this Act, the Costello estate was sold to the 269 tenants in the 1st May 1884. The Costellos had made 3000 acres of mountain bog available to them at no cost. £25,000, that is 25% of the purchase price, was made available to the tenants as an advance. It may well have been that at this point that Pat Halloran and Winifred Morley came into possession of their property.

A man who played a key role in this transfer of ownership was Fr Denis O'Hara. He was treasurer of the local Land League and was frequently on its platforms supporting its activities and direct action by the tenants, including the Plan of Campaign. As a priest, this meant he was in defiance of Pope Leo XIII's rescript forbidding clerical engagement in such activities. However, his work went beyond this. There had been considerable difficulty in apportioning the £25,000 purchase money and the mountain bog land made available to the 269 tenants on the Costello estate. Under the terms of the 1881 Land Act, 25% of the purchase price, £6,250, had to be made up by the tenants. However, they could only make up about £1,500, or £6 each. The rest was raised in the local Hibernian bank on the joint security of the tenants and two Ballaghaderreen traders. Fr O'Hara, it is said by Máire McDonnell-Garvey, was instrumental in bringing about this transaction, and neither the guarantors nor the banks lost out as every penny was paid back on time. She also describes how he walked every section of the land with the purchasers, fixing what each should pay.

It is sad to reflect on the loss of esteem in the minds of the people in modern Ireland, of both the banks and the Roman Catholic clergy. However, when one considers the change in their roles, it is hardly surprising.

After 1909, an offer was accepted by J.P. Costello on over 180 acres of his estate in county Sligo.

---

1 NUI Galway Landed Estates Database, http://www.landedestates.ie/LandedEstates/jsp/estate-show.jsp?id=129, accessed Jan 2011.

The sad case of Catherine Casey

An indication of the difficulties involved in the struggle to obtain the 'three Fs' demanded by the Land Leaguers is illustrated by the sad story of Catherine Casey and her son from Cahir, which is reported in detail by Basis Burke in *The 1897 Cahir Land-grabbing Case, Glór Achadh Mór*, 2007.

In 1897, Catherine Casey of Cahir was jailed in Castlebar for resisting eviction by Colonel Brabazon on April 4th, of the previous year, and 'abusing' the new tenant, a certain Waldron. We are not sure if Colonel Brabazon bought the land in Cahir from the Costellos or O'Gradys.

On her release from prison, the following newspaper reports appeared.

Welcome For Jailed Evictee

Western People, February 3rd 1897

A tremendous welcome awaited Mrs. Catherine Casey, when she arrived by train in Kiltimagh. Mrs. Casey, who was evicted from her holding at Cahir, was jailed for one month for calling the man who took possession of her homestead a "Grabber".

Thousands of people made their way to Kiltimagh to give her a cordial welcome and escort her back to Cahir. Headed by the Kiltimagh band, the procession started for Cahir at 6 pm, a distance of four miles.

The enormous gathering occupied the road for over a mile. There were a large number of torches burning and bonfires were ablaze on the hills. Some thirty members of the R.I.C[1]. were stationed close to the house from which Mrs. Casey was evicted, and remained until 8 o'clock that evening. There was no trouble; good humour and excellent order prevailed throughout. Mrs. Casey having been escorted, the people dispersed quietly to their homes".

The Cahir Grabbing Case Welcome For Jailed Evictee Connaught Telegraph,

Mrs. Casey, after returning from jail, went back into the possession of her old home, and on January 31st, 1897, a public meeting was held on the evicted holding for the purpose of denouncing the conduct of Waldron.

Over 8,000 people attended the meeting, which was addressed by Mr. William O'Brien, the local clergy and other speakers. Waldron was there boycotted and for his protection a police hut was erected at Cahir and five police put inside. Waldron could not get one so mean as to speak to him or to sell him 6d worth of provisions.

September 3rd 1898

The Census of Ireland for 1901 shows that Catherine Casey, now aged 62, was living alone in a one-roomed, third class thatched house with one window at the front. We do not know what happened to her son. She must have lost her battle with Colonel Brabazon, as she was leasing a property from Bridget Costello.

Catherine Casey in census of Ireland for 1901

Later, apparently a bit the worse for wear for drink, she had to be rescued from sinking in boggy land. In 1906, she died alone, forgotten by the politicians and clergy who championed her when it suited them to do so.

This is how local writer P.D. Kenny remembers the event in his book, *The Sorrows of Ireland*:

---

1 Royal Irish Constabulary

Chapter 10 - THE HALLORANS OF RATH, CAHIR AND CORNAGEATHTA

The widow's hut stood by the river at a bend in the bleak road, about half-way between Cill Cheallaigh and Kiltimagh. Driving past in the rain, I saw the hens crouching against the door, and looking hungry. Perhaps they had not been fed, and if not, what of the old lady? I looked through the little window and thought I saw something queer. Then I went on and told the police. They opened the door. On the floor was a mass of dark ashes, in the outline of a human body. At one end was a tuft of grey hair, at the other some charred remains of a boot. A little apart was a human shin bone and there were bits of bones among the ashes. Catherine Casey had been burned to death in her solitude and that was all that remained of her. She had died without a priest. There was a priest to 'lead' her in the war, and to keep her out of her old home, but none when she had to face the Almighty. Mr. O'Brien did not come to the wake. No one came. The remains were left in their solitude for days until her relatives came from a distance and removed the ashes.

Despite political exploitation of individual tragedies like this, by the beginning of the twentieth century, as a result of political agitation by the Land League and the pressure put on Westminster by the Parnellite party, all the residents of Cahir owned their own homes and land. Thus a most radical change had been brought about in Irish life, arguable a more significant change for the rural community than the gaining of Irish independence two decades later.

Reference to map	Name		Description of tenants	Area	Rateable Valuation		Tot. Annual Value
	occupiers	Immediate Lessors			Land	Buildings	
1	CORNAGEAGHTA. (Ord. S. 81 & 82.) George Horken,	Lambert Rutledge,	Land,	84 0 27	25 0 0	—	25 0 0
			Total,	84 0 27	25 0 0	—	25 0 0
1 a	MOUNTAIN-COMMON. (Ord. S. 81, 82, 92, & 93.) Bridget Burke (of 3 b),	Sir Compton Domville, Bart.,	Land,	9 1 35	0 15 0	—	0 15 0
2 a	Patrick M'Guire,	Same,	Land, house, and office,	18 3 15	2 0 0	0 10 0	2 10 0
3 a	William Phillips,	Same,	Land, house, and office,	33 3 15	5 0 0	0 10 0	5 10 0
.. b	Bridget Burke,	Same,	House and office,	—	—	0 5 0	0 5 0
4 a	James Scarry,	Same,	Land, house, and office,	31 2 18	8 5 0	0 10 0	8 15 0
5 a	Thomas Grogan,	Same,	Land, house, and office,	33 3 29	5 10 0	0 10 0	6 0 0
6 a	Luke Walsh,	Same,	Land and house,	17 1 30	4 10 0	0 10 0	5 0 0
7 a	John Duffy,	Same,	Land and house,	36 3 35	4 5 0	0 10 0	4 15 0
8 a	Thomas Costelloe,	Same,	Land, houses, and office,	8 3 15	1 10 0	0 5 0	1 15 0
9 a	Mary Grourke,	Same,	Land and house,	10 2 22	1 10 0	0 5 0	1 15 0
10 a	Bryan Lyons,	Same,	Land and house,	11 1 5	2 5 0	0 5 0	2 10 0
— b	Thomas Lyons, (See lot 12.)	Same,	House,	—	—	0 5 0	0 5 0

Griffiths Valuation record of the townland of Cornageaghta and Mountain-common

Again, although the Griffith Valuation does not record any Hallorans in Cornageaghta, we find a number of them in the townland in later Aghamore parish records, suggesting that they moved into the townland after the famine or were landless labourers or very small land holders before that. In the Griffiths Valuation records we notice the area of land held by each tenant is larger than in the other townland and is rented directly from the landlord, Sir Compton Domville Bart, in Mountain and Lambert Rutledge in Cornageaghta. There are only two cases of secondary letting, one clearly within the Lyons family. The land was used primarily for sheep farming and there are no mills, schoolhouses or cottages, suggesting it was an isolated life where one shepherd farmer held a number of acres of mountain grazing and few if any labourers were required from outside the family.

Cornageaghta or Mountain / Mountaincommon

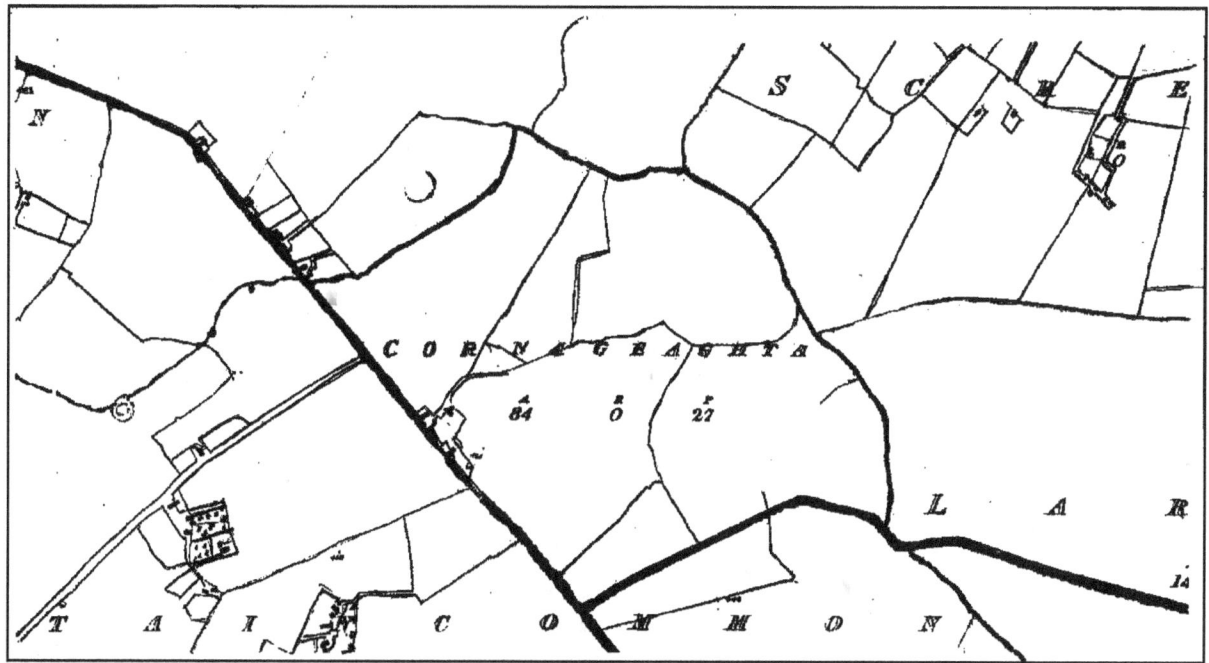

The townland of Cornageaghta circa 1837

Aghamore parish records (APR) and grave yard inscriptions

In Cahir we found in the APR that a Thomas Halloran and Sally Coyne were married on 18th Feb 1867, witnessed by James Hopkins (?) and Mary Stenson. We have records of the baptism of two children:

- Bridget Halloran, baptised on 25th January 1868, and was sponsored by Martin Halloran, Mary Stenson.

- Mary Halloran, baptised on 29th May 1869, and was sponsored by Ned and Mary Adams.

Through the same records we discover that Thomas Halloran and Sarah Kyne had their son Michael baptised on 15th January 1881, and that Anthony Lohan and Catherine Nyland were his sponsors. This family is recorded as from Mountain. It is possible, given the similarity of the names, that this is the family earlier found in Cahir and that they had moved to Mountain and subsequently to Cornageaghta. Michael was baptised thirteen years after their first child, Bridget.

Irish census 1901

According to the 1901 census, we further discover that Thomas Halloran (b. abt. 1839) was aged 62, and is recorded as head of the household in Cornageaghta. Thomas was James' son. He recorded his father's death in 1882. His wife Sarah Kyne (b. abt. 1842) was aged 59. They were married on 18th Feb 1867. They now had two sons: Michael, now aged 20, and Thomas (b. abt. 1886), aged 15. There is no record of Bridget or Mary, who, if they had lived, would have been in their mid-thirties by this time.

Census of Ireland 1901- Cornageaghta

Thomas was a shepherd. His son, Michael, was an agricultural labourer, and young Thomas was recorded as being at school. Thomas and Sarah could not read or write though the sons could. The whole family were speakers of Irish and English.

Chapter 10 - THE HALLORANS OF RATH, CAHIR AND CORNAGEATHTA

They are recorded as the only residents of Cornageaghta; and though the family were recorded as of Mountaincommon in parish records, Mountaincommon and Cornageaghta are adjoining townlands and may not always have been differentiated. They lived in a stone 2 to 4 room dwelling with a non-perishable roof. It had 2 front windows and the family occupied 2 rooms. They must have concentrated solely on sheep as there was only one outhouse in the entire townland, and that was a stable. At this time they were the only known members of the family who are still renting their land. Their landlord was T. Dillon-Leetch, who we discovered living in Cahir in the only 1st class dwelling.

Irish census 1911

We learn more of the family in the Irish census of 1911. Here we find Thomas Halloran, now estimated to be aged 75, though he was recorded as 62 ten years earlier. He was still working as a shepherd, but sadly, he is now a widower, his wife Sarah having died. His youngest son, Thomas, was still living with him and was 26, but at that young age, is also recorded as a widower. Thomas had probably taken over the sheep farm at this time; 10 years earlier he was recorded as a farm labourer. Michael, his elder brother by five years is not recorded.

The house had not changed significantly in the previous decade. A major change, however, was that Thomas was now the landholder, presumably having bought T. Dillon-Leetch out.

Census of Ireland 1911- Cornageaghta

A grave inscription in Aghamore cemetery reads:

> *In Loving Memory Of THOMAS HALLORAN Mountain Died Feb. 2nd 1951 His Wife MARY Died March 19th 1952 Their Son RODDY Died Nov. 26th 1983 R.I.P. - Erected By Daughter-in-Law Peggy and Grandchildren*

If this is the young Thomas of the 1911 census, he would have died aged about 66 having remarried after being made a widower so young. His second wife Mary died within a year of him.

We have been told by Martin Joe Halloran of Carrowbaun and Swinford that Roddy's death in Nov. 26th 1983 saw the disappearance of the last Halloran to live in Mountain (Mountaincommon, Cornageaghta). Some of Roddy's family now live in Manchester and we would be happy to hear from them. Roddy's grave is also to be found in Aghamore cemetery.

The landlord - Sir Compton Domville Bart

The landlord at the time of the Griffith Valuation (about 1856) was Sir Compton Domville Bart, a member of the Domville family who bought the county Mayo estate of the Trench family of Heywood, county Laois in 1833. Following the death of Sir Frederick William Trench in 1859, the Domvilles inherited his estate in county Roscommon. Sir Compton Domville had married Helena Sarah the eldest sister of Sir Frederick W. Trench in 1815[1].

At the time of Griffith's Valuation the Domville Mayo estate was located mainly in the parishes of Manulla, barony of Carra; Killasser, barony of Gallen and Aghamore, barony of Costello. It was around

---

[1] http://www.landedestates.ie/LandedEstates/jsp/family-show.jsp?id=511

this time the son of Sir Charles Compton, William Domvile the 2nd Bart, assumed the title (Jill Dale, 2010)[1]. Sir Compton Domvile Bart was the primary landlord in the following townlands in Aghamore Civil Parish: Casheltourly, Falleighter and Mountaincommon; Clooncleevragh, Darhanagh, Dromada (Joyce), Drumalooaun and Loobnamuck in Killasser Civil Parish; Lakill and Tawnagh More in Templemore Civil Parish; and Cregg, Drumloughra, Lisnolan, Prison East, Prison North, Prison South, Rush Hill and Smuttanagh in Manulla Civil Parish (Jill Dale, 2010).

His generosity as a landlord was described in the J. F. Quinn's *History of Mayo* (1996). Apparently, at a meeting held in Balla in February 1848 he forgave the rents of the tenants of Prizon, Drimlooher, Cragaga, Lisnolan, Castletoorly and Loobnamuck. He also sent them blankets, clothing and food, (Quinn, 1996, Vol IV, Ch 9, p. 265 quoted in Jill Dale, 2010). The consolidated nature of the farms of Mountaincommon suggests the activity of an improving landlord. The following letter, of November 25th 1846, from the Parish Priest of Balla, Fr Martin Browne, written at the height of the Great Famine, also bears testament to the fact that not all landlords were guilty of avarice and indifference to the condition of their tenants (Swords 1999).

To the Editor of the Mayo Telegraph
  Dear Sir, - I hasten to inform you that during the last week three persons died of actual starvation in this Parish. My curates are toil-worn by their unwearied exertions to minister to the spiritual and temporal wants of the destitute poor in this locality. Any language I am master of cannot adequately convey to you the heart-rending scenes we are compelled to witness. The greater part of the people are wretchedly clad, and almost every poor man possessed of a cow is selling her to purchase a month's provisions for his family. But this, I suppose, is in accordance with the doctrine of Political Economy. ....
  ... [U]nless immediate steps are taken by the Government and Landlords to purchase seed for the poorer tenants, and prepare the soil for receiving it, the ensuing year will be far more memorable than the present. I send you a circular which Sir Compton Domville has addressed to his tenants in Mayo, and ... I trust you will give it a place in the next number of your independent Journal. There is not in Ireland a more indulgent Landlord, or one that has taken more pains to improve his tenants; and his efficient and benevolent agent, Mr. Sherrard, is indefatigable in his endeavour to carry out the benevolent intentions of this excellent Landlord. He has never impounded the tenant's cattle for rent, and whatever improvement is made by the tenant ... will ensure for him not only full and adequate compensation, but also the respect and esteem of this worthy Baronet. If Ireland had hitherto possessed such proprietors, her resources would have been more fully developed, and her many qualities, which now lie dormant, would have been called into active exercise, and productive of innumerable blessings to this country, which is so temperate in her climate, and, up to the present awful visitation, was so fruitful in her fields.

Though tributes to landlords like this bear testament to the generosity of individuals, it should be borne in mind that the system of land tenure which enriched these men was completely iniquitous, even for its time. Small landholders and agricultural labourers in England lived in luxury compared to their Irish counterparts. Their legal situation in regards to security of tenure and compensation for improvements was much better. The granting of compensation to a tenant for improvements made to their dwellings or land was hardly an act of great magnanimity, it was a well-established right in England, and was enjoyed by tenant in Ulster. In the rest of Ireland, if a small farmer attempted to improve his lot, his rent would have been increased. The simple fact was that the Irish landlords demand rents in excess of what the land could provide, and men and women had to go to England for part of the year, or else emigrate entirely. They lived on the edge. A poor crop meant hunger. A crop failure meant famine.

There is an interesting account given by Bernadette Kilduff, in *Glór Achadh Mór* (2005). She tells of how her grandfather came to Mountain View in 1880s having inherited land from his uncle, Pat Waldron, former agent of the Domvilles in the area. The circumstances of the time meant that he had the odd task of having to bury a pile of unused windows. The reason for this was that Domville had donated windows to all his tenants in Mountain. He gave them to Pat Waldron, his agent, to distribute. Pat placed three windows in his own home and sent out a circular to the rest of the tenants that they were there to be picked up. However, no one came to claim them. The reason was quite simple. The tenants feared that installing the windows would increase the value of their holdings and this would result in an increase in

---

1 http://www.rootsweb.ancestry.com/~irlmayo2/comptondomvilebt_mayolandlords.html

Chapter 10 - THE HALLORANS OF RATH, CAHIR AND CORNAGEATHTA

rent. Such was the mistrust between tenants and even well-meaning landlords, and such were the disincentives to the most basic improvements.

It is worth noting, that though windows were taxed in Ireland, it was a tax on the size of the house. Houses having less than seven windows were not subject to this tax.

However, the end of the Great Famine marked the beginning of the decline of the power of the major landlords. In December 1865 the county Roscommon 5779-acre estate of the Domviles in the baronies of Athlone and Moycarn was advertised for sale in the Landed Estates' Court. Most of it was purchased by the Waithmans. In 1876 the Domviles of Heywood, Abbeyleix, owned 6,040 acres in county Mayo and other estates in counties Dublin and Laois. By March 1916 the sale of the estate to the Congested Districts' Board had been accepted by the Domviles[1].

Conclusion

Aspects of the story of the Hallorans of Birstall and Aghamore has been unearthed here and told in order that we may have a better understanding of those who went before us; their terrible privations, extreme trials, courage and capacity for survival. We leave the story in Ireland at beginning of the twentieth century, more than a century ago. Great changes have taken place since then.

One of the most significant of these was the fact that the ownership of Irish land, by and large, was in the hands of ordinary Irish men and women. This, and the massive expansion of education, meant that fewer lived in crushing poverty and many found new levels of prosperity, though Mayo remained poor relative to other parts of Ireland, and emigration continued to be a problem, and has become so again.

Politically, the Civil War, partition and the establishment of the Free State in December 1922, and then the proclamation of the Republic of Ireland in 1949, changed the fundamental nature of life in all of Ireland. However, for the ordinary families that worked the land, none of these developments had the practical impact that of ownership of the land they worked.

Along with these developments was the establishment of a secure sense of Irish identity. The Gaelic League or *Conradh na Gaeilge* was founded by Eoin MacNéill, on 31 July 1893. Among its earliest adherents was the poet and folklorist, Douglas Hyde, the first President of Ireland. He was the son of a Church of Ireland rector from Frenchpark, the seat of the Barons de Freyne, an area that has already featured in this account, situated some 25 miles east of Carrowbaun. The aim of this movement was to revive the Irish language and the ancient culture of Ireland. It attracted some of the most prominent Irishmen of the time. Many revolutionaries were also active in the League, including Patrick Pearse. Members of the Irish Republican Brotherhood actually took over of the League in 1915, prompting Hyde's resignation and thrusting that the League into the republican fight for national independence after 1916.

The reclaiming of the Irish language and culture may not have been as comprehensive as the members of the league would have liked, and it may have come too late in the day to reverse the anglicisation of Ireland, but it did transform the cultural and social landscape, taking the stigma out of being an Irish speaker and fostering a restored pride in the heritage of Gaelic Ireland.

This was also particularly the case in the area of sport. The Gaelic Athletic Association (GAA) or *Cumann Lúthchleas Gael* has the aim of promoting traditional Irish sports such as hurling, camogie, Gaelic football, handball and rounders, as well as Irish music and dance. Huge numbers of people throughout the land and in virtually every parish, follow GAA sports with a passion - nowhere more so than in County Mayo.

Many now argue that the sense of Irish identity developed through these institutions was too narrow and even bigoted; that they did not allow for the inclusion of those Irish men and woman whose allegiance was to Britain, and whose religious faith was not centred on Rome. The lives of those who have appeared in this history indicate that the very nature of Irish life over the centuries has meant that many of Ireland's daughters and sons have had to accommodate themselves to new and even hostile ways of life, and that this is central to the Irish experience. The sheer depth of their hardship means we should not forget them.

---

1 http://www.landedestates.ie/LandedEstates/jsp/family-show.jsp?id=511

THE HALLORANS FROM BIRSTALL AND AGHAMORE

Kilkelly (Peter Jones)

130 years after his great grandfather left the small village of Kilkelly in Co. Mayo, Peter Jones found a bundle of letters sent to his great grandfather by his father in Ireland. The letters tell of family news, births, death, sales of land and bad harvests. Peter Jones used these letters to write this song.

The "trouble" in verse two is probably the Fenian rising of 1867. What is of additional interest is that Kilkelly is hardly three miles from Carrowbaun. It is where Betty Halloran's people, and indeed many of the Irish from around Birstall, came from. Their families shared the experiences expressed in this song and many probably even knew this family[1].

Kilkelly, Ireland, 18 & 60,
My dear and loving son John,
Your good friend, the schoolmaster, Pat McNamara's so good as to write these words down.
Your brothers have all gone to find work in England,
The house is so empty and sad.
The crop of potatoes is sorely infected,
A third to a half of them bad.
And your sister Brigit and Patrick O'Donnell
Are going to be married in June.
Your mother says not to work on the railroad
And be sure to come on home soon.

Kilkelly, Ireland, 18 & 70,
Dear and loving son John,
Hello to your Mrs and to your 4 children,
May they grow healthy and strong.
Michael has got in a wee bit of trouble,
I guess that he never will learn.
Because of the dampness there's no turf to speak of
And now we have nothing to burn.
And Brigit is happy, you named a child for her
And now she's got six of her own.
You say you found work, but you don't say
What kind or when you will be coming home.

Kilkelly, Ireland, 18 & 80,
Dear Michael and John, my sons,
I'm sorry to give you the very sad news
That your dear old mother has gone.
We buried her down at the church in Killkelly.
Your brothers and Brigit were there.
You don't have to worry - she died very quickly.
Remember her in your prayers.
And it's so good to hear that Michael's returning,
With money, he's sure to buy land.
For the crop has been poor and the people
Are selling at any price that they can.

Kilkelly, Ireland, 18 & 90,
My dear and loving son John,
I guess that I must be close on to eighty,
It's thirty years since you're gone.
Because of all of the money you send me,
I'm still living out on my own.
Michael has built himself a fine house,
And Brigit's daughters have grown.
Thank you for sending your family picture.
They're lovely young women and men.
You say that you might even come for a visit.

Kilkelly, Ireland, 18 & 92,
My dear brother John,
I'm sorry that I didn't write sooner to tell you that father passed on.
He was living with Brigit, she says he was cheerful
And healthy right down to the end.
Ah, you should have seen him play with
The grandchildren of Pat McNamara, your friend.
And we buried him alongside of mother,
Down at the Kilkelly churchyard.
He was a strong and a feisty old man,
Considering his life was so hard.
And it's funny the way he kept talking about you,
He called for you in the end.
Oh, why don't you think about coming to visit,
We'd all love to see you again.

---

[1] The complete letters are to be found at: http://www.kilkellyirelandorg.org/letters-sent-to-john-hunt-from-home.html

Appendices

Appendix A - Ó hAllmhuráin - the name O'Halloran

There are many different origins for Irish names but the vast majority can be broken down into either of three categories: Gaelic Irish, Cambro-Norman, and Anglo-Irish. *Ó hAllmhuráin*, anglicised as O'Halloran or Halloran, is in origin a Gaelic *Clann* name, Prendergast, on the other hand is Cambro-Norman and is found throughout the British Isles.

All Irish surnames have evolved and changed over the centuries, usually originating from a single given name, which now tend to be used as first names. Gaelic family names started to be used in the twelfth century. In ancient Ireland the population was much smaller and the mass movement of people was uncommon. It was usual therefore for a person to be known only by one name: *Niall, Eoin, Art*, etc. A first name, even today, may be modified by an adjective to distinguish its bearer from other people with the same name. Only a few generations ago our ancestors might well have been a *Séamus Mór* (big James), *Tomás Óg* (young Thomas), *Máire Bhán* (Fairhaired Mary). Adjectives denoting hair colour may also be used, especially informally: *Pádraig Rua* ("redhaired Patrick"). But this seems unlikely in our ancestors, none of us being red haired. Indeed as a boy Seán O'Halloran was often referred to as *Seán Óg* by his mother Eileen to distinguish him from his father, John. His sister Eileen was referred to as *Eileen Óg* to distinguish her from Eileen, their mother.

This single-name-only system began to break down during the eleventh century as the population was growing and there was a need for a further means of identification, especially if taxes and tithes were to be gathered! The solution was to adopt a prefix such as Mac (Mc is an abbreviation) or Ó. *Mac* means 'son of' whilst *Ó/Ua* mean 'grandson of' as surnames in Irish are generally patronymic in etymology. Indeed, Ireland was one of the first countries to adopt hereditary surnames. Nowadays, they are no longer literal patronyms but have become fixed and unvarying from generation to generation.

O'Halloran is an Anglicisation of *Ó hAllmhuráin* (also anglicised variously as O'Halleron, Halloran, Holleran, meaning "descendant of *Allmhurán*". This personal name was derived from *allmhurach* (or *allwuran*, depending on how it's translated), which means "foreigner," "overseas stranger," or possibly "pirate," and is composed of the parts *all* for "beyond" and *muir* for "sea". The *Ó hAllmhuráins* of Mayo appear to have universally chosen the surname 'Halloran' for official purposes which required English and when they emigrated. It would probably have been first written in this way by the local priest who would have been literate in English, when church records started to be kept in English in the early nineteenth century.

In Irish speaking communities, a female's surname replaced Ó with *Ní* ("daughter of the grandson of") and *Mac* with *Nic* ("daughter of the son of"); in both cases the following name undergoes aspiration. The daughter of a man named *Ó hAllmhuráin* has the surname *Ní Ó hAllmhuráin*. When anglicised, the surname can remain O or Mac, regardless of gender, though more recently many Irish woman have reclaimed the female form, just as many families have reclaimed the Irish version of their surnames that were repressed by the authorities under British rule and stigmatised in various way in the past.

If a woman marries, she may choose to take her husband's surname. In this case, Ó is replaced by *Bean Uí* ("wife of the grandson of") and *Mac* by *Bean Mhic* ("wife of the son of"). In both cases *bean* may be omitted, in which case the woman uses simply *Uí* or *Mhic*. However, many women chose not to do this as we see with husband and wife, Martin Halloran and Winnie Ruane, of Carrowbaun. Winnie is referred to as Ruane in the 1911 Irish Census and subsequently in the Aghamore Parish Register on the baptism of her children. We frequently see this in the Mayo side of the family.

Irish surname derived from a variety of sources, often from the personal name of a significant person. In the case of Brian Boru who possessed no surname, being simply "Brian, High King of the Irish", his grandson *Teigue* called himself *Ua Briain* in memory of his illustrious grandfather, and the name became hereditary thereafter, now anglicised as O'Brian. Similarly, the O'Neills derive their surname from *Niall mac Aoiodh*, who died in 917.

The origins of many of the personal names such as Niall or Brian, which form the stem of the surname remain obscure, but two other broad categories of surname can be distinguished: those which are descriptive of the person and those which reflect an occupation. In the first category, we can guess that the progenitor of the Traceys (Ó *Treasaigh*) was a formidable character, *treasach* meaning "warlike", while the ancestor of the Duffs must have been dark featured, since *dubh*, the root of the name, means black or dark. Among the occupations recorded in names are churchmen, clerks (Clery, Ó Cleirigh, from *cleireach*), bards (Ward, *Mac an Bhaird*, from bard), spokesmen (MacCloran, Mac Labhrain, from the Irish *labhraidh*), and smiths (McGowan, Mac Gabhainn, from *gabhann*). The name Ó hAllmhuráin, could belong to either of these categories; 'strangers from beyond the water' being descriptive while, more interestingly, piracy is an occupation.

When single names became surnames, new forms of first names appeared. Traditionally these were Christian names taken from the Bible and the names of saints. A new system of first names developed, and it may be useful when looking at possible relationships between family members up to and including the 19th Century. In many communities, the oldest son was named after the father's father. The 2nd son was named after the mother's father the 3rd son named after the father and the 4th son named after the father's oldest brother.

The same pattern applied to the daughters, with the oldest named after the mother's mother, the 2nd daughter named after the father's mother, the 3rd daughter named after the mother and the 4th daughter named after the mother's oldest sister. This, of course, was not an absolute rule and there were probably many differences, depending upon the community. However, the practice is worth mentioning in relation to Irish family genealogy, especially as the same names crop up frequently within families:

The influence of the church, dating from this period, can still be seen in many common modern Irish surnames, in particular those beginning with "Gil" or "Kil", an anglicised version of the Irish *Giolla*, meaning follower or devotee. Thus Gilmartin, in Irish *Mac Giolla Mhairtin*, means "son of a follower of (St.) Martin". Similarly, the church is the origin of all of those names starting with "Mul", a version of the Irish *Maol*, meaning bald, and applied to the monks because of their distinctive tonsure. Thus Mulrennan (Ó *Maoilbhreanainn*) means "descendant of a follower of St. Brendan". One category of name, common in English, which is extremely rare among Irish names, are those deriving from the name of a locality. For the Gaels, who you were related to was much more important than where you came from.

Although the immediate reason for the early adoption of hereditary names in Ireland may have been a rapidly expanding population, it can also be seen as the logical outcome of a process at work from the times of the earliest tribal names. Originally, these indicated identification with a common god, often connected with an animal valued by the tribe, in the case of the *Osraige*, or "deerpeople", for example. Next came identification with a divine ancestor, the *Boandrige*, for instance, claiming descent from the goddess *Boand*, the divinised river Boyne. Later the ancestor was merely legendary, as for the *Eoghanachta*, while later still the tribe claimed direct descent from a historical ancestor, as in the case of the *Ui Neill*. This slow emergence of kin relationships out of religion and myth into the realm of history would seem to reach its logical conclusion with the adoption of hereditary surnames, permanent proof of verifiable ties of blood. On a more mundane level, of course, such proof was a valuable political asset, since it demonstrated membership of a powerful kin-group. Even today, the fact that all Gaelic names, without exception, begin with Ó or *Mac* is continuing proof of the significance of family and kin for the Irish.

As the population grew and new families were formed, they sought to consolidate their identity by adopting hereditary surnames of their own, usually by simply adding Mac to the first name of the founding ancestor. In the course of this process, then, many surnames were created which are in fact offshoots of more common names. Thus, for example, the MacMahons and the McConsidines are descended from the O'Brien family, the former from Mahon O'Brien, who died in 1129, the latter from Constantine O'Brien, who died in 1193. The continuing division and subdivision of the most powerful Gaelic families like this is almost certainly the reason for the great proliferation of Gaelic surnames.

The name Prendergast, a Cambro Norman name, is particularly associated with decedents of Prenliregast, a follower of Duke William of Normandy during the Norman conquest of England in 1066. A member of this family played a prominent part in the invasion of Ireland in 1169. In Ireland they were awarded a baronetcy, and became Viscounts Gort of Castle Gort in Galway. Another branch acquired New Castle near Clonmel, in County Tipperary, and this was the family seat for several centuries.

Appendices

Appendix B - Distribution of Hallorans

Mayo.[1]

Aghamore	1	Ardagh	1	Ballinchalla	3	Ballinrobe	1
Cong	6	Crossmolina	3	Islandeady	1	Kilcolman	1
Kilgarvan	1	Killasser	5	Mayo	1	Oughaval	1

Ireland

Clare	214	Cork city	8	Antrim	2
Galway	159	Sligo	8	Longford	2
Cork	82	Kilkenny	8	Kildare	1
Tipperary	77	Laois	4	Down	1
Kerry	57	Dublin	4	Dublin city	1
Limerick	54	Louth	3	Donegal	1
Mayo	26	Offaly	3	Carlow	1
Limerick city	14	Tyrone	3		
Waterford	12	Fermanagh	2		

Worldwide

To become even more fanciful, below is a table indicating the number of Halloran/O'Halloran families per million in various countries around the world[2].

Halloran	FPM	O'Halloran	FPM
Ireland	208.45	Australia	158.69
Australia	65.76	New-Zealand	73.36
United States	27.65	Canada	71.52
New-Zealand	12.34	United Kingdom	33.53
United Kingdom	11.83	Luxembourg	8.5
Canada	2.98	Denmark	1.95
Switzerland	1.28	Switzerland	1.28
Netherlands	0.21	United States	0.78
Germany	0.14	Netherlands	0.43
Spain	0.1	Spain	0.42

Name variants [1].

Hallaran	5	Halleran	15	Halloran	747	Halloren	1
Haloran	2	Holleran	38	Holloran	33	Holoran	3
O'Halloran	73	Hollaran	9				

---

1 http://www.irishtimes.com/ancestor/surname/index.cfm?fuseaction=Go.&UserID=

2 http://www.publicprofiler.org/worldnames/Main.aspx

Appendix C - Family names in Aghamore Parish and Birstall

Every name in Table 3 above is shared by families living in the Birstall area in Yorkshire and in Aghamore parish Co. Mayo at the time of Griffith's Primary Valuation (1856)

Surname	Townland
Brenan	Barnagurry, Carrowneden Aghamore, Mountaincommon, Crossard, Derryclaha, Rath, Carrowneden
Frain	Rath
Feeny	Falleighter, Mountaincommon, Tooreen
Giraughty	Falleighter
Halloran	Carrowbaun
Henry	Cappagh, Crossard, Corhawnagh, Scardaun, Cloongawnagh
Higgins	Caher, Rath, Cloongawnagh, Casheltourly
Kilkenny	Falleighter, Addergoole, Ballyhine, Scregg, Caher, Carton, North Falleighter, Liscosker, Liscat, Lismeegaun
Kelly	Carrowbaun, Derrycoosh, Derrynarud, Derrycashel, Liscat, Cloonturk, Rinn, Addergoole, Derryclaha, Meeltran, Derrynaned, Doogary
Linskey	Cappagh, Aghamore, Scardaun, Aghataharn, Carrowbaun, Carrowscoltia, Crossard
McCue	Caher
McNamara	Annagh, Cloongawnagh, Coogue, South Carton, Liscat
Stenson	Carrowbaun Falleighter, Arderry, Carrowscoltia
Swift	Meeltran, Carrowscoltia
Waldron	Rath, Mountaincommon, Aghamore, Caher

Appendices

Appendix D - Halloran families in Birstall according to English censuses 1851-1901

Michael Halloran and Hannah (Stinson)

1851	1861	1871	1881	1891	1901
Haliron	Allen	Hallaron	Holleran	15 Gelderd Road	
Low Lane Birstal Gomersal	Gelderd Road, Birstall	Church S, Birstall	5 Coach Lane		
Thomas and Judy: Michael, 23, labourer, b. Mayo, Ireland, 1828 Hannah Stinson, 14, visitor, to Pat Frain	Michael, 33, farm labourer b. Mayo, 1828 Honorah, 28 ? b 1837? Mary, 7 b. Birstal 1854 Thomas, 3, b. Birstal 1855 John, 6mnths Catherine Gallagher, 64, widow, boarder Michael Kenny, 20, farm labourer visitor Anthony Stenson, 55, farm labourer, widower, visitor	Michael44, Labourer b. 1827 Oughamore, Mayo Hannah, 38, b. 1833 Clamfullough, Mayo Mary, 17, birler b. 1854, Birstall Thomas 15, coal miner, b. 1855, Birstall Patt 13, coal miner b. 1858, Birstall John, 10, scholar, b. 1855, Birstall James, 8, scholar b. 1863, Birstall Ann, 3, b.1867, Birstall Bridget, 1 b. 1870, Birstall	Hannah, 50, widow (Thomas boarder with Henry fam, Br'hill James, 19, coal miner, b. Birstall, Hannah, 13, scholar b. 1867, Birstall Bridget, 11, scholar b. 1869, Birstall + James Mcdonagh, 22, miner, lodger b. Ireland James Kilkenny, 22 miner Lodger, b. Ireland	Hannah, widow, 60 Daspery hawker Thomas, 34 b. 1855, Birstall Ann, 23, rag picker b. 1867, Birstall Bridget, 21, cloth machine feeder, b. 1869, Birstall + Martin Flanaghan26, miner, b. Ireland Thomas Mat, 25, coal miner, b. Dublin	
Michael m Honorah Stinchin in 1854		Ann born 16/11/1872 Mary married John Smith on 4/10/1873 Michael Halloran died 15/10/1877	Pat married Mary Stenson in Oct 1883		

Thomas Halloran and Judy (Stenson)

1851 - Haliron/ Halizon79, Low Lane, Birstal	1861 - Halleron,101 Common Rd, Batley	1871 - Hallaron,184, Brownhill, Batley	1881 - Allen, Brownhill, Batley	1891	1901
Thomas, 42, Labourer, b. 04, Mayo Judith, 40 b. 08, Mayo James(Thomas)Labourer b. '37, Mayo (14) Paterick, 12 b. '39, Mayo Michael, 10 b.1841, Mayo Thomas, 9 b. '42, Mayo Mary, 7 b. Mayo, 44 Bridget, 5 b. '46, Mayo Catherine, 3 b. '48, Mayo Michael, labourer, brother b.1828, Mayo (23) Thomas Brennan, labourer b. '17, Mayo (34) Ann Brennan, 26 b.'23, Mayo Margaret Brennan, 11 b. '40, Mayo Patrick Brennan, 3 b. 1850, Mayo James Brennan, 7months b. 1851, Mayo	Thomas, 57, Ag lab b.04, Mayo, Ireland Judith, 61, b. 1810,Mayo, Ireland Patrick, 24, miner b. '37, Ireland Michael, 22, miner b.'39, Mayo Thomas, 20,miner b.'41, Mayo Mary, 18, wool fact worker, b.'43, Mayo Catherine, 12, wool fact worker, b. 47, Mayo Bridget, 7, scholar, b. 54, Batley Catherine Convey, 24, wool fact wkr, b. 37Mayo	Thomas, 63, Hawker b.08, Ireland Judy, 61, b. 1810, Ireland Kate, 23, Rag sorter b. '47, Ireland Bridget, 17, fuller b. '54, Batley Kate Conove, 30, ragsorter, b. 41, Ireland Michael Mallon, 22, visitor Labourer, b. '49 Ireland Thos. Prendergast, 20 Labourer, b.'51, Ireland James Hallaron, 3, visitor b. '68, Batley Patrick Hallaron, 2, visitor b. '69, Batley Mary Hallaron, 2months b.1871, Batley	Thomas, 72, rag sorter? b. Ireland Bridget, 26, rag sorter married, b. Batley Bridget B 11, scholar Ann C 11/2, dau, sch		
	Cath m Thomas Moran, 3/66	Judy died 18/12/1878 Bridget m. Peter Coyne, 5/74	Thomas died 17/02/1887		

James Halloran (son of Thomas) and Bridget (Higgins)

1851	1861	1871	1881	1891	1901
Haliyon/ Haliron					
Low Lane Birstall	20, Gelderd Rd	20, Gelderd Rd	8, Coach Lane	113 Leeds Rd	113 Leeds Rd
James (as Thomas?/) 14, labourer, b. '37, Mayo	James, 25, miner b.'36, Co. Mayo Bridget, (nee Higgins),21 b. 1840, Mayo Thomas, 2 months b. 17/02/61, Birstall	James, 33, miner b. 38, Ireland Bridget, 29 housewife n. '41, Ireland Thomas, 11, scholar b. 17/02/1861, Ireland ? James, 9, scholar b. 06/02/63, Birstall John, 7, scholar b. 5/10/64, Birstall Michael, 5, scholar b. 2/1/66, Birstall Mary, 4, b. 21/11/67, Birstall Ann, 2 b. 8/04/69, Birstall Catherine, 3 months b. 6/01/71, Birstall John Naifsy Thomas Stinton	James, 44, miner b. 37, Ireland Bridget, 40 b. 41, Ireland Thomas, 20, miner b. 1861, Birstall James, 18, miner b. 63, Birstall John, 16, coal harrier b. 64, Birstall Michael, 15, coal harrier b. 66, Birstall Mary, 14 b. 67, Birstall Annie. 12 b. 1869, Birstall Catherine, 10 b. 71, Birstall Martin, 8 b. 14/02/1873, Birstall William, 4 b. 18/06/1877 George, 2 b.29/04/1879	(Record not found)	James, 65, Gen Labourer b. 1836, Ireland John, 36, harrier b. 64, Birstall Michael, harrier b. 1866, Birstall Anorah, 20, dressmaker b. 24/08/1881
	M. 1859 3/4, Dewsbury 3/12/60, James: citation for uttering counterfeit coin, 1 yr imprisonment		Bridget died 1884, 2/4 or 21/08/87 (Dewsbury, 9b 414) George died, 1886 3/4		

Patrick Halloran (son of Thomas) and Bridget (Lyons)

1851	1861	1871	1881	1891	1901
		Halloran	Halleran		
		(77) Chandler's Alley	23 Coach Lane		
		Patrick, 34, miner b. 1837, b. Co. Mayo Bridget, 32, mill operative, b. 1839, Co. Mayo Mary, 8, Scholar b. 13/07/63, Birstall James, 5, scholar b. 1865 Michael, 4, scholar 20/09/67 Sarah, 1 ? 05/02/70? (Honora)	Patsey, 45, miner b. 1837, Ireland Bridget, 44, b. 1837, Ireland Mary, 18, rag sorter b. '63, Birstall James, 16, miner's labourer. b.1865 Michael, 14, miner's lab b. 1867, Birstall Annie, 9 scholar ? 05/02/70? (Honora) Thomas, 7, scholar b. 26/03/1874 John Lyons, 9 nephew b. 1872, Durham John Lyons, 60 farm lab (unempl'd) wid. f-in-law Annie Lyons, 24, burler Unmar b. Birstall	James m. Catherine Kelly : Mary, b1888, Pat, b1890 Michael, miner,lodger w. Cunningham, Batley	Mich, miner, Back Richmo St. Bat. + Honora
	Patrick Hallarian married Bridget Lyons 18622/4		Pat died Sept 1883 Bridget died 18842/4 or 21/08/87		

Michael Halloran (son of Thomas) and Mary (McGuire)

1851	1861	1871	1881	1891	1901
		Hollaron	Halleran		
		Brownhill	Cross Street	Coach Lane	23, Leeds Road, Batley
	Michael	Michael, 33 Miner b. 1838, Mayo, Ireland	Michael, 40, miner b. Ireland	Michael, miner	
		Mary, 35, burler b. 1836, Ireland	Mary, 40 b. Ireland	Mary	Mary
		Thomas, 5 scholar b. 1866, Batley	Thomas, 16, Horse driver in coal pit, b. Batley	Thomas, 25, miner	Thomas, 33, coal hewer
		John, 3 b. 1868, Batley	John, 13, Horse driver in coal pit. b. Batley	John, 22, miner	John, 30, coal hewer
			Mary, 9, scholar	Mary, 19, cloth weaver	
			Frank, 6, scholar	Frank, 16, harrier	Frank, 28, coal hewer, b. Birstall
	Michael, married Mary McGuire, 1863/4				

Appendix F - Prendergast families in Birstall according to English censuses 1851-1901

1851	1861	1871	1881	1891	1901
Frain	Prendegast	Prendergast	Prendergast	Prendergast	
3 Oak St, Bury	Paradise St Bury	6 High St, Birstall	6 High St, Birstall	Copley Hill, Leeds Rd., Bir	
Honor Frain, 57, widow Thomas, 30, labourer b. Ireland Michael, 28, tailor b. Ireland Barny, 24, labourer b. Ireland James, 20, tailor b. Ireland Richard, 14, back teater b. Ireland Dominic, 12, back teater b. Ireland Mary, 12, cotton drawer b. Ireland Catherine, 18 cotton drawer	Thomas, 26, Ag Lab b. Ireland Catherine 25, factory op, cotton, b. Ireland + 4 Horrocks	Thomas, 36 quarryman b. Ireland Catherine, 35, rag sorter b. Ireland Mary, 7, scholar b. Bury, Lancs Margaret Ann, 5 b. Birstall John Edward, 1 b. Birstall	Thomas, 45, mason's lab, unemployed, b. Ireland Catherine, 44 layer-on, worsted mill b. Ireland Mary, 18, layer-on b. Bury, Lancs Margaret-Ann, 15 b. Birstall	Thomas, 52, stone quarry man, b. Ireland Catherine, 51	Thomas, 63, labourer and pensioner, Catherine, 60
				Margaret-Ann, 25 wool cloth weaver, b. Birstall John E. 22, miner b. Birstall	*Margaret-Ann, 32, rag sorter,
					Thomas, 30, rag grinder
	17 Livesey St Bury: John Frain, 35 Tailor b. Ireland Bridget, 36, Fact oper. b. Ireland John, 14, fact. Op, b. Bolton Lancs James, 12 fact op b. Rochdale, Lancs Mary Ann, 10, favt op. b. Bradford, Yorks Hannah, 8, scholar b. Bury, Lancs Sarah, 1, scholar Hannah, 70, mother b. Ireland	Honora Frain, m-in-law formerly laundress, b. Ireland Ellen O'Neil, 17 rag sorter b. Ireland	Thomas, 9. Scholar b. Birstall Elizabeth, 6, scholar B Birstall	Thomas, 19, condenser minder, fact b. Birstall Elizabeth, 16, woollen cloth weaver, b. Birstall Thomas Scally, 4, grandson, b. Birstall	Elizabeth, 28, rag sorter
					Thomas Scally, 15, coal hewer, grandson
				+	+
				31 Brownhill, James Scally 29 miner b. Willington, Durham Mary 26 b. Thomas, 4, b. Birstall Ellen, 3, b. Birstall Patrick. 1, b. Batley Catherine, 6m, b. Batley	John E, 31, coal hewer Catherine, 29 (Nee Kelly) Mary, 3
					+
					James Scally, 39 Mary, 38 Ellen, 13 Pat, 11 Catherine, 10 Winifred, 8 Ann, 6 Sarah, 9m Sarah, 69, m-in-law, b. Mayo *married in 1914, age 44 to William H Keenan
18603/4 Bury: Catherine Frain m. Thomas Pendragast					

Appendices

Appendix G – Hallorans of Birstall - Baptisms and Births

Origin of info	Date	Baby	Father (Halloran)	Mother	Sponsors	Other info	Family
St Mary's	1854	Bridget Haleron	Thomas	Judy Stinchin	Michael Henry + Mary Higgins	(m.at Jacob Wells)	T
St Mary's	1855	Julia Halloran	Patrick	Bridget McNamara			?
St Mary's	1857 ¾	Thomas	Michael	Honoria Stinchin	James and Mary Frain		M
St Mary's	02/03/1857	John	Patrick	Sarah O'Brian	John Mulligan Helen Manning	Went to Wigan '58?	?
St Mary's	1857	Michael	Patrick	Bridget McNamara	Pat Sullivan Bridget Grace		?
St Mary's	11/01/1858	Patrick	Michael	Honoria Stinchin	John Kelly Judy Stinchin		M
St Mary's	04/10/1860	John	Michael	Honoria Stinchin	John Brannon Mary Frayne		M
St Mary's	17/021861	Thomas	James	Bridget Higgins	Pat Halloran Honoria Higgins		TJ
St Mary's	1862	James	Michael	Honoria Stinchin	James Higgins Mary Stinchin		M
St Mary's	06/02/1863	Mary	Patrick	Bridget Lyons	John and Catherine Halloran		TP
St Mary's	18/09/1864	Catherine	Michael	Mary McGuire	Pat Stinchin Mary Higgins		TM
St Mary's	05/10/1864	John	James	Bridget Higgins	Pat. Conboy Margaret Higgins		TJ
St Mary's	1865	Catherine	Michael	Honoria Stenchin	Pat Stinchin Mary Higgins		M
St Mary's	1865	James	Patrick	Bridget Lyons	Thomas Halloran Mary Lynch		TP
St Mary's	1865	Mary	Thomas	Ann Henry	Patrick and Bridget Halloran	? died Mar 1866 BMD	TT
St Mary's	02/01/1866	Michael	James	Bridget Higgins	Pat Stinchin Honoria Higgins		TJTM
St Mary's	08/02/1866	Thomas	Michael	Mary McGuire	George Booth Catherine Haleron		TM
St Mary's	24/11/1866	Thomas Holloren	Thomas	Ann Henry	Patrick and Bridget Haleron		TT
St Mary's	1867	Helen	John	Elizabeth Connor	James Lee Margaret Watherson		?
St Mary's	20/09/1867	Michael	Patrick	Bridget Lyons	John Lyons Judith Halleron		TP
St Mary's	15/10/1867	Ann	Michael	Honoria Stenchin	John Kelly Catherine Brennan		M
St Mary's	21/11/1867	Mary	James	Bridget Higgins	Michael Halloran Catherin Moran		TJ
St Mary's	10/04/1868	John	Michael	Mary Mc/Guire	John McGuire Hannah Burke	At Brownhill	TM
St Mary's	08/04/1869	Ann	James	Bridget Higgins	Mich. Stinchin Honor Conway		TJ
St Mary's	26/09/1869	Bridget	Michael	Honoria Stinchin	Michael Kenny Bridget Halloran		M
St Mary's	05/02/1870	Honora	Patrick	Bridget Lyons	Pat Stenson Catherine Lyons	Known as Ann?	TP
St Mary's	12/11/1870	Thomas Hallaron	John	Elizabet O'Connor		At Staincliffe, Kilpin Hill	?
St Mary's	06/01/1871	Catherine	James	Bridget Higgins	James Frain Bridget Halloran		TJ
St Mary's	22/03/1872	Mary	Michael	Mary McGuire	Michael Stenson Ann McGuire		TM
St Mary's	10/08/1872	Michael	John	Elizabeth Connor		Heckmondwike	?
St Mary's	16/11/1872	Ann	Michael	Honora Stenson	Michael Frain Hannah Grady		M
St Mary's	14/02/1872	Martin	James	Bridget Higgins	Pat Adams Mary Phillain		TJ
St Mary's	26/03/1874	Thomas	Pat	Bridget Lyons	Michael Walsh Mary Frain		TP
St Mary's	24/12/1875	Francis	Michael	Mary McGuire	Thomas and Julia Halloran		TM
St Mary's	07/08/1876	Catherine	Patrick	Bridget Lyons	Andrew Cox Catherine Cairns	Bpt at home 8/8 + 13/8	TP

Origin of info	Date	Baby	Father (Halloran)	Mother	Sponsors	Other info	Family
St Mary's	18/06/1877	William	James	Bridget Higgins	John Stinson Mary Higgins		TJ
St Mary's	29/04/1879	George	James	Bridget Higgins	Thomas Stinchin Cather. Conway		TJ
St Mary's	24/08/1881	Honora	James	Bridget Higgins	John Higgins Ann Brannon		TJ
St Mary's	11/11/1884	Michael	Pat	Mary Stenson	Thomas Stenson Ann Halloran		MP
St Mary's	27/11/1886	James	Pat	Mary Stenson	John Kenny Bridget Halloran		MP
St Mary's	08/06/1887	John	James	Catherine Kelly	John Halloran Mgt O'Brian		TPJ
St Mary's	12/05/1888	John	Thomas	Ann Brennan	Michael and Mary Halloran	Live at Bruntcliffe	TJT
St Mary's	29/09/1888	Mary	James	Catherine Kelly	John Halloran Mgt O'Brian		TPJ
St Mary's	23/12/1888	John	James	Helen Cuddy	Pat Adams Mgt Cuddy	m.Gertr Walker 1/1/18	TJJ
St Mary's	13/05/1890	Patrick	James	Catherine Kelly	James Halloran Mary Duffy	Batley	TPJ
St Mary's	18/08/1890	William	James	Helen Cuddy	Pat Cuddy Catherine Halloran		TJJ
St Mary's	29/08/1890	Mary	Thomas	Ann Brennan	Thomas Brennan Ann Halloran		TJT
St Mary's	10/04/1892	Thomas	James	Catherine Kelly	Thom. Halloran Catherin Walsh		TPJ
St Mary's	28/07/1892	Phalem	Thomas	Ann Brennan	Thomas Graily Mary Mullvany		TJT
St Mary's	10/08/1892	Mary	James	Helen Cuddy	Martin Halloran Ann Cuddy		TJJ
St Mary's	20/08/1893	Margaret	Michael	Mary McCarthy	John Kelly Mgt McCarthy		TJMi?
St Mary's	03/01/1894	Ann	James	Catherine Kelly	Thomas and Catherine Duffy	m.Abr Elsworth 6/11/16	TPJ
St Mary's	20/03/1894	Ann	James	Helen Cuddy	William Halloran Mary Higgins		TJJ
St Mary's	07/11/1894	Ann	Thomas	Ann Brennan	Matthew Brennan Cath Halloran	Morley	TJT
St Mary's	09/11/1894	Catherine	Martin	Ann Sheridan	Michael Halloran Jemima Hudson	m.J Gavaghan 22/5/20	TJM
St Mary's	23/09/1895	Thomas	James	Ellen Cuddy	James Adams Mgt Ann Pren'gast		TJJ
St Mary's	29/11/1895	Thomas	Michael	Mary McCarthy	Simon and Mary Lyons		TJMi?
St Mary's	04/12/1895	James	James	Catherine Kelly	John Cox Anna Murphy	Batley	TPJ
St Mary's	29/02/1879	Helen	Thomas	Ann Brennan	John Lyons Mary Mulhearn	m.E. Pickard 12/8/22 Morl	TJT
St Mary's	07/11/1896	George	Martin	Ann Sheridan	Thomas and Honora Halloran	m.A Kilbride 14/9/18Bat	TJM
St Mary's	20/10/1897	James	Michael	Mary McCarthy	Simon and Bridget Kelly		TJMi?
St Mary's	19/05/1898	Catherine	James	Catherine Kelly	John Lyons Mary Kelly		TPJ
St Mary's	10/08/1898	Margaret	James	Ellen Cuddy	John Kenny Bridget Giblin		TJJ
St Mary's	02/02/1899	Bridget	Martin	Ann Sheridan	Will Halloran Mary Sheridan	m.A Curley 07/01/23	TJM
St Mary's	17/04/1899	John	Michael	Mary McCarthy	John Halloran Catherine Tigue		?
St Mary's	24/12/1899	Thomas	John	Mary Kelly	Simon Lyons Mary Snee	Brookroyd	?

Appendices

Origin of info	Date	Baby	Father (Halloran)	Mother	Sponsors	Other info	Family
St Mary's	15/02/1900	Honora	Michael	Helen Pren'gast	Thomas Halloran Bridget Kilkenny	Boro' Rd Batley	TPM?
St Mary's	03/05/1900	James	James	Ellen Cuddy	Thomas Pren'gast Margaret Hunt	Partington Sq	TJJ
St Mary's	17/07/1900	Mary	Michael	Mary McCarthy	Simon Kelly Mary Frain	High St Birstall	?
St Mary's	20/03/1901	Joseph	James	Catherine Kelly	John Duffy Honor Halloran	Birch St Carlinghow	TPJ
St Mary's	29/07/1901	Ellen	Michael	Helen Pren'gast	Tim Meague Anna Gledhill	Borough Rd Batley	TPM?
St Mary's	01/09/1901	Honora	Martin	Ann Sheridan	John Halloran Honor Cox	Cross St m.J Sword '23	TJM
St Mary's	29/10/1902	Ellen	James	Ellen Cuddy	Thomas Halloran Mary Hunt	Partington Sq	TJJ
St Mary's	18/01/1903	James	Michael	Helen Pren'gast	James Cunningham Mary Gladhill	Back Richmond St, Bat	TPM?
St Mary's	1904	Thomas	Michael	Ellen Kilkenny	Thomas and Ann Halloran (Mor)		?
St Mary's	1905	Henry	James	Ellen Cuddy		(died as infant)	TJJ
St. Pat, Birstall	1905	James	William	Elizabeth Pren'gast		(died as infant)	TJW
St Mary's	1906	John					
St Pat. Birstall	06/04/1907	Joseph	James	Ellen Cuddy			TJJ
St Pat, Birstall	10/01/08	James Gerard	John	Margaret Kelly			?
St Pat, Birstall	27/02/1908	Thomas	William	Elizabeth Pre'gast		Brownhill	TJW
St Pat, Birstall	1908	Michael					
St Pat, Birstall	17/04/1910	John	William	Elizabeth Pren'gast		Farrah's Bdgs	TJW
St Pat, Birstall	1912	Bernard	John	Ann Corbett		Morley, mNorah Kelly	TJTJ
St Pat, Birstall	28/12/1913	William	William	Elizabeth Pren'gast	Thom. Pren'gast Margaret Snee	m. Bgt Walsh 26/06/41	TJW
St Pat, Birstall	17/05/1916	Bernard	William	Elizabeth Pren'gast			TJW
St Pat, Birstall	09/11/1917	Mary Veronica	Martin	Susan Lyons		m.Henry Hinchliffe '47	?
St Mary's	1919	Honor					
St Pat, Birstall	03/05/1920	Mary	Patrick	Catherine Lynskey	Martin Lynsky and ?	m.Ed Pickering 24/7/48	?
St Mary's	1921	Catherine					
St Pat, Birstall	24/07/1922	Aileen	John	Gertrude Walker	John Mullins(exHalloran) + Mary	Church St (m.1978)	TJJJo
St Pat, Birstall	30/12/1922	Teresa	Patrick	Catherine Lynskey	James Grayson Mary Adams	Gelderd Rd	?
St Pat, Birstall	08/04/1924	Ann	Patrick	Catherine Lynskey	Michael Frain Norah Lynskey	Gelderd Rd	?
St Mary's	1924	Mary					
St Pat, Birstall	30/04/1927	James Dermott	William	May Clifford	John Mullins Gertrude Moore	Industrial Ave m.M Kay	TJJW
St Mary's	1927	Ellen					

Origin of info	Date	Baby	Father (Halloran)	Mother	Sponsors	Other info	Family
St Mary's	1927	James F					
St Mary's	1828	George					
St Mary's	1930	Mary					
St Mary's	1930	Patrick					
St Mary's	1932	Ann					
St Mary's	1932	Michael					
St Mary's	1933	Peter					
St Mary's	1935	Joseph M					
St Mary's	1935	John					
St Mary's	1945	Anthony					
St Pat, Birstall	12/03/1948	Mary	William	Bridget Walsh	Thomas Halloran Ellen Fenton	11 Kings Drive	TJWW
St Pat, Birstall	08/06/1951	Bernard	William	Bridget Walsh	Joseph Halloran Mary Mullins	11 Kings Drive	TJWW
St Mary's	1961	David Christopher					
St Mary's	1963	Kevin					
St Pat Birstall	08/10/1885	Kyle	Mark	Christine Hopkins	Ronald and Angela Fenton	Tyndale Walk, H'wik	

Family Key:

1st Generation	T = Thomas/JudyStenson/Stinchin	M = Michael and Honor Stinchin/Stenson	
2nd Generation	TJ = James/Bridget Higgins	TP = Patrick/Bridget Lyons	TM = Michael/Mary Maguire	TT = Thomas/Ann Henry
3rd Generation	TJT = Thomas/Ann Brennan	TJJ = James/Ellen Cuddy	TJJo = John/Mary Gillespie?	TJMi = Michael/Mary?
	TJMy = Mary/Martin Duffy	TJA = Ann/Thomas Higgins	TJC = Catherine/Chas McCarthy	TJM = Martin/Norah Sheridan
	TJW = William/Eliz Prendergast	TJH = Honorah and Stephen Frain		
	TPJ = James/Catherine Kelly	TPM = Michael/Ellen Prendergast	TPT = Thomas/Honor Durkan	TJTF = Frances/Mary Cox
4th Generation	TJTJ = John/Ann Corbett	TJTE = Ellen/?	TJTT = Thomas/Kathleen Borough	
	TJTH = Honora/John Reynolds			
	TJJJ = John/Gertrude Walker	TJJW = William/May Clifford	TJCJ = John McCarthy/	TJCA = Annie and DavidTully
	TJMC = Cath/James Gavaghan	TJMG = George/Ann Kilbride	TJMA = Ann/?	
	TJWJ = John/Eileen Sheehan	TJWW = William/Bridget Halloran	TJHMy = Mary/Stephen Frain	

Appendix H - Knock (Aghamore) Parish Baptism Records – 1864 to 1903

Aghamore's LDS Film# 0926214 1864-1882

Date	Name	Parents	God parents / Sponsors	Townland
1864 Baptisms				
December 4	Patt	Patt Halleran and Catherine Tighe	Pat and Judith Tigue	Raith
1865 Baptisms				
March 6	Pat	Austin Morley and Bridget Mulkeen	Pat Halleran, Sarah Morley	Cloonahulty
1866 Baptisms				
January 27	Bridget	Pat Halloran and Winifred Morley	Thomas and Bridget Mulkeen	Auher? (Cahir)
November 4	Mary	David Duffy and Catherine Nolan	Pat Halleran, Bridget Nolan	Cahir
1867 Baptisms				
January 13	Margaret	Michael Toughy and Mary Halloran	Thomas Lyons, Mary Stenson	Raith
December 29	Mary	Thomas Kenny and Bridget Kelly	Martin Kenny, Bridget Halloran	Aghamore
1868 Baptisms				
January 25	Bridget	Thomas Halloran and Sally Coyne	Martin Halloran, Mary Stenson	Cahir
February 16	Mary	Pat Halloran and Winnie Morley	Martin Grogan, Bridget Halloran	Cahir
December 13	Michael	Pat Halleran and Catherine Tighe	Tim Kelly, Bridget Stenson	Raith
1869 Baptisms				
February 14	Pat	Michael Toughy and Mary Halloran	Martin Halloran, Bridget Stenson	Raith
May 29	Mary	Thomas Halloran and Sally Coyne	Ned and Mary Adams	Cahir
1870 Baptisms				
June 19	Honor	Thomas Stenson and Margaret Snee	John Halloran, Margaret Snee	Ballinaclocha
1871 Baptisms				
January 15	Catherine	Pat Halloran and Catherine Tigue	James Halloran, Bridget Stenson	Raith
May 18	Winifred	Pat Halloran and Winifred Morley	Michael Hunt, Mary Morley	Cahir
October 15	Catherine	Pat Tigue and Mary Freeman	James Halloran, Ann Fremman	Balinaclogha
1872 Baptisms				
May 25	Catherine	Thomas Halleran and Cecilia Coyne	Michael Connelly, Sally	??
October 16	Martin and John	Michael Touhy and Mary Halloran	John and Bridget Halloran, James and Catherine Halloran	Raith
1873 Baptisms				
July 25	Pat	Pat Halloran and Winny Morley	John and Winny Egan	Cahir
August 3	Margaret	Pat Halloran and Kate (?)	Thomas and Bridget Halloran	??
1874 Baptisms				
January 7	Pat	Pat Tighe and Mary Freeman	John Freeman, Mary Halloran	Ballinaclocha
January 28	Ellen	James Kelly and Anne Freeman	James Halloran, Bridget Beirne	Raith
1875 Baptisms				
February 10	James and Pat	Thomas Halleran and Cecelia Coyne	(respectively)Pat and Bridget Halleran, Thomas and Mary Nyland	??

Date	Name	Parents	Sponsors	Place
July 2	Honor	Pat Halleran and Winifred Morally	Austin Waldron, Mary Morally	Cahir
1876 Baptisms				
January 21	James	Michael Touhy and Mary Halloran	Thomas and Bridget Lyons	Raith
October 30	Martin	Pat Halloran and Winifred Morley	John and Catherine Halloran	Cahir
December 21	Catherine	Thomas Kenny and Bridget Kelly	James Kenny, Bridget Halloran	Aghataharn
1877 Baptisms				
October 14	Martin	Pat Tighe and Mary Freeman	Austin Freeman, Mary Halleran	Raith
December 23#	James	Martin Halleran and Winifred Ruane	James and Catherine Halleran	Ballinaclocha
December 29	Mary	Michael Touhy and Mary Halleran	Thomas Touhy, Bridget Cox	Raith
1879 Baptisms				
February 23	Honor	Pat Halleran and Winifred Morley	Thomas Halleran, Catherine Nolan	Cahir
October 19#	Catherine	Martin Halloran and Winifred Ruane	Patrick Ruane, Mary (?)	Ballinaclocha
November 5	Michael	Pat Niland and Catherine Halleran	John Niland, Mary Mulloy	Mountain
November 26	Mary	Michael Boyle and Ellen Creton	Pat Boyle, Mary Boyle	Shanvaghera
1881 Baptisms				
January 15	Michael	Thomas Halloran and Sarah Kyne	Anthony Lohan, Catherine Nyland	Mountain
1882 Baptisms				
August 13	Catherine	Michael Touhy and Mary Halleran	Thomas and Bridget Lyons	Raith
September 10	Mary #	Martin Halleran and Winifred Ruane	James Ruane, Bridget Kelly	??
October 12	Sarah A.	Pat Halleran and M.Morley	Martin Flanigan, B.Waldron	Cahir
October 22	Anne	Patrick Nyland and Catherine Halleran	John and Margaret Nyland	Mountain
Baptisms 1869				
August 11	Bridget	Michael M (?) and Mary Malee	Edward Hallinan (?), Judith Egan	
June 20	Mary	Pat and Mary Muldoon	Mathew Carney, Bridget Halleran (?)(Notationmarried to Thomas Carney,	Liscat
November 3	Mary	John and Bridget Coleman	Thomas Hallinan (?), Mary Curry	??
1892 Baptisms				
September 4	Catherine	Denis Begley and Margaret Halloran (?)	Bridget Kilduff, Pat Kilduff	??
1895 Baptisms				
November 17	Michael	John Lee and Kate Hallinan	Pat Lee, Bridget Lee	Liscat- dob. 15
1897 Baptisms				
July 28	Patrick	John Lee and Kate Halloran	Mary Lavan, Thomas Conway	- dob. 26??
1898 Baptisms				
January 2	Bridget	Tom Forde and Julia Halloran (?)	John Jordan, Bridget Cunniffe	Breen
1899 Baptisms				
August 27	Martin	John Lee and Kate Halloran	John Mullins, Mary Mulline	Liscat- dob. 22
1901 Baptisms				

Appendices

September 18	John James	John Lee and Kate Halloran	John Lee, Winnie Morley	Liscat - dob. 14
1903 Baptisms				
July 12	Thomas	John Lee and Catherine Halloran	Thomas Halloran, Kate Niland (?)	Liscat

Appendix H - Knock (Aghamore) Parish Marriage Records - Sept. 1, 1864 - June 24, 1882

Aghamore s LDS Film# 0926214 1864-1882

Date	Marriage partners	Sponsors	Townland
1864 Marriages			
September ?	Pat Holleran to Winifred Morley	John Kenny, Bridget Mulloy	
1867 Marriages			
February 18	Thomas Halloran(?) to Sarah Coyne	James Hopkins(?), Bridget Halloran	Cahir(?)
1872 Marriages			
January	Michael Hunt to Anne Duffy	John Halloran, Margaret Doyle	Falleighter
1872 Marriages			
February	John Kenny to Mary Lynsky	John Halloran, Elizabeth Forkin	Falleighter
1877 Marriages			
January 10	Certificate of marriage to Martin Halloran		
1878 Marriages			
May	Patrick Niland to Catherine Halloran(?)	John Nally(?), Bridget Touhy	

References

Berkeley, George, (1871), A Word to the Wise: Or, an Exhortation to the Roman Catholic Clergy of Ireland, in A.C. Fraser (ed.) The Works of George Berkeley, D.D. (Oxford, 1871)

Jordan Jr., Donald E, (1996), The Famine and its aftermath in County Mayo County Mayo from the Plantation to the Land War. Great Britain, Cambridge University Press.

Local Government Board, Ireland, (1876), Land Owners in Ireland (Return of Owners of Land of One Acre and Upwards, in the several Counties, Counties of Cities, and Counties of Towns in Ireland). Baltimore: Genealogical Publishing Co, Inc. 1988.

Baine, Edward, (1970), [Originally 1858], Woollen Manufacture of England, edited by KJ Pointing, Extracted from 'Yorkshire Past and Present', Newton Abbot: David & Charles

Beaumont de, Gustave, (1839), Ireland: Social, Political and Religious Parts , Harvard University Press

Becker, Bernard H., (1881), Disturbed Ireland: Being the Letters Written during the Winter of 1880-81, London: Macmillan and Co.

Binns, Isaac, (1882) Village To Town: A Random Reminiscence of Batley During The Last Thirty Years, from reprinted articles edited by F. H. Purcas in the Batley News

Blassingame, J.W. (ed.), 1979, The Frederick Douglass Papers, Series One: Speeches, Debates and Interviews, Vol. 1, 1841-46, New Haven

Byrne, Joe, (2002), *Páirc an Teampaill*: The Ancient Cemetery of *Achadh Mór*, in *Glór Achadh Mór*

Clegg, Malcolm, (1994), A History of Birstall, The Last 200 Years, Batley: Clegg

Clegg, Malcolm, (2007), Echoes from Birstall Past, Batley: Clegg

Coulter, Henry, (1862), The west of Ireland: its existing condition, and prospects, Dublin:Hodges and Smith, Google Books, http://www.archive.org/details/westirelanditse00coulgoog

Cousens, (1961), Emigration and demographic change in Ireland, 1851-1861, in Economic Historic Review, 2nd series, xiv, 2 pp 278-88

Devon Commission: appointed to inquire into the occupation of land in Ireland, (1845), Dr. McParlan and Fr. Durkan's Deposition on behalf of the Royal Dublin Society in Sobolewski, Peter & Solan, Betty, (no date), Kiltimagh: Our Life and Times, Eds., Kiltimagh Historic Society

Donnelly, James, S., (1996) 'Irish Property must pay for Irish Poverty': British public opinion and the great Irish Famine, in Fearful Realities, (eds. Morash and Hayes), Dublin: Irish Academic Press.

Dorian, Hugh, (2000), The outer edge of Ulster: A memoir of social life in Nineteenth century Donegal, Ed. Breandán Mac Suibhne and David Dickson, Dublin, Lilliput

Dutton, Hely, (1824), A statistical and agricultural survey of the county of Galway, http://books.google.co.uk/books

His Majesty's Commissioners, (1835), First Report Inquiring into the Condition of the Poorer Classes in Ireland, http://www.clarelibrary.ie/eolas/coclare/history/poverty/poverty_before_famine_index. htm

Fitzpatrick, D., (1995), Flight from Famine in The Great Irish Famine, Cathal Póirtéir (ed.), Mercier Press:Dublin

Fitzpatrick, David, (1985) Marriage in Post-Famine Ireland, in Art Cosgrove, ed., Marriage in Ireland Dublin: College Press

Fox, J.A., (1880), Reports on the Condition of the Peasantry of the County of Mayo, during the Famine Crisis of 1880 Dublin Mansion House Committee

Freeman, T.W., (1957), Pre-famine Ireland, Manchester: Manchester University Press

Geary, L.M., (2000), The Late disastrous Epidemic: Medical Relief and the Great Famine, in Fearful Realities, (eds. Morash and Hayes), Dublin: Irish Academic Press.

Griffith, Richard, (1847-1864), Griffith's Valuation; Eneclann LTD and the National Library of Ireland. Retrieved in June, 2010, from http://www.askaboutireland.ie/griffith-valuation/index.xml.

Hack Tuke, James, (1847) A visit to Connaught, Society of Friends, Dublin

Hall and Hall, S, 1841, Ireland: its scenery and character, London: Jeremiah Howe

Head, George, (1836), A Home Tour through the Manufacturing Districts of England in the Summer of 1835, London: Murray, http://www.archive.org/details/hometourthroughm00head.

Henry, Cathal, (2009), The Charlestown Chronicles, Dublin: Nonsuch Publishing

Hill, George Augustus, (1887), Facts from Gweedore, LSE Selected Pamphlets, Stable URL: http://www.jstor.org/stable/60217301

Inquiry into the State of the Poor in Ireland, (1836), Parliamentary Commission

Jordan Jr., Donald, E. (2000) Land and Popular Politics in Ireland County Mayo, in Fearful Realities, (eds. Morash and Hayes), Dublin: Irish Academic Press.

Jubb, Samuel, (1860), The History of the Shoddy-trade: Its Rise, Progress, and Present Position, Holston and Wright, http://www.archive.org/details/historyshoddytr00jubbgoog

Lewis, Samuel 1837. Lewis's Atlas, Comprising the Counties of Ireland and a General Map of the Kingdom. London: S. Lewis and Company; 2009 Kessinger Publishing.

Lewis, Samuel, 1837, (1984). A Topographical Dictionary of Ireland- volumes 1 and 2. Baltimore: Genealogical Publishing Company, Inc.

MacLysaght, Edward, (1972), Irish Families Their Names, Arms and Origins. New York, Crown Publishers, Inc.

MacRaild, Donald, (1999), Irish Immigrants in Modern Britain, 1750-1922, New York: St. Martin's Press.

McDonald-Garvey, Marie Lecture, (2007), The Towey Clan, http://www.toweyclan.com/MarieGarvey Lecture.pdf

McDonald-Garvey, Marie, (1995), The Ancient Territory of *Sliabh Lugha*: Mid-Connacht, Nure, Manor Hamilton, Dublin:Drumlin Publications

McGlinchey, Charles, 2007, The Last of the Name, Cork: Collins Books

McParlan MD, James 1802., Statistical Survey of County Mayo, http://www.askaboutireland.ie/reading-room/digital-book-collection/digital-books-by-county/mayo/mayo-statistical-survey/index.xml

Mitchel, John, (1876) The Last Conquest of Ireland (Perhaps), UCD Press, Classics of Irish History series

Morash, Chris, (2000) Literature, Memory, Atrocity, in Fearful Realities, (eds. Morash and Hayes), Dublin:Irish Academic Press.

O'Dowd, Anne, (1991), Spalpeens and Tattie Hokers: History and Folklore of the Irish Migratory Agricultural Worker in Ireland and Britain, Dublin, Irish Academic Press

Orser, Charles E. Jr. (2000) An Archaeology of the Great Famine, in Fearful Realities, (eds. Morash and Hayes), Dublin:Irish Academic Press.

Poirteir, Cathal, (1996), The Great Irish Famine (Thomas Davis Lecture Series), RTE:Mercia Press

Poor Inquiry (Ireland), 1836

Quinn, J.F. 1996. History of Mayo- Volumes I-V. Ballina, Ireland: Brendan Quinn.

Sobolewski, Peter & Solan, Betty, (no date), Kiltimagh: Our Life and Times, Eds., Kiltimagh Historic Society

Swift, Roger (ed.), (2002), Irish Migrants in Britain 1815-1914: Documentary History, Cork University

Press

Swords, Liam, (1999), In their own words: The famine in North Connaught, Dublin:The Columba Press

The Society of Friends, 1847, Distress in Ireland: Extracts from correspondence, The Central Relief Committee of the Society of Friends, II.

Trevelyan, Charles, Edward, (1848), The Irish Crisis, London: Green & Longman, Google Books, http://books.google.co.uk/books Trevelyan,+Charles,+Edward,+(1848),+The+Irish+Crisis

Whelan, Kevin, (1995), Pre and post Famine Landscape Change, The Great Irish Famine, Cathal Póirtéir (ed.), Mercier Press: Dublin

Useful Web pages

Aghamore - http://www.aghamoreireland.com/history/overview.htm

Aghamore Online http://www.aghamoreireland.com/history/overview.htm

Blank, Maggie, (2004) http://maggieblanck.com/Land/Birstall.html: Latest update, July 2010

Costello family - http://www.nanglemedieval.com/BaronyCostello.pdf

Costello Heritage: http://skehana.homestead.com/newsletter.html

Dale, Jill, (2010), http://www.rootsweb.ancestry.com/~irlmayo2/comptondomvilebt_mayolandlords.html

East Mayo - http://eastmayo.org/Aghamore_Marriages_1864_1882.htm

East Mayo - http://www.eastmayo.org/Aghamore_1864_1883_and_Knock_1869_1905_Baptisms.htm

Goireland - http://www.goireland.com/genealogy/family.htm?FamilyID=56

Hansard - http://hansard.millbanksystems.com/commons/

Irish hollocast - http://irishholocaust.webs.com

Irish Times Website 2010. irishtimes.com. Dublin, Ireland. Accessed website 8/5/2010

John Nussey, Introduction to the Birstall Parish Register by the Yorkshire Archaeological Society – http://www.maggieblanck .com/Land/Birstall.html

Mayo Ireland, http://towns.mayo-ireland.ie

Mayo Ireland, http://towns.mayo-ireland.ie

NUI Galway Landed Estates Database - http://www.landedestates.ie/LandedEstates/jsp/estate-show.jsp?id=129, accessed Jan 2011.

Rootsweb - http://www.rootsweb.ancestry.com/~irlmayo2/comptondomvilebt_mayolandlords.html

St Mary's Batley - http://www.stmarybatley.co.uk/about%20us.html

St Patrick's Birstall - http://www.birstallstpatrick.org.uk/history.htm

St Patrick's website: http://birstallstpatrick.org.uk/history.htm

The Irish Times - http://www.irishtimes.com/ancestor/surname/index.cfm?fuseaction

The Irish-American – New York City newspaper - http://www.irishinnyc.freeservers.com/photo2.html

Vivian Thompson - http://vivientomlinson.com/batley/ui54.htm

Westminster Orders of the Day - http://yourdemocracy.newstatesman.com/parliament/orders-of-the-day /HAN1 030300 S

www.ingramcontent.com/pod-product-compliance
Lightning Source LLC
Chambersburg PA
CBHW081349160426
43196CB00014B/2698